# THE CUBAN IMAGE

## Cinema and Cultural Politics in Cuba

Michael Chanan

BFI Publishing, London
Indiana University Press, Bloomington, Indiana

First published in 1985 by the British Film Institute
127 Charing Cross Road
London WC2H OEA

Published in the United States of America by
Indiana University Press, Bloomington, Indiana

Illustrations from Cuban films reproduced by courtesy of the
Instituto Cubano de Arte y Industria Cinematográficos (ICAIC)

**British Library Cataloguing in Publication Data**

Chanan, Michael
   The Cuban Image
   1. Moving-pictures—Cuba—History
   I. Title
   791.43'097291    PN1993.5.C/
   ISBN 0–85170–137–X
      0–85170–138–8 Pbk

**Library of Congress Cataloging-in-Publication Data**

Chanan, Michael
   The Cuban Image
   1. Moving-pictures—Social aspects—Cuba
   2. Moving-pictures—Cuba—History
   I. Title
   PN1993.5.C8C48   1986   302.2'343'097291   85–45505

ISBN 0–253–31587–5
     0–253–21261–8 Pbk

Cover design: John Gibbs
Typeset by Computerset (MFK) Ltd and Bemrose Security Printing.
Printed in Great Britain by Bemrose Security Printing, Derby.

# CONTENTS

*In memory of*
*Luis Espinal and Miguel Cabezas*
*and for*
*Margaret and Duncan*

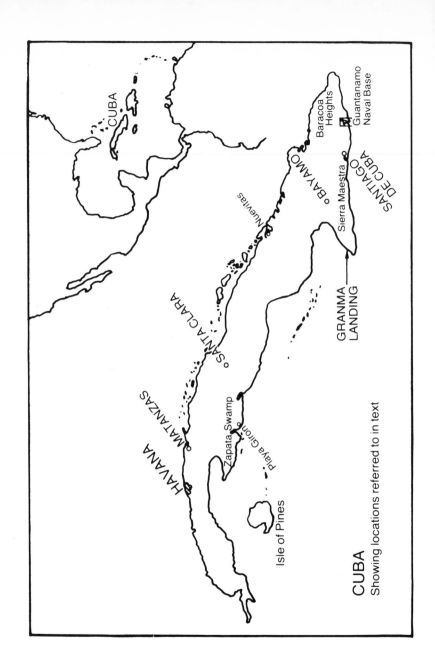

CUBA

Showing locations referred to in text

CUBA

HAVANA

MATANZAS

SANTA CLARA °

Nuevitas

BAYAMO °

Baracoa Heights

Guantanamo Naval Base

SANTIAGO DE CUBA °

Sierra Maestra

GRANMA LANDING

Zapata Swamp

Playa Girón

Isle of Pines

# FOREWORD

There is a sense in which this book is a labour of love. Like many people of my generation who grew to political consciousness during the 60s, after the Cuban Revolution, I cannot say when exactly I became aware of Revolutionary Cuba, but over the course of time I began to realise that it was there, and that it represented a focus of identification for all sorts of socialist ideals that were gradually forming in my mind. I had first gone to Latin America in the early 70s and became deeply involved with Chile solidarity work very shortly after the coup. Within a few years this involvement led to a signal interest in Latin American cinema, and when, finally (except that it was really the beginning of something new in my life) the opportunity presented itself for a visit to Cuba not as a tourist but under the auspices of the Film Institute, ICAIC, I grabbed at it.

At first I didn't know whether the chance for such a visit would be likely to repeat itself (in fact I've been back many times since), so I spent a very intense month watching films, six or seven hours a day, and talking to as many people as I could. For the same reason I decided not to pull any punches, but to wade in with questions about everything I could think of. Some of these questions were definitely awkward. For one thing, I was strongly influenced by the degree to which the women's movement, and my friendships with women who were involved in it, had affected my own political thinking and my conception of the body politic. Cuba is a very macho country, and feminism was seen by men and women alike as a divisive trend. But some questions were more awkward than others, and not all of them stemmed directly from this pro-feminist orientation: I also had my due share of suspicions, as a graduate of the Dialectics of Liberation at the Round House in 1967, of the authoritarianism associated with orthodox communism. So sometimes my questions met with a certain resistance, including some which touched on Cuba's relationship to the Soviet Union; after all, I was a European, drunk, as one Cuban director described it, on ideology. But more often than not they were answered more than courteously, and on several occasions at great length.

Returning from this first visit I was rapidly confronted with a problem. I went from the airport to my brother's house, and within a matter of hours became involved in a heated discussion with a friend of his who was a member of the International Socialists group. I was gushing with enthusiasm, which he countered by calling me – it was, in his vocabulary, a term of abuse – a third-worldist. I learnt that I had to keep quiet, to choose where and when to talk of my experiences, and with whom. I gradually acquired more confidence but still, for a long time, among people who didn't know me, I was lumbered with a certain reputation for being, let's say, an unreconstructed zealot. Being fairly thick-skinned by nature I didn't worry too much, especially since the problem wasn't just to do with Cuba, and I'd been struck with it before after six months in Bolivia. Several friends of mine with extended first-hand experience of third world countries reported similar experiences. Returning to your own country and leaving behind the smell and the taste of the country of your sojourn, you felt disoriented and set apart by your experience of the reality of underdevelopment. The difficulty is that this is something you have to take on in the course of then writing the piece of work which has been your reason for going.

The strange thing about that month in Cuba was that because my subject of investigation was cinema, I had seen both more and less than any other visitor might in a month. Less, because I was sat in a viewing theatre much of the time. But it had been very intense, and had seemed not like one month but like six, at least, because I had been watching the country go by on the screen: you couldn't possibly see so many things, visit all those places, listen to all those people in the space of a month in any other way; but film transports you, and condenses time.

Yet no-one could possibly have taken in so much from such relentless viewing unless for another quality of film, which that experience so forcefully taught me: that although the film as a material object is exactly the same wherever you watch it, the film you see depends – among other things – on where that is. The image that is projected is everywhere the same, but the space between the screen and your eyes is different.

In fact I had felt this very strongly once before, when I had seen a work of 'underground' cinema, Carolee Schneeman's *Fuses*, first on a large screen at the ICA, and then not long afterwards, projected on the wall of her own flat at a party. I had not much liked it the first time, but very much the second, and it seemed very clear to me that this was because of the kind of film it was: the dull space of the cinema deadened something in the image, which on the contrary, was very much alive in the film-maker's home. I felt something similar in Havana. Abroad, these films often communicate very powerfully. Film is an incomparable means, in the right hands, with which to show the way things are (whatever the theoretical status you ascribe to the image in its quality as a sign). But there are also always aspects of reality that remain unexpressed, and in some way cannot be communicated, when geography intervenes. The image of your own country looks different to you when you see it abroad.

The thing struck me particularly vividly on a day two weeks after first arriving in Cuba. I had watched, the day before, Octavio Cortazár's marvellous documentary, *Hablando de punto cubano* ('Speaking of Typical Cuban Music'), which

2

explains all about a song form called the *controversia*, the controversy, a kind of competition in which singers improvise alternate verses (I discuss it in Chapter 13). I had wondered after seeing it to what extent the art was really still alive, or whether the film-makers had had to search hard to find these obviously very accomplished practitioners. The next day I was taken off to Varadero for a weekend at the seaside (Cuban hospitality is rightly legendary). On the way, we stopped for a drink at a beauty spot. It was mid-afternoon, and the only other people in the bar were a group sitting at a table in the garden at the back who, judging by the number of empty beer bottles, had been there a good while. As we sat down we heard singing, and they gestured us to come and listen. An older man and a younger were engaged in a *controversia*. There was a cheerful round of laughter as the older man declared himself the winner, because, he sang, his opponent had slipped up, and used the same word twice in the same verse. I knew at once, of course, the answer to my doubts of the previous day, and at the same time became suddenly more aware of all sorts of other continuities between what I was seeing on the screen and what lay outside the viewing theatre.

This sense of contact with the reality has served, I hope, to animate this book. If it hasn't, the book is lacking. It is not just an advantage that one has over the historian investigating times before living memory, which needs a certain leap of imagination; it provides criteria for the interpretation of the testimonies of the people who have lived the events you're investigating – and I approached Cuban cinema not as just a series of products but as a living historical process, in which those films were related to a series of events in the life of the institution that made them, and the life of the institution to the events of the Revolution.

In the course of my inquiry I was struck by, and tried always to remember, the fact that Cuban cinema had become a most powerful force in the collective memory of the Cuban people, popular historian of the Revolution second only to Fidel, and thus a force for social cohesion. It was very impressive to discover how much ordinary viewers were excited and stimulated by it, for within very few years it had become one of the most imaginative cinemas being produced anywhere, and this showed that it was possible for artistic experiment and popularity to go together even though in other respects popular taste hadn't changed a lot. It was an invigorating discovery. But it has also been necessary to ask if in the mid to late 70s Cuban cinema did not begin to be too conformist, as if the film-makers were finding it more difficult to bear the weight of the cultural influence that they carried. Probably this is a question that cannot yet be answered, particularly since recent changes in the institution and its policies – ICAIC acquired a new head, Julio García Espinosa, at the beginning of the 80s – are only just beginning to bite. I have therefore not tried to bring the book up to date while revising it; the account presented here reaches the late 70s.

As of the moment, however, the film people have lost their vanguard position among Cuba's cultural producers. The most experimental work is that of the plastic artists, who are working in idioms that incorporate those of the political avant-garde galleries of the metropolis; and there is lively aesthetic debate accompanying the exploration of conceptual art and multimedia work. There are also a number of Cuban composers producing notable avant garde scores; two of them have recently won first and second prizes in France for electro-acoustic works. Not that comparability with the metropolis or its approval are proper indications of the nature of this activity. Nor do Cuban or other Latin American artists need to pay homage to the Old World, though they often do. But their situation is not so very different in one respect: their audiences, like everywhere, are much smaller than those for cinema. Be that as it may, of one thing I'm certain. The question of the Film Institute's loss of initiative has nothing to do with accusations by Cuba's enemies that there is no artistic freedom in Cuba. Patently there is. All kinds of artistic creation thrive, as long as the work produced isn't manifestly counter-revolutionary. (As the documentarist Santiago Alvarez, on a visit to Britain, explained to a BBC radio interviewer, 'Yes, we have censorship. We don't allow works that are racist, or fascist, or Zionist... ') The Cubans believe, in the words of Fidel, that the enemy is imperialism, not abstract painting. Nor is it a question of 'yes, but it has its limits'. Apparently the limits are expanding. Writing which was earlier allowed to go out of print is now beginning to be republished (unless the author has left the country) – and writing is usually thought of as a particularly dangerous medium. In many ways, therefore, this book is a reasoned argument against such accusations. It's also meant to be more: a detailed history which is also a case study in cultural politics, intended to contribute to the clarification of the issues which cultural politics involves.

From the historian's point of view, it was necessary to investigate what people who had left Cuba had to say, and I have consulted all the sources I could find; but I did so, as my professors of philosophy had taught in another ideological context, in a spirit of scepticism. It was also necessary, of course, to treat the immediate reality with a certain caution, and to remember that the excitement it generates can be no substitute for good old-fashioned scholarship; and I hope I provide sufficient historical evidence for the way I tell the story of ICAIC. I have no excuse if I haven't, because I was given every facility, and a great deal of generous help.

I do not believe, however, that any apologia is needed for showing commitment. The agenda is set by the wider circumstances in which a book like this is written. A perfect illustration of the problem confronts me as I complete my revisions of the text and write this foreword, in the shape of the arrival of a film by one of the significant characters at a certain point in the story. The emigré cinematographer Nestor Almendros and New York Cuban film-maker Orlando Jimenez-Leal have made a documentary called *Improper Conduct*, which demonstrates clearly enough that there has been a sad history of repression of gay people in Cuba since the Revolution came to power in 1959. This is incontrovertible. However, the film is highly tendentious in its manner of presentation. Beginning with interviewees whom Almendros himself describes as naive – ordinary people without higher levels of education – it gradually mixes in among their moving individual testimonies others which contain a number of, to begin with, relatively small untruths. As B. Ruby Rich comments in her review of the film ('Bay of Pix', *American Film*, Vol.IX No.9, July-August 1984, pp.57-9), the interviews begin to ring true in inverse proportion to the viewer's knowledge of Cuba today, so that for any viewer with such knowledge there comes a point where the film begins to defeat its own purpose. (It is mostly a matter of exaggeration; yes, tourists are accosted by youths offering them black market exchange rates for their dollars, but no, not by prostitutes offering their bodies for a pair of jeans. Taxi drivers do not take down your hotel room number, and no one stops a tourist going wherever they want.) In this way, the film progresses to the more articulate accusations of the artists and intellectuals. But these also begin to test the viewer's credulity, especially if anything is known about the people who make them. A number of the interviewees in the film are people with a vested interest in spreading calumny in order to defend their own reputations as people who were wronged. (For example, Heberto Padilla; see Chapter 13. Or Armando Valladares, who claimed to have been paralysed as a result of ill-treatment in a Cuban prison, but arrived in Madrid, as we see in the film, propelling himself on his own two feet.) These interviews are assembled with relentless disregard for dialectical argument, with no exploration of the contradictions they pose, or respect for the viewer's powers of discrimination. In the end, one has to doubt whether all of these stories can be true.

I recount in this book that when Fidel Castro went to the USA for the first time in 1959, one of the people he met was Richard Nixon, and Nixon wrote a report of his meeting with Castro saying that he was either extremely naive or else under communist discipline. Something similar is true of this film. The film-makers are either ingenuous, or else they set out to make a film intended to serve the forces of darkness which reign in the White House, which conducted the invasion of Grenada and threaten to invade Nicaragua and maybe Cuba again too. Almendros commented in a discussion after the screening of the film at the 1984 London Film Festival that the film is strongly disliked by the right wing because they sympathise neither with gays nor with the ideals of free speech. Yet the film falls very neatly into one of the five types of propaganda described by the theorists of the military state and the fight against what they call the internal enemy, a theory and a concept which go back to the Nazis (see *De l'usage des médias en temps de crise* by Armand and Michèle Mattelart, Alain Moreau, Paris, 1979); namely, tactical propaganda, propaganda addressed to a particular group of the population who, because of their special susceptibilities, are not open to easy persuasion by more overt or general forms of propaganda, and which, where appropriate, uses the truth, but presents it dishonestly. In short, the method of this film is emotional blackmail. It relies on the putative critic being prepared to be branded anti-gay.

However, here is what a gay critic sympathetic to Cuba, Richard Goldstein, has to say about the film in *Village Voice*, 24 July 1984:

*Improper Conduct* arouses ... empathy the way left-wing documentaries always have. It ... consists, for the most part, of passionate personal testimonies, warmly lit and intimately framed . . . For all that homosexuals have suffered on the silver screen, *Improper Conduct* is the first film to present gay people as social victims. For that reason, it's a giant step toward our legitimation.

But there's another agenda in this film, perhaps more central than its liberationist aims and surely more problematic. That agenda involves the delegitimization of the present Cuban government, a prospect we may well be forced to contend with if Reagan is reelected . . .

Two decades of ostracism have taken their toll on Cuba. Defensive macho – with its cornered response to homosexuality – may have less to do with any 400-year-old tradition than with the anguish of contemporary politics. *Improper Conduct* hardly promotes the process of normalization that must accompany any meaningful critique. On the contrary, it feeds our most bellicose intentions and inflames the paranoia that prevents Cuba coming to terms with its past and risking change.

It should also be said that there are one or two moments in the film which raise substantial doubts about the film-makers' real feelings about their subject. Most distasteful is the moment in the interview with Heberto Padilla when he describes the attitude of a Cuban official he had dealings with towards lesbians, and the titillation of imagining two women in bed together. The picture cuts emphatically to the interviewer, sharing Padilla's ribald laughter, as he and the film-makers savour the idea.

Particularly scurrilous is the film's use of a critique proposed by Susan Sontag (once an enthusiastic supporter of the Revolution) of gay repression as an expression of militaristic virility; scurrilous not because it may not be correct (though I suggest in the course of this book that militarism isn't very strong in Cuba) but because it is used to close off any further discussion of the reasons for the phenomenon. And yet these things, as psychoanalysis teaches – especially in matters of sexuality – are always overdetermined. For myself, it seems to me far more probably the result of the advancement of women within the Revolution, which has been very considerable, however much still remains to be won. But especially in a society as intensely machista as Cuba, the advancement of women represents a threat to men, or a certain kind of man, and men whose own sexuality is thus threatened are all too liable to start taking it out on other men. This, of course, is an argument the film is hardly likely to use, since it requires admitting that the Cuban Revolution indeed has positive achievements to its credit, and this it is nowhere prepared to do.

All that remains to be added on the subject of this film, from my own enquiries, is that in the context of a history of Cuban cinema, an attack on the grounds of gay repression is in certain crucial respects misplaced. First, although Cuban cinema has not yet provided any positive image of gays, nor has it fanned any homophobic flames; it can be criticised only for ignoring the subject altogether, and rendering gays invisible. Secondly, even during the worst periods of gay repression in Cuba, ICAIC, together with one or two other cultural organisms, refused to have any truck with what was going on, and protected its

6

own gay members. A final dishonesty in the film is that it leaves the impression that there are no longer any gays in Cuba living openly as gays, and this is false. It may not always be easy for them, but they have evidently made a choice which this film dishonours, in the same way that film-makers and other artists who left Cuba because their work was suppressed are not prepared to admit that there are others, who suffered the same suppression, but have chosen to remain, convinced that the Revolution is fundamentally positive, in spite of even serious aberrations. As Tomas Gutiérrez Alea has put it, in replying to Almendros in a debate about the film in the pages of *Village Voice*, 'We do not live in a paradise on earth. We're not yet the people of the future we would like to picture in our minds. Prejudice, injustice and ineptitude are still with us, and we know our struggle against that to be part and parcel of the struggle against those bent on destroying us, on wiping us off the map.' That is why, if anyone wants to call this book a partisan history, I will make no apology for it.

The act of writing is a lonely one, but over the years of writing this book, I've never felt alone. Too many people have given me their help, their time and their encouragement. First of all, the members of ICAIC: Alfredo Guevara, Julio García Espinosa, Tomás Gutiérrez Alea, Santiago Alvarez, Humberto Solás, Ambrosio Fornet, Pastor Vega, José Massip, Jorge Fraga, Manuel Octavio Gómez, Sergio Giral, Enrique Pineda Barnet, Hector García Mesa, Idalia Anreus, Daysi Granados, Miguel Torres, Manuel Pérez, Octavio Cortazár, Juan Padron, Jesus Díaz, Gerardo Chijona, Jorge Pucheux, Eusebio Ortiz, José Antonio González, Enrique Colina, Norma Torrado, Francisco Leon, Sergio Nuñez, Romualdo Santos, Mario Piedra, Manuel Pereira, Raúl Rodríguez, Roberto Roque, Jorge Sotolongo, and others. Also the composers Leo Brouwer and Harold Gramatges. For helping to organise my activities, special thanks to Olga Rios, Maria Padron, Lola Calviño; and for their courteous assistance, the projectionists of ICAIC and the staff of the library of the Cinemateca.

I have also benefited from many people apart from the members of ICAIC. In Cuba, in some cases in between films during successive Havana Film Festivals, and in other countries, they include Jorge de la Fuente, Nina Menéndez, Jean Stubbs, Pedro Sarduy, Lionel Martin and Adrienne Hunter; Julianne Burton and Zuzana Pick; Fernando Birri, Settimio Presutto, Miguel Littin, Patricio Guzmán, Joris Ivens, Jorge Sanjinés, Octavio Getino and Jorge Denti; Hector Schmucler, Ana Maria Nethol, Emilio García Riera, Jorge Ayala Blanco, Dennis de la Roca; Lino Micciché, Peter Chappell, John King, Alastair Hennessy, Nissa Torrents, Robin Blackburn, Angela Martin, Anne Head, Olivia Harris, Alan Fountain, Rod Stoneman, Chris Rodriguez and people at the South West Arts Weekend School on Cuban Cinema in 1982; thanks also to Simon Hartog for drawing my attention to a number of bibliographical sources, and to Ed Buscombe, Geoffrey Nowell-Smith and others at the BFI, particularly Jim Adams and Erich Sargeant who prepared the frame stills.

Material from this book has previously appeared in the form of articles and essays in a number of places, including *Framework*, *Areito* and *Third World Affairs 1985*, and in *Guerres Révolutionnaires, Histoire et cinéma*, ed. Sylvie Dallet, Editions l'Harmattan, Paris, 1984; the bulk of the material in Chapter 10 previously appeared in *Santiago Alvarez*, BFI Dossier No.2, 1980.

Cartoon by Juan Padrón

*Were you able to see Cuban films down there?*

Any films we wanted to see. We would just sit in the screening room and they would run anything we wanted.

*What did you think of them?*

I thought they were very good. I have been travelling around and I know very well the pain of a country like Australia that's a wealthy civilised place and yet has no film industry, because it's cheaper for them to buy our old television shows and our old movies. You see them struggling to have a little bit of a film thing. Yet here you have Cuba, which is a small place by comparison, and they have healthy, real, ambitious films.

*Are they doing experimental things?*

A person who considers himself an artist approaches a socialist society worrying about, well, the art has to be really simple and follow a certain line and make a certain point, but my impression was that there's a lot of latitude. The Cuban authority acknowledges the complexity of the human experience and their films explore that. My first impression when I saw *Memories of Underdevelopment* years ago was that it was complex and had different shades of feelings about the Revolution. They acknowledge that. They're very eloquent about it. They're not pretending that it's just child's play to put together this new kind of society; it's really hard. And for all their many successes, they've had many failures. But they feel they're right, so it's worth pursuing it.

They know that it's hard on people – the man at the mental institution says that the incidence of neurosis is much higher than before the Revolution. They are very honest about the difficulties of creating the socialist society – people rethinking questions of property, the fact that you're not rewarded monetarily. They have a very elaborate system of competition which does reward workers materially. If you do better at your job than the next person, you get to buy the washing machine. The lowest paid person might make $150 a month and Fidel makes $700 a month. So, I mean, there are some differences in pay. We asked most of the smart-ass questions. For example, let's say you don't want to be a street cleaner any more. How do you get out of it? And the key word was education. If you're a street cleaner and you want to be a draftsman or an electronics engineer, you have the opportunity to study three hours a day; you don't get paid any less. The state encourages it. It's made available to them and they are not docked in pay. That, to me, is a really exciting idea...

*Did you ask questions about the problem of artistic freedom?*

Yes. No one is permitted to criticize the government, other than through the channels that are provided for them. If you're a worker or if you're a writer, you can do it in your various workers' groups. In a factory they get together a couple of nights a week and discuss problems – how to make things better, what's unfair and stuff like that. So in other words, there are channels that allow you, not to criticize the idea of the society, but to figure out how to make it better. I like the honesty of it. They say no, you cannot criticize the government – that freedom, no, you don't have.

Here in America you can write or say anything you want – and many people in Cuba are very impressed when you tell them this. They are surprised when they see something like *Godfather II*. They wonder: 'How can you make a film that says nice things about our Revolution?' But the truth is, I believe, that the freedoms we have here are possible because they do not even come close to jeopardizing the real interests that govern our country. If there were someone who really came close to jeopardizing those interests, I believe our freedoms would vanish, one way or the other. If there were a man, a political candidate, who was elected to office and began implementing real programs that were counter to the big interests, there would be a coup or a murder or whatever was necessary.

In Cuba they don't even have the illusion of that kind of political freedom. It's as though they're saying, 'Our Revolution is too fragile, it has too many enemies, it is too difficult to pull off to allow forces inside or outside to work to counter it.' I understand the implications of what I'm saying, the dangers. But I put it to you: If they are right – if their society is truly beautiful and honest and worthwhile – then it is worth protecting, even with this suspension of freedom. In Chile, that newborn, elected society was not protected in this way, and so it was destroyed. Ironically, the government that replaced it is not taking any chances and is controlling the press and opposition in a way that Allende did not.

*It seems that what you're saying is that in Cuba, for instance, people suddenly had the freedom to do something very positive like create a mental institution or a school, which in some sense is a freedom we don't have. Basically our freedom is still limited freedom.*

We don't have the freedom to live in a society that is healthy. *That* is real freedom. We don't have the freedom to live in a society that takes care of people . . .

# 1
# FOR THE FIRST TIME

*By way of introduction*

The screen comes to life. Three men wearing the working clothes of a tropical country are grouped around the front of a truck with its bonnet open. One of them stands more or less facing the camera, another is sitting on the mudguard and the third is working on the engine. An unseen questioner is asking them about their job, and as they speak, the picture cuts to the interior of the truck, to show us the fittings they describe, including projection gear and stowaway beds. For this is a *cine movil*, a mobile cinema unit, and the job consists in showing films in small and isolated communities, in the schools during the day and for everyone in the evenings. Do they know of any place where movies have not yet been shown? 'Yes,' says one, 'I know of a place that is so entangled and the road is so bad that it's almost completely cut off. It's called Los Mulos, in the Guantanamo-Baracoa mountain region.'[1]

Then comes music and the title sequence, incorporating travelling shots taken from the cabin of the truck as it drives to Los Mulos, which is discovered lying in a valley. We are watching *Por primera vez* ('For the First Time'), a prize-winning ten minute black-and-white documentary made in 1967 and directed by Octavio Cortazár, a young Cuban director who – untypically – trained at the Prague film school.

We meet the people in the village, beginning with the children. In the schoolroom, the teacher explains about the arrival of the mobile cinema. Then a woman explains that she's lived in the village for seventeen years and they have no entertainment there. Another woman tells us, 'No, I never saw films during the time of the other government, because we couldn't go to see them and neither did they come here to the country.' The off-screen voice asks her, 'What do you think films are?' and she replies, 'They must be something very important, since you're so interested in them, they must be something very beautiful.' Another woman muses, 'Film is... well, lots of things happen in the cinema. You see snakes and you see beautiful girls and you see weddings, horses, war and all that.' 'Well,' says one of the others, 'I've never seen a film, you know, but I think maybe you get a fiesta or a dance or something like that, but I want to see one so nobody has to describe it to me.'

And then we see them watching a film – Chaplin's *Modern Times*. The sequence with the automatic lunch machine has them in tears of laughter. We see faces gazing in wide-eyed amazement and delight – the camera filming is positioned in front of them just under the screen so we see them full face. Old men and women look as if they cannot believe the cinema has really come to them, and a little girl bites her finger in excitement.

What we seem to see and hear in their conversation with the screen is what anyone must have been able to see and hear anywhere at the turn of the century, when the first teasing reports circulated about the wonders of the cinematograph machine, until finally some itinerant entertainer or adventurous small entrepreneur arrived and announced a film show. Or is it? It is said that early film viewers sometimes reacted as if the projected scene were physically before them. Gorki wrote of the Lumière film, *Teasing the Gardener*, that the image carried such a shock of veracity that 'you think the spray is going to hit you too, and instinctively shrink back'.[2] The earliest audiences, in other words, didn't always see the screen as a screen, a barrier, as it were, between them and the pictured world. But they soon learnt eagerly to accept the screen's power of illusion. This illusion hangs on the peculiar relationship which arose between the camera and the audience, which the development of narrative cinema came almost entirely to depend on: the camera as an invisible surrogate for the human observer that enables the audience to see without being seen, to feel that it is present but disembodied within the projected view – a condition which nowadays is largely taken for granted.

The viewer's naive identification with the camera becomes possible because paradoxically there is a sense in which the camera is outside the scene that is being filmed – in the same way that the eye, as Wittgenstein mentioned, is outside the view that it sees, on the edge of it, and can never see itself except in reflection. But in another sense the camera is part of, inside the scene, occupying the same area, the same space, in which it moves around, taking up first one position and then another. The effect of film depends largely on the interaction between these two viewing conditions, for it is their fusion that gives the viewer the impression of disembodiment, being present but unseen. But this state of affairs hardly impinged on the early film-makers, for whom the profilmic event – the scene they were filming—was still set apart like the scene within a theatrical set. The image reproduced on the screen was consequently also set apart, it was a world which at one and the same time reproduced reality and also swallowed it up and regurgitated it magically. This screen world looks the same as the one we live in but turns out to behave according to its own logic, its own laws, which have their own form of rationality. Whether or not, however, an audience is disposed to see the screen world as a magical one or as an authentic representation of the real world is another matter, not logical but ideological and political.

To approach the question another way: just as the classical economists regarded the act of consumption of commodities as something that occurred after all the economic transactions involved were duly completed and therefore of no

*Por primera vez*

technical interest to them, so too the act of watching a film. The film industry regards the way in which the film makes contact with the audience exclusively under the rubric of marketing. Reaching an audience is only a question of marketing it effectively; this is what brings the audience in. But there's entirely another way of seeing this relationship: as the reception by an audience of an aesthetic object. The film lives not through people paying money to see it, but through the sensual, sentimental, psychological and intellectual gratification they are able to draw from it and the significance they are able to grant it.

This aesthetic relationship is supposedly the sphere of criticism, but the marketing business is so all-embracing that too often the critic becomes merely its adjunct, a kind of glorified advertising copywriter to be quoted on the billboards. (Or else an oppositional and marginalised figure, whom the billboards sytematically exclude.) No matter that at the beginning film wasn't considered an art form. About a decade after its birth in 1895 it started to acquire the characteristics and capacities of narrative and visual expression and began to claim critical attention. But along came the big production companies that emerged after about another decade of growth, and they rapidly learnt the publicity value of claiming for their product the status of art, if only to draw in past the ticket window the more respectable classes of society who were not among the early enthusiasts for the medium. In this way old assumptions about aesthetic consumption passed to cinema, and one of the big studios even emblazoned the formula round the head of its roaring lion: *Ars gratia artis*, Art for art's sake. But it was bluff.

An Italian theorist, Antonio Banfi, has described the atomised condition which the film industry imposed on its audiences, and which, in an industry that suffered substantial risks of financial loss, it reinforced above all other possible relationships with the screen, as an insurance policy against the unpredictability that, in spite of everything, audiences continued to manifest. The book of his from which the following passage is taken was published by the Cuban Film Institute, ICAIC, during the 60s, as one of a series of texts on cinema and aesthetics which established the terms of reference for critical and theoretical discussion of these issues in revolutionary Cuba. Banfi describes the situation in the countries of the metropolis, and what he says is often much less true of the attitudes of audiences in underdeveloped countries where traditional popular cultures still have force and a more collective relationship obtains. But then his account serves as a warning:

> The cinema public is the anonymous everyday crowd of every extraction which enters with no particular social disposition or commitment, at an hour neither fixed nor anticipated, and leaves to plunge back again into the course of everyday life. As a spectator, seated among the rows, each person in the audience is enveloped in darkness, alone; there is no communication, nor reciprocal reflection. The spectator absorbs the spectacle that much more effectively and avidly as an individual.
>
> Withdrawn from inter-subjective relations, the spectator does not find the representation cathartic. Nor is there a feeling of being dominated; not only because of the impressionist and suggestive character of the representation itself and the technical artifice of which cinema avails itself with the aim of simplifying and stereotyping the action and determining the meaning, but also because of the isolation and passivity which envelops the spectator in the absence of collective participation in the spectacle. First and foremost, the spectator, more in a state of fragmentation than organic wholeness, accepts the elements of the spectacle just as they are served up. Rather than an integrated personality the spectator is more often a bundle of instincts with silent unconfessed demands, finding satisfaction in the commonplaces of rhetorical positions and solutions, the vulgar attitudes, rowdy incidents, cheap humour and banalities which make up the pastiche of cinema... At the centre is the fixation – sometimes obsessive – of types, gestures, tones and values which the spectator absorbs and unconsciously imitates, seeing, or wishing to see, life refracted in them.[3]

*Por primera vez* marks a change in all that. Cuban cinema has done more in this film than simply capture something which evaded the first film-makers. It has produced for its audience a vision of its own self-discovery *as* an audience. These simple and least portentous of images, presented without any special tricks or cleverness, communicate to a Cuban audience the most concrete possible signs of their own activity. For a non-Cuban audience too they may carry the indication of profound changes in the conditions of consumption. We see, first, that the

moment of consumption is also a moment of production – not only the production of wonder, laughter and all those other reactions, but the production of,
precisely, an audience, subjects for the film which is the object of their attention.
Secondly we see that there is nothing private about this. The experience of the
audience, the excitement that enthuses them, is contagious.

At the same time, *Por primera vez* embodies a process which is hardly present
in capitalist society, a circuit from consumption to production and back again to
consumption *such that it raises the act of consumption on to a new level*. An audience
consumes a film, a camera films them and a film is produced; the film is then
consumed by a new audience in circumstances which give them a new awareness
of their own status. The circumstances in capitalist cinema generally always leave
the audience in the same condition of naive consumption they began in. This is a
film which even outside Cuba may give audiences a rare experience of intense
vicarious delight, but for us the delight is tinged with a kind of nostalgia. For the
Cuban audience it becomes a living analogue of the development of cinema
within the Revolution, because here the audience has become, together with the
film-makers, participant observers and observant participators in the same
process.

It was the naive enthusiasm that people brought to the moving pictures at the
first encounter which led Lenin to sign the decree of 27 August 1919 which
nationalised the businesses that made up the Czarist film industry. The revolutionaries recognised this naive enthusiasm as a force to be mobilised. In conversation with Commissar of Education Lunacharsky a couple of years after the
nationalisation, Lenin expressed the belief that 'for us, film is the most important
of all the arts'. The remark is often quoted in works on the history of cinema by
people who have no real notion of what he meant and why he meant it. They
think that Lenin, who once revealed that he was suspicious of the beauty of the
music of Beethoven, was nothing but a cold propagandist. What Lenin was
talking about, however, can be seen in the way early Soviet cinema responded to
its mission with fantastic creative energy, bringing forward in the process the
first serious theoretical considerations on the medium. Something close to this
has also happened in Cuba. Cuba's leading documentarist, Santiago Alvarez,
considers the parallel extremely apt. Commenting on the comparison that has
been made more than once between his own work and that of Dziga Vertov, he
explained in a conversation with the present author, that since the comparison is
obviously correct but he didn't know Vertov's work until the early 70s, the
explanation must lie in the similarity of the situations. In other words, the
discovery of cinema in both countries in and through the revolutionary process.

With the Revolution, cinema in Cuba became, in a word, highly animated.
The mobilisation of the audience's enthusiasm in turn enthused the film-makers.
In complete contrast, in the developed countries during the same period, the
magic of cinema was wearing off. Television had invaded the home and the thrill

of the discovery of the moving image which was so strong in the early years of cinema now lay as if buried in some unconscious memory. Nowadays the child becomes accustomed to the constant presence of a miniaturised world of images constantly in motion – a very different experience from first beholding the enormous image of the cinema screen – even before it has learnt to talk. It is a world it learns to recognise perhaps no later than it learns to recognise its own reflection in a mirror.

In Britain, the loss of the cinema audience has been particularly steep. In 1945, 35 million attendances were recorded by the country's cinemas *each week* – in a country with a population of roughly 45 million. By 1978 attendance had fallen to a mere 119 million *for the whole year* (and it has since fallen to half of that). The country's population had meanwhile grown by about 10 million, which happens to be roughly the same as the present population of Cuba.

Until the start of the 80s, annual admission figures for Cuban cinema tell a very different story. By the late 1940s the figure had reached about 57 million; box office earnings in 1949 were 16.69m pesos (the Cuban peso was valued at 1 US dollar at the time of the Revolution). It was in the late 40s that cinema audiences in the US began to fall, a little later in Britain. A principal cause of this fall, television, was introduced into Cuba in the early 50s, earlier than most Latin American countries, but it made no incursion on cinema audiences because it was hardly accessible to any but the better-off classes. And indeed cinema attendance in Cuba continued to grow until 1956, when box office earnings reached 20.99m pesos. A small fall in attendance in 1957 and 58 was due to political conditions and the effects of the guerrilla war (cinemas were a target of bomb attacks). Then, the moment the Revolution took power, and its economic policies increased people's purchasing power, box office earnings shot up again and reached 22.8m pesos in 1960. This very high level – roughly 120m admissions a year – represented a national average of about seventeen cinema visits per person in a year; but since a fair proportion of the population had no access to cinema the actual attendance for those who did works out even higher. Attendance was sustained during the 60s but fell during the 70s to around 86.5m, or an average of twelve annual cinema visits per person. One reason for this reduction, however, is an increase in alternative opportunities for entertainment and cultural participation. During 1977, for example, there were 46,704 professional performances in the different arts, which recorded an attendance of 11,837,300; there were also 269,931 aficionado performances with an attendance of 47,874,800.[4] Taken together, these are almost three-quarters the number of paying cinema attendances. ICAIC was not therefore too worried by the loss in attendance. But the early 80s have seen a sudden huge fall in paying attendance, to less than half its previous level. The cinema audience has fallen not only in Cuba but in a number of other Latin American countries too, like Chile and Brazil, where colour television has now reached the mass of the audience – or rather, been planted on them. In Cuba, the spread of television has been slower, but it seems to be finally catching up on cinema there too. The reason appears to be not an improvement in the quality of television, which is poor, so much as an increase in the number of new films shown on television, which developments in video have made more easily available. Yet in the cinemas, Cuban films themselves have retained their popularity. A successful Cuban film may nowadays be seen by a million people or more in the space of its first two months' exhibition. In 1984, a first feature by Rolando Dìaz, the comedy *Los pajaros tirandole a la escopeta* ('Tables Turned') drew an audience of two million in its first two months. It is clear that cinema in Cuba has remained one of the most powerful instruments of both social cohesion and social debate.

In many ways the problem for cinema is primarily economic. There are approximately five hundred 35mm cinemas in the island, with extremely low admission prices which remain roughly the same as twenty-five years ago. A good number of these cinemas are new, either replacing older structures or situated in new locations, though the total number has remained more or less constant. At the same time, the population of Cuba has grown by about three million since the Revolution, which helped to keep the cinemas full. Additionally, a part of the increased cinema audience in the early 60s was made up of those sections of the rural population who before 1959 had virtually no access to cinema at all. The new regime decided to take cinema to them and the mobile cinemas were set up; but their showings were free. Nor was this a stop-gap policy. They still operate today and number about 100. The largest expansion, however, was in non-commercial fixed location 16mm exhibition outlets, located in cultural centres, film clubs, schools, colleges and so forth. These too collect no box office. On the last count, there were a total of 741 16mm outlets including mobile cinemas, which held 332,700 showings between them to an audience of 33,400,000. In sum, as one Latin American commentator has put it: 'By enormously expanding the cinema public and multiplying the opportunities of access to a variety of presentations, conditions for the diversification and enrichment of taste have been set in motion, also leading to intercommunication between regions of the country which used not to know each other, and the construction of an organic national culture.'⁵ If cinema isn't the only medium involved in this process, it is certainly one of the main ones.

There is a related set of figures whose careful interpretation is also revealing. The number of features now released annually is about 130. This is just over a quarter of the annual release figure at its height before the Revolution. Unsympathetic commentators would hold this reduction as evidence of the autocratic designs of the communist government. The truth is rather different. In the first place, the previous figure was primarily the result of one of the standard methods by which Hollywood ensured its control over foreign screens: by oversupplying them (the mechanisms they used are analysed in a later chapter). Secondly, the lower figure of today is partly a result of the nefarious designs of successive US administrations in maintaining an economic blockade against Cuba, which, among other things, makes it almost impossible for the Cubans to obtain those North American movies they might want to show; and which, because of the economic constraints which the country suffers as a consequence of the blockade, also requires them to economise on the purchase of films from other capitalist countries. Yet these difficulties also have a positive effect: fewer films means that each film has a potentially larger share of the audience than was previously true for all but the most successful pictures. And this contributes to the role which cinema has had in Cuba in nourishing social cohesion.

Indeed there has been a remarkable growth in Cuba of national consciousness of and through cinema. There is another film by the same director as *Por primera vez* which gives a clue as to why: *El brigadista* ('The Teacher', 1977), a feature movie, which portrays Mario, a 15-year-old member of one of the 1961 literacy brigades (*brigadista* literally means 'brigade-member') who goes to teach in a small village in a remote part of the Zapata swamp to the south of Havana. The boy's arrival is greeted with suspicion on the part of many in the village who do not believe that a kid of his age could be a teacher – including Gonzalo, the village leader, in whose house the boy is billeted. Little by little, however, Mario's tenacity and the events of the struggle against the counter-revolutionary bandits, the *gusanos* – 'worms' – hidden in the swamps, brings the boy and Gonzalo closer together. A profound friendship develops between them, as Mario teaches Gonzalo to read and write and Gonzalo teaches Mario to overcome his adolescent fears. The film is not without its problems. It represents Cuban cinema at its stylistically most traditional, with an orthodox narrative form that inevitably emphasises a certain naive *machismo* in its young hero, which is already strong enough in the story as it is. This may even have been one of the reasons why the film was so popular – it was one of the most successful ICAIC has yet made. (On the other hand, another has been *Retrato de Teresa* – 'Portrait of Teresa' – directed by Pastor Vega in 1979, which is highly critical of machismo.) However, and just as important, it was a film which had an equally strong appeal across the different generations. It stimulated the memories of both teachers and taught, bringing back to them the profound changes in their lives which the 1961 campaign had rendered; while it explained to those too young or not yet born why the literacy campaign occupied such an important position in revolutionary history. It also dealt with practically the same cultural operation, says its director, as his earlier film *Por primera vez*: the *brigadistas* brought literacy where the mobile cinemas brought the movies.[6] Both are means whereby the popular classes in Cuba have been able to discover their own reality and their own history. *El brigadista* shows a process of cultural exchange between a peasant and a boy from an urban middle class background. The portrayal is idealised but the film could not have been made without the very same process having taken place within the development of Cuban cinema itself. The experience of taking films to new audiences was instrumental in making Cuban cineastes responsive to the cultural needs of the popular classes. While they thrilled at their own good fortune in being able to make films for the first time, they were also enthused by the parallel thrill of an audience *seeing* films for the first time, and seeing things in them that had never previously been shown on Cuban cinema screens. One of the themes of the present study is the exploration of this process and its implications.

The birth of a new cinema with the Revolution in Cuba in 1959 was sponsored by the force that overthrew the dictatorship of Batista – the Rebel Army that grew out of the 26th July Movement. With the victory of the Revolution, the Cubans set about the construction of a new film industry even more rapidly than did the October Revolution. The Cuban Institute of Cinematographic Art and Industry (*Instituto Cubano de Arte e Industria Cinematográficos* – ICAIC) was created less than three months after the Rebel Army, led by Che Guevara and Camilo Cienfuegos, entered Havana on 1 January 1959, while Fidel Castro, at the other end of the island, led the rebels' entry into Santiago de Cuba. ICAIC was set up under the first decree concerning cultural affairs passed by the Revolutionary Government, signed by Castro as Prime Minister and Armando Hart as Minister of Education (now Minister of Culture). Alfredo Guevara (no relation), a young activist in the urban underground which had supported the guerrillas and a *compañero* of Fidel's since student days, was appointed to head the new organisation.

The new cinema which the Revolution promoted was not entirely without antecedents, either in Cuba, where the first political film dates back to the production of a newsreel by the Communist Party newspaper in 1939, or elsewhere in Latin America. The founder, in Argentina in 1956, of the Documentary Film School of Santa Fe, Fernando Birri, was one of a number of Latin Americans – others included the Cubans Tomás Gutiérrez Alea and Julio García Espinosa – who had studied film in Rome at the Centro Sperimentale at the beginning of the 50s, and who brought back with them to Latin America the ideals and inspiration of Italian neorealism; because, as Birri has explained, neorealism was the cinema that discovered amidst the clothing and rhetoric of development another Italy, the Italy of underdevelopment. It was a cinema of the humble and the offended which could be readily taken up by film-makers in the underdeveloped countries.[7]

At the same time, especially given the limited resources available to them and the difficulty of entering the industry in those countries where a film industry existed, there were other influences to manifest themselves as well. Birri also speaks of John Grierson, who visited the documentary and experimental film festival of the SODRE in Montevideo in 1961, of his idea of the social documentary, and of documentary as a hammer with which to mould reality; ideas which were also taught in Rome. The first film to emerge from Santa Fe, Birri's *Tire die* ('Throw Us a Dime'), completed in 1958, represents a new documentary paradigm along these lines for Latin America, a film based on a lengthy investigation (which Birri called the process of 'successive approximations to reality') among the shanty town dwellers with whom it deals and who were closely involved in its completion.

Cinema Novo in Brazil established a new paradigm for the feature film in Latin America, with examples such as *Rio, quarenta graus* ('Rio, Forty Degrees') and *Rio, zona norte* ('Rio, North Zone'), which appeared in 1955 and 1957 respectively, directed by Nelson Pereira dos Santos. While the Documentary School of Santa Fe was born, according to Birri, out of the cultural and industrial disintegration of the period – Perón was deposed late in 1955 – Cinema Novo in Brazil came about partly under the stimulation of the populism of João Goulart, Vice President during the government of Juscelino Kubitschek and then President from 1961 to 1964, when he was overthrown by a military coup. This political atmosphere, one of the Cinema Novo directors, Ruy Guerra, has said, provided a rationale within which it was possible for a number of young directors centred in Rio de Janeiro to challenge both established Brazilian commercial cinema and the European-oriented artistic production coming out of Sao Paulo.[8] But these are only the most prominent examples of the beginnings of a movement which developed in a number of countries during the 60s, in whatever way local conditions permitted, and which came together for the first time at a Meeting of Latin American Film Makers in Viña del Mar in Chile in 1967.

Before the Revolution, conditions in Cuba were hardly more favourable than in most of the rest of Latin America. The film which ICAIC regards as its principal precursor, *El Megano*, dating from 1955, was made in conditions of clandestinity and was seized at its first screening by the dictator Batista's secret police. However, the decree which established ICAIC in 1959 was not strictly speaking a straightforward act of nationalisation. It envisaged an autonomous body, empowered to 'organise, establish and develop' a national film industry, and it handed over to this body properties and facilities connected with the film business which passed into the hands of the Revolutionary Government because their owner, a certain Alonso, had been one of Batista's henchmen who fled the country after the rebels took power. The decree further empowered the new body to take over other film properties which might be further confiscated from members of the dictator's entourage. Perhaps the acquisition of a studio egged the young revolutionaries on, except that they had already been egged on precisely by the fact that the thing had been in the hands of the tyranny they had been fighting. In fact, on close examination, the decree that established ICAIC cannot be mistaken for the kind of law which would be passed by a government which just happened to acquire a film studio and didn't really know what to do with it. Both the preamble and the law itself clearly show that its authors understood the character of the forces that had prevented the growth of an independent film industry in Cuba until then, and it contains an analysis of the structure needed to set up an industry which might be able in the future to escape those forces. The preamble begins by declaring cinema an art, an instrument for the creation of individual and collective consciousness, accordingly able to contribute to the deepening of the revolutionary spirit and to feeding its creative inspiration. But then it goes on clearly to speak of the need to establish an appropriate technical infrastructure and a distribution apparatus. In sum, the text tells us a good deal about the political understanding, intelligence and intentions of its authors, members of the revolutionary vanguard which stood behind the Provisional Government. This Provisional Government was seen by the international media at the time as a novel kind of bourgeois nationalist social democratic grouping, which was precisely the revolutionaries' purpose. This decree, though couched in language which does not openly contradict such an impression, is on closer examination good evidence that whatever the appearances, there were people at work here intent on the creation of socialism.

But how far back should we go, trekking through the historical undergrowth, in order to answer the question how it was that the Cuban revolutionaries learnt to place such a high value on cinema. What do we need to know about the history of cinema in Cuba before 1959? What do we need to know about the history of Cuba apart from its cinema? And about the cultural and political history of the revolutionaries who promoted the decree and set up ICAIC?

## References

1.  Throughout the book, quotations from films have been made either from dialogue scripts provided by ICAIC or, as in this case, by direct transcription from the film on a viewing machine. Some of the dialogue scripts were supplied in English translation, otherwise all translations are my own. This also applies to all foreign language texts unless an English translation is cited.
2.  M. Gorki, 'You Don't Believe Your Eyes', reprinted in *World Film News*, March 1938. (Place of publication for English sources if none is given is London.)
3.  Antonio Banfi, *Filosofía del arte*, Ediciones ICAIC, 1967, p.72. (Place of publication for Spanish sources if none is given is Havana.)
4.  Figures compiled from the *Anuario Cinematográfico y Radial Cubano*, the pre-revolutionary film trade annual; Francisco Mota, '12 aspectos economicos de la cinematografía cubana', *Lunes de Revolución* 6 February 1961; Armando Hart, *Del trabajo cultural*, Editorial de Ciencias Sociales, 1978, p.338.
5.  Néstor García Canclini, *Arte popular y sociedad en América Latina*, Editorial Grijalbo, Mexico 1977, pp.247-8; 16mm exhibition figures supplied by ICAIC, 1983.
6.  Mayra Villasis, interview with Octavio Cortazár, 'El documental, Cortazár, El brigadista', *Cine Cubano* No.93, p.76.
7.  Fernando Birri in *New Cinema of Latin America, I – Cinema of the Humble*, dir. Michael Chanan 1983. See also F. Birri, 'Cinema y subdesarrollo', *Cine Cubano* No.42-43-44, p.13.
8.  Interview with Ruy Guerra, 'El cine brasileño y la experiencia del Cinema Nuovo', *Octubre* (Mexico) Nos.2-3, January 1975, p.46.

# 2
# BACK TO THE BEGINNING

*The films of the Cuban-Spanish-American War of 1898*

In 1972, a full-length documentary appeared ironically entitled *Viva la Republica* ('Long Live the Republic'), directed by Pastor Vega. An historical compilation juxtaposing a variety of old newsreels, photographs, political cartoons and similar visual material, and narrated with a wit that makes the most of the very crudeness and limitations of such stuff, the film elegantly traces the history of the Republic set up under US tutelage at the beginning of the century, following the expulsion of the Spanish after their defeat in the Cuban-Spanish-American War in 1898. Close to the start we see two of the very earliest newsreels (actualities, as they were then called), scenes of the war as issued by the Edison company. One of them pictures Teddy Roosevelt's Rough Riders disembarking on the island. They were among the very first films to be shot in Cuba, and were probably filmed by Albert E. Smith, pioneer of actualities and co-founder of the New York Vitagraph company. Like all the earliest films, they're hardly more than moving photographs.

Brief and crude as they are, these fragments should not be underestimated. However minimal they are as images – the camera remains distant from its subject and there is very little detail – they were already capable of satisfying a more than simple demand by the audience for spectacle, mere wonder at the magic of the moving image. They were made not for Cuban audiences, but for those of North America in the epoch of the robber barons, where, however naive, their interest had been carefully nurtured by the new mass press of the day – especially by the two leading newspaper chains of Pulitzer and of Hearst.

William Randolph Hearst provided the model for Charles Foster Kane in Orson Welles' famous first film *Citizen Kane* of 1940. A scene early in the picture makes passing reference to the role of Hearst's New York *Journal* (Kane's *Inquirer* in the film) in fomenting popular encouragement for the Cuban war. Kane's ex-guardian Thatcher protests at a headline which reads 'Galleons of Spain off Jersey Coast'. 'Is this really your idea of how to run a newspaper?' Thatcher asks Kane. 'You know perfectly well there's not the slightest proof that this armada is off the Jersey Coast.' Bernstein, Kane's general manager, interrupts with a cable from a correspondent called Wheeler whom Kane has sent to Cuba, modelled on the real Richard Harding Davies sent by Hearst. 'Girls delightful in Cuba stop,' reads the cable. 'Could send you prose poems about scenery but don't feel right spending your money stop. There is no war in Cuba. Signed Wheeler.' 'Any answer?' asks Bernstein. 'Yes,' says Kane, 'Dear Wheeler, you provide the prose poems, I'll provide the war.' One of the ways Pulitzer and Hearst competed against each other was by building sensationalist press campaigns around the Cuban War of Independence.

This kind of real historical reference, and not just the film's virtuosity, is one of the elements that made *Citizen Kane* a radical movie; yet its attitude towards Cuban history – 'there is no war in Cuba' – is cavalier. The newspapers of both press barons published releases by the Junta of Cuban Exiles in the United States, from the moment it was established in 1895 with the aim of winning recognition for Cuban belligerency. People certainly knew there was a war going on ninety miles from Miami, indeed a revolution – and at that time, North Americans weren't yet afraid of the word. Their own revolutionary origins were still alive in popular memory, and the Cubans attracted a good deal of sincere sympathy. But they also attracted, says the North American historian Philip Foner, 'elements... who viewed the Revolution as an issue suited to their own purposes, such as American traders and investors who were directly connected with Cuban affairs and wished to protect their trade and investments in the island; expansionist elements who were seeking foreign markets for manufactured goods and for the investment of surplus capital; businessmen and politi-

*Viva la republica*: Batista with US Ambassador Sumner Welles

cians who cared nothing for the revolutionary struggle in Cuba but saw in it an opportunity to divert popular thinking away from the economic and social problems arising from the depression which had begun in 1893; and newspaper publishers who saw in the Cuban Revolution an opportunity to boost circulation.'[1]

Throughout 1897 and 98, atrocity stories flowed north from the island, both fabricated and exaggerated. Another historian: 'Vivid language, striking sketches drawn by men who never left New York, lurid details composed in bars and cafes mingled with the truth about Cuba until the whole fabric dazzled millions into a stunned belief. Reporters rescued damsels in distress and upheld the American flag in filibustering expeditions. Artists furnished pictures from the palm-fringed isle and toured incognito in the devastated cane fields and sickened cities... An elaborate system of spies and rumor mongers spread lies.'[2]

When the USS *Maine* exploded in Havana harbour – it was moored there supposedly on a good-will visit – on 15 February 1898, killing over 250 officers and crew, the newspapers didn't wait for the naval report on the cause of the explosion (which might just have been an accident). A few days earlier, Hearst's *Journal* had published a photographic reproduction – another new technology – of a private letter by the Spanish ambassador in Washington insulting the American president. The *Journal* now coined the slogan 'Remember the *Maine*, To hell with Spain' and offered $50,000 for the 'detection of the perpetrators of the *Maine* outrage'. With more than eight pages devoted to the incident every day, the circulation of the *Journal* more than doubled in the space of a week. In fierce competition, Pulitzer sent deep-sea divers to the scene of the wreck, and the circulation of his *World* also rose hugely. The site of the wreck was filmed by Cuba's own film pioneer, José G. González. In France, Méliès made a reconstruction of the scene, typically delightful and fantastical, fish swimming around in a glass-walled tank with a disproportionate cut-out of a ship resting on the bottom.

As pressure for US military intervention had mounted, wrote Albert E. Smith in his autobiography, *Two Reels and a Crank*, he and his assistant Blackton went to film the preparations for war at Hoboken, 'where New York's famous old 71st National Guard Regiment was gathered to entrain for Tampa, assembly point for the invasion troops. We found the soldiers shuffling willy-nilly from ferryboat to train and called this to the attention of an officer. "We can't take pictures of your boys straggling along this way. You wouldn't want a New York audience to see this sort of marching on the screen." The officer assembled a hundred men in tight lines of eight, marched them briskly by our camera.'[3] A revealing incident. Clearly Smith had an eye for what constituted a 'proper' picture. And evidently even the earliest film-makers knew they were doing more than just taking moving snapshots. On the contrary, Smith was already prepared to intervene here in order to produce a certain image, he was ready to do a bit of stage managing, to work the image up in order to get what we can properly call an ideological effect. (Notice, however, that precisely the same kind of work is needed for what may also properly be termed the aesthetic labour required by the new art form.)

Nonetheless, the early film-makers were often surprised by their own work – something that is bound to happen in any art form when the frontiers of expression are under exploration. Because they were starting from scratch, the creative conditions in which the early film-makers worked were precisely what artists in other media engaged in the modernist revolution were themselves looking for, but for them a struggle was needed to explode the traditional parameters of expression and throw the traditional criteria of aesthetic judgment and reasoning into question. There were all sorts of things, however, that film-makers did spontaneously and unselfconsciously which had precisely this effect; so that in a strange way, film, which had no traditions because it was utterly new, was to become the most deeply characteristic of modern art forms.

Albert Smith was taken by surprise at the very first projection of his images of the 71st. 'The film was developed in time for a special showing at Tony Pastor's that night. One factor had escaped us, and we were unprepared for the demonstration that took place. Public indignation over the *Maine* had taken on another form. Now the public was crying out its confidence in American strength; the spirit of patriotism was a rousing aria on every street corner . . . That night at Pastor's the audience, enthralled with the idea of a war with Spain, saw their boys marching for the first time on any screen. They broke into a thunderous storm of shouting and foot stamping. Hats and coats filled the air. Never had Pastor's witnessed such a night!'

Theodore Roosevelt was Assistant Secretary for the Navy and one of the strongest advocates of us military intervention. Thanks to his great zeal for publicity, Smith and Blackton soon found themselves travelling to Cuba with the famous Rough Riders, a cavalry regiment but on this occasion unhorsed. Once there, Smith filmed them in action in what came to be known as the Charge up San Juan Hill. Roosevelt, who knew a thing or two about promoting his image, at one point in this Charge halted and struck a pose for the camera.

An hour or two out of port as they left the island with their film in the can, Smith and Blackton heard the low distant thunder of heavy guns. In Florida, they learnt that the Spanish admiral, bottled up in Santiago de Cuba by us warships, had tried to make a run for it. It was the Fourth of July and the us navy had sunk the Spanish fleet. New York was buzzing with the news when they got back there. Unsure exactly what their footage was like, they at first resolved to keep mum about what they had actually filmed. But reporters hungry for information gathered round them and they were asked if they'd got shots of the sea battle. 'At this precise moment,' wrote Smith, 'flushed with triumph, I think we would have taken credit for any phase of the Cuban campaign. "Certainly, certainly," I said, and Blackton nodded solemnly as if I had spoken a simple irrefutable truth . . . Once in our office, we knew we were in trouble. Word had spread through New York that Vitagraph had taken pictures of the Battle of Santiago Bay.'

The only way out, they decided, was to fake it. They bought large sturdy photographs of ships of the US and Spanish fleets that were on sale in the streets of New York. They cut them out and stood the cut-outs in water an inch deep in an inverted canvas-covered picture frame, with blue tinted cardboard painted with clouds for a background. They nailed the cut-outs to small blocks of wood and placed small pinches of gunpowder on the wooden blocks. They pulled the cut-outs past the camera with a fine thread and used cotton dipped in alcohol at the end of a wire, thin enough to escape the camera's vision, to set off the gunpowder charges. To complete the effect, assistants blew cigarette and cigar smoke into the picture.

The result, seen today, is clearly a model, but not then: 'It would be less than the truth to say we were not wildly excited at what we saw on the screen,' Smith continued. 'The smoky overcast and the flashes of fire from the "guns" gave the scene an atmosphere of remarkable realism. The film and the lenses of that day were imperfect enough to conceal the crudities of our miniature, and as the picture ran for only two minutes there wasn't time for anyone to study it critically. Deception though it was then, it was the first miniature, and the forerunner of the elaborate "special effects" techniques of modern picturemaking. Pastor's and both Proctor houses played to capacity audience for several weeks. Jim [Blackton] and I felt less and less remorse of conscience when we saw how much excitement and enthusiasm were aroused by *The Battle of Santiago Bay* and the thirty-minute long *Fighting With Our Boys in Cuba*. Almost every newspaper in New York carried an account of the showings, commenting on Vitagraph's remarkable feat in obtaining on-the-spot pictures of these two historical events.'

Smith and Blackton were not the only people to fake a Battle of Santiago Bay. Two Cuban writers on cinema, Sara Calvo and Alejandro Armengol, mention another in a passage on the relations between politics and the new-born film business:

The principal North American companies – Edison, Biograph and Vitagraph – exploited this war for ideological, political and economic ends. Biograph enjoyed the financial assistance of the future president McKinley, at that time Governor of Ohio. This company, under the flag of the Monroe slogan, provided the politician's personal propaganda and was to specialize in actuality and documentary material. Vitagraph was *Tearing Down the Spanish Flag* in 1898, on the day hostilities between Spain and the United States broke out. Scarcely had military operations begun than hundreds of copies of fake documentaries on the war were circulating through America. One of the most famous was shot in Chicago by Edward H. Amet, using models and a bathtub to show the naval battle... Amet dealt with the problem that the battle had occurred at night by claiming very seriously that he had a film 'supersensitive to the light of the moon' and a telephoto lens capable of recording images at a hundred kilometres' distance. It is said that the Spanish Government managed to acquire a copy of such an 'important' graphic 'document' for its archives.[4]

Neither such supersensitive film nor telephoto lens existed then – they have only been developed recently for use in surveillance satellites – but it seems that the question didn't even occur to the press in New York. Calvo and Armengol conclude that films like this 'offered a stereotyped image of the war, devoid of the participation of the Cubans, who suffered discrimination and not a few humiliations in the struggle.'

It isn't difficult to understand why audiences should have been taken in by faked images. Smith makes it clear in what he writes that whatever the publicity claims of the early film business about the way the cinematograph reproduced the world in all its detail and sharpness, the early film-makers themselves were quite aware of the limitations of their apparatus. Audiences, however, had nothing effectively to compare with these images that might reveal them as fakes, except perhaps for photographs. But photographs were not a sufficient test. Apart from any other consideration, photographs themselves carried an ideological charge which also contributed to the inclination of the audience to see the war uncritically. Photographs of countries like Cuba – everywhere in the Americas south of the Rio Grande – generally came into the category of the exotic. The very idea of the exotic is a creation of imperialism. It expresses the point of view of the metropolis towards its periphery. The concept of exoticism identifies the gulf between the self-proclaimed civilisation of the metropolis and ways of life beyond it: primitive societies full of strange and unfamiliar features, the stranger the more interesting – as Lukács once observed, speaking of certain 19th century French novels – like the curious use of dogs milk and flies' feet as cosmetics.

The history of the exotic image goes back to the 1590s, when Theodore de Bry published more than a dozen volumes of engravings of the Great Voyages, the *Historia Americae*. Between them, de Bry and the authors of the accounts whose drawings he copied gave visual form to the world discovered by the *conquistadores*, enfolding it within the mythological vision of a Europe still emerging from the middle ages. The fantastical images of *Historia Americae* wove spells over those who looked upon them. They evidently included Shakespeare, who doubtless found de Bry in the library of one of his patrons. Describing one of the most haunting of these images, he has Othello speak of

> travel's history
> Wherein of antres vast and desarts idle,
> Rough quarries, rocks and hills whose heads touch heaven . . .
> And of the Cannibals that each other eat,
> The Anthropophagi and men whose heads
> Do grow beneath their shoulders.

But, as Shakespeare, with the prescience of his genius, intimates in his last play, *The Tempest*, where he repeats the image of the 'men whose heads stood in their

From the *Historia Americae*

breasts', the strange forms and behaviour of which these images tell are the projections of the colonisers – a reaction to encountering, in those they proceeded to conquer, creatures disturbingly like themselves who nonetheless, like his own creation Caliban, did not fit their own ideas of what it is to be human.

The image of the exotic undergoes a transformation and intensification in the nineteenth century with the coming of photography, not just because of the new conditions for the production of images but also because photography became a vehicle of nineteenth-century empiricism. 'The view of reality as an exotic prize to be tracked down and captured by the diligent hunter-with-a-camera has informed photography from the very beginning,' writes Susan Sontag. 'Gazing on other people's reality with curiosity, with detachment, with professionalism, the ubiquitous photographer operates as if that activity transcends class interests, as if its perspective is universal.'[5] The camera collects the facts. A Frenchman with a daguerreotype was already roaming the Pacific in 1841, two years after the invention of photography had been announced to the world. Painters soon realised how the camera would undermine the credibility of their foreign landscapes and adopted it as an ally instead. Already in 1841 in Mexico,

Frederick Catherwood took photographs in Yucatán where he had been painting for several years. And in 1844, Arago, the man who persuaded the French parliament to purchase the invention for the nation because of its scientific importance, promoted a daguerreotype expedition to photograph the aborigines of Brazil. The very authenticity of such images contributed to their exoticism, because of lacking any context in which to read them. As a scientist, the early photographer was locked into the tabulating methods of empiricism, engaged in making inventories of everything, and the naturalism of the camera fitted; this was a different form of endeavour from, say, the imaginative synthesis, in Darwin, of the theoretical naturalist. The photographic intelligence in its infancy was more like that of the utilitarian minister with bible in one hand, magnifying glass in the other (in E.P. Thompson's phrase), whose illusion of productivity in the pursuit of knowledge consisted in nothing more than the patient assembly of detail upon detail without ever being able to show their connections. In the same dissociated way, the exotic image made no connection with the immediate reality of those who looked upon it. The camera conquered geographical, but not cultural distance.

With the coming of moving images, venturing to obtain the exotic image for the audience back home went hand in hand with opening up a market for the invention in the countries of the exotic themselves. Moving pictures were first brought to Cuba by Gabriel Veyre, agent for the French company of Lumière Frères, early in 1897. He arrived in Havana from Mexico, where he'd unveiled the *cinématographe* on 14 August 1896 – eight months after its Paris debut, six months after another Lumière agent, Félicien Trewey, introduced it in London. The Lumières sent a team of agents around the world on planned itineraries designed to sweep up on the fascination the new invention created everywhere, preferably in advance of competitors – the Havana debut of the *cinématographe* on 24 January was quickly followed by the arrival from the USA of Edison's version on 13 February and the rival North American Biograph on 10 April. The Lumière machine served as both projector and camera and the agents were briefed to bring back scenes from the countries they visited. Since these films were developed on the spot, they were also exhibited immediately, and thus provided the first examples of local imagery in moving pictures. In Mexico, Veyre filmed at least thirty scenes, ranging from the President and his entourage to local dancing and groups of Indians. In Cuba, as a condition of being allowed into the country, he was required by the Spanish authorities to take military propaganda scenes, views of the artillery in action and of troops on the march.[6]

The content of the images of the Cuban-Spanish-American War was, above all, the projection of the power of the state – like the content ever since of the images of US landings in Latin America, from Nicaragua in the 1920s to Grenada in 1983. The spectacle of war, of the military, and of state display – coronations, state visits, imperial ceremonial – were all popular subjects in early cinema. (British film-makers excelled at the ceremonials, but they also made effective films of the Boer War, where Smith contributed his expertise too.) For as Thomas Hobbes once observed, power is the reputation of power. It was sufficient for early audiences to be presented with the crudest images, little more than the reputation of the reputation, and they were engaged by them. If scenes like these became a genre, an established term in the vocabulary of screen rhetoric, this is because they functioned first and foremost not on the level of information but like religious icons: they aroused the devotion of an audience to an idea.

This is the source of some of film's first ideological functions, and it comes from something more than the automatism of the camera, its mechanical capacity to record whatever it's exposed to – as Albert E. Smith, for one, realised very rapidly. Yet although Smith's fakery was deliberate, it's not that it arose exactly from a desire to deceive, or only in a superficial sense. Their 'invention' of the miniature was a discovery in what the medium lent itself to, as well as an organic response to an eager audience that made them feel they were only satisfying a 'natural demand'. And they were. Because in consuming moving pictures the audience stimulated their production not merely economically but also, through their ready surrender of self to the content of the image, on the level of symbolic exchange.

This does not, however, authorise us to say that the ideological effects of film were ingrained in the image itself, as if they were part of the chemical process. In fact, they arise in the relationship of the screen with the audience, in the space between the screen and the spectator. The ideological disposition of commercial cinema saw to it that the emerging screen vocabulary was formalised and pressed into service in ways that seemed to lock the ideological message on to the screen. Nevertheless it would be a very undialectical approach which took the effects of film to be so fixed – and the relationship of the screen to the audience to be so mechanical – that they cannot change with different audiences and in different situations and circumstances. Pastor Vega's *Viva la Republica* is a film which plays on this possibility, in particular upon the altered perspective of an audience which has seen the Revolution triumph and then the defeat of the invasion of the Bay of Pigs sponsored by the CIA, which left the reputation of US power irretrievably tarnished.

Cuba's revolutionary cinema has sought to undermine that power further, by building on the audience's new attitude towards the screen to create both a more critical disposition in the audience, and a radical film language. The experience both of guerrilla warfare and of the popular militia that the Revolution created after it took power provide the underpinning for a number of films which use experimental cinematic techniques explicitly to demystify the iconography of warfare as portrayed in conventional Hollywood cinema. Over the same years that saw the invention of film, Cuban patriots were engaged in a War of Liberation against Spain, a struggle dating back to 1868. The events of that year are recreated in *La primera carga al machete* ('The First Machete Charge'), directed by Manuel Octavio Gómez, one of the films which ICAIC produced at the end of the 60s to celebrate one hundred years of struggle. Highly experimental both visually and narratively, shot in black and white to imitate the high contrast of very early film stocks, it is constructed as if it were a piece of contemporary documentary reportage on the events, including interviews with the participants, and sections of explanatory documentary.

But it is not as if the conventional iconography of warfare was a secret. Albert E. Smith's account of his Cuban adventure includes a pertinent comment on the way the image of the Charge up San Juan Hill came to be embroidered: 'Many historians,' he wrote, 'have given it a Hollywood flavour, but there was vastly more bravery in the tortuous advance against this enemy who could see and not be seen.' In other words, not only does the Hollywood image not correspond to reality, but it over-dramatises; intending to produce the image of super-heroism, it ends up negating the quiet heroism of the real situation. (This seems to be true of the conventional anti-war movie as well). To expose these genres for what they are, the Cubans have also produced films like Manuel Herrera's feature-length documentary reconstruction of the Bay of Pigs, *Girón*, made in 1972, a film testimonial which builds up an account of what happened through the recollections not of experts, analysts and leaders, but of ordinary people who made their contributions on the day and then returned to their regular lives. Their testimonies are filmed in the real locations of the events, and the film reconstructs their stories behind them as they speak. A member of the militia at the time of the invasion remembers the moment when he had to throw a hand grenade for the first time: 'I tried to pull the pin out with my teeth, because I thought I would try and copy what they did in the cinema, but that way I'd only have broken my jawbone. I realised that using your teeth is strictly for the movies...' And to top it, a woman then relates how she too imitated the movies: she was on her way with a message to headquarters from her militia unit, walking along a beach, when she heard suspicious noises, which she was afraid might have been invading mercenaries. To be sure they wouldn't get the message if they captured her, she decided she'd better eat it. It was harder to chew, she says, than she expected.

Cuban cinema hasn't always abandoned the portrayal of war in the idealised forms of genre cinema. A number of films, like *El brigadista*, set out to use, rather than subvert, the iconography of Hollywood. They are not dishonest films, but they sometimes run into trouble, reproducing unwanted elements of genre uncritically, like *El brigadista*'s reinforcement of the individual macho hero. *La primera carga al machete* and *Girón*, however, are films of a different instinct, more central to the development of ICAIC, which is to try and relocate the point of view of the film upon the narrative which it relates, in order to find ways to communicate the popular experience of real situations without falling into the traps of populism.


The invention of cinematography had required a lengthy period of gestation, but once achieved, its basic principles were easily enough grasped by people anywhere who had moderate mechanical skills, no more than a smattering of scientific knowledge, and some acquaintance with photography. This combination existed wherever the machines of the industrial revolution had penetrated, and the task of maintaining and repairing them had produced practical knowledge. The lines of communication with the metropolis brought the rest. Local film-makers took no longer to appear in Cuba than in most of Latin America. English machinery came into use on the sugar plantations in the 1830s, and increasing trade with the United States after the mid-century made much of the latest mechanical equipment available. A Spanish traveller found a us-made sewing machine in a remote Cuban village as early as 1859. One of the men who filmed the scene of the sinking of the *Maine*, José G. González, tried his hand, like many film pioneers the world over, at many things. He constructed, for example, illuminated commercial signs. He had a competitor who apparently attempted to project signs on to clouds in the sky, an idea subsequently toned down to projection on to the façades of buildings, as was done in London in the early 1890s. A fancy anecdote, perhaps, but it shows that the principles of the magic lantern were perfectly well known in Havana. Similarly the other fashionable forms of popular visual entertainment. At the moment film made its Cuban debut there were, in the city, numerous photographic establishments and a couple of Panoramas – the *Panorama Soler* specialised in war scenes, and other optical illusions were on display at the *Salón de variedades*. There was also a range of temporary and open-air attractions.

After their intervention against Spain, the North American style of urban commercialism was transmitted rapidly to Havana. Havana had always been an open city, a busy port on the routes in and out of destinations throughout the Caribbean and the Gulf of Mexico, a cosmopolitan city open to European influences. It had suffered occupation by the British in 1762, but culturally much more important was the French presence during the nineteenth century in Louisiana and in Mexico. (There are even Hollywood movies of the 30s and 40s starring people like Nelson Eddy, in which expatriate French aristocrats roam the Caribbean from New Orleans to Martinique.) The mark of French culture survived in Cuba right into the twentieth century, but at the moment when cinema was born, Havana was poised to pass under North American influence, which though already present, intensified greatly with the establishment of the Republic. The early years of the century saw the Havana bourgeoisie coming increasingly under the sway of North American ideas and uneasy with the revolutionary nationalism to be found particularly in the eastern parts of the island. Following the defeat of the Spanish, the United States left a military government in Cuba which tried to resist nationalist pressures but was forced, after two years, to call a constituent assembly to draw up a constitution for a new republic. This assembly was expressly instructed to make provision in the constitution for us-Cuban relations, which they initially declined to do on the grounds that such provisions had no place in a constitution. But there were forces in Washington determined to curb patriotic resistance in the island and ensure that the constitution gave formal recognition to their demands. Their only concern was to give their threats and ultimatums a semblance of legality. This was contrived by means of an amendment to an Army Appropriation Bill which carried the name of Senator Platt, and which stated the conditions the US would require to see fulfilled before the occupation was ended. The Platt Amendment fooled nobody. There was a certain amount of doubletalk about just intentions, but the *Washington Post*, in those days a Republican and pro-administration paper, offered the truth. An editorial under the headline 'Let us be Honest' declared:

Foolishly or wisely, we want these newly acquired territories, not for any missionary or altruistic purpose, but for the trade, the commerce, the power and the money that are in them. Why beat about the bush and promise and protest all sorts of things? Why not be honest. It will pay. Why not tell the truth and say what is the fact – that we want Cuba, Puerto Rico, Hawaii and Luzon [all acquired through the defeat of the Spanish] . . . because we believe they will add to our national strength and because they will some day become purchasers at our bargain counters?[7]

The Constitutional Assembly acceded to the Platt Amendment by only a narrow majority, but it was the Havana bourgeoisie with their northward orientation that won the day with the argument that conditional independence was better than continued occupation. In Europe, Cuba was now seen as a US dependency. Following official independence celebrations on 20 May 1902, the London *Saturday Review* commented:

It is true that the American troops and officials have been withdrawn, the American flag hauled down, and a republic of sorts inaugurated. But it is not true that the republic is independent even in the management of its internal affairs, while so far as foreign relations go, it is undisguisedly under the thumb of Washington. The republic has been obliged to cede naval and coaling stations to the United States; it has no power to declare war without American consent; it may not add to the Cuban debt without permission; even its control over the island treasury is subject to supervision. Moreover, the United States retains a most elastic right of intervention.[8]

Which they exercised twice in the following decade, between 1906 and 9 and again in 1912.

This was the atmosphere in which the first film-makers in Cuba began to work. Compared with, say, Mexican cinema, Cuba was a bit slow off the mark, but this is probably only because the market was so much smaller. Nevertheless, and despite the difference in size, the two countries show similar characteristics, most of them typical of early film activity almost anywhere, such as the links with fairground entertainment and popular comic and musical theatre. But there's one trait they share which is particularly interesting. The uses of film in Mexico constitute, even before the turn of the century, a catalogue of initiatives in the techniques of marketing. In 1899, for example, the newspaper *El Imparcial* was offering its readers free film shows if they smoked a certain brand of cigarettes. Indeed the link between film and advertising can be found right at the start: another paper, *El Nacional*, reported in the very year film arrived in Mexico, 1896, a project to set up temporary premises in the city centre with free film shows of *vistas pintorescas* – picturesque views – financed by including colour-slide advertisements in the programme.

There is a temptation to call such examples prophetic, for the way they seem to anticipate the symbiotic relationship between programme and advertisement in commercial broadcasting, but there is also something odd about them, because film wasn't destined to develop in this way. Radio and television learnt to make advertisements pay for programmes because they are forms of diffusion where you can't make the audience pay directly, or couldn't until pay-TV was developed. There are other methods available to pay for broadcasting of course – licensing, sponsorship, straight state subsidy – and it is always significant which method a society chooses. In the same way, it says something about conditions in Mexico that such hare-brained schemes were thought up for the early film. It says that film found it difficult there for some reason to capture the audience that awaited it; and the reason must be an economic one – probably the fact that the vast majority of people had hardly any spare cash to spend on such things, and therefore needed special inducement. Conditions for working people in the metropolis, bad though they were, were already better than this: the last quarter of the nineteenth century had brought, in countries like England, a real increase in purchasing power.

Most of the desirable conditions for launching film successfully could be found in most Latin American countries, and its early development took place in similar circumstances in different countries. In Cuba, too, there was a close link, from the start, with the ideology of marketing. One of the very few early Cuban films of which records survive is *El brujo desapareciendo* ('The Disappearing Magician') – the title suggests it must have been a trick film of the kind that was perfectly typical of early cinema. It was made, prior to 1906, by a certain José E. Casasús. Casasús was a pioneering exhibitor who began his career travelling round the island with an Edison projector and a portable electric generator, exactly like the 'town hall' showmen in Britain at the same time. This film they made turned out quite successfully – copies were purchased by the French Lumière company, and by Edison in the United States. But it was made with money subscribed by a beer merchant.

In 1906, to celebrate the opening of Cuba's first purpose-built cinema, the *Teatro Actualidades* ('Theatre of Actualities'), another pioneer, Enrique Díaz Quesada made a scenic film, *La Habana en agosto 1906* ('Havana in August 1906'), and in the same year, *El Parque de Palatino* ('Palatino Park'), showing scenes of Havana's principal entertainment park. The Cuban film historian J.M. Valdés Rodríguez described this second film as a distinct achievement 'which at moments conveyed irony and humour'.[9] It seems, nevertheless, precisely in this film that an ideological fusion with the function of publicity took place: the film was commissioned by the entertainments park company for its publicity campaigns in the United States. Two years later Díaz Quesada made another film in the same vein, whose title was quite explicit: *Un turista en la Habana* ('A Tourist in Havana'). Obviously these films presented a highly selective picture of the city, since they were meant to show it as a commodity on the tourist market.

But this would hardly have required any great effort on the part of anyone with the minimum photogenic sense of the time. The link between tourism and photography was well established. Susan Sontag calls this the predatory side of photography, and it follows upon the exploitation of the exotic. The alliance between photography and tourism, she says, becomes evident in the United States earlier than anywhere else:

> After the opening of the West in 1869 by the completion of the transcontinental railroad came the colonization through photography. The case of the American Indians is the most brutal. Discreet, serious amateurs like Vroman had been operating since the end of the Civil War. They were the vanguard of an army of tourists who arrived by the end of the century, eager for 'a good shot' of Indian life. The tourists invaded the Indians' privacy, photographing holy objects and the sacred dances and places, if necessary paying the Indians to pose and getting them to revise their ceremonies to provide more photogenic material.[10]

The selective and tendentious imagery which is produced in this kind of cultural operation cannot escape having an invisible shadow, the underside of the innocuous attractions of tourism, and of the mysteries of the exotic: the menace of what these constructs render invisible; like the underworld pictured by Francis Ford Coppola in *Godfather II*, in which Havana is a city prostituted to the gangsterism of the brothel, the sex show and the gambling den. It was indeed an ineluctable part of the city's image, which Graham Greene satirised in his spoof spy novel *Our Man in Havana*. It has also been captured by a Cuban director, Oscar Valdés, in a film made in 1973 called *El extraño caso de Rachel K.* ('The Strange Case of Rachel K.'), a fictionalised account of an incident which occurred in 1931, when a French variety dancer was murdered during an orgy attended by politicians and prominent society leaders. A few years later, President Roosevelt was advising the Cubans to clean the city up, but the corruption only grew, until the Mafia were able to congratulate each other (in Coppola's depiction) for finding in Cuba what they couldn't find in the USA itself – a government prepared to work with them as partners.

# References

1. Philip S. Foner, *The Spanish-Cuban-American War and the Birth of American Imperialism*, Monthly Review Press, 1972, Vol.1, pp.167-8.
2. H. Wayne Morgan, *America's Road to Empire: The War with Spain and Overseas Expansion*, Wiley, 1965, p.13.
3. Albert E. Smith, *Two Reels and a Crank*, Doubleday, 1952, p.55 (subsequent quotations chapter five *passim* and p.148).
4. Sara Calvo and Alejandro Armangol, *El racismo en el cine*, Serie Literatura y Arte, Dpto. de Actividades Culturales Universidad de la Habana, 1978, p.27 (note 16).
5. Susan Sontag, *On Photography*, Farrar, Straus and Giroux, New York 1977, pp.54-5.
6. For details in this paragraph and below, see Aurelio de los Reyes, *Los origenes del cine en Mexico (1896-1900)*, UNAM Cuadernos de Cine (Mexico), 1973, p.178; Arturo Agramonte, *Cronologia del cine cubano*, Ediciones ICAIC, 1966; articles in the *Anuario Cinematográfico y Radial Cubano*; and Rolando Díaz Rodríguez and Lazaro Buria Pérez, 'Un caso de colonización cinematográfica', *Caimán Barbudo* No.85, December 1965.
7. Quoted in Foner, op.cit. Vol.II, p.562.
8. Ibid., p.669.
9. J.M.Valdés Rodríguez, 'Algo en torno al cine y la República Cubana' II, *El Mundo*, 19 April 1960.
10. Sontag, op.cit., p.64.

# 3
# THE NINETEENTH-CENTURY HERITAGE

*Cuban culture from Romanticism to* Modernismo

José Casasús and Enrique Díaz Quesada were not the only Cuban film pioneers who made commissioned publicity films. In 1906, Manuel Martínez Illas made a picture about sugar manufacture called *Cine y azucar* ('Cinema and Sugar'). It was sponsored by the Manatí Sugar Company, which was in the process of trying to raise further capital. Now sugar was Cuba's principal crop. The island wasn't quite monocultural, tobacco and coffee were also important export crops. But it was above all sugar which was responsible for Cuba's economic deformation, the imbalance in its productive forces which created so much poverty and misery. It would not be possible to understand the peculiar susceptibility of the Cuban film pioneers to commercial sponsorship without considering the effects of the pursuit of sugar on ideological and cultural dispositions in nineteenth-century Cuba.

A number of films produced by the Cuban film institute during the 70s – among them Sergio Giral's trilogy, *El otro Francisco* ('The Other Francisco'), *Rancheador* ('Slave-Hunter') and *Maluala*, and Tomás Gutiérrez Alea's *La ultima cena* ('The Last Supper') – investigate the nineteenth-century Cuban social formation and the role of sugar in shaping its character, and that of the different social classes by which it was constituted. The picture these films combine to produce is of a deeply troubled colonial slave society with a class of largely Spanish-born plantation owners, grimly determined to prevent the overthrow of their rule by slave rebellion as in Haiti. Their attitudes, opinions and political alliances were all directed to this end, with the consequence that while Bolívar and his followers brought independence from Spain on the mainland, powerful forces in Cuba preferred to keep the island under Spanish rule and maintain the institution of slavery.

A dissident group, however, began to appear within the landowning class in the 1830s, which linked up with the emerging creole bourgeoisie in the belief that slavery was holding back the island's modernisation. But precisely because Cuba was still under colonial rule, the creole bourgeoisie was unable to constitute itself as a fully fledged national oligarchy; and the country was exposed to the highest levels of exploitation not only by the Spanish colonial power but increasingly by her competitors. Opposition to the Spanish grew progressively more militant, and, spearheaded by the fiercely independent coffee-growing small landowners who were largely concentrated in the eastern part of the island, a War of Independence broke out in 1868. In the first phase of this struggle, the independence movement was defeated. The Cuban historian Francisco López Segrera suggests that these circumstances encouraged the creole bourgeoisie, who owned less than a third of the riches of the oligarchy as a whole, and lacked the solid foundations for political activity, to play the role of intermediary with competing foreign capital, simply in order to defend their position.[1]

Yet paradoxically, Cuba's historical idiosyncrasies served not so much to distinguish it from the rest of Latin America as to intensify a number of traits that could be found throughout the continent, especially in relation to cultural experience and behaviour. The process of cultural development in Latin America does not fit easily into European terms of explanation. The Peruvian José Carlos Mariátegui (founder of the Peruvian Communist Party), in a seminal work published in 1928, *Siete ensayos de interpretación de la realidad peruana* ('Seven Essays of Interpretation of Peruvian Reality'), puts aside both the standard bourgeois periodisation of art into the Classical, the Baroque, the Romantic and so forth, and also the orthodox Marxist classification of feudal or aristocratic, bourgeois and then proletarian art, because neither of these systems is appropriate either to Peru itself or to Latin America as a whole. Instead he suggests his own brilliantly simple schema: he distinguishes three periods, the colonial, the cosmopolitan and the national. In the first, the literature of the country concerned is not that of its own people but of the conquistador. It is an already evolved literature transplanted into the colony, where it usually continues to exert an influence beyond the overthrow of the colonial power. During the second period, which is ushered in by the establishment of the independent republic, elements from various foreign literatures are assimilated simultaneously, and the unique cultural hold of the original colonial power is broken. Finally, in the third period, which implicitly only arrives with proper economic as well as political independence, a people 'achieves a well-developed expression of its own personality and its own sentiments'.[2]

The transition to cosmopolitanism in these new republics is clearly echoed in Cuba even though it remained a colony. The first manifestations of a new Cuban literature date from the end of the 1830s when a number of short-lived literary journals appeared and the first Cuban novels were written. Just as elsewhere in Latin America, they reveal the influence of European Romanticism. For instance, the novel *Francisco* by Anselmo Suárez y Romero, unpublished till later in the century, on which Sergio Giral's *El otro Francisco* is based.

At the same time as these cultural developments, the creole bourgeoisie in many places succumbed to the doctrines of free trade which the British were seeking to impose upon the continent. The Chilean historian Claudio Véliz has suggested that the acceptance of foreign economic principles was due primarily not to intellectual conviction but to the common sense of self-interest: payment for exports was made in foreign currency, which allowed the exporters to purchase both machinery to expand production, and manufactured and high quality consumer goods, all at very low prices. They were advantages which favoured increasing private consumption and sumptuary display. As Véliz puts it:

> They clothed their cowboys with ponchos of English flannel, rode in saddles made by the best harnessmakers of London, drank authentic champagne and lighted their mansions with Florentine lamps. At night they slept in beds made by excellent English cabinet makers, between sheets of Irish linen and covered by blankets of English wool. Their silk shirts came from Italy and their wives' jewels from London, Paris and Rome.[3]

And of course they sent their children to Europe to be educated, just as they nowadays send them to the United States.

The Cuban bourgeoisie was in no way deprived of similar 'progress' just because they remained colonial. Of course, the cultural configuration of the island took its own form. The influence of the English was rather less than in many Latin American countries, and that of the French rather stronger, both because of the influx into Cuba of French whites fleeing the Haitian revolution and then the renewed French presence in the region during their period of rule in Mexico. But in any case, by the 1840s, according to the Cuban literary historian Ambrosio Fornet (who is now ICAIC's literary adviser and has worked on a number of film scripts, both fiction and documentary), by the 1840s 'social life demanded new and more sophisticated forms of consumption, similar to those of the great European capitals: the privileged classes enjoyed their leisure at soirées and operatic performances where they could show off how well-informed they were, at least according to the dictates of fashion and the latest news.'[4]

As the most leisured sector of the leisured classes, women played an important role in this process, making themselves socially useful in the only sphere of activity allowed them. Already in 1829 there was a Cuban journal called *La Moda o Recreo Semanal del Bello Sexo* ('Fashion or the Weekly Amusement of the Fair Sex'). Its pages included salon music – songs and *contradanzas* – and 'pleasurable literature'. From then on, says Fornet, no journal could manage without lavishing its attention on literature, which now became another item of sumptuary consumption. The success of the Romantics in Europe helped make literature fashionable in Cuba, creating a new market and a new merchandise.

Confirming the link between fashion and literature, the editor of *La Moda* was a leading literary figure, Domingo del Monte, the host in years to come of the literary circle which succoured the first generation of Cuban novelists. The opening scene of *El otro Francisco* takes place in del Monte's salon. Del Monte has invited Suárez y Romero to read his new novel to a visiting Englishman by the name of Richard Madden, an agent of the British government with a commission to investigate violations of the treaty between Britain and Spain on the suppression of the slave trade. The members of del Monte's circle were

*El otro Francisco*

liberal intellectuals opposed to slavery and in favour of social reform: *Francisco* is the first anti-slavery novel written in Cuba. The image of the slave which the novel presents is a romantic one – the film is called 'The Other Francisco' because it sets out to show what the suffering hero, the slave Francisco, might have been like, what kind of life he would really have led, had he been an historical figure. But the members of del Monte's salon were neither unworldly, nor unversed in the realities. Between the scenes in the film which narrate the novel and reconstruct it to show the contrast between romantic fiction and historical reality, we are shown the progress of Madden's investigations (the different strands come to together in a brilliantly imaginative stroke, when Madden, travelling round the island, visits a plantation where he meets the characters in the novel). In one of these scenes, Madden is conversing with del Monte:

MADDEN: Tell me, del Monte, how many whites and blacks are there on the island?

DEL MONTE: 300,000 whites and 500,000 coloured; 250,000 of them slaves.

MADDEN: Will abolition have an effect on the sugar industry?

DEL MONTE: Well, so far the slaves are necessary, but with the process of mechanisation, importing new ones will go against progress.

MADDEN: If the problem were in your hands, what would be your solution?

DEL MONTE: In the first place, the immediate end of the slave trade. Then, the gradual elimination of slavery.

MADDEN: How do the enlightened white creoles look upon Independence?

DEL MONTE: Any utterance in favour of Independence involves the end of slavery. Right now it would earn us the hatred of the white population... Remember that here even the poorest families have slaves.

MADDEN: Does Spain have the power to suppress the slave trade on the island?

DEL MONTE: More than sufficient.

MADDEN: And the desire to do so?

DEL MONTE: None whatsoever.

MADDEN: Then, it's fear of the blacks that holds back pro-independence feeling?

DEL MONTE: Yes, that's the fear.

Literature, in this Cuba, had become a fashionable commodity, but there was no real cultural sensibility among the majority of the dominant class that made up its market, no real cultural awareness, because there was no preparedness to admit critical thinking. Only in the interstices of the growth of luxury consumption, like del Monte's literary salon, did any authentic cultural production take place within the 'cultured' classes. For a creole bourgeoisie of this kind – and this is a trait which Cuba only reveals more starkly than elsewhere – the attitude of 'vulgar' Marxists that art is nothing more than a form of luxury consumption, turns out ironically to be a true description. Culture for them was indeed on a par with linen sheets and silk shirts – the very antithesis of culture as Mariátegui understands it, an active agent and expressive force within society. But this, of course, is not the kind of culture you can acquire by buying it. The culture you buy doesn't stick.

It doesn't stick because the only thing going on in such a transaction is the imitation of outward forms of behaviour. The model, for example, for the socio-cultural role of women was already well-established in London, Paris and other European cities. There, women exerted vigorous leadership in the bourgeois salons in a manner corresponding to the nature of the bourgeois family: the wife presided over the gathering, introduced the guests and led the conversation. The daughters of the family were among the performers because playing an instrument was an accomplishment which demonstrated their eligibility for marriage. The discussion of fashion was a topic of the salon because different styles of dress were deemed appropriate to different types of event. The Cuban bourgeoisie simply copied all this, though rather than fashion being an extension of the salon, the salon became an extension of fashion, a place to show off dresses brought back from trips to Europe like trophies. The portrayal of a salon in the second film of Sergio Giral's trilogy, *Rancheador*, captures the style of the thing to a tee. It was the development of 'cultured' musical life in Cuba after about 1810, which provided one of the principal routes of entry for European Romantic literature. Madame de Staël, Chateaubriand and Lord Byron, Alejo Carpentier tells us, were the main authors to inspire the Cuban romances that were sung in the salons.[5]

But by the time the products of European culture had crossed the seas, they had lost the originality or polemical significance they may have started off by possessing. Indeed very little was left except the function of being a social commodity which could be circulated and cashed in, in order to acquire social status, such as the status that went with hosting the salon. The consequences of this reduction of the symbolic values of cultural objects to the narrowest social exchange value can be seen in the fate of Cuban literature in the course of the nineteenth century. The appearance of a number of literary journals and novels at the end of the 1830s marks the beginning of a national literary renaissance which never fulfilled its promise. There is very little continuity between this brief flowering of literary sensibilities and the appearance of the *modernista* poets at the end of the century. Ambrosio Fornet tells us that the literary journals which appeared at the end of the 1830s had all disappeared by the beginning of 1841, unable to sustain their subscriptions.

The journals demonstrated the existence of a literary market, but the beneficiaries turned out to be not the publishers of journals and books, but the newspapers, who only had to concede space to literature amid the advertisements and mercantile announcements to take this market over. They began to publish novels in instalments. These were not, however, auspicious conditions for literary development, as the papers found it both cheaper and safer to reprint foreign successes rather than risk publication of new and untried works by Cuban authors; safer especially ideologically. Cuban authors, like so many others throughout Latin America, tended towards radical liberalism, and there was even more of a danger in Cuba that the readership would refuse to patronise these works. It was safer, too, to avoid courting censorship. The result was that the market was de-Cubanised, and the Cuban author lost contact with the wider audience.

This situation persisted during the second half of the century and formed the background to the emergence of *modernismo*. (The movement took its name from the description by the Nicaraguan poet Rubén Darío, in 1890, of 'the new spirit which today quickens a small but proud and triumphant group of writers and poets in Spanish America'.[6]) The Mexican *modernista* poet Amado Nervo complained that 'in general in Mexico, one writes for those who write. The literary man counts on a coterie of the selected few who read him and end up as his only public. The *gros public*, as the French say, neither pays nor understands, however simply he writes. What can be more natural than that he should write for those who, even if they don't pay, at least read him?'[7] Not suprisingly, this only increased their predilection for a kind of aestheticism which was already well developed in Europe. Combining a variety of European stylistic influences, *modernismo* is a fine example of Mariátegui's cosmopolitanism, but also a highly sophisticated one.

The *modernistas* imported into Latin America the style of the bohemian, and undoubtedly they show a certain degree of dependency on their European influences. But at the same time, in adopting bohemianism, the *modernistas* were attacking the dependency and conformism of the creole bourgeoisie, claiming the right, even if they couldn't earn a living at it, to live like writers and artists, and asserting the needs and possibilities of cultural self-determination. Moreover, they carried their project through not just with great aplomb but with imaginative originality. The manner in which they chose their paradigms and combined their features created an entirely new aesthetic synthesis which it would be appropriate to call 'syncretistic'. Syncretism is not a word which will be found in a dictionary of literary terms, though Latin American literary and cultural critics have long employed the concept. It is borrowed from anthropology, where although no longer much in use, it used to be applied to the process of synthesis of religious symbolism in Latin America over the period of the Conquest. The imposition of Catholicism did not succeed in simply displacing pre-Colombian cosmologies and their corresponding symbols and practices. Nor was Catholicism simply overlaid upon them. A fusion took place in which the new symbolism was interpreted through the old and acquired some of its attributes and functions, creating a new level of signification fusing elements of both. The small protective three-pronged cross which adorns peasant houses in the Andes symbolises both the Catholic trinity and a mythology of three that comes from the Incas. *Modernismo* was the product of a similar process in aesthetic shape: more than an imitative combination of different stylistic elements, but their fusion in a poetic language with its own creative force. For the *modernistas* used the language in which they wrote with a new sense of birthright, speaking no longer with a Spanish accent but with the rhythms and lilts of real Latin American speech.

Anti-materialistic sentiments were almost a determining characteristic of the *modernista* movement. Many of its members came from the fallen bourgeoisie to be found not only in Cuba but throughout the continent. The Cuban Julian del Casal belonged to a family which had been forced off its land by large scale competition in sugar production following the abolition of slavery, while in Colombia José Asunción Silva spent much of his energy trying to refloat the family business which had been ruined by civil war. The parents of the Argentinian Leopoldo Lugones were forced to abandon their family estate because of financial difficulties and the Uruguayan Julio Herrera y Reissig saw his family lose their wealth and influence by the time he was twenty. Jean Franco, who compiled this list, comments that 'it would be absurd to suggest that these men became poets because their families lost their money (indeed, there were also wealthy dilettantes among the modernists... ) but these reversals almost certainly hardened that hatred of contemporary society which is one of the constants of their writing.'[8] A figure like Julian del Casal, living the life of the bohemian aesthete, collecting Chinese and Japanese knick-knacks and burning incense in front of an image of the Buddha, is indeed the very model of defiance towards material fate. And paradigmatic *modernista* writings, like Rubén Darío's story *El rey burgues* ('The Bourgeois King'), are allegories of the fate of the artist who rejects bourgeois values and ends up forced to live the life of a beggar, which expresses, among other things, the fears of material insecurity which are never so great as among the petty bourgeoisie, especially those who are newly poor.

The *modernistas* find their antithesis in the materialism of the film pioneers, that new kind of image-maker who now emerges like the poet's shadow, the double who represents exactly what the *modernistas* fear within themselves – submissiveness to the material interests of their class. And all the more so in Cuba, where it seemed to the writer Jesus Castellanos in 1910 that materialism had become the main preoccupation since the emancipation from Spanish rule. For defenceless against the influence of North American commercialism, and exposed like nowhere else in Latin America to the penetration of the new advertising and publicity businesses, Cuba is once again the country where the reality of Latin America is least masked.

It wasn't long before the early film reached the stage where sustained narrative became possible, and at this point new ideological tensions appear. From the point of view of its aesthetic development, the cosmopolitanism of early Latin American cinema, if you can call it that, was inevitable. It was a function of the medium. Since film was already international at the moment of its birth, because the film trade was necessarily international – nowhere was supply equal to demand without importing films from abroad – so nowhere in the world was film immune from the most diverse range of influences. And since everyone was starting from scratch it is impossible to imagine that it could have been otherwise. Indeed not until the film idiom has arrived at a greater stage of elaboration and technical development is it possible to conceive of such a thing as a national style in the cinema, and hardly even an individual one, for that matter. The apparent exceptions, like Méliès, prove the rule. They have been inscribed in the history of film less as conscious artists with their own personal style than as ciphers of supposedly inherent possibilities within the medium – Albert E. Smith is another example. But the development of narrative introduces a new dimension.

In Europe, the development of film narrative during cinema's second decade joined with a desire to prove the respectability of the new medium to produce the first, and as yet far overstretched adaptations of the classics of stage and fiction. In Latin America, this same desire for respectability expressed itself in the choice of patriotic themes. Examples are the large-scale reconstructions, *La batalla de Maipú* ('The Battle of Maipú') and *La revolución de mayo* ('The May Revolution'), produced by the Italian expatriate Mario Gallo in Argentina in the centenary year of his adopted country's emancipation from Spain. In Cuba, Enrique Díaz Quesada found his subjects in the popular themes of more recent anti-colonial struggle. In 1913, after several more shorts, he produced his first full-length picture, *Manuel García o el rey de los campos de Cuba* ('Manuel García or the King of the Cuban Countryside'), based on a book by Federico Villoch concerning a bandit popularly identified with anti-Spanish nationalism. A contemporary newspaper account of the film suggests that, as one might expect, the treatment was highly melodramatic. It ended, for example, with the bandit's ghost appearing above his tomb.[9] Other nationalistic themes followed – such as, in 1914, *El capitan mambi o libertadores y guerrilleros* ('The Mambi Captain or Liberators and Guerrilla Fighters'). *Mambi* was the word that identified a Cuban rebel. Derived from the name of a black Spanish officer who changed sides and joined the guerrillas in Santo Domingo in 1846, Spanish soldiers sent from Santo Domingo to Cuba in 1868 brought the term with them. Intended pejoratively to lump the white freedom fighters with the blacks, the liberation movement proudly accepted the equation.

It would seem natural to suppose that such films represented popular feeling against authority in a pseudo-republic of such obvious servility towards the neocolonialists of the north. This is the way Valdés Rodríguez describes them. 'From his first film... to the last,' wrote Valdés Rodríguez of Díaz Quesada,

> ... the themes and characters were firmly rooted in social reality, historical and contemporary. In some cases, such as *La zafra o sangre y azucar* ('The Sugar Harvest or Blood and Sugar'), relations of property, social problems, the worker and peasant struggle for human conditions of work and of living, are present in a manifest way if rather confused, disoriented and without deliberation. It was the innate feeling of justice, expression of the spirit of rebellion and equality, radically democratic, of the Cuban people.[10]

The films are now lost, but historical sense urges caution here. Valdés Rodríguez may be giving these films the benefit of the doubt, since there were no films anywhere at this time that were not, by later standards, confused and disoriented – even *The Birth of a Nation* and *Intolerance* are not completely free from these limitations of the early film idiom. But for the same reason, the images would have been more ideologically ambiguous – as in Griffith's films too. The evidence for this is that authority didn't unequivocally condemn them as dangerous embodiments of popular feeling. On the contrary. The fact is that a regime as shaky as that of the Cuban Republic had every need of the means to legitimise itself, and film was clearly a candidate for this job. Both *El capitán mambi* and Díaz Quesada's next film, *La manigua o la mujer cubana* ('The Countryside or the Cuban Woman') were given direct assistance by the government of President Menocal. For the first, the army supplied equipment and soldiers for the battle scenes; for the second, Menocal, educated at North American universities, chief of Havana police during the military occupation, then administrative head of the Cuban American Sugar Company and now head of a staunchly pro-imperialist government, himself intervened to allow filming to take place in the Morro Castle, the Spanish fortification – the oldest in Latin America – which overlooks Havana protecting the harbour.[11] The closing scenes of the film which were thus vouchsafed represented that historical moment when the Spanish flag was lowered for the last time and the Cuban flag was raised for the first. Perhaps Menocal was hoping that these images would obscure the more ambivalent memory of similar scenes when the lowered flag was the Stars and Stripes, the day the puppet republic he now headed was officially born.

# References

1. Francisco López Segrera, 'La economía y la política en la república neocolonial (1902-1933)' in *La república neocolonial, Anuario de estudios cubanos 1*, Editorial de Ciencias Sociales, 1975, p.130-132.
2. José Carlos Mariátegui, *Siete ensayos de interpretación de la realidad peruana*, Casa de las Americas, 1975, p.21.
3. Quoted in Andre Gunder Frank, *Capitalism and Underdevelopment in Latin America*, Penguin, 1971, p.115.
4. Ambrosio Fornet, 'Literatura y mercado en la Cuba colonial (1830-60)', *Casa de las Americas*, No.84, p.48.
5. Alejo Carpentier, *La música en Cuba*, 1946, p.90. On nineteenth-century musical culture in Europe, see William Weber, *Music and the Middle Classes*, Croom Helm, 1975.
6. Quoted in Gordon Brotherstone, *Latin American Poetry*, Cambridge 1975, p.56.
7. Quoted in Françoise Perus, *Literatura y sociedad en America Latina: el modernismo*, Casa de las Americas 1976, p.99.
8. Jean Franco, *The Modern Culture of Latin America*, Penguin 1970, p.31.
9. Quoted in Agramonte, op.cit. p.32.
10. J.M. Valdés Rodríguez, 'Algo en torno al cine y la República Cubana', III, *El Mundo*, 21 April 1960.
11. Agramonte, op.cit. p.33.

# 4
# MELODRAMA AND WHITE HORSES

*The underdevelopment of Cuban cinema before the Revolution*

Two Cuban investigators of early cinema in their country, Rolando Díaz Rodríguez and Lázaro Buria Pérez, have divided the years 1897-1922 into three periods. The first, 1897-1905, is the period of cinema as simple spectacle in as yet unequal competition with theatre. The second, 1906-1918, is the stage of the consolidation of cinema both as a spectacle and as a business, but under European domination. In the third period, 1919-1922, the spectacle becomes increasingly ideological in nature, the Europeans are displaced by the North Americans, and the incipient national cinema is killed off.[1]

Early exhibition in Latin America was substantially an activity of *comicos de la legua*, itinerant showmen, just like everywhere else. In most Latin American countries, however, the geographical spread of film was generally restricted to the reach of the railways and only a little beyond. Along the railway lines, a regular supply of new films from the capital city encouraged permanent cinemas. There was a limited hinterland where travelling showmen found places to set up in, like barns and yards, but transport and surface communication throughout Latin America were underdeveloped and there were vast remote areas which they never visited at all.

In any case, rural populations in Latin America offered very little scope for making money out of them. There is no reason to suppose that peasant communities wouldn't have been just as receptive to films as urban workers, only they existed beyond the cash nexus and were economically marginal. (Their labour was still largely extracted by the quasi-feudal means inherited and evolved from the Spanish Conquest.) In this respect, Cuba stood out among Latin American countries. It had an extensive rural proletariat rarely found elsewhere, the workers in the *ingenios*, the sugar mills attached to the large plantations in the sugar growing areas, which were all well served by lines of communication constructed to get the sugar out. They were also a way for film to come in.

In the years 1906 and 7, at the start of the second period, cinemas began to spread from the centre of the capital to both the popular districts and the interior of the country. Every kind of mechanism was used to attract the audience. Stores offered customers free film shows, there were free gifts and car rides home (cars were also a novelty). In these ways, and in spite of the technical and expressive limitations of the early film, cinema soon became the most widely distributed and available form of commercial entertainment in Cuba. By 1920 there were 50 cinemas in Havana and more than 300 in the rest of the country. The average number of seats in a Havana cinema was 450, with a total of 23,000 seats for a population of half a million. The total seating capacity in the country as a whole was in the region of 130,000 to 140,000 for a population of around four million.[2] There were large areas of the country where people were out of reach of a cinema, but for the majority of the population the evidence is clear: the market for cinema in Cuba was not only more intensely developed than over most of Central and South America, penetration was roughly as intense as in many regions in the metropolitan countries where film had been invented. Not as intense as in the industrial conurbations, of course, but equal to rural districts like, in Britain, East Anglia, or to the less developed European countries like Greece, regions where cinemas were generally small but quite frequently placed.

The spread of cinema in Cuba was largely due to the overall intensity of foreign exploitation on the island and especially that of the USA, but it was accomplished through intermediaries. The emerging pattern of exploitation in the film industry didn't require that the dominating country actually own the cinemas, it was enough for them to dominate the mentality of the economically dependent tribe of creole capitalists. In Cuba, as in other Latin American countries, the cinemas came to be owned by the commercial classes, the same local business people who later also set up the multitude of small commercial radio stations. Commercial broadcasting spread throughout the continent during the 30s, following the model of exploitation developed north of the Rio Grande, and again Cuba became one of the most intensely developed Latin American markets. Radio depended considerably on a supply of recorded music, for which it provided an aural shop window, and it grew in symbiosis with the record companies. This was a field where the North Americans supplied the technology and local producers put it to work. In Cuba, Mexico, Argentina, recording industries took the rich national popular music and entered it in international competition across the continent, proving that they were all good pupils. In Cuba (where Segovia made his first record in 1927) RCA was the first to come along with a modern electrical recording factory, and by the end of the 30s popular Cuban recording artistes like Benny Moré and the Trio Matamoros were known throughout Central America and the northern parts of South America. With cinema, where the costs of production were very much higher, local production as a result was minimal. The exhibitors were much more dependent upon the US distributors than radio was upon North American record producers. And those distributors that were not themselves North American were still dependent on the North Americans for a regular supply of new films.

Yet in cinema the USA had been a late starter. Their entry into international competition was constrained during cinema's first twenty years or so by the ravages of the Motion Pictures Patents War, in which the companies battled viciously against each other to establish legal ownership of the industry's patents (the basis of the technological rents which formed a significant ingredient in profit rates). At one point, it seems that independents needing to flee the attacks of the would-be monopolists thought of Cuba as a possible scene of operations, before moving right out of reach to California and establishing the colony that became Hollywood. But at this time the dominant foreign film companies in Cuba were French. Although at home the Lumière Company was progressively eclipsed by competitors, its careful preparations had given the French a firm foreign footing, which Pathé and Gaumont fought it out to turn to advantage. Cuba was one of the places where they competed. In 1906, Havana's *Teatro Actualidades*, the country's first purpose-built cinema, began to acquire films from Pathé on a regular basis. The island's first film distributors, Santos y Artiga, established in 1904, were agents for Gaumont. Around 1909, they took over the *Teatro Actualidades* and dropped Gaumont in favour of an exclusive contract with Pathé. The arrangement was from Pathé's point of view part of the fightback against the growing danger from the North Americans; back in Paris, the Kodak entrepreneur George Eastman was trying, on behalf of the Patents Company, to stymie Pathé's leadership in the manufacture of raw film stock in Europe. Gaumont's response to the North American threat was to withdraw from international markets and consolidate at home (it sold its British operations to British buyers during the same period). Pathé were able to hold their own in Cuba and other foreign territories until the First World War. But the war entailed a cut-back in European production, leaving a space which the North Americans, with the Patents War now behind them, were eager to fill.

Film, a new invention, became a major branch of what the Frankfurt sociologists in the thirties, Adorno and the others, identified as the culture industry, a segment of production financed by entertainment capital. This industry is characteristically imperialist; entertainment capital is dominated by North American interests and closely linked with the electrical industry, which for Lenin, in his pamphlet, *Imperialism, the Highest Stage of Capitalism* of 1917, was the very model of capitalism in its highest stage of development. Even at the beginning, when the technology was still primitive and the expressive means still poor, the infant film business in each country was only able to satisfy demand with difficulty, and through the international character which its trading patterns even then revealed, cinema showed itself a child of late capitalism, just like the giant electric companies with their transnational structure which Lenin described. So explosively did film catch on that rates of growth were unprecedented, and for several years there was no country able to produce enough for its own home market. If the colonisers of Hollywood were able to turn these conditions to their especial advantage, this is because they were the first to obtain the backing of finance capital. The process upon which the North American film business then entered altered the prospects of creole capital more rapidly and radically than it affected the big European film companies. These had been seriously weakened by the war but they still had an industrial base and national roots. In the countries of the imperialised periphery such advantages were entirely absent, and the local operators either left the business or rapidly gravitated into exhibition. Distribution concentrated on a small number of companies, principally North American subsidiaries. Production was left to a few adventurists.

José Agustín Mahieu has characterised the first period of cinema in his own country, Argentina, as one of 'empirical adventurism'.[3] The term could equally well be used for Cuba. In Argentina, this period lasted about fifteen years and its end was signalled, says Mahieu, in 1912, with the founding of the *Sociedad General Cinematográfica*, the first film dealers in the country to move from selling films to exhibitors to rental instead. In Cuba this transition had been reached five or six years earlier, with the company of Hornedo y Salas.

This change-over lays the basis for subsequent market domination by the North American distributors. They became the majors because they had understood that control of distribution was the dominant position in the industry. As the economic historian of cinema Peter Bachlin has explained:

> The distributor takes over the risks of purchasing the films while the exhibitor only has to rent them; the distributor's mediation improves economic conditions for the exhibitor by allowing a more rapid change of programmes. For the producers, this development signals a growth in the market, with films able to reach consumers more rapidly and in greater number, whilst also constituting a kind sales guarantee for their films. In general, the distributor buys the prints of one or more films from one or more producers and rents them to numerous exhibitors; in the process he's able to extract a sum considerably greater than his costs.[4]

The balance of power thus shifts to the distributor. But since cinemas in the capitalist system exist to provide not films for audiences, but audiences for films, so exhibitors in turn serve as fodder for the distributors, and the producers behind them.

The twenties, in the North American film industry, became the period in which dealers-turned-distributors learnt the tricks of the trade and battled for control of the exhibition market with the emerging Hollywood studios, who were trying to extend their own control over the industry. It was the period when the peculiarities of the film as a commodity first clearly emerged. The film is consumed *in situ* not through the physical exchange of the object but by an act of symbolic exchange, the exchange of its projected impression. William Marston Seabury, a North American film lawyer, explained that 'in the picture industry the public may be regarded as the ultimate consumer but in reality the public consumes nothing. It pays an admission price at a theatre from which it takes away nothing but a mental impression of whatever it has been permitted to see.'[5] Correspondingly, the exchange value of the film is realised not through physical exchange of the object itself, but through gate money, the price of admission, in this way manifesting its affinity with various other forms of cultural production and entertainment. But if it doesn't need to pass physically into the hands of the consumer, nor does the film need to pass into the legal ownership of the exhibitor. He need only rent it.

By this means, the exhibitor becomes the prey of the ways the distributors find to manipulate the conditions of rental. 'Block booking' and 'blind booking', for example, in which they force exhibitors to take pictures they don't want and sometimes haven't seen in order to get the ones they do want. None the less, Seabury insists that film is entirely different from the commercial operation of the chain stores with which people had begun to compare the cinema. Bachlin is in agreement with this. It is, he says, 'of great importance for the forms of concentration and monopoly which arise within the industry. The principles of price fixing and ways of dominating the market will be different from those which relate to products which involve only a single act of purchase by the consumer, that is to say, products which disappear from the market in one transaction.'[6] In Europe, the North American distributors found resistance to their various malpractices, and European countries progressively during the 20s erected legal barriers to protect their own film industries, with varying degrees of success. They were barriers of which it was practically impossible to conceive in underdeveloped countries. Even had governments had the will, what should they try to protect? The only Latin American country which in those days ever tried it was revolutionary Mexico, in the early 20s, angry at the offensive representation of their country which they began to find in the Hollywood picture.

The taste of the Cuban public is rapidly becoming more educated – the highly sensational film has had its day and interest now centres on the drama with what is called 'a strong love interest'. The public is now accustomed to the very best type of film, indeed to a better type than in England. Comic films are not popular and even Charles Chaplin, who combines comedy with genius, is not as popular as previously. The action must be quick and the ending happy. Italian films have lost ground in Cuba owing to alleged slowness of action, while as an illustration of the need for a happy ending can be mentioned the *Prisoner of Zenda*, a first class film which indeed became a great success but which was shown with some trepidation and caused some criticism by its 'renunciation' scene in the final act.

The market in Cuba is known as a 'star' market, i.e. producers' names are rarely if ever known and advertising follows the same lines, calling the film a 'Mary Pickford' film, or a 'Douglas Fairbanks' film. These names are so well known to the public that it is quite sufficient to advertise the name of the star in order to fill the theatre.

Just because these are the quaint observations of His Britannic Majesty's Consul-General in Havana, that is no reason to discount this report on the taste of Cuban audiences in 1923.[7] The Consul-General's comments are concise and very much to the point:

The proximity of the United States is almost fatal to the films of other countries. Not only are all the American film stars well known to the Cuban public, but both the Spanish and American papers in Havana constantly grant publicity and a number of American cinema magazines are in circulation in Cuba. Advertising is intense. Theatre owners and others have only to run over to Florida (some 96 miles) or even up to New York (60 hours) to see the latest films and purchase them on the spot, and most of them have agents and correspondents in the United States who send particulars of all new films and report on their suitability for the Cuban market.

In fact the US majors began to move in on Cuba while the First World War was in progress: Paramount was first, in 1917. By 1926, Cuba represented one-and-a-quarter per cent of US foreign distribution, according to the tables published in the Film Year Book. It isn't much in comparison with Europe, where Britain commanded a huge 40% and Germany came a distant second with 10%, although several European markets were much smaller than Cuba: Switzerland, Holland, Czechoslovakia and Poland were only one per cent each, while Yugoslavia, Rumania, Bulgaria, Turkey and Greece represented one per cent between them. In Latin America, Brazil had two-and-a-half per cent, Mexico two, Panama and Central America three-quarters, and Argentina, Uruguay, Paraguay, Chile, Peru, Bolivia and Ecuador, six per cent between them.[8] None of this made it easier for Cuban producers. The director of a film made in 1925, *Entre dos amores* ('Between Two Loves'), commented that if the film failed commercially while the public had applauded it, this was because of the foreign distribution companies who were anxious to prevent the development of Cuban film production.[9] 'Foreign' is a euphemism for North American.

How did the distributors achieve this kind of market dominance, from which they could dictate their will? They engaged not only in the malpractices already mentioned. Seabury quotes the comments of an independent exhibitor in the US upon the variants of the rental system, who complains that they're designed to provide the distributor with a guarantee plus a percentage, which makes the percentage 'excess profit'. But the bigger such excess profits, the more investment you can attract. The industry leaders knew this perfectly well. According to one spokesman, discussing before an audience at the Harvard Business School in 1926 the question of 'how we are trying to lessen sales resistance in those countries that want to build up their own industries':

We are trying to do that by internationalising this art, by drawing on old countries for the best talent that they possess in the way of artists, directors and technicians, and bringing these people over to our country, by drawing on their literary talents, taking their choicest stories and producing them in our own way, and sending them back into the countries where they are famous. In doing that, however, we must always keep in mind the revenue end of it. Out of every dollar received, about 75¢ still comes out of America and only 25¢ out of all the foreign countries combined. Therefore you must have in mind a picture that will first bring in that very necessary 75¢ and that secondly will please the other 25% that you want to please. If you please the 25% of foreigners to the detriment of your home market, you can see what happens. Of course, the profit is in that last 25%.[10]

Or rather, the excess, or surplus, profit. This is cardinal, because it is not ordinary but surplus profit that attracts investment capital, and this is ultimately how Hollywood came to dominate world cinema. They gleaned a surplus profit from the market which gave them the backing of Wall Street, which was already fast becoming the most substantial and modern fund of investment capital in the world.

The North American film industry underwent in the 20s a rapid process of vertical integration, in which not only did the production studios and the distributors combine, but they began to acquire their own cinemas. This was intended to combat the formation of circuits among independent exhibitors, where booking arrangements were pooled in retaliation against the methods of the renters. But abroad in Latin America the distributors faced no such organised resistance, since the exhibitors had neither the capital resources nor the bargaining power to fight, and there the distributors had no need to acquire cinemas to break the exhibitors' backs and bully them into submission. They acquired no more than a handful in each country, simply to serve as showcases. When foreign-owned cinemas were taken over in the Cuban nationalisations on the weekend of 14 October 1960, there were no more than eleven of them.

The film as a commodity has another peculiarity, which has been observed by the North American economist Thomas Guback. He points out that the cost of making prints for distribution is an extremely small fraction of the total costs of production, what the industry call the 'negative costs' – the costs of getting to the finished negative of the complete film from which the prints are made. (The prints then become part of the distribution costs.) Indeed this proportion has grown progressively smaller over the course of the history of cinema, as production budgets have grown larger and larger. It means, above all, that films can be exported without having to divert the product away from the home market (whereas with many commodities, especially in underdeveloped countries, the home market must be deprived in order to be able to export). In Guback's words,

'The cost of an extra copy is the price of the raw stock, duplicating and processing – incremental costs... a motion picture is a commodity one can duplicate indefinitely without substantially adding to the cost of the first unit produced... a given film tends to be an infinitely exportable commodity; prints exported do not affect domestic supplies nor the revenue resulting from domestic exhibition... We can have our film and foreigners can have it too.'[11]

When you add that the United States soon developed into the largest internal film market in the world at the time, it's clear why they were irresistible. Because it was so big, US producers were able to recover negative costs on the home market alone, and the distributors were therefore able to supply the foreign market at discount prices that undercut foreign producers in their own territories. They also undercut European competitors. The Consul-General's 1923 report commented that 'British prices are said to be too high'.

Guback doesn't quite get things right, however. He has an empirical approach which is misleading over the shape of Hollywood's foreign policy. He somehow thinks that the overseas offensive of the US film industry dates only from after the Second World War, when the contraction of the cinema audience following the introduction of television made foreign revenue increasingly necessary for profitability. He claims that before that 'American films were sold abroad but the resulting revenue hardly compared to what the domestic market yielded'. This is true, it was around 25%. He continues that 'Foreign revenue was simply an additional increment, extra profit upon which the American film companies did not depend'. But we saw that they depended on it for surplus profit. His conclusion is that 'The foreign market did not warrant enough attention to force Hollywood to modify significantly the content of its films to suit tastes abroad, nor to induce the film companies to maintain elaborate overseas organisations.'[12] This is what is misleading: they didn't have to. Their methods, in spite of the differences revealed by detailed economic analysis, were still those extolled in the *Washington Post*'s declaration at the beginning of the century about wanting the territories acquired from the defeated Spanish 'because they will one day become purchasers at our bargain basements'.

Hollywood was never entirely, however, without international competition. The 1923 British Consul-General's report, for instance, said that after North American pictures, the order of popularity from various countries went: Italy, Germany, France, Spain. ('The British film is unknown... The fault lies with the British producer who has never attempted to work the market, and now there is a grave doubt whether it is worthwhile to do so.') At the end of the Second World War things looked rather different. The main competition facing Hollywood on Cuban screens came from Mexico, and to a lesser extent Argentina.

The success of Mexican pictures in Cuba is an ambivalent phenomenon, for essentially they were no different from the Hollywood product in their idiom, and usually rather inferior. They testify to the ideological as well as the economic effects of Hollywood domination. A US Government market report from 1947 informs us about the films Cuban audiences were then watching:

> Film distributors and theatre owners say that Mexican movies are more popular in Cuba outside the two large cities of Havana and Santiago than the productions of any other country except fast-paced action films with a readily understood plot from the United States. Action films of this type are the only United States movies which ordinarily outrank Mexican films in popularity in theatres in cities and towns of less than 50,000 population. The preference for action pictures from Hollywood is measurably greater if their locale, stars, and supporting casts can be easily identified by patrons, as the titles suggest. An action picture in an unfamiliar setting is not as popular as a Mexican movie which does not have wave after wave of turbulent activity... More than a dozen distributors, including branches of United States studios, unanimously agree that Mexican movies hold a unique, high place in the affections of the representative Cuban theatregoer... Hearing Spanish instead of having to read or being unable to read Spanish subtitles of English language movies is an important but not the fundamental reason for the partiality shown Mexican movies... Artistically and technically Mexican movies are not comparable with United States and European pictures. However, Mexican movies have been able to portray the national spirit, institutions, character, and social organism of Mexico, which to a large degree are similar to those in Cuba. Nearly all of the dozen or so Cuban features made to date were produced with the help of Mexican directors and stars.[13]

Perhaps this was the price Hollywood had to pay for not modifying the contents of its films to suit tastes abroad? This would miss the point again. The author of this report has an idea of the 'national spirit' etc. in Mexico and Cuba which can only be taken with a large pinch of salt – a dose of *salsa* is a good idea too. It is not untrue that there were certain similarities between the 'social organism' ('social formation' perhaps?) of the two countries. But since before the talkies, and the documentary material of the Revolution, the Mexican film industry had hardly succeeded in putting anything of its country on the screen with authenticity. On the contrary, as one commentator has put it, 'By the 1920s, the "hits" produced and exported by Hollywood exerted a growing influence and even sharper competition. The Mexican film-makers fell under the cultural sway of their northern neighbour and, to the degree that they did, their filmic concern with national reality diminished.'[14] A generalisation which, he adds, is by no means unique to Mexico.

The aesthetics of the adaptation of Hollywood values to Latin American cinema has been analysed by the Cuban cineastes Enrique Colina and Daniel Díaz Torres, in an essay in *Cine Cubano* in the middle 70s, entitled 'Ideology of Melodrama in the Old Latin American Cinema':

> During the silent period... Hollywood fabricated and disseminated the myth of the 'American Dream' by making the image of reality presented in its films

conform to reflections of a falsely optimistic and promising universe. Skin-deep features of different cultures were fitted into novelettish stories which created a stereotypical image, exotic and picturesque, of the underdeveloped countries. This image showed a sub-world dominated by the instincts, by a tendency towards irresponsibility and licentiousness, enveloped in a stereotyped mythical atmosphere. The primitive was counterposed to the aseptic order of civilisation, and thus the screen mediated the frustrated desires of a bourgeois universe which demanded conformity and equilibrium. This discriminatory content, offered to popular consumption, opened the floodgates to a manifold process of cultural colonisation which would end up resonating throughout the various 'national' cinemas of the hemisphere.[15]

Colina and Díaz Torres proceed to pinpoint the leading characteristics of the Latin American film melodrama to be found in the paradigms of the Argentine and Mexican film industries in the 30s and 40s. 'Melodrama' is taken broadly, since the cinema of these two countries, together with that of Brazil, which the language barrier kept out of Cuba, created a number of distinctive genres of their own. Their variety, however, amounted to little more than different ways of treating the same basic set of conventions. The Mexican critic Jorge Ayala Blanco, who has analysed the genres of Mexican cinema in great detail, has observed that a number of the genres thrown up in the 30s were hybrid and artificial, and their apparent consolidation in the 40s, in swashbuckling adventures, historical biographies, adaptations of novels of the kind that used to be serialised in the nineteenth century newspapers, all these had no other function than to substitute hurriedly for Hollywood product during the Second World War, when Hollywood was much given over to wartime propaganda that had little to do with the Mexican audience. There were other genres, however, which deserve more attention, because they elicited a more firmly based popular response: 'they answered to a truly national need and can be considered as a collective expression, albeit secondhand.'[16] These include the comedies of ranch life and the epics of small town communities; the almost folkloric narratives of the Mexican Revolution and its revolutionary heroes; various films of family life; above all those films which nostalgically idealised the Porfirian *hacienda*, the semi-feudal relations and paternalistic benevolence of the Mexican ranch in the years of the pre-revolutionary dictator Porfirio Díaz.

There was obviously more melodrama, so to speak, in some of these genres than in others, but if they elicited a popular response it was because, like the classic Victorian melodrama which dominated the London stage for much of the nineteenth century, they were just about the only dramatic forms available to the audience to deal at all with the dreams and needs of the popular classes. Inevitably they were clumsy and emotionally over-simplified, and again like Victorian melodrama, thoroughly moralistic. Like the Hollywood paradigms it followed, the Mexican film melodrama was an art which proclaimed the predominance of the individual over the milieu, at the same time as subordinating the individual to the given order. It diluted awareness of social problems by installing a Catholic-inspired 'spiritual' realm in parallel to the social order. It reduced life to a single dimension, that of love and the 'sentimental life', it belittled social equality by alleging that human beings were all equal before the designs of the heart. But how did the heart behave? Entrenched in a world which was instinctively defensive and defensive about instincts, the dominant characteristic of this artless art was sentimentality; which, to give it a more precise meaning, is the disguised return of repressed feeling through the obsessive exaggeration of ordinary sentiment.

Sometimes all this took the form of the costume picture, in which case, as the Cuban writers explain, the spectator was presented with a cast of supposedly popular characters who had been reduced to caricature and given a dose of paternalistic moral chauvinism. Return to the primitive past was seen as a journey to the fountain of authenticity, and the blemishes of underdevelopment were celebrated as old popular values. True popular values were nowhere to be seen. The idea of the nation itself became completely general and empty, an ahistorical archetype which was detached from the evolution of society and real social conditions. God, Fatherland and Home comprised the inseparable triad which social equilibrium demanded and depended on.

Since morality in such a system is no more than a badge, its presence or absence can be read on the faces and in the bodies of the actors, in the iconography of villains, suffering mothers, prodigal sons, innocent girls and women of the streets. Typecasting was taken to its extreme in the Latin American film melodrama. Sara García's long-suffering face made her the mother incarnate; Maria Felix and Tita Morello embodied the enigma and diabolical attraction of the female sinner, their deep voices and caressing manner the expressions of shameful amours (which never needed actually to be seen – everything was achieved by suggestion and innuendo); Carlos López Moctezuma's grim looks and disagreeable features spelled out his villainy. Cinema has always – perhaps by necessity – sought its primary iconography in the physiognomy of the actors. The actor in cinema, instead of having to project, is projected (as Stanley Cavell, the North American philosopher, has felicitously put it). This is why the non-professional actor, when appropriately cast, makes such important contributions to film art. But it also explains how and why the genres of Hollywood cinema were constructed to make the star system – as vehicles for the character-types which the stars variously embodied. (In the process, the stars were turned into valuable pieces of property, which the studios bought and sold and rented among themselves.) The system was sophisticated enough in Hollywood and other more artistically developed cinemas to make it possible to treat films as vehicles for the stars as well as vice versa. In the imitation of the star system that developed in Latin America, however, the personality of the actor was sacrificed to the abstractions of the genre. The result – to return to the Cubans' analysis – was that relationships between the characters on the screen reduced reality to a series of artificial cause-and-effect mechanisms.

The entire semiotic system of the Latin American film melodrama is based on this. In such a world, the anecdote becomes the principal narrative form, with an oversimplified structure which makes the linearity of the average Hollywood picture into a veritable labyrinth. It typically consists of variants of no more than two or three continually repeated themes, many fewer than the basic plots available in Hollywood cinema. Whenever the film is set in the past, history remains quite alien, merely ornamental, and of course idealised. Past or present, the film stands outside real historical time; it is the product of a dichotomy between social and affective life. The mechanisms of cause and effect, the expression of reductive one-dimensional ethics, give a narrative form which is only apparently dynamic.

There can be no real audience identification with the complexities of character and behaviour, no exploration by the film viewer of the ambiguities of intention, since there are no complexities and ambiguities in this universe except by unintended accident. (Jean Renoir once said that technique is a way of doing again deliberately what you first did by accident. But this implies a strong and highly structured artistic tradition where ambiguity and accident are cultivated and encouraged; here it merely signifies lack of control over the medium or awareness of the complexities it can be made to yield.) Consequently the argument of these films proceeds by a succession of climaxes which are really like escape valves that need to be decongested of accumulated emotion in order that in the end equilibrium can be restored. The imagery comes from Colina and Díaz Torres: 'In this persistent correction of the level of dramatic tension,' they explain, 'and in the way the unusual is made to appear banal, this cinema finds its regulatory mechanisms, which prevent anything sudden revealing the undercurrent contained by their hypocritical conventions.' Dramatic development—this will hardly come as a surprise – is essentially verbal, and the organisation of visual elements is subordinate to the primacy of the verbal text:

> This kind of hierarchy can be explained by the fact that the suggestive value of images provokes interpretation which would go beyond the unambiguous significations of this type of filmic schema. However, a lack of aesthetic expression in the visual components of these films prevents any transcendence of the immediate, merely functional significance of locations, decor, dress, make-up, props and so forth, which are used to reaffirm the dramatic conventions carried by the formalised gestures and standardised message.

With the comming of sound also came a development which, were Guback right, would be rather strange: Hollywood began making films in Spanish. The first was actually an independent production by a successful Cuban actor, René Cardon, with the title *Sombras habañeras* ('Shadows of Havana'). But then the big Hollywood companies got involved and spent two or three years making Spanish-language versions of regular Hollywood movies. They weren't dubbed, this was beyond the technical means the talkies started with. They were remakes in Spanish, with Spanish speaking actors and a Spanish speaking director, but otherwise exactly the same. *The Big House*, directed by George Hill in 1930 with Wallace Beery and John Gilbert, became *El presidio*, with Juan de Landa and Tito Davison; Tod Browning's 1931 *Dracula* with Bela Lugosi was remade under the same title with Carlos Villarías and Lupita Tovar; and there were many others.[17] They just went in and took over the sets and the shooting script and did exactly the same thing but in Spanish.

These films didn't make money directly. They were essentially a sales device for selling the talkies, for goading Latin American exhibitors to convert to sound. The talkies represented a major investment by the US film industry, the product of an intricate history of competition between the studios, which was undertaken in the face of the threat of falling audiences. It was an investment which Hollywood needed to recoup as fast as possible. It was essential that exhibitors abroad were rapidly induced to spend the money necessary to convert their cinemas, otherwise the 25% surplus profit from the foreign market would begin to drain away. In the case of Britain, William Fox was smart enough to persuade the Gaumont circuit into it by arranging for £80m for the purpose to be subscribed by banks in the City of London. A very large part of that was the purchase of equipment from the United States. This kind of finance was much more difficult to achieve in Latin America, but the fact that here too the cinemas were owned by local capital – though there were very few significant circuits – served the exporter's purposes. Making Spanish-language films and putting them into their showcases served to bully the local cinema owners to find the means or risk going under. They made these films for this purpose as a loss-leader, and it ceased as soon as the techniques of re-recording were brought to the point, in the mid-30s, that allowed the original production to be dubbed into any foreign language required.

One of the directors recruited to Hollywood, by Twentieth Century-Fox, to direct (supervise would be a better word) these Spanish-language versions, was the Cuban Ramón Peón. Peón's career is an excellent illustration of the fate of Cuban cinema from before the talkies to the fifties, and not only because his name crops up in connection with almost all the attempts that were made to create a basis for regular production in Cuba. Peón and the others he was involved with were optimistic opportunists. Arturo Agramonte, summing up Cuban production in the interwar years, says that it gave the impression of 'photographed theatre': 'weak themes and deficient shooting gave the viewer the sensation that something was lacking. In fact this was due to an almost total want of close-ups as well as an insufficient variety of angles, which made the films monotonous. It was a rude shock for the technicians and for serious investors, for whom all opportunities were closed off. This situation left the door open rather more to adventurers, who were less well-intentioned than the traditional "white horse" (*caballo blanco*).'[18] What in Latin America is called a 'white horse' is what is called in English an angel, a theatrical backer. In Cuba, says Agramonte, they didn't usually put money into films. Peón, however, managed to persuade one or two of them to do so. He became the nearest thing to a professional film director in Cuba. The subjects of his films, however, were no different from anyone else's. It is true that the French film historian Sadoul praises his *La virgen de la caridad* ('The Virgin of Charity', 1930), one the last Cuban silent pictures, as almost neorealist, but everything else the present author has been able to discover about him suggests that this must have been an exception to his general level of achievement.

Peón was an energetic operator. He was associated with most of the attempts to set Cuban film production on a regular basis between 1920 and 1939. It will come as no surprise that none of these businesses lasted very long. Agramonte says that apart from lack of confidence on the part of always cautious Cuban investors, the failure to establish sustained production was due above all to a total lack of support from the banks. In these conditions, the backing of *caballos blancos* was essential. Peón began his career with a trip to the United States in 1920 with the money of a stable full of them in his pocket, to purchase several thousand dollars' worth of equipment. It was duly installed in new studios belonging to a company calling itself Estudios Golden Sun Pictures, whose first production he then directed himself. He managed to make a further six films over the next five years before embarking on a new collaboration in 1926 with a certain Richard Harlan, who later worked in Hollywood with Cecil B. De Mille. This was the Pan American Pictures Corporation, a grand name for a shoestring operation. Its short run of productions were mostly directed by either Harlan or Peón. Absolutely typical was Peón's *Casi varon* ('Almost Masculine') of 1926. It is hard to imagine a more inconsequential but thoroughly sexist absurdity: an adventuress is obligated to a villain who proposes to rob a rich mansion. She disguises herself as a chauffeur and goes along to teach the *señorito* of the house to drive. The deceit is discovered, of course, and once restored to womanhood she is forgiven by the young gallant, and all live happily ever after.

It was in Hollywood that Peón really learnt his trade, churning out the remakes. They provided a certain training, especially in speed, and when Hollywood no longer had any work to offer him, Peón went and put this training to use in Mexico, where production values were so constrained that every film had to be a quickie. A little legend grew up around Peón that his 'greatest achievement' was to complete ten films in 126 days of continuous production.[19] This is doubtless an exaggeration, but García Riera confirms that he did indeed make more films than any other director working in Mexico at the time. He was the champion, says García Riera, of the melodrama.[20] The methods which were used to keep the costs of shooting down have been described by another director of Mexican quickies – they weren't much different from the methods employed on similar productions in Britain in the same period: 'In the first place, I reduced the use of the clapper to a minimum. Second, I didn't bother with framing up, which seemed to me unnecessary... I filmed like this: a wide shot with one camera, and when I called "cut" I only stopped the main camera and left the lights burning; then I approached the actors with a hand-held camera and took close-ups. In the third place, I never repeated a scene. If an actor made a mistake it didn't worry me. I changed the position of the camera and went on filming from the point where the mistake had been made.'[21] It isn't difficult to imagine the outcome. The clapper is used to mark the point of synchronisation between picture and soundtrack – without the clapper synchronisation can be imperfect; not bothering to frame up but only pointing the camera in the right direction with an appropriate lens annihilates composition and gives the picture a sloppy look; as for hand-held close ups and only changing angles when there's a mistake, this is to discard the entire artistry of *découpage*, the articulation of visual rhythm and dramatic flow. The advantage of his Hollywood experience was that Peón could do all these things a bit more efficiently than others. He had a good line in potboilers, ranging from swashbuckling adventures set in the time of the viceroyalty, to films like *Tierra, amor y dolor* ('Earth, Love and Distress', 1934) and *El bastardo* ('The Bastard', 1937), both of them vehicles for 'artistic nudity' – Jorge Ayala Blanco's nicely ironic term for one of the subgenres of 1930s Mexican cinema.[22] On the other hand it would be unfair to deny that Peón had his pretensions: in 1933 he directed *Tiburón*, an adaptation of Ben Jonson's *Volpone*, the first such enterprise in the Mexican cinema. García Riera says of it that 'in this Volpone transformed into a modern and mundane tragicomedy, Peón's timid formalist intents are shipwrecked on the verbose dialogue elaborated by a Bustillo Oro in the desire to demonstrate his culture, in homage to a cast composed of true champions of overacting.'[23]

Returning to Cuba at the end of the 30s, Peón again attempted to create a production base in Havana and succeeded in bringing together another group of backers. The resulting company, Pecusa (Peliculas Cubanas S.A.) installed itself in new studios in 1938, and managed to make six films before giving up the ghost before the following year was out. Some of these films – though none of the ones directed by Peón – were musical comedies, and these represent perhaps the most distinctive (but not distinguished) product of the struggling Cuban cinema of the pseudo-Republic. This type of film was hardly unique to Cuba, of course. On the contrary, the coming of sound gave Latin American producers the opportunity to enlist local popular music, and employ musical artistes with a commercial track record already proven by radio and records. The answer Hollywood found to this competition was what the audience in the Harvard Business School had already learnt in 1926: they poached the talent and the music. They already had Fred Astaire *Flying Down to Rio* to meet Dolores del Rio (real name: Lolita Dolores de Martinez, and not Brazilian but Mexican) in 1933. As for Pecusa, Valdés Rodriguez explained that the reason for its collapse was 'undoubtedly its films, as much for their content as their form... Pecusa had been the foremost exponent of the mistakes and lack of bearings of Cuban cinema... [their films were] a transplant onto the screen of the Cuban *bufo* theatre in its later years at a time when it was already a lesser genre, which represented the vernacular theatre at its least worthy.'[24]

In the 40s and 50s Cuban production efforts were dominated by the Mexican film industry in the form of co-productions using Mexican directors and stars. Occasionally there were similar efforts with Argentina. At the beginning of 1952, however, just before Batista's coup, the government of Carlos Prio set up a film finance bank and executive commission for the film industry (*Patronato para el Fomento de la Industria Cinematografica*). According to a report in the US trade journal *Variety*, this commission was authorised to advance producers up to 33% of the costs of production: 'this provision, in effect, underwrites up to 33% of losses should that picture lay an egg since repayment shall only be from its earnings.'[25] It added that the commission was to be financed by a national lottery (not inappropriately, one might say). Such arrangements could make no essential difference to the state of film production in Cuba. The most distinguished films made in Cuba in the years before the Revolution were North American productions on location, including one Errol Flynn movie, one Victor Mature, and *The Old Man and the Sea*, directed to begin with by Fred Zinneman, who was replaced by Henry King, who in turn was replaced by John Sturges.

Only one other Cuban film of this period calls for special comment: *La rosa blanca* ('The White Rose'), subtitled *Momentos de la vida de Martí* ('Moments from the Life of Martí'). A co-production with Mexico, it was a government-sponsored official tribute to the Cuban national hero, who was played by the Mexican actor Roberto Canedo under the direction of one of Mexico's leading directors, 'El Indio' Fernandez. Canedo bore not the slightest resemblance to Martí, physically or spiritually. The commission charged with supervising the production, which succeeded only in offending national dignity with their sentimentalising, was composed of right-wing intellectuals like Francisco Ichazo, the man who warned Julio García Espinosa a few years later about US Embassy concern over the clandestine *El Megano*.


In 1958, an article appeared in the Havana journal *Carteles* entitled 'The Possibilities of a Film Industry in Cuba: Considerations'.[26] The central question which the article raised was 'is the home market sufficient to sustain a film industry?' The author, one Oscar Pino Santos, began his answer by pointing out that the average Cuban expenditure at the cinema over the years 1948-1957 was 0.7% of the national income, as against 0.5% in the United States. (His figures differ from those covering the same period given in 1960 by Francisco Mota, from which an even higher average expenditure of 0.9% can be derived.)[27] There were 15 people for every cinema seat in Cuba, which had no film production of its own to speak of; while in Mexico and Brazil, with substantial industries producing, in their best years, as many as a hundred features a year, there were 18 and 25 respectively. The fact was, said Pino Santos, the Cuban market simply wasn't big enough, even if they did spend more on cinema than in the mecca in the north. The total average income for a film exhibited in Cuba he estimated at some 26,000 pesos. Out of this sum, for a Cuban film, about 15,600 pesos went to the distributor, about 6,300 to the producer, the remaining 4,100 to the exhibitor. Was it possible to make films on this little money? No way.

Again the figures which Mota gives are a bit different, though he's talking about imported films, for which, he reported, the royalty was said to be 40%, although only half this sum actually left the country after various deductions. (In 1954, *Variety* reported that a new tax threatened the US film industry in Cuba, a 20% levy on top of the existing 3% they had previously always managed to avoid. The article mentioned that Cuba rated as a 3 million dollar market for the US companies.)[28] Pino Santos's figures gave the exhibitors' share at 16%; Mota estimated 20% to the exhibitors. But even this difference isn't material. The point is that unless a *very* much higher sum – double or even more – had gone back to the producer, not even a cheaply made film could recoup its cost. Even the 33% which the commission established by Prio effectively granted against losses was insufficient. It could only really serve as a subsidy to attract foreign, mainly Mexican, co-production.

What chances then for ICAIC? What cheek the Cuban revolutionaries had, if they thought they could really create a film industry that wouldn't need constant and enormous subsidy! Could an underdeveloped country afford such luxuries? The answer is that this line of reasoning only applies under capitalist conditions: conditions in which the middlemen (the distributors), and the retailers (the exhibitors), rake off the profits before anything gets back to the producer. The provisions that are made in the decree by which ICAIC was set up envision and empower it to intervene not only as a production house but also as both a distributor and an exhibitor, in order to alter these conditions, knowing that unless indeed they were altered, films produced in Cuba would never stand a chance.

Of course ICAIC has needed subsidy. Not however, because Cuban films don't make enough money at the Cuban box office. They do so, as already noted, sometimes very rapidly. In general, their own films make more than enough money at the box office to cover the costs of production – except for one thing: the problem of foreign exchange. The exclusion of Cuban films from many parts of the foreign market prevents them earning enough freely exchangeable currency entirely to cover the inevitable foreign costs of the enterprise. These foreign costs are of two main kinds: first, the costs of purchasing films for distribution; and second, in order to make their own, the costs of the industry's most monopolised resource, film stock (of which there are no more than half a dozen manufacturing companies in the world). Some of the foreign exchange ICAIC needs is saved by trade agreements with socialist countries which supply up to about 40% of the new films distributed annually; and by the expedient of purchasing film stock for distribution copies of their own films from East Germany. Even then, they have to make do with only six or eight copies for the entire country, with the result that programming still has to be carried out centrally, and copies have to be kept in circulation after they've been scratched or damaged and should have been withdrawn. They would prefer to shoot their films on Eastmancolor, which the US blockade makes it difficult and expensive for them to obtain, so they generally shoot instead on Fuji, but this is Japanese and still requires foreign exchange.

ICAIC, for much of its existence, has been financed according to what socialist economic planning calls the system of central budgeting. Profitability plays no role in this system in the evaluation of the enterprise, which instead receives a pre-arranged sum; any net income is returned to the treasury from which central budgeting funds are allocated. In recent years ICAIC's annual production budget has stood at seven million pesos. In other words, its entire production programme, which has averaged out at around three or four feature-length movies a year, more than 40 documentaries, a dozen or so cartoons and the weekly newsreel – all this is accomplished on less than the cost of a single big-budget movie in Hollywood, or under half the cost of quite a few individual blockbusters.

Since the basic peculiarities of the film industry also apply within socialist economies, ICAIC's financial system includes special arrangements. Apart from the *Cinemateca* and a small circuit of first-run houses of its own, the commercial cinemas are run, since the instigation of the system of Popular Power in the mid 70s, by the local administrations, which also run such facilities as shops and petrol stations. Box office earnings pay for running the cinemas and for renting the films from ICAIC's distribution wing. The net takings go back to the central bank.

The system could be improved, but it has clearly shown that it works. Internally, the costs of production are recovered from the home market successfully enough. Two important factors contribute to keeping production costs down, both of them the fruits of the Revolution in the relations of production. One is that the economics of the star system no longer exert any influence. Since the Revolution has established control over inflation and rationalised salaries and wages, there is no longer any pressure to keep putting up the pay of actors and specialised technical personnel – a major factor in the constantly increasing costs of production in the capitalist film industries. At the same time, the plan for ICAIC to become a fully equipped production house envisaged and accomplished the elimination of the different individual companies which buy and sell each other their services and facilities in every capitalist film industry, each one raking off its own profit. Under such a system the costs tend upwards, production is risky, employment uncertain. In ICAIC today, where about a thousand people are employed in production, such uncertainty, which was always worse in Cuba because production was underdeveloped and fragile, has become a thing of the past.

# References

1. Rolando Díaz Rodríguez and Lázaro Buria Pérez, 'Un caso de colonisación cinematográfica', *Caimán Barbudo* No.85, Dec. 1975, pp.6-7.
2. See Mota, op.cit., (Ch.1).
3. José Agustín Mahieu, *Breve historia del cine argentino*, Editorial Universitaria, Buenos Aires 1966, p.5.
4. Pierre Bachlin, *Histoire Economique du Cinéma*, La Nouvelle Edition, Paris 1947, p.21.
5. William Martson Seabury, *The Public and the Motion Picture Industry*, Macmillan, New York 1926, p.39.
6. Op.cit., p.127.
7. *Report on Market for Cinematograph Films in Cuba* (furnished by His Majesty's Consul-General in Havana, 13th March 1923), typewritten copy, Library of the British Film Institute.
8. Seabury, op.cit., p.283.
9. Quoted in Agramonte, op.cit., p.42.
10. 'Distributing the Product' in J.P.Kennedy, ed., *The Story of the Film*, A.W. Shaw & Co., 1927, pp.225-6.
11. Thomas Guback, *The International Film Industry*, Indiana University Press 1969, pp.7-8.
12. Op.cit., p.3.
13. *World Trade in Commodities*, November 1947, Motion Pictures and Equipment, p.3 (Report by Byron White, United States Embassy, Havana).
14. E. Bradford Burns in Introduction to Beatriz Reyes Nevares, *The Mexican Cinema, Interviews with Thirteen Directors*, University of New Mexico Press, Albuquerque 1976, p.xii.
15. Eduardo Colina and Daniel Díaz Torres, 'Ideología del melodrama en el viejo cine latinoamericano', *Cine Cubano* No.73-4-5, p.15.
16. Jorge Ayala Blanco, *La aventura del cine mexicano*, Ediciones Era, Mexico 1968, p.48.
17. See Emilio García Riera, *Historia documental del cine mexicano* Vol. 1, Ediciones Era, Mexico 1969.
18. Agramonte, op.cit., p.65.
19. Raimond del Castillo, 'Cuban Cinema', *Sight and Sound*, September 1947.
20. Emilio García Riera, *El cine mexicano*, Ediciones Era, Mexico 1963, p.28.
21. Quoted by Colina and Díaz Torres, op.cit., note 12.
22. Ayala Blanco, op.cit., p.156.
23. García Riera, *Historia documental*, cit., p.51.
24. Valdés Rodríguez, 1960, op.cit., III (24 April).
25. 'Cuban to back film production setup', *Variety*, 11 February 53.
26. Oscar Pino Santos, 'Las posibilidades de una industria cinematográfica en Cuba: Consideraciones', *Carteles*, 30 November 1958.
27. Mota, op.cit.
28. 'Cuba Tax in New Vexation', *Variety*, 27 January 54.

# 5
# AMATEURS AND MILITANTS

*Aficionado cinema in the 1940s and 50s*

'Perhaps more interesting than the professional cinema,' said an article entitled 'The Cinema in Cuba' in the North American magazine *Film Culture* in 1956, 'is the experimental cinema in 16mm and the intense action of the cine-clubs'.[1] The author of this article, Nestor Almendros, the son of an exile from Franco's Spain, was himself a member of this movement. Like most of the *aficionados* he was writing about, he worked at the Film Institute when it was first set up, but he was also one of the first film-makers to leave Cuba as a result of disagreement with ICAIC's policies. Meeting with success in Paris as a cinematographer with the new wave directors, and later internationally, Almendros has published his own version of these disagreements in his autobiography *Días de una cámara* ('Days of a Camera').[2] He rapidly became disillusioned with ICAIC, he says, because ICAIC rapidly became bureaucratic and intolerant of differences of opinion. To be fair, he was already experimenting with new styles of cinematography which were not yet appreciated, and felt frustrated that the value of his experiments was not being recognised. But there was clearly more to it than this, and to understand more fully, one needs to go back to the *aficionado* movement which ICAIC grew out of. This movement involved a whole generation of Cuban artists and intellectuals, for whom the attempt to create an independent cinema was a symbol of cultural resistance and a way of forging a sense of unity in their cultural aspirations. As the head of ICAIC, Alfredo Guevara, later wrote:

> Only the Cine-Clubs, brave in their narrow field, denounced the apologia for violence [of the Hollywood movie] and supposed American superiority, and opened a gap for a cinema of quality, discovering for the public the significance of schools and currents, the work and value of particular directors, and the necessity, above all, of sharpening the critical spirit. But in a closed ambience, and in the face of the hostility of the distribution companies and in some cases subject to police vigilance and pressures, there was little they could do.[3]

However little, it included laying the foundations of a future film culture. 'Police vigilance and pressures' records the close links of many of these aesthetic militants with active political opposition; but whatever held the movement together, it was mainly a union of convenience, in which certain rifts opened up when the inevitable political divisions were brought out into the open after the victory of the Revolution. Not that this impugns those who were trying to use film as part of the political struggle. On the contrary, it can be argued that the artistic openness of the most militant members of the movement helped to win people over.

The movement first developed during the 40s. In 1945, the us Department of Commerce publication *Industrial Reference Service* (later *World Trade in Commodities*) reported on the development of a new market in Cuba:

> The market potentialities for the sale to amateur users in Cuba of United States motion-picture cameras and projectors are fair. It is estimated that upon termination of the war about $3,500 worth of 16mm sound projectors and $2,400 worth of silent 16mm projectors can be sold. Sales of 8mm motion picture cameras are expected to be somewhat higher.[4]

This was the last paragraph in a detailed report that examined prospects for the sale of various kinds of equipment in both the theatrical and the non-theatrical markets. Non-theatrical users included schools, the army and navy, commercial users and amateurs. The expected sales were not particularly large, even allowing for the higher value of the dollar at the time. However, Cuba had been of interest to the United States for some time as a kind of offshore testing laboratory for trying out new technologies and techniques in the fields of media and communication.

Back in the mid-20s, Cuba was together with Puerto Rico the birthplace of the now massive communications corporation ITT – the same ITT that offered the CIA $1m to 'destabilise' the Popular Unity Government in Chile at the beginning of the 70s. ITT was set up by sugar brokers Sosthenes and Hernand Behn after they acquired a tiny Puerto Rican telephone business in settlement of a bad debt. The company was then built up on the success of the underwater cable link they laid between Havana and Miami.[5] At the same time radio arrived; the first transmissions in Cuba took place in 1922[6] and Cuba quickly became one of Latin America's most intensely developed broadcasting markets. By 1939 it had no less than 88 radio stations and about 150,000 receivers. Mexico, by comparison, though many times larger, had only 100 stations and no more than 300,000 receivers. Argentina had about 1.1m receivers, but only about 50 stations. This gave Argentina the best ratio of sets to inhabitants in Latin America, approximately 1:12, but the Cuban ratio, 1:30, was better than the Mexican, 1:64. The ratio in the USA at the same time was 1:3.5 and in Europe between 1:6 and 1:11.[7]

Because of the inherent problems of media programming and the opportunities provided by language and national musical idioms, local capital found that it was relatively easy to enter certain parts of the culture industry while other areas remained the prerogative of foreign capital. The two media of radio and records – which are intimately linked – were also cheaper to enter and to operate than film production after its earliest years. The Cuban commentators Rodríguez and Pérez say that during the 20s, after the great collapse of sugar prices in 1920 and the resulting depression which ruined many small businessmen – including the foremost film business, Santos y Artega, who only survived by returning to their earlier activity as circus proprietors – that after this, local capital preferred to look to the new activity of radio. (The circus of Santos y Artega crops up in Tomás Gutiérrez Alea's comedy, *Las doce sillas* – 'The Twelve Chairs' – of 1962.) As for records, early technology was almost artisanal and easily permitted small-scale local production, and it remained so for longer than film. Record production was already well-established in Cuba before the advent of electrical recording in 1925. What electrical recording did was give the North American companies new ways of moving in on the Latin American market, but their control was still necessarily indirect. They built factories for the manufacture of records made by local musicians and produced by local companies who knew the market, and used radio stations both as their aural shopwindow and to discover new talent.

These media, taken together, are different from telephones and cables and electricity which were ninety per cent in the hands of US companies in Cuba at the time of the Revolution, who owned and controlled them directly; in the entertainments sector, a large part of the infrastructure belonged to local capital. Electricity is a universal energy source requiring powerful and expensive generators as well as a guaranteed constant fuel supply; telephones and cables are first and foremost, as well as being luxury items for personal use, instruments of communication for commercial and industrial intelligence and traffic. But the general availability of telephones and cables in underdeveloped countries, like that of electricity, is always restricted. The entertainments media, in contrast, are primarily directed to the exploitation of something nowadays called consumer leisure time, across the widest possible social spectrum. They aim in underdeveloped countries to include the people who do not have electricity and telephones in their homes – or used not to. Radio enjoyed a second vogue after the invention of the transistor in the 50s, though nowadays the shanty towns which encircle the cities increasingly have electricity, and hence television, even if they still lack not only telephones, but also a water supply and drainage system.

Every communications technology and each entertainment medium manifests its own peculiarities and idiosyncrasies as a commodity, which vary with the precise conditions of the environment in which they are installed. The telephone everywhere accelerated, increased and extended commercial intercourse, but in Cuba it also served to let North American companies run their Cuban operations not as fully-fledged overseas offices but like local branches. It made it unnecessary for them to hold large stocks of raw materials or spare parts when they could get on the phone and have them rapidly shipped or flown in from mainland depots when they were needed. The same methods are nowadays employed by trans-national corporations throughout the world on the much larger scale made possible by computerisation, satellite communication, and jet air transport. The advantages are not only economic: the corporations are also in this way lifted beyond the control of the countries in which their various branches are situated. Even in its simpler form twenty-five years ago in Cuba, this system confronted the revolutionaries with difficult problems, for the companies concerned were easily able to operate an embargo on supplies in the attempt to destabilise the new government.

Radio also has peculiarities. The first is that, for the listener who has bought a receiver, the programmes themselves are not commodities – they do not have to be purchased individually. That is why radio becomes an aural shopwindow for records, but also why it is different from them too; for the record which radio feeds off has the peculiarity of being linked to the gramophone on which it is played. The record cannot go where the gramophone does not go, just as the light-bulb cannot go where there is no electricity. In this way the development of advanced technologies creates a greater and greater degree of interdependence of commodities.

But this interdependence is ideological as well as economic – the ideological and the economic are two faces of the same process. Because, in the case of radio, strictly speaking the programme is not a commodity that yields an exchange value from the consumer, other ways must be found of raising revenue to produce the programmes without which the receiver is pointless. The commercial broadcasting system created in the United States and exported to Latin America does this by trading in a new commodity – the air space which is bought up by sponsors and advertisers. (Or the slice of the audience which it sells them, if you prefer.) The values of the commercial publicity industry in this way invade and dominate the medium.

The development of commercial broadcasting in Latin America, however, was not a natural phenomenon, but the result of inducement by the captains of industry in the United States. They encouraged local capital to adopt the system on its own account, to promote its own preservation and reproduction. This is not to suggest some kind of conspiracy: little capitalists naturally imitate big capitalists and big capitalists naturally encourage them to do so – though they also hedge them in to prevent real competition. But the result is still that the media become channels of ideological penetration even when the programmes they carry are not themselves produced abroad. They still automatically imitate the same values. These values, however, are as foreign in Latin America and other dependent countries as the technology that carries them, and can hardly fail to deform the material that goes into the programme, even if it is locally produced. The result is a central feature of the process that has been designated cultural imperialism.

We already know that cultural imperialism is not just a phenomenon of the contemporary world. Before the flooding of the market with the products of the trans-national entertainments corporations, there was, for example, the colonisation of literary taste, the process described by Mariátegui. The whole process started with the arrival of the *conquistadores*. As Alejo Carpentier explains in the opening lines of his classic historical study of music in Cuba:

> The degree of riches, vigour and power of resistance of the civilizations which the *conquistadores* discovered in the New World always determined, one way or another, the greater or lesser activity of the European invader in the construction of architectural works and musical indoctrination. When the peoples to be subjugated were already sufficiently strong, intelligent and industrious enough to build a Tenochtitlán or conceive a fortress of Allanta, the Christian bricklayer and chorister went into action with the greatest diligence, with the mission of the men of war scarcely fulfilled. Once the battle of bodies was over, there began the battle of the symbol.[8]

The power of the symbol, make no mistake, is a material power; though intangible and subject to ambiguity, it has the durability of generations. It operates frequently in the guise of myths, including the modern myths which take on their paradigmatic forms in the movies, in the genres of the western, the gangster movie, the thriller, the romance, the stories of rags-to-riches and all the rest. It is possible that the situation of the Hollywood film industry gave it special insight into the ideological needs of imperialism. In any event, as the film-makers mastered the new narrative art, it and they were pressed into telling tales which, to fulfill the function of a modern mythology, suppressed, as Roland Barthes has put it, the memory of their fabrication and origins. The control of this symbolising, mythologising faculty has been as much the object of the Hollywood monopolies as control of its economic functions, however unconscious and disguised their purposes become by ideological rationalisations. (For in Hollywood, as the critic Paul Mayersburg has somewhere said, conscience doth make heroes of them all.)

This ideological manipulation reaches beyond commercial cinema and the feature film into other uses of film which began to appear. The Industrial Reference Service 1945 Report speaks of the development in Cuba of the use of 16mm 'sub-standard' film equipment both in education and by private firms, not to mention the armed forces. It mentions with approval the example of a local cigarette manufacturer who had begun an advertising campaign using portable 16mm equipment. This kind of use of film was already extensively developed in the metropolis. The English cigarette manufacturers Wills showed a one-reel sub-standard sound-on-disc film, *How Woodbines Are Made*, some 8,000 times in 1934 alone around working men's clubs.[9]

The 16mm gear that such activity employed was classed as sub-standard, to distinguish it from those means of production which were deemed appropriate for producing commercial movies in 35mm. Yet whatever the gauge, a camera is still a camera, and a means of production of films, and the same thing happened in Cuba in the 40s and 50s as happened in the 30s in Europe and North America with the creation of the workers' film movements. The same thing is happening again with the diffusion of sound-on-film super-8 and the growing availability of three-quarter and half-inch video. Such equipment comes within the grasp of people in countries as far apart as Britain and Bolivia who are in a position to conceive other purposes for its use, artistic or political, than those which the market and dominant ideologies license. The medium's power of persuasion has never been a secret.

There were historically two main reactions to the growing power of cinema as an ideological institution, the aesthetic and the political. In capitalist Europe, the aesthetic was the first to arise, in the form of the avant-garde cinema of the 20s; it was followed within a decade by the creation of the workers' film movements. The accent of the avant-garde of the 20s was that of expressionism, cubism, futurism, surrealism and atonality; it incorporated film into the modernist revolution which had begun before the First World War. Revolutionary Russia, at the same time, produced a confluence of artistic with political imperatives and created the first consciously revolutionary cinema; a paradigm for the workers' film movements in the west, though the model it provided was, except in the matter of montage, beyond the scope of independent political film-makers. On the other hand, its influence has never died, and is very strongly felt beyond the metropolis; in Latin America, for instance, wherever an organised and self-educated proletariat emerged, and engaged in film distribution – if only of the Soviet classics – as part of its propaganda work.

In Cuba, political and artistic uses of film were born at around the same moment, together with the appearance of amateur cine, in the early 40s. By the end of the decade, there were both artists and militants among the Cuban *aficionados*. Sometimes the same person was both. The historical detail is quite intricate; three main groups can be distinguished: the political militants, those with artistic aspirations, and the children of the *nouveaux riches* who were neither. The first two had common ground in their anti-imperialism. To be an artist in Cuba was almost always to be a progressive artist, because, except for a few sycophants, to want to be an artist at all was to struggle for the same right to speak that the struggle for political expression involved. The children of the *nouveaux riches* were concerned with neither. Film for them was purely diversion. The ICAIC director Miguel Torres has described them as 'those thousands of "white-collars" of our American countries, who launch themselves on Sundays into feverish filming with amateur cameras and equipment to assuage the oppression of their jobs'.[10] Their aesthetic attitudes were essentially no different from the few of them who invested spare money in the shoestring companies which made publicity films and newsreels.

The newsreel business in Cuba was quite considerable. According to the Industrial News Service of 1945:

There are six newsreel companies with laboratories which together produce an average of one-and-a-half million feet of positive newsreel a year, and about 50,000 feet of commercial advertisements. The newsreel companies do not intend to purchase new equipment but have some photographic lighting equipment which they would like to dispose of.

(Perhaps someone had taken them for suckers and managed to sell them more lighting equipment than they needed in that sunny clime.) But what actually were all these companies doing? Two years later, in 1947, *World Trade in Commodities*, the successor to the Industrial Reference Service, revealed:

Dissemination of propaganda and publicity for individuals, clubs and other groups, and the Government, is a chief function of Cuban newsreels. News as understood in the United States is only an incidental phase of newsreels. The propaganda arises from the fact that one or all persons appearing in practically all newsreels pay the producer for this privilege or else an organisation pays for them. Fees from newsworthy notables are an immeasurably larger source of studio incomes than rental from theatres. Productora Nacional does not charge theatres any rental. Noticiero Nacional has a sliding scale: $5 weekly to first run Havana theatres to as low as $5 monthly in some other places.
The father of a bride or the groom reimburses a producer for making a newsreel record of a wedding. A nautical club pays to have pictures made of some sporting event it sponsors. The official of a government agency will pay to have included in a newsreel shots of construction work on some public project. Large payments are made to newsreel companies by political parties during a national election campaign. No producers deny they are subsidized in the manner described by news-significant personages. [11]

The truth is that the newsreels were an ideological protection racket. Their method was straightfoward blackmail. One of ICAIC's founder members, Tomás Gutiérrez Alea, recalls it as 'a very dirty business': 'if a newsreel cameraman were to happen upon a car crash, he'd be sure to take shots of the smashed up car with its brand-name in close-up, and blackmail the company to pay for them not to be shown.' [12] There was only one commercial producer operating in Cuba in the 50s, says Alea, who was a serious and honourable person, the Mexican Manuel Barbachano Ponce. He had produced three Mexican pictures of some quality and importance: *Raices* ('Roots', 1954), *¡Torero!* (1955) and Buñuel's *Nazarin* (1958). *Raices* was a four-episode film which the French film historian Sadoul calls 'a striking portrait of contemporary Mexican Indian life [which] avoids the extravagant pictorial style of many previous Mexican films'. [13] Directed by Benito Alazraki, it was scripted by a team that included Barbachano himself and the documentary film maker Carlos Velo, an exile from Franco's Spain. Velo also directed *¡Torero!*, a fictionalised documentary on the career of a well-known matador, which Sadoul regards as 'a brilliant achievement'. It is a formally experimental film in its use of newsreel footage, including footage of the matador, Procuña, regaining his fame in the last sequence, mixed with re-enacted scenes in which Procuña played himself. Future head of ICAIC Alfredo Guevara worked for a period with Barbachano in Mexico; he was assistant director on *Nazarín*. In Cuba, Barbachano produced *Cine Revista*, a ten-minute film magazine made up of brief advertisements and short items of reportage, documentary and sketches, distributed throughout the island. Alea, as well as Julio García Espinosa, gained experience through *Cine Revista* in both documentary and working with actors. (The sketches, said Alea, gave him a certain taste for comedy.) The two of them had studied film at the beginning of the 50s in the Centro Sperimentale in Rome, at a time when the school itself was already in decline, and the most important part of the experience was the effervescent political atmosphere in the country. The two of them also went to Eastern Europe, in different years, to attend Youth Festivals. Back in Cuba, they were both harassed and arrested, along with other cultural activists, by Batista's anti-communist squad.

The roots of the sense of protest against cultural imperialism in Cuba go back to the revolt of the Cuban intelligentsia in the 1920s, which was spearheaded by the University Reform Movement. Its mood is portrayed in Enrique Pineda Barnet's historical feature *Mella* of 1975, a dramatised biography of the student leader Julio Antonio Mella who became one of the founders of the Cuban Communist Party. The Cuban students who held the first Revolutionary Students' Congress in 1923 shared the burgeoning consciousness of students in many places in Latin America. The University Reform Movement was born in Cordoba, Argentina, and quickly spread not only to Cuba but also to Chile, Uruguay and Peru, rallying students in an attack upon old teaching systems and the elitism of the academies. The continental character of the movement was in part an expression of generalised hostility towards the new Washington doctrine of Panamericanism, to which the political leaders of the day had widely succumbed in spite of some misgivings. It was also an expression of the unease of a new generation in the process of discovering what was later to be called underdevelopment. A number of emergent radical political leaders cut their teeth in the movement, like Haya de la Torre in Peru, founder of the *Alianza Popular Revolucionaria Americana* (APRA – American Popular Revolutionary Alliance). This was a radical party pledged to an anti-imperialist programme which rejected political, economic or social structures based on foreign models. And was Hollywood cinema, then, not to be anathema?

APRA became, through its successful populism, an obstacle to Communist politics, and was condemned by Moscow in 1928. Does this mean that Mella and the Cuban Communists surrendered their independence to the Moscow decree? Whatever the historical evidence about this from a political point of view, the Cuban Communists clearly manifested a distinctive understanding of the nature of cultural imperialism, which included cinema, and linked it with the control of information and the denial of authentic artistic expression. Mella himself wrote a review of Eisenstein's *October* in a Mexican newspaper (where he was assassinated in 1929) in which he explained:

> The public, accustomed to the bourgeois style of the yanqui film, will not be able fully to appreciate the proper value of this effort from Sovkino. It doesn't matter. It would be asking as much of them to comprehend the Proletarian Revolution after hearing about it through the cables of United Press, or the revolutionary movement of our own country and our national characteristics through the interpretations given them by Hollywood. However, here the ideological vanguards have the opportunity to enjoy one of the most intense pleasures the present epoch can offer in the terrain of art, through the youngest and most expressive of the modern arts: motion photography.[14]

This analysis was further developed during the 30s by J.M.Valdés Rodríguez, who in the 40s went on to set up a film studies department at the University of Havana. Hollywood, he said, in an article under the title 'Hollywood: Sales Agent of Imperialism' in the North American journal *Experimental Cinema*,

> presents the Latin American people as the lowest, most repulsive scoundrels on earth. A Latin, or Latin American, is always a traitor, a villain. Years ago, there was not a picture that was without a Spanish or Spanish-American villain. In *Strangers May Kiss* they present a little Mexican town: the owner of the old 'posada' (inn) is a drunkard and the 'mozo' (servant, waiter) is a similar character; the streets with three feet of mud; countless beggars; licentious girls.
>
> I remember, too, the picture *Under the Texas Moon*, openly offensive to Mexican women, the projection of which in a movie-house in the Latin section of New York City provoked a terrible tumult. The tumult was caused by the enraged protest of a few Mexican and Cuban students, in which one of the former... was killed...[15]

The whole population of Cuba, he continued, suffered drastically from the influence of Hollywood pictures: workers, peasants and artisans, petty bourgeois and bourgeois all alike. The bourgeoisie, so complete was their identification with the American Dream, no longer accepted European films, as their better education might lead one to expect, while young people were induced to imitate the youth they saw in the North American pictures. From this there arose, said Valdés Rodríguez, a conflict, between the traditional patriarchal society of Cuba on the one hand, and on the other, new imported values which young, and even adult people, were beginning to adopt in matters such as family relationships and (heterosexual) love. The image of the American Dream produced only 'wild parties, "necking" orgies, licentiousness, miscomprehension of what "free love" really means, gross sensuality, lack of control over the lower passions, and a narrow, American, utilitarian conception of life, the ardent praise of those who "win", no matter how.' A degenerative influence on Cuban society was also to be seen in the Hollywood treatment of the black. Cuba, said Valdés Rodríguez, had not previously suffered the same terrific racial antagonisms:

> The first act of the Cuban patriots of 1868 – the majority of them were slave owners – was to declare their Negroes free. So in both wars of independence . . . Negroes and whites fought for liberty, shoulder to shoulder, against the tyranny of Spain, their old enemy . . . But things are changing, owing to the Hollywood pictures and to the Cuban youth in America. In American films, Negroes are cowards, superstitious, dumb . . . This depiction of their race has evidently affected the Negroes' confidence in themselves . . .

Intellectual and artistic rebelliousness in Cuba in the 20s found its voice not only in the University Reform Movement but also in the Grupo Minorista, with its journal *Revista de Avance*, and in the artistic movement of Afrocubanism, which expressed itself most strongly in music and poetry. The Grupo Minorista met in Havana in the Hotel Lafayette, a gathering of writers and painters, poets, sculptors and musicians. Some of them were involved in an incident in May 1923 at the Academy of Sciences, remembered as the 'Protest of the Thirteen', when the writer Rubén Martínez Villena spoke out in the presence of a cabinet minister against bureaucratic embezzlement on behalf of a group of thirteen protestors, a demonstration for which they were prosecuted. In 1927, the year in which the group's *Revista de Avance* appeared, they again linked the demand for freedom for cultural development with political protest in a roundly anti-imperialist manifesto; it condemned 'the outrage of pseudo-democracy' and 'the farce' of elections without effective participation, calling at the same time for 'the revision of false and threadbare values,' the reform of education, and for 'vernacular and modern art'.[16]

Afrocubanism began as a quest for the roots of a Cuban national culture, and the elements that made it distinctive. Another member of the Grupo Minorista, Juan Marinello, explained that a return to the roots in Cuba, in the same way as elsewhere in Latin America in the 20s, produced different results, because in Cuba the indigenous Indian population had not survived. Certainly Cuba was part of Latin America, indeed it was where Columbus first set foot in 1492. The native population, however, had been wiped out in the space of fifty years almost without the *conquistadores* noticing what they were doing – only the churchman Bartolomé de las Casas observed and condemned. Consequently, where throughout most of Latin America the new artistic explorations of the 20s became indigenist in character, in Cuba there were no indigenous roots to be found; they were African, because they lay in the culture of the population with which the slave trade replaced the missing native when workers were needed to develop the plantation economy. The same thing had happened in the English and French speaking Caribbean, but they had a different colonial history, and slavery there was abolished earlier. A similar phenomenon is also found in certain other Latin American countries, such as parts of Brazil and Venezuela, in regions where indigenous populations were wiped out or driven back.

In Cuba, however, being an island, the cultural consequences were particularly acute. Because of continuing Spanish rule, slaves continued to arrive in Cuba for much longer than in the rest of the Caribbean, though the abolition of slavery in Brazil was also delayed. The traits of African culture and its symbolisms, though modified, remain in many ways more immediate in Cuba than elsewhere in the Caribbean. Up till today there are people who can speak an African language because they learnt it from a grandparent, and even after twenty-five years of Revolution, the practice of *santería*, in which Catholic saints are worshipped like African deities, is still widespread.

In Cuba, declares Marinello, the black participated in the liberation struggle against Spain, in fact black participation was decisive. General Antonio Maceo and the journalist Gualberto Gómez were two of the acknowledged leaders, and they are not the only ones. In fact, there are two respects in which the nineteenth-century Cuban independence struggle was a model, the participation of black people and its internationalist character: it attracted a number of liberation fighters from the Spanish Caribbean and beyond. Both these factors gave Cuba great advantages in subsequent stages of struggle. The political orientation of the Grupo Minorista owed a great deal to the independence movement. The movement had the support of the Federation of Cuban Workers, in which Cuban trade unionism was born, and its leaders, although not fully formed as socialists, were passionate adherents of the idea of the Social Republic represented for them by the Paris Commune of 1871 or the Spanish Federal Republic of 1874-5.[17]

From a cultural point of view black participation was equally decisive. The black, said Marinello, is 'the marrow and root, the breath of the people... He may, in these times of change, be the touchstone of our poetry.'[18] And in the poetry of Nicolás Guillén which began to appear at the end of the 20s, the Afrocuban movement found a native voice. Guillén brought earlier experiments in Afrocubanism to flower. In imitating the rhythms of Afrocuban dance, and borrowing the verbal patterns and repetitions of voodoo and *santería* ceremonies, this poetry is imbued with a sense of social reality and criticism, and speaks with the voices of real characters in real situations, with their argot and accents. The result was a new and shocking linguistic authenticity.

Something similar happened in music. Alejo Carpentier wrote the scenario of an Afrocuban ballet composed by Amadeo Roldán, *La Rebambaramba*, which they researched in visits to the ceremonies of the Abakuá, a secret religious society of African origin. It was the first of a series of works through which Roldán achieved international renown, alongside composers like Varèse, as an *enfant terrible*. Carpentier has recorded that one of the influences was Stravinsky:[19] the extraordinary rhythmic pulse of *The Rite of Spring*, which they got to know from the score – something quite unprecedented in European art music – showed Roldán how to 'compose' the difficult crossrhythms involved, in other words, how to notate and thereby carry into the theatre and the concert hall the inflections and fusion of African rhythms with the melodic lines of the Spanish and French dance forms, which in another variant also lies at the root of jazz.


The Cuban Communist Party did not remain content with critical and theoretical observations about cinema. At the end of the 30s they undertook to make films of their own. The earliest political films made in Cuba date from 1939-40, when the newspaper *Hoy*, organ of the Partido Socialista Popular (PSP), as the Party was then called, produced its first newsreel, to be shown at union meetings and in the open air. The cameraman was José Tabío, who twenty years later joined ICAIC.

Tabío was one of a group that set up a small production company, Cuba-Sono-Films, at the beginning of the 40s, whose first film was another collaboration with Carpentier. According to Agramonte, the protagonists of this film, *El desahuicio* ('The Sacking') were the workers building Route 20, and 'it showed scenes of high emotion around the social theme it dealt with'.[20] The list of Cuba-Sono-Films titles amounts to a catalogue of Party activities, though it didn't survive for long. But they took to making films again at the end of the decade, and again a future member of ICAIC was involved. Tomás Gutiérrez Alea was not a Party member. He was a law student at the University with the ambition to make films. He worked on two films for the PSP, one of a First of May demonstration which had been banned but went ahead anyway, the other on the World Peace Movement.[21] His name also figures among the non-political *aficionados*, those other radical intellectuals of the educated middle classes whose aspirations were mainly artistic. His first films were made on 8mm in 1946 (*La caperucita roja*, 'Little Red Riding Hood') and 1947 (*Un fakir*), when he also teamed up with Nestor Almendros, the Spanish exile's son, to make an adaptation of a Kafka story called *Una confusion cotidiana* ('An Everday Confusion').

The Photographic Club of Cuba held the island's first amateur cine competition in 1943. Something of its character can be gleaned from the titles of films that were shown in it. They included *La vida de los peces* ('The Life of the Fish'); *Varadero* (the name of one of Cuba's finest but, before the Revolution, private beaches, sited on the same promontory where the North American chemicals millionaire Du Pont built his mansion); and *Desfile gimnastico femenino* ('Feminine Gymnastic Display') which won the gold medal! Competitions like these are part of every amateur cine movement. Similar titles with appropriate differences would be found in any ten best list of British amateur cine in the 30s, when it was a province of the upper classes – even, in Britain, the aristocracy, who made up little amateur dramatics for the cine camera and filmed their favourite pastimes. The only exception among the Cuban amateur cine films of 1943 seems to have been *Vida y triunfo de un pura sangre criollo* ('Life and Triumph of a Pure Blood Creole' – a play on words: creoles in a country like

Cuba are often of mixed descent) which Valdés Rodríguez described as the only one of the films with social and economic implications.[22]

Valdés Rodríguez is a much more reliable guide in these matters than Almendros. He was the mentor of the oppositional film culture which was developing during this period: Alfredo Guevara speaks with warmth of the influence he had both on himself and others of his generation in stimulating an awareness of film. He had followed a 'beg, borrow and steal' policy, Guevara recalls, to build up an archive of films which never entered commercial distribution in Cuba.[23] Agramonte records that Valdés Rodríguez went to the USA in 1941 armed with a letter from the University to Nelson Rockefeller, as a result of which the Museum of Modern Art started sending them films. Later he made similar arrangements with the French Cinémathèque.[24]

The University of Havana, where Valdés Rodríguez introduced film studies, had been one of the focal points of the country's political ferment since the days of Julio Antonio Mella and the University Reform Movement. In the same conversation in which he spoke of Valdés Rodríguez's influence, Alfredo Guevara also mentioned that he had only just discovered, from a book he was reading, how many of the professors when he was a student in Havana had unbeknown to him at the time been active in the political struggles of the 30s, not just the historian Raúl Roa whom everyone knew about because he had emerged as a leader of the Revolution. The whole generation had been politicised by a revolutionary struggle in which a small vanguard of the Cuban proletariat had seized the moment to declare their own short-lived soviets: fruit of the opposition to the dictator Machado whom Batista displaced when he seized power for the first time as a young sergeant.

In the late 40s, when Fidel Castro was a politically active law student, the University was frequently the scene of violent political confrontations between rival factions, in which gun-slinging solutions to political quarrels were a constant liability, a product of the disintegration of Cuban political life. Castro once remarked that his four years at the University were more personally dangerous than the whole time he spent fighting Batista from the Sierra Maestra. Yet in 1950 the University was also the location where a group of students set up a radical cultural society with the name 'Nuestro Tiempo'('Our Times'). They belonged to the students' union cultural group and included Alfredo Guevara.

Guevara – the son of a railway engineering worker who was one of the founders of the railway workers' union – began his political career as a schoolboy adherent of anarcho-syndicalism in the struggle against Batista's first government in the late 30s. By the late 40s he had joined the Communist Party and it was then, while at university, that he first came into contact with Fidel Castro. They first knew each other as political rivals in Student Federation elections in which Castro failed to get elected but Guevara succeeded. Fidel was on the list of a group called the UIR, *Union Insurecional Revolucionaria* or Revolutionary Insurrectional Union, which had formed an alliance with a number of Catholic students: Fidel had already distinguished himself at one of the country's leading Jesuit schools. The UIR was criticised by the MSR – *Movimiento Socialista Revolucionaria* or Revolutionary Socialist Movement – to which Guevera belonged, as too adventurist, and therefore in effect counter-revolutionary. But the two became friends when they went to Colombia together in April 1948, as members of a small delegation to a meeting of Latin American students which was being sponsored by the Argentinian regime of Juan Perón. The Cubans were due to meet the Colombian Liberal Party leader Jorge Gaitán, to discuss his possible participation in the Student Congress which the meeting in Bogotá had been called to plan. On 9 April, just before this meeting with Gaitán was due to take place, the Colombian politician was assassinated. The popular uprising which was sparked off in protest is known to history as the *Bogotazo* – the 'Bogotá explosion'. The Cuban students joined in, and took part in an attack on a police station from which rifles were taken and distributed among the people; they escaped arrest by taking refuge in the Cuban embassy, and returned to Havana in a Cuban government-chartered plane.[25] Though Castro and Guevara followed different political courses over the next few years, the *Bogotazo* constituted a shared moment in both men's political development. Their mutual first-hand knowledge of a moment of popular insurrection gave them a common point in their understanding of the political pulse of their own country. Recalling the episode in conversation, Guevara emphasised how formative an experience it was for them by comparing it with the events which took place almost exactly twenty years later in Paris in 1968, of which, this time a representative of the victorious Cuban Revolution, he also happened to be a first-hand witness.

Nuestro Tiempo came to play a central role in the cultural politics of the Cuban Communists during the 50s. The policy of the Society included a radical programme of activities both within the University and in the local community beyond its precincts – the campus was on the edge of a working-class neighbourhood. These activities were such that following Batista's coup in 1952 members of the society were considered, says Agramonte, 'subversive agents'.[26] José Antonio González, author of an article in *Cine Cubano* called 'Notes for the History of a Cinema Without History', says of Nuestro Tiempo that 'the organisation of the film club and the film cycles it mounted, the pamphlets and the magazine it produced, in reality masked clandestine and semi-clandestine work by the Communist Party among the intellectuals, and organised opposition to the National Institute of Culture set up by the tyranny'.[27] The composer Harold Gramatges, President of Nuestro Tiempo, has explained:

Nuestro Tiempo fulfilled an historic role during the Batista dictatorship. Formed at the beginning of 1950, [it] brought together young people who were pursuing their artistic or cultural activities in dispersal and in hostile surroundings... in a domineering republic consisting in a regime of semicolonial exploitation and misery, the art-public relationship was limited to a privileged class... and aided by the presence of a number of members of

79

the Young Communists, Nuestro Tiempo embarked... with considerable impetus on what was designated the job of a united front [*trabajo de frente - unico*]... the task of proselytising among the youthful masses... We organised ourselves into sections: film, theatre, puppetry, music, dance, plastic arts and literature... [we] produced publications on cinema, theatre and music, and... the magazine *Nuestro Tiempo*.[28]

In 1953, the year of Martí's centenary and of the abortive attack on the Moncada barracks in Santiago de Cuba led by Fidel, Nuestro Tiempo was reorganised and its work extended by the Party committee responsible for cultural work, which was composed of Juan Marinello, Mirta Aguirre and Carlos Rafael Rodríguez. As the repression sharpened, the society was attacked in the press by local apologists for the United States. Its directors were interrogated by Batista's intelligence agencies, the SIM (*Servicio de Intelligencia Militar*, the Military Intelligence Service) and the BRAC (*Buro para la Represion de las Actividades Comunistas*, the Office of Repression of Communist Activities). But Batista never quite dared to close Nuestro Tiempo down.

However, he entertained considerable cultural pretensions. To round off the official celebrations of the Martí centenary, he decided to bring to Havana the Bienal exhibition from Franco's Spain, adding to it the cream of Cuban plastic arts, for which he offered the incentive of large prizes. But, as José Antonio Portuondo, an intellectual of the 30s generation, has recalled, the great majority of Cuban artists refused to collaborate in this salon and a large counter-exhibition was organised. Older and younger artists all participated, not, says Portuondo, for formal reasons, but out of defiance, and a refusal to let Cuban art serve the interests of a hispanic concept of Cuban culture. 'Batista held his Bienal in January 1954 to inaugurate the Museum of Fine Arts, but the most estimable Cuban artists exhibited instead at the Lyceum, went off to the Tejada gallery in Santiago de Cuba, and returned to Havana by way of Camagüey. It was a truly rebel exhibition...'[29]

Portuondo adds that this exhibition was made up predominantly 'not of art with political content but essentially of abstract art, reaffirming the condition of abstract art as an expression of protest in the face of capitalist decadence'. Behind the rhetorical formulation, it is significant that these views were held in the 50s, during the Cold War, by Communist Party members, when the Moscow orthodoxy was that abstract painting was itself the very expression of capitalist decadence. Evidently this is not quite the same orthodox and even collaborationist Communist Party that various anti-communist left-wing commentators have held it to be. The united front approach to cultural politics made it possible to create a bond within the cultural movement of the 50s between artists and intellectuals of different political extractions. It is hardly surprising to find that they included some who later turned out to have supported anti-imperialist objectives principally because this appeared the best route to personal artistic aims, offering the promise of liberal freedoms that did not and could not have existed under the dictatorship. Naturally they came into conflict with those who had come to be revolutionaries first and artists second, who gave their political engagement primacy over their aesthetic ambitions because they regarded the second as impossible to achieve without fulfilling the first.

But these splits were only incipient during the 50s, a time when official culture was on the defensive, powerless to resist the cultural penetration of North American imperialism. The work of Nuestro Tiempo and similar groups had the effect of intensifying ideological confrontation in the domain of cultural activity, and the Catholics too entered the cine-club field. The Church in Cuba had set up a Cinema Commission just before the Second World War which afterwards became a member of the international Catholic cinema organisation. Their strategy seems to have taken a new turn in the early 50s, when they started setting up cine-clubs of their own, in which they showed major films accompanied by cine-debates. The chronology suggests that this was at least in part a response to the initiative of the leftist militants. The Catholic cine-clubs in turn stimulated further development of the idea, spawning cine-clubs around the country which were not directly under their control and only loosely linked with the central organisation. A report presented to the Congress of the International Catholic Office of Film which was held in Havana in 1957 listed forty-two such clubs.[30]

These were the ways in which film came to occupy its key position in radical cultural consciousness in Cuba. Because of its special nature – an industrialised art and agent of cultural imperialism, on the one hand; on the other, the indigenous art form of the twentieth century and the vehicle of a powerful new mode of perception – because of this dual nature, film readily and acutely synthesised the whole range of cultural experience for a whole generation. Cinema was at the same time an instrument of oppression and an object of aspiration. What happened was that the monopolistic practices of the Hollywood majors and their local dependents not only created a frustrated cultural hunger among aficionados of cinema in Cuba, but, combined with their own attempts at making films, this turned cinema into a battlefield of cultural politics. The cine-club movement represented a breach in the defences of cultural imperialism, and in this battlefield lie the origins of ICAIC.

Nuestro Tiempo was one of two principal recruiting grounds for future members of ICAIC: Alfredo Guevara, Tomás Gutiérrez Alea, Julio García Espinosa, José Massip and Santiago Alvarez were all active members; Manuel Octavio Gómez contributed short stories to the society's magazine. There was also the Cine Club Vision, situated in a working class district of Havana, which drew its membership not only from radical intellectuals but also the local people. The composer Leo Brouwer made his debut as a young guitarist under its auspices, and other members who were later to join ICAIC include the film editors Norma Torrado, Nelson Rodríguez and Gloria Arguelles, and the cameraman Luis Costales. The director Manuel Perez recalls that through the club you could get hold of books on cinema that came from Argentina, by

Sadoul, Kuleshev, Balazs, Pudovkin and Chiarini, and it created a cultural ambience where discussion on the films was of a strongly political nature.[31]

Of the *aficionado* films of the 50s the most significant is *El Megano*, directed by Julio García Espinosa, a documentary using neorealist reconstruction to denounce the miserable conditions of the charcoal burners in a region of the Zapata Swamps after which the film is named. García Espinosa started off in theatre, rapidly moving from bourgeois melodrama to the popular vernacular stage, where he acted and directed. But then he went to work in radio, for a commercial station, producing adaptations for a programme called *Misterios en la historia del mundo* – 'Mysteries of World History'. It was in Italy, he recalls, following the debates of the Communist leader Togliatti and talking with other Latin Americans – there was a group of them that published a small cultural magazine with anti-imperialist politics – that he first developed a proper idea of Marxism. He had gone there because some neorealist films they had shown in Cuba had excited him. He did not at that time yet have much of an idea of the relationship between politics and art. But a chance experience made him think hard about it. At an open-air meeting in Rome which Togliatti was addessing, he met the man who had played the lead in De Sica's famous *Bicycle Thieves* of 1949. He learnt what a miserable life this man now led, and how he'd felt frustration and indignity when he was approached to figure in an advertising campaign for a bicycle firm! People talk about the aesthetics of non-professional screen acting, said García Espinosa, but no-one ever asks what happens to these people in their real lives afterwards.[32]

*El Megano* became something of a *cause célèbre* when it was seized by Batista's police after its first screening at the University of Havana. Julio García Espinosa, as head of the group that made it, was taken away for interrogation. He was released on condition that they brought the film to the police. They used the breathing space to look for a way of getting a copy made. Francisco Ichazo, a prominent intellectual with official contacts, warned him that the US Embassy was concerned. Finally, he was interviewed by the head of the secret police. 'Did you make this film?' the man asked, 'Do you know this film is a piece of shit?' 'Do you know,' replied García Espinosa, 'that it's an example of neorealism?' and proceeded to explain. The man, he remembers, listened patiently and then said, 'Not only is the film a piece of shit, but you also talk a lot of shit. Stop eating shit and go and make films about Batista!' 'That', he recalls, 'was my first intervention as a theorist!'[33]

With music by Juan Blanco, *El Megano* had taken a year to make, shooting at weekends on location and then borrowing facilities in Havana for post-production, including dubbing sessions for which the peasant-actors in the film came up to the big city. Neorealism was a powerful element in the film's style, in the shaping of the narrative and the use of non-professional actors. But *El Megano* also has the feel of a documentary in the tradition of Buñuel's *Land Without Bread* (1932), films by Joris Ivens like *Borinage* (1933) or *Spanish Earth* (1937), or Pare Lorentz's *The Plow That Broke the Plains* (1936), as well as some of the work of the British documentary movement of the 30s.

At the same time, an understanding of the media, and taking them into account when thinking about political strategy, had become generalised within Cuban political life in proportion to the intensity with which the Cuban market had been developed in its role as offshore testing laboratory. In a book full of statistics purporting to show his achievements which he published in Mexico in 1961, Batista boasts of Cuba's leading position in Latin America in radio and television: 160 radio stations and one radio set to every five inhabitants in 1958, and 23 television stations and one set to every twenty.[34] Regarded by Batista as one of the indices of how advanced Cuba was and therefore how unjust the rebellion, the presence of the media in fact contributed to his downfall through the variety of uses they were put to in the unfolding of the struggle against his dictatorship. As Lionel Martin has reported:

The July 26th Movement, which had strong backing among professionals, penetrated some of Cuba's publicity agencies. Cubans still laugh about the advertisements for Tornillo Soap that followed the official newscasts. After the Batista government handouts were read, the announcer would burst in with 'Don't believe in tales, woman – Tornillo Soap washes best of all.' Also memorable were the Bola Roja bean advertisements that followed the news. The word *bola* as used in Cuba can be variously translated 'ball' (like a round bean) or 'rumor' [hence *bola roja* – 'red rumor'].

Just a week before Batista fled, a two-page advertisement for Eden cigarettes showed a man with a pack of Edens in one hand and a book in the other entitled *High Fidelity*. Newspapers were ordered to stop running another advertisement showing a man with a watch on his wrist, above the caption 'This is the watch that went to the Antarctic.' The man's face closely resembled Fidel Castro's, complete with beard and military cap.[35]

The best known example of the revolutionaries' use of the media is the radio station, Radio Rebelde, set up by the guerrillas in the Sierra, which kept the population, friend and foe, informed of the course of the struggle from the rebels' point of view. The achievement of Radio Rebelde was that even those who rejected its propagandistic voice knew that what it said impugned Batista and his censorship.

Castro had already envisaged the use of radio at the time of the attack on the Moncada Barracks in 1953. The attack was supposed to instigate a provincial uprising in which local radio stations would be taken over and used to win the support of the masses throughout the country. This was not a scheme that Castro dreamt up out of nothing. He already had first hand experience of radio and its powers and limitations. He had broadcast a regular series of political talks on a sympathetic radio station while practising law and trying every legal means to expose the corruption of the government. Moreover he had been a follower of Eduardo Chibas, leader of the populist and reformist political party known as the *Ortodoxos*. Chibas, too, was a well-known broadcaster, who maintained that radio broadcasts were as deadly in the political sphere as weapons. He took this belief to the ultimate conclusion when he reached the end of his political tether in 1951: unable to defend unscrupulous charges that his opponents had made against him, he took out a gun at the end of a broadcast and shot himself. Castro was in the studio watching. It was a futile gesture, but after Batista seized power the following year, the media kow-towed by promising to bar 'demagogues' from using them.

Nor was this the first time a politician had died on the radio. In 1947, Emilio Tró, leader of a left-wing terrorist group with which Castro was said by some to be associated, was caught by a rival group at dinner with the chief of police in a house in the Havana suburbs. A fantastic three-hour gun battle which ended in Tró's 18-bullet hole death was broadcast live by an enterprising station. Television, introduced into Cuba in 1950, was also drawn into the political arena, as images of political violence inevitably began to reach the television screen. In 1955, for example, the Cuban national baseball championship was interrupted by students rushing on to the field with anti-Batista banners, who were savagely beaten up by the police in full view of the cameras.[36]

Fidel's use of television after the Revolution is famous, and was certainly significant. He never had any difficulty appearing when he wanted to although both radio and television remained, to begin with, in private hands. But then Fidel made very good TV, and he used the medium extremely creatively. Television not only extended the reach of his speeches beyond the enormous public he attracted in person, it was also a means that could be used between the big rallies. The way Fidel used television shows what nonsense Marshall McLuhan was talking when he declared that 'the medium is the message' and the 'message' of a medium is 'the change of scale or pace or pattern that it introduces'.[37] From this one would have to suppose that what mattered was not what Fidel said but only that he used television at all. But he didn't appear on television to perform a mime act, he used it to speak to the greatest number of people, to inform about developing situations, to announce and explain decisions or make policy declarations. Obviously some people will call this demagogy, but what Fidel actually achieved was something else. There is with television a frustration in the impossibility the viewer normally feels of participating. Fidel, in speaking on television not only to the people but also for them, performed a vital vicarious role, and his appearances became the confluence of politics and entertainment. It is a role he has repeated in a number of ICAIC's films, films which yield a great deal of insight into Fidel's relationship with the people. But that is something we shall come back to.

For their part, the leaders of North American society had emerged from the Second World War more aware than ever of the ideological as well as the commercial functions of the communications media. Things had come a long way from the earlier days of modern communications technology when the leading capitalists had first become aware of the need to take control of the channels of communication for their own intelligence purposes; for example, when the banker J. Pierpont Morgan bought into the Western Union Telegraph Company in 1882 in order to safeguard the secrecy of his cables. By the end of the

Second World War, North American capital fully understood the significance for them of controlling communications on a global scale: in 1944 the business magazine *Fortune* declared that upon the efficiency of us-owned international communications 'depends whether the United States will grow in the future, as Great Britain has in the past, as a center of world thought and trade... Great Britain provides an unparalleled example of what a communications system means to a great nation standing athwart the globe.'[38] The United States thus embarked on new offensives after the war, including the establishment in Mexico in 1946 of the *Asociación Interamericana de Radiofusión* (InterAmerican Radio Association), with its acronym, AIR: an organisation bringing radio stations across the continent under its wing, ostensibly in the name of freedom, and to combat attempts at interference in broadcasting by governments in the countries to which the member stations belonged. Behind the ideological smokescreen, AIR was an instrument of cold-war propaganda.

At the other extreme from such grandiose schemes, the Cuban rebels were adept at the imaginative use of the small scale communications equipment available to them. What must have been the sensation of the soldiers of the dictator in the field in 1958, finding themselves addressed by Fidel Castro himself through loudspeakers?[39] The rebels knew how to take advantage of the mass media. In December 1956, shortly after the disaster that occurred when the expeditionary force on the *Granma* landed, Batista's army declared that the rebels had been defeated. A few days later, while the rebels regrouped, one of them went to Havana to contact the media and set up an interview with the rebel leader. Against the wishes of the Cuban authorities, Herbert Matthews of the *New York Times* obliged. A week later, Castro, who had been in desperate need of publicity, was known throughout the world. Batista denied the interview had really taken place. The *Times* replied by publishing a photograph of Matthews with Castro. The regime's credibility was destroyed and its principal officials humiliated.

Che Guevara spoke about the use of the media to a meeting of Nuestro Tiempo very soon after the victory of the Revolution. Of the early days in the Sierra he said, 'At that time the presence of a foreign journalist, American for preference, was more important to us than a military victory.'[40] It should not surprise us that he spoke of this to this particular audience, or that in this address he launched many of the ideas he afterwards developed into a more consistent philosophy, ideas which had a crucial influence on the development of the Revolution.

## References

1.  Nestor Almendros, 'The Cinema in Cuba', *Film Culture* Vol.2 No.3, 1956.
2.  Nestor Almendros, *Días de una cámara*, Seix Barral, Barcelona 1982, p.44ff. (Now published in English as *The Man with a Camera*, Faber and Faber, 1985.)
3.  'Una nueva etapa del cine en Cuba', *Cine Cubano* No.3.

4.  'Postwar Market Potentialities for Motion Picture Equipment in Cuba' by Nathan D. Golden, Motion Picture Unit Chief, in *Industrial Reference Service*, August 1945, Vol.3 Part 3, No.7.
5.  See Anthony Sampson, *The Sovereign State, The Secret History of ITT*, Coronet, 1974.
6.  See Rolando Díaz Rodríguez and Lazaro Buria Perez, Part 3 of 'Un caso de colonisacion cinematografica', *Caimán Barbudo* No.87, February 1975.
7.  Figures extrapolated from Warren Dygart, *Radio as an Advertising Medium*, McGraw Hill, 1939, pp.231-233.
8.  Alejo Carpentier, *La música en Cuba*, 1946, p.1.
9.  Cf. Rachael Low, *Films of Comment and Persuasion of the 1930s (The History of the British Film 1929-1939)*, Allen and Unwin, 1979, pp.128-130.
10. Miguel Torres, 'Respuesta', *Cine Cubano* No.54-5, p.19.
11. *World Trade in Commodities*, November 1947, 'Motion Pictures and Equipment', p.4.
12. Conversation with T.G. Alea, Havana, January 1980.
13. For this and the next citation, see the appropriate entries in Sadoul's *Dictionary of Films*, tr. & ed. P. Morris, University of California Press, 1972.
14. Julio Antonio Mella, 'Octubre', *Tren Blindado*, Mexico 1928, reprinted *Cine Cubano* No. 54-5, pp.111-112.
15. J.M. Valdés Rodríguez, 'Hollywood: Sales Agent of American Imperialism', *Experimental Cinema* No.4.
16. See Max Henriquez Urea, *Panorama histórico de la literatura cubana*, Editorial Arte y Literatura, La Habana 1979, Vol.II, p.421.
17. Cf. Robin Blackburn, 'Class forces in the Cuban Revolution: a reply to Peter Binns and Mike Gonzalez', *International Socialism* Series 2 No.9.
18. Quoted in Jean Franco, *The Modern Culture of Latin America*, Penguin, 1970, p.134.
19. See Zoila Gómez, *Amadeo Roldán*, Editorial Arte y Literatura, 1977, p.63.
20. Agramonte, op.cit., p.156.
21. Conversation with T.G. Alea, Havana, January 1981.
22. See Fausto Canel, op.cit., p.8.
23. Conversation with A. Guevara, Havana, September 1979.
24. Agramonte, op.cit., pp.80-1, 86-7.
25. Cf. Rolando E. Bonachea and Nelson P. Valdés, *Revolutionary Struggle 1947-1958, Selected Works of Fidel Castro* Vol. 1, Massachusetts Institute of Technology, 1972, Introduction pp.24-25.
26. Agramonte, op.cit., p.159.
27. 'Apuntes para la historia de un cine sin historia', *Cine Cubano* No.86-7-8.
28. 'La música en defensa del hombre', *Revolución y Cultura* Nos.52/53/54, 1976/7.
29. José Antonio Portuondo, *Itinerario estético de la Revolución Cubana*, Editorial Letras Cubanas, 1979.
30. Agramonte, op.cit., pp.160-162.
31. Conversation with Manuel Pérez, Havana, January 1980.
32. Conversation with Julio García Espinosa, Havana, January 1981.
33. Conversation with Julio García Espinosa, Havana, January 1980.
34. Fulgencio Batista, *Piedras y Leyes*, Ediciones Botas, Mexico 1961 pp.73, 80.
35. Lionel Martin, *The Early Fidel: The Roots of Castro's Communism*, Lyle Stuart, Secaucus NJ 1978 p.227.
36. Cf. Bonachea and Valdés, op.cit., Introduction, *passim*.
37. Marshall McLuhan, *Understanding Media*, Signet, 1966, p.24.
38. Quoted in Herbert Schiller, *Mass Communications and American Empire*, Beacon Press, Boston 1971, p.1.
39. See Bonachea and Valdés, op.cit. p.109.
40. Che Guevara to Nuestro Tiempo, 27 January 1959, in *Oeuvres Révolutionnaires 1959-1967*, Paris 1968, p.25.

# 6
# THE COMING OF SOCIALISM

*The first documentaries – the Lunes Group and P.M. – Fidel's 'Words to the Intellectuals'*

The victory of the Revolution on 1 January 1959 brought about a flurry of documentary film making. Two commercial producers brought out feature-length compilation films, *De la sierra hasta hoy* and *De la tirania a la libertad* ('From the Sierra to Today' and 'From the Tyranny to Liberty'), the latter an expanded version of a film first seen the previous year under the title *Sierra Maestra*. Shorts to celebrate the Revolution were produced by bodies such as the Municipality of Havana (*A las madres cubanas* – 'To Cuban Mothers') and the Ministry of Education (*Algo mas que piedra* – 'Something More Than Stone'), the former based on a letter of Jose Marti's to his mother in 1869, the latter on a poem of the popular poet El Indio Nabori dedicated to Marti.

Meanwhile the trade annual, in what was to be its last edition, reprinted from the newspaper *Prensa Libre* an article called 'The Second Movement', rhetorically voicing the faith of the anti-Batista business community in the new beginning. The title of the article is a reference to what was ironically known as the 'Movement of the Second of January', the grouping of established bourgeois politicians who, as a distinguished foreign visitor, Jean-Paul Sartre, later observed, 'stole assistance from the victory'. These people 'put in a good word for themselves to the victors, letting it be known that they would accept the burden of power if it were ever so slightly offered to them.' Sartre compared them with 'those uniforms smelling of moth balls that one saw appear in September 1944 on the streets of Paris'.[1]

The article from *Prensa Libre* roundly declared that 'in this glorious and necessary hour... Work is the order of the day. If there aren't sufficient technicians, bring them in, because posterity accepts no excuses.' It advocated 'the reintroduction of constitutional rights, not salvationism, which could degenerate into repugnant totalitarianism. And not to impede it, the leader of the revolution must turn himself into a political leader, and bring the citizen to the ballot box with the same faith as last year, when he led them into combat.'[2] This from a publication which two years earlier had announced: 'We have not for many years had an economic perspective as promising as that of 1957... because cinema – like few other activities – depends for its progress on the country being content and the money supply in the streets being fluid and consistent... Thus everything seems to indicate that 1957 will be a bonanza year for the film trade.'[3] In fact most Cuban capitalists did well that year, but not the film business. The urban underground began bombing cinemas. Some of the audience was frightened away.

But the Rebel Army was not about to abdicate its responsibilities and return the country to the anarchy that immediate civil elections would inevitably entail. Masses of people decidedly declared their support on the streets. They greeted the rebels with a nationwide general strike which frustrated the salvage attempts of the old order to grab back power sans Batista. And in the months that followed, as the former bourgeois opposition to the dictatorship opposed every piece of revolutionary legislation, the masses filled the squares in huge rallies to approve the Revolution.

The Rebel Army in the Sierra had done more than just fight. They had informed and encouraged the population through their radio station *Radio Rebelde*, and demonstrated their principles through introducing, in the areas they controlled, the first real administration of justice the Cuban campesino had ever seen. They had gained experience in how to organise both supply lines and popular campaigns. They had brought to the Cuban countryside for the first time both medical attention and education. Over the two year campaign they had set up thirty schools, where both the campesino and their own ranks sat down to learn at the same time. And thus they were poised to engage the political tasks created by their victory.

These tasks were formidable. The existing bureaucratic administration was riddled with Batista collaborators. The biggest fish fled immediately, followed by a growing flood of frightened rich, the incorrigibly bourgeois and the retinue of professionals, operatives and technical engineers who depended on them. The atmosphere is portrayed in Jesus Díaz's *Polvo Rojo* ('Red Dust') of 1982, the story of a technician at a North American owned nickel plant who remains in Cuba to run things when not only the other technicians and administrators but even his family leave for the States.

The Rebel Army established order, occupied radio stations, arranged for the publication of newspapers. They manifested from the outset an awareness of the importance of the means of mass communications. They brought to their tasks a zeal and an optimism, indeed a euphoria that sometimes bordered on over-optimism, which impressed every honest visitor. A North American economist, Edward Boorstein, who worked with the planning agencies set up by the Rebel Army, has recorded that the atmosphere 'intoxicated almost everyone, Cubans and foreigners alike'.[4]

And they improvised. At the Agrarian Reform Institute, says Boorstein, 'there was no comprehensive, detailed and finished agricultural policy... nor could there have been. There were many ideas. And there was also the method that Napoleon explained when he was asked how he determined the tactics to be followed in a battle. *"On s'engage, et puis – on voit."* You get into the action, and

Filming *Historias de la Revolución*: T.G. Alea, Tomás Rodriguez, Che Guevara

then – you see.' Boorstein holds that for all their limitations, the initial ideas were of great value because they began the process of grappling with the problems, '... and "even a poor hypothesis," Charles Darwin said, 'is better than none at all".' Even those which later had to be altered or discarded began the testing of hypotheses, the piecing together of interrelations between different parts of the economy, the attainment of a view of the whole.

This infectious enthusiasm wasn't limited to questions of economics. The Rebel Army had quickly gone in for making films. Che Guevara opened a military cultural school on 14 January 1959 at the fortress of La Cabana in Havana where until a fortnight earlier Batista had held his political prisoners. Armando Acosta, a leader of the Communist Party, headed the outfit and its predominantly young staff included Santiago Alvarez, Julio García Espinosa and José Massip. García Espinosa was put in charge of producing two films for the Dirección de Cultura (Cultural Directorate) of the Rebel Army under Camilo Cienfuegos. One of them, *Esta tierra nuestra* ('This Land of Ours'), which García Espinosa scripted and Tomás Gutiérrez Alea directed, dealt with the Agrarian Reform and gave an explanation of the legislation to be introduced in May and why it was necessary. The other, *La vivienda* ('Housing'), was directed by García Espinosa himself, and dealt with urban reform.

Until the Agrarian Reform law was promulgated, the USA seemed ready to tolerate the new government, since their first measures caused no sharp internal divisions which could be used to try to legitimise attacks upon it, though Washington was wont to launch military invasions throughout its hinterland – its 'backyard' – with less excuse. The Revolution reduced the price of medicines, telephones, electricity, and rents below $100 per month.

89

It introduced measures to root out corruption from government and business, to suppress gambling (except, at this stage, in the luxury hotels and nightclubs), to reform the tax system. It introduced, say a pair of visitors, leading North American marxists Leo Huberman and Paul Sweezy, 'New Deal-type programmes in such fields as education, housing and health. As long as legislation was confined to such matters as these, no insuperable difficulties arose, though it is clear that friction began to develop quite early between radicals and conservatives, represented chiefly by Fidel on the one side and Urrutia on the other.'[5] Urrutia was a judge who had played an honourable role at the time of Moncada. When the rebels triumphed, Fidel placed him in the presidency and waited the short wait until Urrutia had no alternative but to name him Prime Minister. Six months later Fidel forced him out, by resigning as Prime Minister in protest against his vacillation.

The Agrarian Reform was the turning point because it was the first piece of legislation to expropriate North American property. When Fidel went to Washington and New York in April, before the law was decreed, he was given, Huberman and Sweezy record, a friendly reception, and even received a good deal of favourable publicity in the press and on TV. There were some wary people around too, of course. 'I had a three hour conference with Castro when he visited Washington, back in April 1959,' wrote Richard Nixon shortly afterwards, in his notorious piece of self-glorification, *Six Crises*. 'After that conference, I wrote a confidential memorandum for distribution to the CIA, State Department, and White House. In it I stated flatly that I was convinced Castro was "either incredibly naive about Communism or under Communist discipline" and that we would have to treat and deal with him accordingly.'[6] But, say Huberman and Sweezy, it was not until after the Agrarian Reform that Fidel's stock in government and business circles declined. But now he was 'assigned the role of *bête noire* (or perhaps red devil would be more accurate)', while in Cuba itself, supporters in the upper and middle classes – the Second Movement – began to fall away and moved into a posture of opposition.


Bourgeois though they might have been, and only a minority of them already committed to socialist ideals, the mood of the country's artists and intellectuals was strongly anti-imperialist, and when the Film Institute was set up by decree at the end of March, it offered for those inclined towards cinema an opportunity that had never existed before. The Revolution, according to Julio García Espinosa, 'represented, initially for everyone, both rupture and at the same time continuity, even for many who today are no longer with the Revolution. Everybody felt it was inseparable from their own individual history, and people put themselves at the service of the moment which they felt as the source of creativity for the future.'[7] The new institute's principal problem was to find funding. It needed all sorts of equipment in addition to what it acquired by decree if it were to function efficiently and effectively. But investment was still controlled by reactionary men sitting in banks which were controlled by the USA, who resisted them. The Government, however, honoured its commitment to the creation of a Cuban cinema as fully as it could. Fidel and his brother Raúl arranged for the first credits to be provided from funds controlled by the Agrarian Reform Institute, INRA, and the films begun by the group at the Rebel Army cultural school passed with them to ICAIC for completion. When Che Guevara visited Tokyo in July 1959 in search of new foreign trade agreements, he took time to investigate the purchase of equipment for ICAIC. A letter he wrote to ICAIC's chief Alfredo Guevara gives the flavour of the time – and also of Che's inspiring personal intelligence:

Azuba-Prince Hotel
Honmura-cho Minato-ku Tokyo

26th July 1959

My dear Alfredo,

Hardly had I received your letter than I made contact with a company through people here and put forward the following proposals: the installation, by Japan, of a self-sufficient studio, with a capacity of three films a month, equipped with all apparatus except cameras, and of a cinema belonging to the studio seating 2500, paid for in sugar. I included this last proposal myself because I consider that the Institute should make itself independent of the cinemas and have its own film theatre. I was struck by several surprises; first, all the studios use North American and German cameras, above all the North American Mitchell. The job of sending you all the pamphlets I've given to the ambassador, because it's large and these people work slowly; I'm sending you with the envoy a book which may be of service to you, I don't know its value because I neither speak English nor understand about cinema. On the concrete questions you gave me I can give you the following answers: the Japanese studios are made for interior filming, they only go outside when there's no remedy and they calculate a third of the film in these conditions. Yes it is possible to buy plans of the studios, and they offered them to me, but they haven't been back to see me again. Japanese cinema consists three-fifths in modern day films with little scenery and low cost ($50,000); the remaining two-fifths use large sets, are generally cinemascope, and an extremely expensive film in Japan costs $250,000. According to the businessmen, they are very interested in the Latin American film market but they didn't demonstrate it, since they didn't come back to speak to us again nor send the catalogues I requested. I indicated to the them the interests of the Film Institute in distributing Japanese films. I shall try again before leaving (I depart tomorrow) and will get the embassy to communicate the results to you officially. Forgive me the plainness of this letter but I haven't got enough grey-matter for psychological disquisitions; yours, on the other hand, interested me greatly, but the two pages you dedicated to the analysis of Pedro Luis I can sum up in three words: *hijo de puta*.

*Recibe un abrazo de tu amigo*
Che[8]

If larger political developments at this time caused no dissension within ICAIC, there was nonetheless a growing rivalry between ICAIC and a group led by Carlos Franqui, one of the leaders of the 26th July Movement. During the 50s, Franqui had been prominent in the aficionado film movement. He belonged to a group that included German Puig, the future ICAIC cameraman Ramón Suárez, and the writers Edmundo Desnoes and Guillermo Cabrera Infante, which revived the Cinemateca; and he had made, together with Puig, a short publicity film (*Carta a una madre*, 'Letter to a Mother'). Puig and Desnoes made a short which was produced and edited by Suarez. Suarez and Cabrera Infante made a film together about the artist Amelia Pelaez which got shown on television. All of them except Desnoes were to leave Cuba before the 60s were over – in the case of Ramón Suárez, not before he had served as cinematographer on T.G. Alea's renowned *Memorias del subdesarrollo* ('Memories of Underdevelopment').

Franqui was not, however, among Fidel's closest followers. In the Sierra, Franqui had been responsible for Radio Rebelde and the rebel newspaper *Revolución*. When the Revolution took power, he gave up the radio station and devoted himself fully to the paper, because, he has written, 'a newspaper is a good vehicle for fights' and he 'wanted to start a revolution in Cuban culture'.[9] He added that, in his eyes, Fidel 'looked askance at culture', a doubtful remark in the face of other evidence. It is clear, however, that Franqui himself looked askance at the Communists with whom he had been involved in Nuestro Tiempo – which, himself a member of the Party at the time, he had helped to found – who were now embarking on the Revolution's first cultural undertakings with Fidel's support; in the case of Alfredo Guevara, there was, it seems, considerable personal animosity. Both of them, at a period during the 50s when the Communist Party had viewed the 26th July Movement with suspicion, regarding Fidel as an adventurist, had nonetheless chosen to join. Franqui, in doing so, had gone to the Sierra and cut his political ties, while Guevara retained his Party links and worked in the underground. According to Guevara, Franqui had 'developed a phobia against the Party, which I could understand; but it grew to the extent that when the Revolution took power, he refused to believe that Fidel was capable of developing socialism in his own way.'[10] What is certainly clear from Franqui's own writings is that after the overthrow of the dictator, he saw the Communists exclusively as infiltrators into a Revolution they had done nothing to make. The situation, according to Alfredo Guevara, was that the evolution of the Revolution towards socialism was for many people a great surprise, which created many anxieties. At the beginning, many people found it easy to be progressive. The condemnation of corruption, for example, was a matter of national pride: corruption wasn't Cuban, it was something created by the *gringos*. That a process had been set in motion, however, leading towards socialist solutions, was something relatively few comprehended, and Franqui took advantage of the situation, adopting an antagonistic stance towards the participation of Communists in this process.

Franqui certainly understood more than many the prime importance of the mass media, and determined to build a force around *Revolución* which, among other things, would rival the influence of ICAIC. In the random manner in which the process of revolutionary expropriation distributed its acquisitions, ICAIC at this time came into possession of a record factory and an advertising studio, while *Revolución* found itself with a television studio. The young aficionado intellectuals of the 50s began to divide up. In particular, participants in the urban underground gravitated towards ICAIC, though its only criterion for recruits was that they should not be tainted by association with Batista. Those around *Revolución*, on the other hand, tended to be politically less experienced and correspondingly more bewildered by the course of events. Ten years later, Ambrosio Fornet recollected: 'We had got hold of a terrain – that of high culture – as a piece of private property in the middle of a revolution that didn't believe in private property.'[11]

Fidel soon curbed the newspaper's attacks on the Communists, whom he clearly regarded critically, but as necessary allies – some, of course, had always supported him, like Alfredo Guevara and his own brother, Raúl. But the editorship of *Revolución* – and Franqui knew this well – remained a key position on the ideological battlefield. By early 1960, printers working in the commercial press were inserting *coletillas* – 'tails' – in the other papers to protest against their antagonism towards the Revolution.[12] *Revolución*, on the other hand, was a paper people knew they could trust, and Franqui attracted a group of writers, reporters and photographers, some with more experience than others, whom he knew were hungry for the opportunity to participate.

Many, however, hardly comprehended what was happening: Guillermo Cabrera Infante, for example, an old friend of Franqui's, who now edited *Revolución*'s cultural supplement, *Lunes de Revolución*. According to Julio García Espinosa, Cabrera 'was a friend, but he wasn't with us politically. We called him to become part of the directorate of ICAIC, but he chose to remain with Franqui. He was very talented but also very ingenuous: there were some among the *Lunes* group who had been associated with Batista's director of culture, even if they hadn't been closely involved. These people he kept company with were lacking in direction, while ICAIC set out from the beginning to create a communist political awareness. This was before Fidel defined the Revolution as socialist, and not surprisingly ICAIC soon became the target of attacks. The initial unity of the artists and intellectuals began to crumble.'[13]

By the end of 1959, ICAIC had embarked on regular documentary production and had completed four films. Apart from the two already mentioned, García Espinosa also directed *Sexto aniversario* ('Sixth Anniversary'), about the half a million campesinos invited to Havana to take part in the sixth anniversary celebrations of the attack on the Moncada barracks; this was the first great 26th July demonstration, one of the dates in the revolutionary calendar on which Fidel, in the years to come, was to make some of his major speeches. Fourthly, the writer Humberto Arenal, who went on to make a number of didactic films, directed *Construcciones rurales* ('Rural Construction') about improvements in conditions for the campesino through the building of houses, schools and hospitals.

The tendency in these first few films reflected the dominant character of the Rebel Army, its orientation towards the campesino. And it was enough for these films to touch this orientation for them to evoke a response from the audience that was both demonstrative and emphatic. The audience at the premiere of *Esta tierra nuestra* gave the film a standing ovation. Later the following year Alfredo Guevara wrote that 'each showing of the film had the same significance as a plebiscite ... *Esta tierra nuestra* released a series of forces and made them explosive.'[14] Not that in their style these films made any special appeal to popular culture, rural or urban. Neither did they attempt a radical aesthetic, popular or otherwise. For example, Juan Blanco's music for *Esta tierra nuestra* is simply a modern orchestral film score, and like *El Megano* before it, the film has very much the feel of the classic documentary of social concern. In addition to well-composed if static documentary shots it included enacted scenes, some of them picturing guerrilla warfare. Running nineteen minutes in black-and-white, it also uses a conventional commentary. While the film has a certain artistry and technical control, this commentary – the way it addresses its audience – tells us that this audience is still an amorphous one. Cinema attendance in Cuba in 1959 more than recovered the loss it had seen during 1957 and 58, and this confirmed that going to the movies was the dominant form of popular entertainment; but this had little as yet to do with the efforts of ICAIC and there was very little the new film-makers could safely assume about the audience beyond its powerful popular support for the Revolution. Nor had they sufficient experience to begin immediately to experiment. To be making films at all was experimental enough, and a dominant part of the experience of these first months.

Moreover they had to contend with the speed of events and the state of flux they were trying to capture with their cameras. In June 1959, counter-revolutionary attacks began to take place, with small planes flying in from Florida and dropping incendiary bombs on cane fields and sugar mills. In the following months the country found increasing difficulty in purchasing arms and in March 1960 an explosion occurred in Havana harbour aboard the Belgian vessel *La Coubre*, as an arms shipment was being unloaded, causing dozens of deaths and injuries. The British Prime Minister conceded in the House of Commons that the USA had been exerting international pressure to try and stop the sale of arms to Cuba. Ten years later, Octavio Cortazár reconstructed the events in his documentary *Sobre un primer combate* ('On a First Attack'), showing that it could only have been an act of sabotage. The incident occurred during Sartre's visit to Cuba. 'I discovered' he wrote, 'the hidden face of all revolutions, their shaded face: the foreign menace felt in anguish.'[15]

After the burial of the victims the following day, Castro called for indissoluble unity. The criminal act of the evening before, said Sartre, already united the people in rage and in the mobilisation of all their energies:

If, two days before, there still remained in the depths of some soul a little laxity, a desire to rest, a lazy negligence, or a comfortable optimism, the affront swept away all those cowardly ideas: one had to fight an implacable enemy; one had to win. Castro identified himself with the people, his sole support; the people at the same time manifested their approbation and intransigence. The aggressor had taken the initiative, but the counter-blow provoked by his insensibility was the radicalisation of the people through their leaders, and of the leaders through the people – that is to say, the least favoured classes. At that moment I understood that the enemy, because of his tactics, had only accelerated an internal process which was developing according to its own laws. The Revolution had adapted itself to the acts of the foreign power; it was inventing its counter-thrusts. But the very situation of this country which was strangled for so long, caused its counter-blows to be always more radical, conceding more strongly each time to the just demands of the masses. By trying to crush the Revolution, the enemy allowed it to convert itself into what it was.[16]

Che Guevara's visit to Japan in July 1959 was only one of several he made to various countries with the aim of finding new markets for Cuban produce. He also went to Egypt and India and several socialist countries. Sales of sugar to the Soviet Union were announced later that year and to China the following January. The United States raised objections, and threats to use the Cuban-US sugar quota as a weapon of intimidation became more and more open. Seeing behind this the even greater threat of armed intervention, the Revolutionary leadership took the first steps, in October, towards its most radical measure – the formation of a people's militia. The following month, Che Guevara became president of the Cuban National Bank and immediately took charge of conserving the country's dollar reserves. By the end of the month the importation of many non-essential goods was halted and a system of import licences introduced. Many North American exporters were by now beginning to insist on immediate cash payments instead of the ordinary short-term credit normally allowed to Cuban buyers. These developments led to further disaffection among the middle classes, as they saw their own personal position and comforts increasingly threatened while the popular classes grew in strength.

For the time being the Revolutionary Government allowed its ideological position to remain publicly undefined, but its socialist orientation was an open secret among groups like ICAIC, and a threatening rumour among the nationalist bourgeoisie. 'What is at first suprising,' Sartre wrote in *Lunes*,

– especially if one has visited the countries of the East – is the apparent absence of ideology. Ideologies, however, are not what this century lacks; right here they have representatives who are offering their services from all sides. Cuban leaders do not ignore them. They simply do not make use of them. Their adversaries formulate the most contradictory reproaches. For some of them, this absence of ideas is only a deception; it hides a rigorous Marxism which does not yet dare to reveal its name: some day the Cubans will take off their mask and Communism will be implanted in the Caribbean, just a few miles from Miami. Other enemies – or, at times, the same ones – accuse them of not thinking at all: 'They are improvising,' I have been told, 'and then after having done something they make up a theory.' Some politely add, 'Try to speak to the members of the government; perhaps they know what they are doing. Because as far as we are concerned, I must confess that we know absolutely nothing at all.' And a few days ago at the University, a student declared, 'To the extent that the Revolution has not defined its objectives, autonomy becomes all the more indispensable to us.'[17]

This was the attitude among many artists and intellectuals. They entertained great concern for their own personal freedom, although nothing was threatening them. On the contrary, as Ambrosio Fornet later described it, here was a situation in which if no-one could guarantee that the artists and intellectuals were revolutionaries, nor could anyone say that they weren't, 'except for a quartet of night-prowling tomcats who still confused jazz with imperialism and abstract art with the devil'.[18] There was, he said, a tacit agreement with the intellectuals which was later to cause problems, that allowed them to paint, exhibit and write as they wished, disseminate their aesthetic preoccupations and polemicise with whom they wished, as long as they didn't step outside their own territory. It was, of course, a contradictory situation, because it implied that they should *not* become too politicised. Indeed it was said in some circles that the best cultural policy was not to have one. But this allowed many artists outside such groupings as ICAIC to get cut off, forcing them to follow the course of political development somewhat in isolation; a condition which resulted in a very uneven development of consciousness among them.

A Soviet mission arrived in Cuba in February 1960, and trade and credit agreements were signed within a few days; similar agreements with other socialist countries followed. In April, Cuba began to purchase crude oil from the USSR under the February agreements, enabling them to save foreign exchange. But Cuba's US-owned refineries refused to process Soviet crude and in the last few days of June, before a serious shortage could develop, the government took them over. Within days, President Eisenhower announced the inevitable and expected retaliation: cancellation of Cuba's sugar quota. Khrushchev immediately declared his support for Cuba and the Soviet Union undertook the purchase of the cancelled quota.

The CIA had by this time already begun to deliver weapons and radio

Warner Brothers bite the dust

transmitters to anti-Castro agents, who according to two US journalists quoted by Boorstein, 'all... had contact with the American embassy in Havana... the CIA and the United States government had thus firmly entered the conspiracy to oust Castro.'[19] In this atmosphere, and demonstrating the principle described by Sartre as making the counter-blows against the enemy always more radical, Fidel announced at the beginning of August the nationalisation of key North American properties in Cuba: thirty-six sugar mills and their lands, the electric and telephone companies, and the refineries and other oil properties which had already been requisitioned. In September, Cuban branches of US banks were nationalised, and the following month nationalisation was extended to practically all other large or medium sized industrial, commercial and financial enterprises, railroads, port facilities, hotels and cinemas. Nationalisation of the major film distribution companies followed in May 1961. Three remaining smaller distributors were nationalised at the beginning of 1965 and the stocks of these companies which could not be legally shown were thereby taken over.[20]

As the nationalisations proceeded, however, and the disaffected continued to leave, trained personnel became scarcer and scarcer. Enrique Pineda Barnet, who later joined ICAIC and directed an experimental feature-length documentary *David* in 1967, chanced to be the first person to respond to a call by Fidel during a TV broadcast for volunteers to serve as teachers in the Sierra Maestra – because he lived close to the TV studio and was only waiting like so many others for such an opportunity. When the nationalisations came about

97

some months later, Fidel picked eighty-two of the volunteer teachers, and they were asked to be ready to move in overnight as the new managers. Pineda Barnet found himself in charge of a sugar refinery. Recalling these events, he remarked that he not only in this way came into proper contact with workers for the first time, but he also learnt a good deal about the ousted sugar bosses. He even discovered a hidden cache of soft-core porno movies.[21]

A new organism was now set up, the Bank of Foreign Commerce, to function as a government foreign trade agency, with instructions to import large quantities of goods as rapidly as possible in order to reduce the impact of the embargo by the USA which the Cubans now anticipated. ICAIC was thus able to acquire several crucial pieces of equipment: a Mitchell camera, an optical camera (for special effects work), an animation table and laboratory equipment, all from the USA. The animation table enabled it to set up a cartoon section, staffed by Jesus de Armas, Eduardo Muñoz and the Australian Harry Reede, a Cuban resident, and the first two cartoons were completed before the end of the year. Each lasting four minutes and directed by de Armas, *El mana* ('Manna') is a moral tale about a campesino who believes everything falls from the heavens like manna and ends up with nothing because his neighbours take it all; *La prensa seria* ('The Serious Press') deals with misrepresentation by the supposedly serious newspapers.

The documentaries made during 1960 fall into three groups. The first comprises didactic films aimed mainly at the campesino, dealing with agricultural methods (films on the cultivation of rice, tobacco and the tomato), the dangers of negligence in handling drinking water, or the advantages of the co-operatives and schools and other facilities established by the Revolutionary Government. The second group is made up of films recording the principal mass mobilisations of the year. The third group is more diverse. It includes films that record various other aspects of the revolutionary process or which deal with aspects of Cuba's social and cultural history. Manet's *El negro* is a short history of racial discrimination in Cuba from the time of slavery to the triumph of the Revolution and its prohibition (another of the Revolution's first measures). Grado's *Playas del pueblo* ('The People's Beaches') celebrates the opening up of the island's private beaches. Nestor Almendros made *Ritmo de Cuba* ('Rhythm of Cuba') on Afro-Cuban folk music (and also, in his spare time, using, as he himself admits in his autobiography, film 'short ends' which he filched from ICAIC, *Gente en la playa* – 'People at the Beach'[22]). Some of these films are more personal than others but for the most part the subjects and themes of the films in all three groups were chosen according to the needs of ideological struggle in the revolutionary situation. Historians of the Revolution would do well to watch these films carefully: they serve as an excellent guide to what many, if not all, of these issues were, and at the same time indicate the lines that were being drawn at each moment for the next phase. For since films take time to make, they are also evidence of how closely the leadership at ICAIC was integrated from the outset with thinking at the centre of gravity within the revolutionary leadership.

Ugo Ulive, the Uruguayan film-maker who worked at ICAIC during its early years, singles out Manet's film as 'the only worthy thing accomplished by the Franco-Cuban writer during his stay in Cuba', also mentioning a film by the Puerto Rican Oscar Torres (who like Alea and García Espinosa had studied at the Centro Sperimentale in Rome) called *Tierra olvidada* ('Forgotten Land'), a kind of *El Megano* revisited. The Zapata swamp is being transformed: the Revolution has come to the swamp and the wretched lives of the charcoal burners are undergoing a complete transformation. 'Torres, without doubt one of the more promising directors of this initial stage, undertakes to express the change with a style which fearlessly blends a certain gratuitous grandiloquence with an occasionally moving epic scope... In the culminating sequence [he] juxtaposes the invasion of machinery which has come to dredge the swamp with a peasant woman giving birth in a nearby hut. The absence of false diffidence with which Torres accomplishes a sequence so full of traps as this is without doubt the mark of a director who could have been very important in the later development of ICAIC.'[23] The film won second prize at the Festival of the Peoples in Florence, and an Honourable Mention at the Leipzig Film Festival, both in 1960 – two out of five international awards achieved by Cuban films that year, the year in which (with one exception) they made their first international appearance. Torres went on to direct a feature film for ICAIC, *Realengo 18* ('Plot 18'), a year or two later and then returned to Puerto Rico, where he died young.

These foreign awards were hugely important to ICAIC, for international recognition of this kind vindicated the somewhat crazy project of creating a film industry and provided an answer to critics; moreover they helped the promotion of the image of the Revolution abroad. Not that they were made with an eye to foreign approval. On the contrary, the guiding principle was that foreign recognition would follow, where it will, if the films were authentic expressions of the Revolution's own needs.

The other two films to win international distinctions in 1960 were Alea's *Esta tierra nuestra* and García Espinosa's *La vivienda*. The following year there were collective awards for Cuban films at two German film festivals, Leipzig in the east and Oberhausen in the west. Four films were included: the film by Torres; Alea's *Asamblea general* ('General Assembly'), recording the mass meeting of 2 September 1960 at which the first Declaration of Havana was proclaimed; and two films by José Massip, *Los tiempos del joven Martí* ('The Times of the Young Martí') and *Por qué nació el Ejército Rebelde* ('Why the Rebel Army Was Born'). The second of the Massip pair uses non-professional actors and runs eighteen minutes (the year's longest documentary, García Espinosa's *Un año de libertad*, 'A Year of Freedom', runs twenty-seven minutes). In terms of narrative, wrote Alfredo Guevara, 'Massip found very simple solutions. He decomposes reality in order to recompose it in a succession of frescoes, some of which offer the greatest clarity.'[24] But although the film was structurally uneven, he said, it was undeniably effective because of the power of the theme and the sincerity with which it was treated.

The criticism is interesting because it indicates something of the values which

ICAIC was trying to develop. At the top of the list is judgment in the choice of subject matter, together with that elusive quality, sincerity. It was to give these criteria body, so to speak, that an understanding of formal aesthetic procedures was encouraged. Aesthetic experiment was felt to be thoroughly desirable, but not formalist preoccupation.

The first of Massip's films incorporates a score by Harold Gramatges, who had been president of Nuestro Tiempo and was now serving as a kind travelling ambassador based in Paris. Like Alea's *La toma de la Habana por los ingleses* ('The Taking of Havana by the English' – an event which occurred in 1762), this film originated before the Revolution. Using paintings, period engravings, even magazine illustrations to describe the period of Martí's youth, Massip had started making it in 1956. He was able to complete it during ICAIC's first months, and in July 1959 Hector García Mesa took it to the World Youth Festival in Vienna, where it became the first film of the Cuban Revolution to be seen internationally. It has the distinction of being also the first film seriously and sensitively to tackle the recovery (*el rescate*) of Cuban nineteenth-century political history, a theme that was to be given great prominence in ICAIC's future output.

By the end of 1960 a number of difficulties had begun to appear in the country's economic condition. Edward Boorstein later wrote:

> The management of the Cuban economy during the first two years of the Revolution was made easier than usual by the existence of a large amount of reserves – using this word in the broad sense given to it by economists in the socialist countries. There were unutilized resources: idle land and labour and unutilized capacity in the manufacturing plants and the construction industry. There were some dollar holdings. There were over five million head of cattle... The rapid progress of the Cuban economy in the early years after the Revolution took power was made possible by the reserves. The very irrationality of the prerevolutionary economy served as a springboard for advance... The reserves cushioned the Cuban economy against the consequences of error... The real cost to the economy of using resources that would otherwise be left idle is zero – not the costs that appear in the conventional accounting ledgers. When you raised the demands on resources to a higher level than the supply, the first consequences were not difficulties in the economy, but reductions in reserves.[25]

This was the stage that had been reached by the end of the year. Dollar expenditure was running three times as high as dollar earnings; if the deficit continued, it would wipe out the dollar reserves in about four months.

Though mistakes had been made, this situation was less a consequence of mismanagement than of the very policies of the Revolution: on the one hand of raising the people's purchasing power, on the other, of buying in foreign goods against the likelihood of further US retaliation. By Spring 1961 the first shortages began to make themselves felt and the question inevitably arises of the extent to which the troubles that now occurred in the field of cultural politics were a consequence of the unequal development of political consciousness among the intellectual community, and hence among many of them a lack of preparedness for the likely developments of the Revolution's third year, which began with the USA breaking off diplomatic relations on 3 January.

'We knew,' says Alfredo Guevara, 'through our intelligence services, that we were going to be invaded. So there were the mobilisations of the people, the creation of the militia, the military training, the civil defence. In this heroic climate there appeared a film which did not reflect any of this. It showed the Havana of the lower depths, the drunks, the small cabarets where prostitution was still going on, where there was still drug trafficking, something like the world of *On the Bowery*'. (*On the Bowery* follows the ups-and-downs of an alcoholic through the bars, flophouses and shelters of New York; it was made in 1956 by Lionel Rogosin and is celebrated as an early example of the new documentary.) Similarly, '*P.M.*, in only fifteen minutes, showed a world inhabited by the mainly black and mulatto lumpenproletariat. Obviously it wasn't made out of any feeling of racial discrimination, but the presentation of these images at this time was nonetheless questionable.'[26] In short, it presented black people in roles associated with the state of oppression from which they were in process of liberation.

The film was made by the painter Saba Cabrera Infante, brother of Guillermo (editor of *Lunes de Revolución*) with Orlando Jimenez Leal as cinematographer, and it became a *cause célèbre* of the liberals of the *Lunes* group when it was banned from public exhibition at the end of May. The significance of the moment is crucial to what happened. The incident took place six weeks after the invasion of the Bay of Pigs, when US-backed mercenaries were routed in the space of three days by the Rebel Army backed by the People's Militia. Not only that. The day before the invasion, at a mass rally called to protest a suprise simultaneous air attack on three Cuban cities, and in the knowledge that that a CIA-sponsored invasion was on its way, Fidel publicly declared for the first time the socialist character of the Revolution. Not that this was exactly unexpected. Fidel has explained that this avowal had been anticipated by the masses and he was only acknowledging an already overwhelming mass sentiment. But the timing is significant. It is inconceivable that at a moment when the Revolution was in mortal danger Fidel would have taken this stand unless he knew it corresponded with popular conviction.[27] Indeed it was precisely in this knowledge that Fidel chose the moment: in order to redouble the energy with which the invaders would be met. Perhaps *P.M.* was only a mildly offensive film, but in the euphoria which followed the defeat of the mercenaries the mood of the country was bound to make it seem worse. Alfredo Guevara admits, 'I reacted to the film as an offended revolutionary. Today I would manage a thing like that better.'

Several accounts of the affair have been published. One is Ugo Ulive's in the article already cited. Another is by a British travel writer, Nicholas Wollaston, in a dreadful (though engrossing) book called *Red Rumba*, about his visit to Cuba in the early 60s.[28] Most recently there is a sort of version from exile, by Guillermo Cabrera Infante, the film-maker's brother.[29] As a writer, Cabrera Infante is a kind of literary Ken Russell, the epitome of bad taste, and his article bends under the weight of so many base, bombastic and bloated puns that it becomes a worm-eaten piece of fiction with about as much relationship to what occurred as Russell's horrific films on Tchaikovsky and Mahler to the real biography of those composers. The Cuban poet Pedro Pérez Sarduy, a culturally hungry student of literature at the University of Havana in the days when all this happened, has commented bluntly on what Cabrera Infante has written that he was 'one of those writers who never did know what happened', a member of 'an incongruous cultural elite unable to grasp the real meaning of change'.[30] Combining and adjudging these accounts, and from conversations in Cuba, what seems to have happened was this:

*P.M.* was a modest film, which was shot – as everyone agrees, but that's about all they agree on – in a 'free cinema' style. It begins with a ferry slipping into Havana harbour from across the water. The camera then wanders into a number of crowded bars in the narrow streets behind the waterfront, where it shows people (Wollaston:) 'drinking, arguing, loving, quarrelling, dreaming... It falls on ecstasy and desperation, it peers blearily through the cigar smoke, singles out a glass of beer, lights for a moment on a smile, winces at a bright electric bulb,' – someone should tell Mr Wollaston cameras don't wince – 'hovers over over a shelf of bottles. A blurred negress stands in front of the lens, and the camera moves back to take in the whole jostling, sweating scene... the only sound is the roar of so many Cuban voices, the clink of glasses and ice from the bar, and the music. In the whole film there is not a single coherent word spoken.' In the end, the 'exhausted revellers' return whence they came.

Guillermo gave his brother money to complete the film, which was spent on laboratory facilities at the TV channel run by *Revolución*. Neither Alfredo Guevara nor Julio García Espinosa could remember having seen it on television, but it was noticed by Nestor Almendros, who, having left ICAIC, now had a film column in the independent cultural weekly *Bohemia*. There he praised the film as 'enormously poetic' and 'a veritable jewel of experimental cinema'. Wollaston considers it understandable that he should have been enthusiastic and may be excused for not having mentioned that it was 'amateurish [and] that much of the photography was not half as good as that of his own films'. But encouraged, the film-makers offered it to the manager of one Havana's remaining privately-owned cinemas, who told them he liked it but they would need an exhibition licence from ICAIC. Assuming this was just a formality, says Wollaston, they were taken aback when the film was 'confiscated'.

But it was the Institute which was taken by surprise, since no-one there knew anything about it. The response was hostile. The film was seen, as Pedro Pérez Sarduy puts it, as 'irresponsible both to the Revolution and the cultural tasks of those privileged to have the costly medium of cinema at their disposal'. ICAIC decided that its distribution should be delayed. They did not expect the explosion which took place. Cabrera Infante, always enamoured, says Pedro Perez Sarduy, of the tawdriest Hollywood movies, writes, 'We had been expecting a showdown with the Film Institute. It was to become a shoot-out.' 'Guillermo,' said Alfredo Guevara, 'came to argue with me, and left crying that this was Stalinism and Fascism.' Almendros used his influence to rally support for the offending film-makers. ICAIC decided to arrange a meeting where the film would be shown and discussed. It was held at the Casa de las Americas, the revolutionary literary institute, and therefore more *Lunes*'s territory than ICAIC's. According to Wollaston, the audience supported the film as at best a piece of original artistic work and at worst an amateurish documentary 'that was politically naive'. He also reports that someone had gone down to the waterfront and done a survey, and found that the people in the film all supported the Revolution and some were even *milicianos* (militia members), so how could the film be counter-revolutionary?

For ICAIC, however – only this is something beyond Wollaston's ken – the issue was both more complicated and more serious. People at ICAIC felt the film failed to register what was really in the air because it followed its chosen stylistic model both too closely and too uncritically. This was not just politically but also aesthetically irresponsible. They had begun to sense at ICAIC that the camera was not the unproblematic kind of instrument the apologists for *P.M.* supposed. It does not – to paraphrase the French film theorist Serge Daney – involve a single straight line from the real to the visible and thence to its reproduction on film, in which a simple truth is faithfully reflected. They were learning this, at ICAIC, from the way, in their own films, they had to struggle to keep abreast with the pace of revolutionary change. Daney says, 'in a world where "I see" is automatically said for "I understand" such a fanstasy has probably not come about by chance. The dominant ideology which equates the real with the visible has every interest in encouraging it.'[31] At ICAIC they were beginning to perceive that revolutionary change required a rupture with this equation, which meant among other things being constantly on guard against received aesthetic formulae. The impression *P.M.* must have created at ICAIC was of a film that segmented social reality, evaded recognition that the screen belonged to the same reality as the scenes it portrayed, which thus indicted the film through its very absence.

For their part, the *Lunes* group (according to Wollaston) accused ICAIC of making 'dreary socialist-realist stuff about *milicianos* and *alfabetizadores* [literacy teachers] that would convince nobody who was not already convinced'. Even more cynically, that they 'allowed the importation of terrible Hollywood trash, Westerns and British epics about battling on the North-East Frontier that portrayed imperialists as heroes and Indians as worse than animals – a far cry from the ideals of the Cuban Revolution. Even some of the Russian and Polish films that were shown in Cuba were freer, more individualistic and subjective than *P.M.*; only the Chinese films were as dreary as the Institute's – and as Almendros said, who wanted to make films like the Chinese?'

There is never, on the part of the liberal apologists, any mention of the real problems of distribution that ICAIC faced. ICAIC, however, twice during this period conducted market investigations, and Alfredo Guevara reported their findings in *Cine Cubano*:

> During 1959, for example, 484 films were exhibited in Cuba, of which 266 were North American, 44 English, 24 French, 25 Italian, 2 Polish, 1 Brazilian, 1 Swedish, 8 Argentinian, 19 Spanish, 3 Japanese, 3 German, 79 Mexican and 1 Soviet. The remaining 8 were Cuban, co-productions or films made in Cuba in previous years and premiered or exhibited during 1959.
>
> As can be seen, the bulk of exhibition remained in Hollywood hands and film industries under its influence...
>
> More serious, however, is the character of the films that are shown. Out of the 484 films, 140 presented sentimental dramas and conflicts, generally of the quality of syrup and magazine serials, sometimes psychological in a visually spectacular way; 34 were war movies and 27 police, 43 westerns and 92 action and adventure... Average taste has been maltreated and certain overriding influences have created 'habits' of cinema difficult to eradicate... the genres together with the star system predominate and their formulae amount to anti-cinema...[32]

The same displacement of cultural values, he continued, could be found in other media. The publishing market, for example, had its genres too: detective novels, which intellectuals delighted in; the *novela rosa* ('pink novels') preferred by solitary ladies and leisured young señoritas; comics; and action novels full of Italian gangsters, Russian spies, African savages, Latin American adventurists and treacherous Asiatics, and always, as the heroes, North Americans.

In the face of this culture of depravity, Guevara argued, the cinema needed new criteria, but they had to be realistically related to the conditions to be found among the audience. The public, he said, was divided between the popular and the exclusive. At one extreme lay the campesino masses, at the other, the extra-refined bourgeois minorities. 'One was denied access to national culture and the other became estranged, indifferent or antagonistic.' But the Revolution had not only liberated campesinos and workers, he said, it had also liberated culture and the artists and intellectuals, liberated them from the prison of an exclusive and narrow public which was maimed and deformed in its taste, and from which it had sought escape in a search for eccentric originality and the repetition of all that was uttered in the great capitals of Art. And indeed the *Lunes* group, according to Ulive, was like a clan with its own enshrined idols and 'an excessive urge to be up-to-date and if possible even ahead of of the moment'. As another commentator put it, 'a bit too exclusively preoccupied with beat poetry and the *nouveau roman*'[33] The divorce, says Pedro Pérez Sarduy, between them and their society had fostered a hyper-critical attitude and a non-conformist intellectual rebelliousness with few roots in social reality. They were like the embodiment of the anti-hero of their hero Sartre – but lacking Sartre's perception. Typically unsure of their social position, too fearful to rise up yet too lucid to accept unreservedly the prevailing state of affairs, they judged their epoch while remaining outside it. Finding little outlet in the precarious and coercive world of publishing and the media under Batista, they had taken refuge in the café talk, cynicism and satire of the intellectual *déclassé*, both spurned and nauseated by society. They did not see, when the Revolution came, what Sartre saw when he came to look at it, that this self-image of the intellectual is subverted by revolution. That it became, one may add, like the pterodactyl, which flew once, but was then condemned to extinction.

ICAIC, faced with disagreement at the Casa de las Americas meeting, proposed that *P.M.* be shown to an ordinary audience made up of assorted members of the revolutionary organisations, since that is what the supporters of the film argued that the people in it were. This of course annoyed them even more. They asked, says Wollaston, what trade unionists or women knew about films? (One of the mass organisations was the Federation of Cuban Women.) Obviously, they said, such people would produce the verdict expected of them; and they went away to sulk and scheme again. ICAIC made a copy of the film for its archive and returned the original to the film-makers with permission for public screening denied. (They showed it to Wollaston after all these events had taken place, privately, without legal offence, but in an atmosphere calculated to reinforce his own paranoiac suspicions.)

Rather than call this the Revolution's first act of film censorship, it is more enlightening to see it as the dénouement of the incipient conflict between different political trends which lay beneath the surface during the period of the aficionado movement in the 50s. The conflict brought the whole cultural sector to boiling point, and clearly it was only resolvable through the intervention of the Revolution's maximum leader. A series of meetings was called which took place in the National Library on 16, 23 and 30 June 1961, with the participation of practically the whole intellectual and artistic community. Fidel and other revolutionary leaders attended, and his closing speech has become known as the 'Words to the Intellectuals'.[34] Though he had not seen the film himself, he approved the decision not to show it, for it was a question of upholding the right of a government body to exercise its function. But this was the least of what he had to say.

Carlos Franqui's account of these meetings is not a trustworthy memoir: it is scarred by general paranoia, and a marked personal hatred of Alfredo Guevara.[35] There is no denying the meetings were highly charged, but Franqui's graphic picture of manipulation by a communist clique just does not square with a proper reading of the speech. Fidel began by apologising for not attending to the issue sooner. Then, he identified the question at issue as fundamentally concerning 'the problem of freedom for artistic creation'. Distinguished visitors to Cuba, he said, including Sartre and the North American sociologist C. Wright Mills, had raised the question and he didn't doubt its importance. But the Cuban Revolution had been made in record time, it had not had time to hold its Yenan Conference, and accordingly he had a lot to learn himself; he did not presume to know more than others. Listening to the discussion, however, he had sometimes had the impression of dreaming a little because it seemed there were people there who thought the Revolution was over, it had won, and now it was going to asphyxiate them. He wanted to assure people that this fear was unfounded, the Revolution defended freedom, it had brought the country a very large sum of freedoms.

Then he went straight to the point. Everyone, he said, was in evident agreement in respecting freedom of form: 'I believe there is no doubt about this problem.' But over the question of content there were people who feared prohibitions, regulations, limitations, rules and authorities. What could be the reason for this worry? It can only worry someone, he said, 'who lacks confidence in his own art, who lacks confidence in his real capacity to create. And one can ask oneself if a true revolutionary, if an artist or intellectual who feels the Revolution and is confident that he is capable of serving the Revolution, can put this problem to himself; that is to say, if there is room for doubt on the part of the truly revolutionary writers and artists. I think not; the area of doubt exists for writers and artists who without being counter-revolutionaries do not feel themselves to be revolutionaries either. (Applause.)'

A remarkable formulation, politically impeccable because it out-manoeuvred not only the liberals but also the revolutionary sectarians, the night-prowling tom-cats mentioned by Fornet who still confused abstract art with the devil. This position of Fidel's was also ICAIC's. It also has an antecedent in the ideas of the *Manifesto: Towards a Free Revolutionary Art*, published in 1938 over the signatures of Diego Rivera and André Breton, which Trotsky is said to have had a hand in drafting: 'True art is unable *not* to be revolutionary, *not* to aspire to a complete and radical reconstruction of society.'

It was correct, said Fidel, for artists who were neither revolutionary nor counter-revolutionary to feel the Revolution as a problem. Only the dishonest and the mercenary found no problem in it and knew where their interests lay. But people who sincerely held a distinct philosophy from the Revolution, like proper Catholics, the Revolution had to respect. Its attitude towards them should be the same that it adopted towards all honest people who were not enemies of the Revolution. Thus he arrived at the much-repeated formula: *dentro de la Revolución todo; contra la Revolución, nada*— 'within the Revolution, everything, against it, nothing'.

At the same time, Fidel defended the *Consejo Nacional de Cultura* (CNC – National Council of Culture), from which ICAIC was also under attack but from the left, for the CNC represented the old guard of the Communist Party whom the Young Communists of ICAIC had criticised during the Batista years. Partly addressing these Young Communists – his own comrades and contemporaries who had the unfortunate experience of having to exercise a cultural authority they did not believe ought to exist – Fidel said: 'The existence of an authority in the cultural field doesn't mean there is any reason to worry about the abuse of this authority, because who is it that hopes this cultural authority should not exist? By the same count one could hope the Militia would not exist and not even the State itself, and if anyone is concerned so much that there should not exist the smallest state authority, well, there's no need to worry, have patience, the day will come when the State too will not exist. (Applause.)'

The aim of the Revolution, said Fidel, was to develop culture into the true heritage of the people; it was a struggle to create the conditions to be able to do this, but that was the CNC's job, just as it was also the job of other bodies the Revolution had created, like the *Imprenta Nacional* (National Printing House), and ICAIC itself. Individuals had the responsibility to integrate themselves within these bodies. He did not want to propose any general rules about this: not all artistic production was of the same nature. But to do this couldn't possibly contradict anyone's artistic aspirations, as long as you suppose, said Fidel, that artists are trying to create for their own contemporaries. There can be no artists, he said, who just go around thinking about posterity, 'because, in that case, without considering our judgement infallible, I think that whoever holds to this is a victim of self-delusion. (Applause.)' The same with the Revolution itself. We're not making it, he said, for the generations to come, but for now. Who would follow us otherwise? As for posterity, how would posterity judge the artist who lived through this epoch but remained outside it, did not form part of it and did not express it?

Alluding to *Lunes* itself, Fidel allowed the need for a cultural magazine, but not that it should be in the hands of one particular group. Only one more issue of *Lunes* appeared. But arising from the discussions at these meetings a new organisation was created, the *Union de Escritores y Artistas de Cuba* (UNEAC – Union of Cuban Writers and Artists). This was to be a professional-interests body rather than a trades union, and one of its first functions was to publish a journal, *Gaceta de Cuba*, in which future cultural debates were to take place.


The confrontation over *P.M.* represents the most visible moment in the process of ideological 'rupture' (*desgarramiento*) of which revolutionary intellectuals all over Latin America have spoken, 'the famous "ruptures" we intellectuals are so addicted to' as the Cuban poet and essayist Roberto Fernández Retamar once put it with affectionate irony.[36] The rupture is 'an ideological conflict, a conflict of growth', which produces a crisis of self-confidence, but may be resolved in a sudden spurt of *concientización* – an untranslatable word: it derives from *conciencia*, which means both 'conscience' and 'consciousness'; hence, more or less, 'conscience-stricken growth in consciousness or awareness'.

The philosophy behind this concept has been lucidly developed by the Brazilian educationalist Paulo Freire. The rupture to which the artist or intellectual is subjected in the course of the revolutionary process is the seed of his or her translation from one social function to another, from the habits acquired under the regime of bourgeois values, through rejecting and refusing the political impotence these values imply, to a new self-image as a cultural worker. The rupture has many aspects. In the words of the Salvadorean poet Roque Dalton:

> In every rupture we intellectuals are accustomed to see first an ideological problem and then, always as a result of this, moral and sentimental problems. These resulting problems can only be resolved through the solution of the fundamental ideological conflict. In this sense revolution is a constant challenge: its uninterrupted advance makes simple overall acceptance of its latest and most general principles insufficient, but requires permanent incorporation of its totalising practice.[37]

The process brings on a crisis of individualism, which the whole weight of bourgeois ideology pushes the artist to defend; after all, the bourgeois myth of the artist was created around it. When this happens, those who resist the challenge are reduced to such things as making personal attacks against the conduct of those who respond to it. This is when they begin to make wild accusations of Stalinism and Fascism.

Here, in Dalton's discourse, the key formulation – incorporation of a totalising practice – corresponds to the concept of 'revolution within the revolution'; not so much Trotsky's, however, as the version which Regis Debray developed around the ideas and example of Che Guevara.

But let the final word on the subject go to Julio García Espinosa:

> *Lunes de Revolución...* did not present itself as a simple alternative. It is undeniable that it... did not represent a socialist option... it is equally undeniable that one should not underestimate the individual talents of some of its members, and not out of unbridled admiration for artistic talent but from the firm conviction that here too was something that could contribute in some way to the development of the Revolution. How should one struggle, then, against an opposition which at the same time should be regarded as an ally? What solution could there be? Could we think in terms of the traditional United Front? But the experience we'd had of frontism was that it had been limited to bringing artists and intellectuals with an openly progressive attitude together only granted an extremely wide and generous meaning to the concept. Besides, 'revolutionary artist' and 'Party artist' had hardly ever meant the same thing. One could say that the only difference between a progressive artist and a Party artist had been that the latter was more committed to essential party tasks and worked with more discipline at the immediate political objectives which the Party defined. The difference was not due to a more revolutionary concept of art. (And of life?) When the concept of socialist realism was raised, everyone broke out in uproar. If the United Front, enmeshed in such ambiguities, was questionable under capitalism, what role could it play with a Revolution in power? Was the union of all revolutionary forces clearly and simply the unification of all progressive artists and intellec-

tuals? The union of all revolutionary forces, yes, but under the direction of the Revolution's most advanced force. And among the progressive artists and intellectuals, who, at that moment, represented the most advanced current? The CNC, ICAIC or *Lunes de Revolución*? If it is difficult to give a definite reply, politically we realised it was ICAIC, and fought against the tendency represented by *Lunes* which was not directing itself towards socialism. Socialism which in reality the Revolution had begun to define. The climax to the situation was produced by the Revolution itself. It did not deny *Lunes* members the right to continue as participants within the Revolution, but took away their opportunity of exercising cultural hegemony. The Revolution in this way established better conditions for different artistic tendencies to engage with each other on more equal terms. This was a correct, a revolutionary solution.[38]

With *Lunes* disbanded, the conditions ripened for the next episode of the cultural struggle, the struggle against sectarianism.

# References

1.  Jean-Paul Sartre, *On Cuba*, Ballantine Books, 1961, p.62.
2.  Sergio Carbo, 'El segundo movimiento', *Anuario Cinematografico y Radial Cubano*, 1959.
3.  Editorial, *Anuario Cinematografico y Radial Cubano*, 1959.
4.  Edward Boorstein, *The Economic Transformation of Cuba*, Monthly Review Press, 1969, p.53.
5.  Huberman and Sweezy, *Cuba, Anatomy of a Revolution*, Monthly Review Press, 1968, pp.85-6.
6.  Richard M. Nixon, *Six Crises*, Pocket Books Inc., New York 1962, p.379.
7.  Conversation with Julio García Espinosa, Havana, January 1980.
8.  *Cine Cubano* No.95 p.13.
9.  Carlos Franqui, *Family Portrait With Fidel*, Jonathan Cape, 1983, pp.9 and 10.
10. Conversation with Alfredo Guevara, Havana, January 1980.
11. In *El intelectual y la sociedad*, Colección Minima No. 28, Siglo Veintiuno Editores, Mexico 1969, p.49.
12. See Tariq Ali in Carl Gardner ed., *Media, Politics and Culture*, Macmillan, 1979, p.152.
13. Conversation with Julio García Espinosa, Havana, January 1980. (During research for this book, I sought to obtain an interview with Guillermo Cabrera Infante, who lives in London, but received no response.)
14. Alfredo Guevara, 'Revisando nuestro trabajo', *Cine Cubano* No.2, p.12.
15. Sartre, op.cit. p.142.
16. *Ibid.* p.152.
17. *Ibid.* p.149.
18. Fornet, 1969, op.cit. p.48.
19. Tad Szulc and Karl E. Mayer in Boorstein, cit. p.29.

20. *Financial Times* 13 May, 1961; *The Times* 6 January 1965.
21. Conversation with Enrique Pineda Barnet, Havana, January 1980.
22. Almendros, cit., p.47.
23. Ugo Ulive, 'Cronica del cine cubano', *Cine al dia* No.12, March 1971, p.9.
24. Alfredo Guevara, 'Revisando nuestro trabajo', cit., p.14.
25. Boorstein, cit., pp.81-4.
26. This and further quotations by Alfredo Guevara on *P.M.*, in conversation, Havana, January 1980.
27. Cf. Robin Blackburn, cit., p.87.
28. Nicholas Wollaston, *Red Rumba*, Readers Union edition, 1964.
29. 'Notes from the Bearded Crocodile', *London Review of Books*, 4-17 June 1981.
30. Pedro Perez Sarduy, 'An Infant in English Breeches: What really happened in Cuba', *Red Letters* No.15, 1983, p.25.
31. 'Sur Salador' in 'Travail, lecture, jouissance', *Cahiers du Cinéma* No.222.
32. 'Una nueva etapa del cine en Cuba', *Cine Cubano* No.3.
33. Michèle Firk, 'Naissance d'un Cinéma', *Positif* No.53, June 1963, p.15.
34. Reprinted in Lee Baxandall ed., *Radical Perspectives in the Arts*, Penguin, 1972.
35. Franqui, cit., pp.130-134.
36. *El intelectual y la sociedad*, cit., p.92.
37. *Ibid., p.92.*
38. Julio García Espinosa, 'Respuesta', *Cine Cubano* No.54-5, p.11-12.

# 7
# THE FIRST FEATURE FILMS

*Historias de la revolución, Cuba baila, El joven rebelde,*
*Cumbite, Las doce sillas*

It was in 1960 that ICAIC made its first feature films. The first to be shown, at
the end of the year, though it was completed second, was *Historias de la
revolución* ('Stories of the Revolution'), a film made up of three episodes directed
by Tomás Gutiérrez Alea. Originally it was intended to comprise four episodes,
two by Alea and two by a director born in Spain and living in Mexico, José
Miguel García Ascot, all four photographed by the Italian neorealist
cinematographer Otello Martelli; Martelli's camera operator was the son of
another leading Italian neorealist, Cesare Zavattini. García Ascot's episodes were
later incorporated into another three-episode film, *Cuba '58*, released in 1962
with a final episode directed by Jorge Fraga, while Alea directed a third episode
for the original film.

The first film to be completed by ICAIC had in fact been Julio García
Espinosa's *Cuba baila* ('Cuba dances'). But *Cuba baila* had as its subject the pre-
revolutionary world of the middle bourgeoisie and it was felt that ICAIC should
make its feature debut with a film about the revolutionary struggle itself. The
three episodes of *Historias...* are *El herido* ('The Wounded Man'), *Rebeldes*
('Rebels') and *La batalla de Santa Clara* ('The Battle of Santa Clara'). These three
stories, wrote Eduardo Heras León ten years later, offered the audience the
chance of identifying with three key moments in the revolutionary struggle: the
assault on the Presidential Palace mounted by the urban revolutionary group
Directorio Revolucionario on 13 March 1957; the struggle of the guerrillas in the
Sierra; and the final battle for liberation. However fragmentary the treatment, he
said, the subjects themselves were enough to engage the audience. 'We didn't
think much at that time about the technique, about the shots, or the direction of
the actors: that was secondary since the film reflected a truth, a living reality for
all of us. We were anxious to relive the history which many of us had not been
able to help make' – Heras León was 18 years old when the film was first shown –
'to allow the imagination fully to run its course and momentarily depersonalise us
by recovering life on celluloid'. 'In a word,' he continued,

we wanted to feel heroes ourselves in some way – at least for an hour and a half – in order to satisfy our appetite for heroism and courage... And naturally we were the wounded man in the first story, beaten but not defeated, as Hemingway said, and we were hurt terribly by the shot in the young rebel's leg during the assault on the palace, and suffered with him while searching for somewhere to hide ourselves; and we began to hate the petty bourgeois full of fear who ran away like a coward in order not to get involved. We felt not even a hint of sympathy for him, not even after he tried to change his attitude. Nor did we feel it was a pity when, victim of his own contradictions and fears, he fell into the hands of the police. We said, 'the coward asked for it,' and that was enough for us. It didn't interest us that the actors were a little artificial (sad reality about our film actors), that the characters were schematic... that the director was clumsy in his use of the interior sets, and that above all, the episode was lacking in what [Alejo] Carpentier calls contexts... We were only interested in the hero and qualities of sacrifice; contexts merely rounded the story off.[1]

In the second story – which Alea based on an anecdote recounted to him by Che Guevara – they became the guerrillas in the Sierra. They decided not to abandon their wounded comrade even before the characters on the screen made the same decision. They felt the film was the clearest of lessons in the humanity of solidarity and again thought the movie was excellent. Yes, there were defects: it

*Historias de la revolución*

moved too slowly; the actors – even though they knew them to be actual rebels – were evidently self-conscious about being filmed. But these and other weaknesses did not obscure the efficacy of the message.

A viewing of the film today confirms that the original critical acclaim given in particular to the last episode was not undeserved. Shot on location in Santa Clara itself, the agile montage gives a clear overview of the course of the battle, all the more notable in that it does so with a minimum of dialogue. And again, according to Heras León, 'The derailment and the capture of the armed train, the scenes with the tank regiment, the fighters throwing Molotov cocktails left and right, the organisation within the chaos of battle, the reception given to the heroes after the battle, and then the tragic finale – which demonstrated that the price of victory is always, above all, paid in human lives – illuminated those moments which get a little lost in legend . . . ' The tragic twist to the episode is the unfortunate death of one of these heroes, after the battle has been won, and unknown to his compañera who joins the funeral cortege amid the celebration of victory honouring the fallen fighter only to discover that the dead man is her own compañero.

The processes of audience identification in this film, however, continue to be basically the same as in the conventional war movie. At first sight the final twist is no different from devices used in conventional war movies for purely sentimental effect, which, on the ideological plane, alienate the viewer's intelligence from the historical significance of the events portrayed. Normally the film says 'this is the eternal, universal content of war', and pushes into the background the question of why *this* war, what are *these* people fighting for. And this isn't just the absence of contexts, it's the brazen rejection of context. But this is not what was happening for that audience of which Heras Leon was part. He says that the film seemed to them to have none of those scenes which however full of emotion, the Cubans habitually found distant either in space or time, as in films of the Second World War; or even the assault on the Winter Palace in 1917 which was already enveloped in the fog of history. Here 'it was our own image, our own history, our own day-to-day fact magnified by legend'. In short, it was successful because a sense of immediacy linked the time and space on the screen with that of the audience in the cinema. This was a rare experience for the Cuban audience, and it didn't combat but rather intensified the regular process of naive audience identification that is associated with the kind of film ICAIC was committed to fighting against.

For the film is clearly conceived in as unHollywood a way as the Cubans could manage at that moment. The paradigm of Italian neorealism is present in its episodic form, a narrative structure introduced by Rossellini in *Paisà* of 1946, which was also shot by Martelli. Ironically, however, Martelli (as well as the inexperienced laboratory workers) failed to give the Cuban film the real quality of the neorealist image. By the late 50s Martelli's photographic style had changed, his lighting techniques had grown closer to Hollywood. The biggest problem was filming the interiors which dominate the film's first episode. They turn out rather flatly lit, perhaps the result of a misjudged compromise.

113

The appeal of the neorealist paradigm did not come about just because Alea and others had studied cinema in Rome in the early 50s. There were certain parallels between the Cuban situation in 1959 and that of the birth of neorealism fifteen years earlier, though not of course in the political sphere. However, the Italians had needed to make a virtue of the lack of resources they suffered as they emerged from the war, just as the Cubans did in setting up a film industry in an underdeveloped country going through a revolution. And then the kind of movie both groups of film-makers were seeking to counter was closely similar. Both had suffered the domination of Hollywood. The Italians had decided to take their cameras out into the immediate photogenic real world in order to counter the fanciful studio space of the 'white telephone' film, the Italian fascist equivalent of the Latin American melodrama.

Revolutionary cinema, or a radical cinema in a critical situation, like Italy just after the defeat of the fascists, has always involved the discovery of a new screen space to unfold in, which transcends the spatial (and socio-spatial) character of whatever cinema it aims to replace. It aims to show the world changing, and the need for change; it must change the way the world looks on the screen in order to do so. One of the most strongly determining factors in the character of Italian neorealism was the starkness of the immediate photogenic world at the end of the war.

As time passed, the neorealists became committed to portraying the indifference of the republic that replaced the transitional government, and suffocated people's hopes and aspirations. If these developments created a very different situation from that of revolutionary Cuba, the ideas behind the neorealist aesthetic were far from theoretically innocent or naive. The Centro Sperimentale, founded in the middle 30s, had been a forum for theoretical as well as practical instruction. Italian fascism was culturally more sophisticated than Nazism; futurism was as much an aesthetic of Italian fascism in the 20s as of the Russian Revolution, and in the 30s Italian fascism considered there was much to learn in the art of propaganda from the communists. At the Centro Sperimentale, an independent-minded man like Umberto Barbaro was able to translate the writings on cinema of Eisenstein, Pudovkin, Béla Balázs and others.

It was Barbaro who gave the neorealist movement its name. He used the term to evoke the realism of early, pre-fascist Italian cinema, not as a model to be imitated directly but to support a conviction that all humanistic art demanded realism. Barbaro and other neorealists greatly admired Soviet revolutionary cinema, but felt it was hardly an appropriate model to be adopted in attempting the renovation of Italian cinema. Its sophisticated style of montage depended on an audience, which even in revolutionary Russia had been limited, geared up to a new kind of imaginative participation in the film, a condition which certainly did not exist in Italy at the end of the war where it had been lulled by two decades of screen escapism. They did not reject Soviet montage as non-realist like the influential French critic André Bazin (but then Bazin was an inveterate idealist, in the mould of the French Catholic intelligentsia). They regarded it as inapplicable for conjunctural reasons: because it was culturally and historically alien.

Barbaro himself argued that montage was the fundamental creative dimension of cinema – the fact that whatever the style of shooting, the film was still constructed by means of editing – and for him the neorealist idea was not intended to negate this but to constitute a particular way of providing the material upon which montage operated. By dialectical reasoning this meant that neorealist montage could not adopt the same appearance, the same rhythms and tempi, as Soviet montage. These arguments were appealing to the Cubans, who had limited knowledge but unbounded admiration of the early Soviet classics, but like the Italians could not imagine, in the Cuban context, simply trying to copy them.

In addition to going out onto the forbidden streets, and into real locations and real houses, it was also part of neorealist practice to find 'natural' actors instead of professionals. It was partly a matter of what might be called aesthetic opportunism. Location sound recording was still at that time physically cumbersome, and severely restricted the mobility of the camera, which the neorealists prized above all else because it enabled them not simply to picture the external reality but also to move through it, to become part of it, as if they belonged there. 'Natural' non-professional actors would improve the effect since they would more easily behave as if they belonged to the spaces in which the film was unfolding – because in large part (not always) that is indeed where they did belong. Professionals were too accustomed to the artificial spaces of studio and stage; nor at that time did they have the facility to represent the popular classes with conviction. The same was true in Cuba. In Italy, they were used only to dub the voices of the non-professionals afterwards. This was partly to provide the films with standard Italian pronunciation and avoid the difficulties of introducing regional accents. It was also a necessity imposed by the constraints of the times: to have post-synchronised the voices of the non-professionals themselves, as the Cubans did in *El Megano* in 1956, would have required too many expensive dubbing sessions; this was not a problem for the Cubans because *El Megano* was made clandestinely, with borrowed facilities and without commercial budgeting. But the Italian audience was in any case used to dubbing: the Fascists had required all foreign films to be dubbed rather than subtitled – it made censorship easier and guaranteed a certain regular flow of work to the dubbing studios.

As Italian neorealism developed, the films they made confirmed that certain themes have a particular affinity with certain kinds of space, and the entry of the camera into new spaces it had not previously been allowed to enter permitted new subjects to be conceived and new kinds of narrative treatment to be evolved. It became easier to break with the conventions of melodrama, with literary influences, with the specifically cinematic trickery of devices like the flashback, and the deceptions of the techniques of suspense. Stories could be developed out of the anecdotes of everyday existence, and narrated by a camera moving with unobtrusive ease among the characters and places of the film, obeying the natural rhythms and order of the events. When the Cubans adopted the neorealist paradigm there was no need for them to use it to expose continuing deprivation and official indifference, for here the government was a revolutionary one. But the neorealist aesthetic still contained many elements that were readily transferable – above all, those which brought to the screen the real social world outside the cinema dream palace.

Even at the beginning, however, the Cubans did not treat neorealism as an exclusive doctrine. While employing non-professional actors, for example, they also searched out professionals to whom they could entrust a good proportion of the lead parts. This wasn't just because they weren't dogmatic, but because they were also thoroughly pragmatic. If appropriate professionals could be found, their experience could help others – including the crew, so many of whom were total beginners. Moreover, in this way ICAIC could begin to build up a team of actors, a company of sorts, which is always in one form or another an integral part of a thriving cinema. What chance otherwise of creating a Cuban school of dramatic film art?

Not only that. If *Historias de la revolución* is clearly conceived in the neorealist tradition, García Espinosa's *Cuba baila* is in certain respects clearly not. For *Cuba baila* is an attempt to exorcise the Latin American melodrama, not by seeking radical alternatives but by taking its conventions and turning them around. From this point of view it has little to do with neorealism except in the way certain scenes were shot. The film was born of what is to become for García Espinosa a perennial concern, that of using a form with which the audience is thoroughly familiar, in order to take them through its surface illusions to the social reality it has conventionally been used to mask. Not too didactically, however, for according to the criteria he later elaborated in his concept of 'imperfect cinema', a film still has to entertain. In the end, it is a question of overcoming the opposition between notions of didacticism and notions of entertainment.

The main originality of *Cuba baila* lies in its treatment of music. When he first conceived it before the Revolution, he thought of it as a kind of Cuban musical but with a difference: where the Latin American musical used music for purposes of evasion, here it would fulfil a dramatic function by becoming a vehicle for the class analysis of the pseudo-republic. He had not been able to find the backing for such a film before the Revolution, even after he'd reworked the film with Cesare Zavattini when the neorealist master had visited Cuba.[2] But ICAIC readily undertook its production and the script was reworked another time by García Espinosa, Alfredo Guevara and Manuel Barbachano Ponce. Visually undistinguished, even plain, the image is nonetheless given another dimension by the music: the film works upon the characteristics of the social spaces, public, private or semi-public, in which the different pieces of music that occur in the film are played and heard. Of course it may well have been neorealism which made García Espinosa sensitive to this way of sensing space.

*Cuba baila*

The premise of the film is that while music of all the popular art forms had sustained the strongest vigour, it was no less susceptible for that to the uses which bourgeois ideology found in it. The story concerns the family of a minor functionary in which the daughter is about to celebrate *los quince*, the fifteenth birthday which is traditionally the occasion for a big family *fiesta*, which the higher up the social scale you go becomes more of a social coming-out party, a girl's launching onto the marriage market. The film moves through all the social spaces which make up the world of such a family, together or separately: from the home to the father's office, through bars and streets and other public areas and into the exclusive milieu of the fiesta hosted by the father's boss for his own daughter's fifteenth birthday.

The mother of the protagonist family is keenly aware of the importance which the music at her daughter's fiesta will play. Though the cost is almost prohibitive, she wants an orchestra like the one that impresses them as minor guests among the upper bourgeoisie. Musically such an orchestra means the Viennese waltz and North American hits, instead of the popular Cuban dances preferred by the daughter herself and her local boyfriend, whom her mother slights. To obtain a loan to pay for it, the father has to ingratiate himself with his superiors at the office by attending a political meeting in a local square. A band is employed to attract the public, but the politicians cannot hold the crowd; vociferous heckling rains down on them and much to the petty bureaucrat's consternation the meeting breaks up in violent disorder. In contrast, the passengers on a bus whistle together a popular tune with politically different overtones. Here the film comes close to suggesting a different paradigm to neorealism, that of the French Popular Front films of the 30s, where songs and dancing also play an important and positive role in portraying the social cohesion of the popular classes.

The parents' plan for a posh party fails to materialise. In the end, and much to the daughter's satisfaction, everyone is forced to go off and celebrate the fiesta in a popular open-air entertainment garden where, although the family's socially superior guests condescend to attend, the mother feels defrauded. The satire in this last scene is gentle but leaves no room for doubt about the hypocrisy of bourgeois values, as the camera watches the awkwardness with which the condescending guests dance to the popular music, while the daughter and her boyfriend mix unselfconsciously with the crowd.

The film has shown how the natural social functions of music – including the way it expresses and creates social cohesion – become corrupted when it is made to conform to corrupt or discreditable social ends. It offers a portrait of the pre-revolutionary Cuban bourgeoisie which superficially conforms to the format of the family melodrama but more deeply, through its careful use of music, mocks the stupidity of bourgeois convention. Perhaps the film's most surprising aspect is how much remains implicit, especially in comparison with the French Popular Front movies of the 30s. It has none of the propagandising socialist content of films like Renoir's *Le Crime de M. Lange*, even though one might expect more rather than less in a film by a revolutionary film-maker in the euphoria just after victory.

It was in his second feature, *El joven rebelde* ('The Young Rebel'), made the following year, that as Ugo Ulive put it, García Espinosa paid his debt to neorealism. The film has an original script by Zavattini, reworked by José Massip, J. Hernandez Artigas, Hector García Mesa and García Espinosa himself, and the story is that of a 17-year old peasant boy, Pedro, who leaves his family to join the guerrillas in the Sierra.

First, however, he needs to find himself a gun of some sort, the new recruit's passport. Together with a friend, he sets off to steal a revolver from the friend's uncle. But the plan misfires, and the friend is sent home again.

Out on the open road, Pedro gets a ride from a wily old peasant who understands full well that the youngster is aiming not, as he claims, to get a job on a coffee plantation but to join *los barbudos* – the bearded fighters in the hills. At a village where soldiers are stopping and searching anyone they suspect of carrying supplies to the guerrillas, the old peasant covers for Pedro. On his own again, the boy enters a bar where he grabs the opportunity to steal a soldier's rifle. The soldier gives chase across the fields and corners him. Pedro fires and the soldier is wounded. The camera lingers on Pedro's face, his eyes alight with a mixture of anxiety and pride at his first unexpected shot at the enemy.

His arrival at the rebel camp, where the troop drills with pieces of wood for guns, brings with it his first set of lessons. To start with, the small girl serving as look-out who brought him into the camp turns out to be a boy. The surprise hardly has time to sink in when the rifle he brought is taken away from him because, he is told, it belongs not to him but to the Revolution. His attempt to resist the loss of what is obviously the proudest possession he's ever had produces his third quick lesson in succession: a new figure appears to resolve the problem, Artemisa, a figure of evident authority – and he's black. Although feeling humiliated, Pedro sumbits. We soon begin to realize that the very obstinacy that brought Pedro to the Sierra is to cause him problems, as he tries to evade the guerrilla school by claiming to be able to read already. But in a gently ironic scene following an air attack, his ignorance is exposed by his failure to read the inscription on an unexploded bomb: 'Mutual Aid USA'.

Then Pedro is sent on an expedition to the coast to steal salt from the salt pans. He dawdles on the way to talk with a young girl washing clothes at a pool. An understandable slackness of discipline, it is also a moment of characteristically Cuban nature symbolism: as the girl asks Pedro to bring her a seashell on the way back, the promise of the sea is associated with a sense of erotic anticipation. At the salt pans, the utmost discipline is needed in order to break cover as soon as the clouds hide the moon, reach the salt, fill the sacks and retire again before the moon reappears. Pedro works fast and then puts down his sack and steals off to the shoreline to search for a shell. He has never seen the sea before and he pauses, looking at it with absorbed fascination. Only as the moon re-emerges does he remember the need for haste, and rushes to pick up his temporarily abandoned sack. Too late, for he has been spotted, and shots ring out. His comrades watch helplessly from the wood, which he finally reaches in safety after a zigzag run pursued by machine gun fire. The scene is directed with impressive restraint, dominated by long shots and a rhythm which corresponds to the slow tempo of the movement of the clouds across the sky. The visually arresting location – the strange dim white of the salt pans – does the rest. It enjoins us to share Pedro's feeling of magic at the seashore while also letting us sense the danger of his dalliance.

Conventional techniques of suspense reduce the conflict of contradictory perceptions to a unidimensional forward pressure with an artificial climax, because narrative convention normally assures us of the outcome in advance. But here the peculiar calmness of the scene gives rise to more complex responses. Given to experience a clash of emotions each of which is positive, we end up understanding the boy far better, and his situation more fully: the way his youthful, naive and so far frustrated appetite for experience is precisely what gives him the self-possession he needed to join the rebels, and how it may lead at times to pride or indiscipline.

The rest of the film is devoted to showing how the guerrilla ethic knows this and is ready to tame it tenderly and constructively. During the return to the camp, just before the expedition is caught in an unexpected air attack, one of the recruits, Campechuelo, complains of hunger. In the rain the next morning the group pass the village where the girl who asked Pedro for the seashell lives. The village has been bombed overnight, the inhabitants are leaving, and when Pedro

*El joven rebelde*

finally finds the girl departing with her family, they are able only to exchange silent looks, as he reaches into his sack for the gift. Back at camp Pedro is still unruly enough that he has to be reprimanded for uttering a racist insult and picking a fight when he volunteers for a dangerous mule-train escort but is passed over for being too inexperienced. When the mule-train arrives it is carrying the body of the comrade Pedro fought with, who died after a fall into a ravine.

Next morning the camp is summoned to an inquiry: during the return of the salt expedition a cheese ration was stolen. The compañero is asked to confess but after a silent pause the *comandante* conducting the inquiry is forced to name him: Campechuelo. Pedro is thunderstruck. Artemisa, prosecuting, asks for punishment according to the regulations. 'Within a few hours,' he says, 'we shall be fighting against an army equipped with tanks, heavy artillery and planes. What do we have? We have the trust that exists among ourselves.' Turning to Campechuelo he continues, 'Now you're suffering but before you lied. Everyone trusted you and you lied. Can you be trusted now? It's easy to say "I'm with the Revolution" but do you know what the word means? It signifies everything changing, beginning with ourselves. You're the same as before. Cuba has a great many things . . . sugar, tobacco, coffee, it's a rich country – with a poor people, because there are thieves, big thieves. How can you judge them if you steal the ration from your comrades?' Campechuelo is duly punished, on the eve of a battle which the camp is informed Fidel has said will be decisive, by expulsion from the Rebel Army. As he is called to prepare for battle, Pedro protests to Artemisa. Artemisa's face shows that he comprehends Pedro's confusion, and he does no more than quietly order him to leave the humiliated Campechuelo and join the others. The film ends in mid-battle, with Pedro taking over the machine gun at which Artemisa has been killed, and we recall Artemisa's last words to Pedro before the battle: 'Now you'll earn your gun.'

Again Heras León recalled the film's original impression; the youthful audience felt themselves to be

> the indisciplined youth, stubborn in the face of orders, anarchic and naive, whose desire to fight justified all his actions, all his rebelliousness and incomprehension... Again the technique didn't worry us. Of course we would have preferred the youngster to have a more expressive face, not so hard, not so withdrawn, especially in the last scene in which his consciousness is awakened and changes from a young rebel into a revolutionary soldier; we would have preferred if Isabel, the naive peasant girl, had had an attitude less like that of an underdeveloped Silvana Mangano; that García Espinosa, the director, had taken care that the photography captured the Cuban countryside with greater veracity; that Pedro had shot the drunken soldier with greater decision; and finally that the last scene hadn't been so much like *La patrulla de Bataan* by reason of its long close up on Blas Mora's face.

'La patrulla de Bataan' was *Bataan*, starring Robert Taylor, George Murphy and Lloyd Nolan, directed in 1943 by Tay Garnett; a Cuban favourite.

Not all these criticisms are equally valid. To criticise Pedro's indecision in shooting the soldier he stole the rifle from, for instance, betrays idealistic impatience in the viewer – it is, in fact, a scene both effectively mounted and acted. But then this idealism of the film's first viewers was an extension of Pedro's on the screen.

At the same time, there are some subtle and significant symbolic shifts and parallels in the final sections of the film which may well have escaped them. In his determination to keep his promise and bring the seashell, Pedro demonstrates an essentially generous spirit which contrasts with Campechuelo's meanness in stealing the cheese ration – all the more so because in the midst of the destruction of the village the symbolic meaning of the seashell changes: it becomes less a sentimental gift than a metaphor for the promise of victory. But then Pedro insults a man and picks a fight and then feels irrationally guilty when the man he fought with dies an accidental death. Complexities like these give the film its most paradoxical and didactic quality: that it is a film about heroism that is anti-heroic, a film about fighting which is anti-militaristic. To recall that the young rebel is a peasant, and to recognise in the film its projection of the peasant character as a paradigm of the spirit in whose name the Revolution was under-taken – the untutored appetite for experience, impetuous but generous – this is to grasp why and in what sense it has been claimed that the Cuban Revolution is not militarist, in spite of its guns and uniforms. *El joven rebelde* is not a paean to the military institution, and not at all about strategies and tactics, but the ethical education of a *guerrillero*.

The other fiction film of 1961 was Oscar Torres's *Realengo 18*, a modest picture of 60 minutes (though *El joven rebelde* is only 83). The title of the film refers to one of the ownerless tracts of land which dispossessed peasants used to settle, and the film deals with an incident during the Communist-led popular rebellion of the mid-30s. It takes place in the sierra in eastern Cuba in which the guerrillas later established their principal liberated zone. The story is one of division within a family. After his father has been shot dead, and against his mother's wishes, the son, in need of a job, joins the local guard. When a North American sugar company decides it wants the village lands, he ends up having to point a gun at the people of his own village with his staunchly defiant mother one of the leaders. The story has a Brechtian simplicity to it; the handling of the camera is unfortunately rather stiff and conventional. Its achievement is that it successfully applies a neorealist approach to an historical subject by using non-professional actors who included survivors of the events portrayed – one of Latin American cinema's first attempts to do this.

With one major exception – Alea's *Cumbite* of 1964 – this is really, from a practical point of view, as far as the heritage of neorealism reaches in Cuban cinema. But this exception is a remarkable one. *Cumbite* is not only ICAIC's last neorealist picture, it is also visually the most striking: its stark black-and-white photography creates a feeling of tropical countryside better than ever before; there is an absence of background music; the narrative has the form of chronological anecdote; it is told with slow deliberate pace to give time for the patient observation of everyday activities. Like *Realengo 18* it employs neoreal-

*Cumbite*

ism in representing an historical period, but this time the film is fictional: based on Jacques Romain's novel *Les Gouverneurs de la Rosée*, it takes place in 1942, and tells about the return of a Haitian, Manuel, to his home village after fifteen years in Cuba. It is the first of a number of Cuban films about Haiti, all of them made with the participation of the Haitian community in Cuba.

Manuel's years in Cuba have given him a knowledge of the world, enough at least to make him critical of the fatalism of the Haitian peasant, product of the fate of the Haitian Revolution, its ossification into a static society and a repressive dictatorship. Returning to his village he finds them facing the problems of drought. 'If water doesn't fall from the sky,' one of them tells him, 'there's no water. We are wretched negroes.' 'It is the lack of the negro,' Manuel tells his mother, 'not of the good Lord.' He knows they can find water and build an irrigation system. He tries to explain to the villagers, 'Look, we are the earth, without us it is nothing.' Many are uneasy with his challenge and regard him an an interfering outsider; they take rancour at his liaison with one of the village girls, Analaisa. This sentimental subplot Alea handles with the greatest restraint.

Manuel's scheme requires a *cumbite*, a general assembly of the village, because it requires collective labour and, moreover, Manuel wants the water to be collective property. Some of his opponents declare his proposals illegal and call him a subversive. Then he is killed in a fatal night-time attack by his rival as Analaisa's suitor. On his death-bed he tells his mother that Analaisa knows where there's a water source – they discovered it together – and his death shocks the village into realising the benefits the scheme will bring.

*Cumbite*, according to a group of Venezuelan critics in 1971, a bit harshly I think,

is characterised by its extreme sobriety. Nothing protrudes, the story is fine, the actors well cast, the images plastic, the narrative advances in spite of everything. But perhaps it's too sober. Incorporated in the film are some sequences showing voodoo ceremonies. They are treated with an almost anthropological vision, with tremendous respect, the gratuitously picturesque is at all costs avoided, but in this way it seems to lose all its force, all intensity in the expressiveness which is worked into the material. The result is a film that is correct but removed, which succeeds neither in stirring, nor surprising, nor convincing, nor entertaining. The exploration by Cuban cinema of a world not its own remains a hybrid experience and apparently without perspective.[3]

Perhaps, since Venezuela has its own black culture, its own versions of voodoo, they are more sensitive to the representation of these things than a European eye, but it is still important to say that the film has its own integrity, and a sense of authenticity which is guaranteed not only by the participation of the Cuban Haitians but also by the way the camera watches their ceremonies, without any trace of voyeurism, but moving around with considerable fluidity. It is this fluidity with the camera that is to become one of Alea's distinctive capacities as a director and an important stylistic trend in Cuban cinema.

In any event, the film has several layers of significance; among them the allegorical. It is a film of solidarity with the Haitain peasant and a lesson in revolutionary ethics and the practice of collectivism. But it is also a film about the cultural complexity of underdeveloped society and its internal contradictions, for the collective spirit which Manuel seeks to mobilise is already present in the traditions of the *cumbite* – and in the form of the religious ceremonial. It is not a film which views these things schematically, or from a position of, as it were, higher revolutionary wisdom. It takes up an aspect of Fidel Castro's thinking that is both characteristic and essential to its revolutionary style: the refusal of the sectarian idea that only the purest proletarian elements in the society are capable of correct revolutionary action. At the very least, this idea is a denial of the capacity to learn which underdeveloped illiterate peasants manifest as much as any other kind of human being; a capacity which in Paulo Freire's idea of cultural action for freedom, is recognised as a powerful social force.[4]

Finally, there is a stylistic paradox, for in *Cumbite* neorealism becomes a kind of farewell to the past. The rapid progress of the Revolution has already, by the time this film was made, created a distance from the conditions only five years earlier. As Alea has recalled:

When we began to make films in a post-revolutionary situation the neorealist mode of approaching reality was very useful to us because in that early stage we needed little more. First of all, we were not developed enough as film-makers to posit other approaches. Secondly, our own national situation at that juncture was . . . very clear. All we had to do was to set up a camera in the street and we were able to capture a reality that was spectacular in and of itself . . . That kind of film-making was perfectly valid for that particular historical moment.

But our revolution also began to undergo a process of change. Though certainly not the same as that which occurred in post-war Italy, the meaning of external events began to become less obvious . . . more profound. That process forced us to adopt an analytical attitude towards the reality which surrounded us. A greater discipline, a much more exact theoretical criterion was then required of us in order to be able properly to analyse and interpret what we were living through.[5]

The theoretical criterion which Alea invokes here is not a particular theory of film or style, but the application to all theoretical and stylistic principles of the new way of thinking that was now established in Cuba, revolutionary marxism – in a Cuban way, of course.


Before *Cumbite*, Alea had revealed another side of his creative personality in his first comedy, *Las doce sillas* ('The Twelve Chairs') of 1962. This is an adaptation to the Cuban Revolution of the comic novel of the early years of the Soviet

Revolution by Ilf and Petrov which has also recently been put on the screen by Mel Brooks in the United States – the story has that kind of crazy comedy. A masterful comedy *auteur* in the true Hollywood tradition that goes back to Chaplin and Mack Sennet, Brooks has made a very serviceable job of it, but with the difference that he did it as a period piece, while Alea does it as a contemporary satire on the world immediately outside the studio. The story concerns the hunt by Hipolito, the scion of a bourgeois family, and his rascally sidekick and erstwhile servant Oscar, for a suite of English period chairs, in one of which Hipolito's dying mother-in-law has hidden the family jewels. This piece of information she delivers at the start of the tale from her death-bed, when the chairs are no longer in the family's possession, and there then follows an increasingly desperate and hopeless pursuit in which Hipolito and Oscar compete against the family priest who administered the last rites for the old woman and has hit the trail on his own. The chairs are among property confiscated by the Revolutionary Government, to be sold at auction; Oscar helps Hipolito raise the necessary money to bid – he presents him to a secret meeting as a counter-revolutionary in need of funds – but things go awry at the auction, and the chairs go to a variety of buyers. Several are sold to a circus, where one is used by a lion-tamer – until the lion tears it to pieces in a typical scene, Hipolito and Oscar watching in desperate impotence for fear of the jewels falling out right there in front of the audience. When they finally track down the last chair, which was bought by the railway workers union, they find them already celebrating the good fortune of their windfall.

Unexpectedly, Alea had the idea for this film before the Revolution, when it wasn't possible to make it. Now it was not only more apt, but the Revolution itself provided the elements of the setting, beginning with the film's Ministry of Recuperation in charge of confiscated property. Sets of initials of official organisations keep cropping up in the film – real ones, INRA, ICP, ICAP, INDER, even ICAIC itself. Then there's the whole ambience of conspiracy, the private settling of accounts within the unsettled bourgeoisie at the moment of its dissolution, the activities of the counter-revolutionaries, the treasures hidden in secret places and – as Alea himself points out – the possibility of making a film about such things. It is an imaginative adaptation, in which neorealist techniques assist the incorporation of the real environment within the inevitable stylisation of the comedy form. It gives you a kind of guided tour of the new society. The conspirators, at one point, unwittingly hitch a lift on a lorry taking volunteers to the fields to cut cane; at another they track down one of the chairs to a blood donor centre where they find the militiaman on duty sitting on it. Both master and servant find this new society topsy-turvy and it upturns their own relationship too. They argue about how to divide the spoils when they find the diamonds: Oscar protests he's only trying to help his erstwhile master but if Hipolito doesn't want his help he, Oscar, will go and find the chairs by himself. Hipolito objects, 'Just a moment – remember those diamonds are mine!' To which Oscar responds: 'Are you still insisting on private property?'

Alea employs a variety of techniques, including documentary insert and intertitles. He also cuts in quick shots which do not advance the narrative but simply provide additional comic sideswipes. A newspaper seller, for example, passes by announcing the latest news – the publication of *Don Quixote*. There are certain bits of satire, however, directly aimed at a rather particular target. At the beginning of the film there's an interpolated newsreel sequence – it parodies ICAIC's own newsreels, which have not yet fully escaped the old formulae: 'ICAIC Social Notes... More hidden treasures found – vanity and selfishness revealed'; and the commentator intoning 'The dark interests of the past maintained our people in ignorance in order to exploit them...' At the end of the film the target is a different branch of official art. Hipolito and Oscar arrive at the Railway Workers' Social Institute to find a mural painter describing to the workers the mural he's going to paint them – they have commissioned him with some of the money they got for the jewels. He describes a tableau picturing the forces of the Revolution against the forces of Imperialism in the style of socialist realism. The workers, listening to his high falutin' ideas, conclude that he is a bit crazy.

It was in the course of making this film that Alea and his crew discovered how rapidly the changes wrought by the Revolution were taking place. 'The Revolution implies a fundamental change in the structure of society,' he said, 'but the appearance of things also changes from day to day. A billboard announcing a luxury hotel in Miami and inviting Cubans to spend their vacation there is substituted by another which declares Cuba a territory free of illiteracy. Suddenly, where a large mansion previously housed counts or marquesses, there is now an art school; where Cadillacs used to be sold, now they sell furniture for workers who have been given houses by the Urban Reform. When we arrived to film a lonely vantage point over a valley we found a large hotel built by the Tourist Institute full of tourists. Inside a building where we had gone to shoot a number of scenes we found walls erected and walls demolished, a new arrangement of furniture and bricklayers at work everywhere, which obliged us to change our plans and to hurry the filming through because of the danger that even during shooting they would transform the scene around us. I think that the general rhythm of the film to some extent reflects the vertigo of the revolution.'[6]

# References

1.  Eduardo Heras León, 'Historias de la revolución y el joven rebelde', *Pensamiento Critico* No.42, July 1970, pp.128-134. Reprinted in *Cine y Revolución en Cuba*, Editorial Fontamara, Barcelona 1975.
2.  See Fausto Canel, op.cit.
3.  'Resultado de una discusion critica', *Cine al dia* No. 12, March 1971.
4.  See Paulo Freire, *Cultural Action for Freedom*, Penguin Education, 1972.
5.  Julianne Burton, 'Individual Fulfillment and Collective Achievement, an Interview with T.G. Alea', *Cineaste* Vol.8 No.1, 1977.
6.  *Ibid.*

# 8
# BEYOND NEOREALISM

*Influence of the nouvelle vague – the struggle against sectarianism – film posters – the Cinemateca – more films*

In an interview he gave to a Peruvian film magazine towards the end of the 60s, Julio García Espinosa spoke of the way the rapid development of the Revolution took them beyond neorealism. Even those who had made *El Megano*, he said, who had been imprisoned and gone to work in clandestinity for the overthrow of Batista's government, had believed that they were preparing only for a multi-class government with the participation of leftists alongside the bourgeoisie, and with a national programme. Nobody thought at first the outcome would actually be a socialist government – even if that is what they dedicated themselves to work for. Neorealism they saw as the model for an appropriate cinema – a humanist and progressive aesthetic that offered a real alternative to the dominant modes of Hollywood and Latin American commercial production. An anti-dictatorial nationalist bourgeoisie could not have objected to it, it was a style that placed the people on the screen as historical actors, but without being too explicit about it. But the rapid radicalisation of the Revolution demonstrated that there was both room and need for a cinema to go further than this: straightforward neorealist ideas could not really catch the speed and depth of revolutionary change. Though what kind of cinema could do this was not yet obvious, and would not emerge for some years.

Alfredo Guevara wrote of neorealism in the first issue of ICAIC's film journal *Cine Cubano* as only one among several options.[1] There was also another film movement on the horizon which was duly to exert its influence in Cuba, the French New Wave. Though yet to reach its peak, it had already been named, and Alfredo Guevara was able to mention in this article the names of some of those linked to it: Molinaro, Malle, Vadim and Chabrol. Also that Simone de Beauvoir described the New Wave directors as 'anarchists of the right'. Nevertheless, he suggested, they offered an interesting and valid lesson: they represented a cinema both youthful and inexpensive, a cinema without stars (substantially true at the time), a cinema that aimed to be rebellious. It was a cinema of protest, aesthetically nonconformist, innovatory and iconoclast, ready to confront 'respectable' values and discard them without hesitation. There was clean, fresh air in the work of the New Wave directors. Sometimes, it was true, they played games with Hollywood formulae, transformed bedroom drama into sexual poetry, or indulged in shallow philosophy and amateur psychology, all of which amounted to little more than rebellion from the armchair or the bed. But some of their films hit the target of a genuinely new cinema: Truffaut's *Les Quatre cents coups*, Resnais' *Hiroshima mon amour*. Most importantly, these were new directors who showed no fear of the technology and technicalities of cinema.

The demise of the Francophile *Lunes* group in 1961 did not mean the influence of the French New Wave was to be curbed within ICAIC. It could be said that, on the contrary, with the establishment of new critical criteria the field was clear only now for its influence to be critically absorbed. And in fact we find, over the next few years, a group of short fictional films clearly influenced by the *nouvelle vague*, by a clutch of apprentice directors who were subsequently to be internationally acclaimed for their very differently styled feature films; including Humberto Solás, Manuel Octavio Gómez, Manuel Pérez and Sergio Giral. None of these films is more than an apprentice work, but they are not without interest. Sergio Giral, reminded of *La jaula* ('The Cage') which he made in 1964, recalls it as 'rather too much influenced by Godard'.[2] It tells of a woman suffering from a paranoid psychosis. The story is told firstly from the husband's point of view and then from that of the patient. Tomás Gutiérrez Alea plays the psychiatrist. *Minerva traduce el mar* ('Minerva Interprets the Sea', 1962) has the distinction of being the only film on which the poet Lezama Lima ever collaborated, contributing the hermetic verses heard on the soundtrack while a pair of ballet dancers perform at the edge of the sea around a bust of Minerva. Solás, who was barely 20 years old when he made this film with Oscar Valdés as co-director, laughs at it now as a naive experiment.[3] A year later he and Valdés made another mysterious short, *El retrato* ('The Portrait'), about a painter seeking inspiration by pursuing an imaginary woman whose image he finds on a portrait in an abandoned house, a tale which clearly reveals (the only thing about it which *is* clear) that good intentions are not enough to banish fascination with ancient myths about the sources of creativity. Then in 1965, this time by himself, Solás directed *El acoso* ('The Pursuit'). This time the subject is less obscure. An escaped mercenary from the defeated invasion of the Bay of Pigs kills a man in the countryside, takes his clothes, comes upon a cabin where he rapes the woman he finds there alone, and finally wanders lost and helpless across endless mudflats. The film is primarily a stylistic exercise, but this time by a student who has gained self-confidence in the handling of the craft. Refusing the technique of cross-cutting which constitutes the conventional chase movie, and with an almost static camera, Solás still builds up an atmosphere of tension and menace, especially inside the cabin after the rape.

These fictional shorts – about a dozen were made altogether, several dealing with episodes from the guerrilla war – were originally intended to be combined into feature length films made up of separate and unconnected episodes. Apart from *Cuba '58* no such film was ever released. In a couple of cases the episodes were not released at all. *Elena*, directed by Fernando Villaverde, and *El final*

('The Ending'), directed by Fausto Canel, both proved problematic. Ugo Ulive quotes someone saying that *Elena* was 'so absurd that it was unprojectable'. Failures were inevitable if the policy was to let untried film-makers experiment.

The problem, in the effort to build a film industry from scratch, was how to train the personnel. As Alea wrote about filming *Las doce sillas*:

> The main collaborators during the filming were young, without much previous experience. The director of photography, the camera operator, the focus-puller and the camera assistants were all working on a feature film for the first time. Similarly the assistant director and the continuity girl. Even the film we were using (Agfa NP20 and Ultrarapid) presented problems which hadn't been technically resolved by our cameramen.
>
> We wanted to launch out with a crew of new people in whom we had hope. Fortunately the lighting technicians, carpenters and production team included compañeros who were old hands and highly disciplined, which gave us relative peace of mind, even though they also had apprentices engaged in this work for the first time. Perhaps not everything would go well. We had accumulated too many risks in the key positions and this at times prevented our always proceeding smoothly . . .[4]

Largely to help deal with this problem of training, ICAIC followed the development of the Revolution in looking towards the socialist countries for assistance, and the years 1962-4 saw three co-productions, one each with the Soviet Union, East Germany and Czechoslovakia. In each case the co-producing country supplied not only the director but other principal personnel too. From the GDR, Kurt Maetzig directed *Preludio 11* ('Prelude 11'). Wolfgang Schreyer wrote the script with José Soler Puig, a story about counter-revolutionaries in the service of the CIA making preparations for the Bay of Pigs. The director of photography and the editor were also Germans. A team of Czechs came to make *Para quien baila La Habana* ('For Whom Havana Dances'), directed by Vladimir Cech, with a script by Jan Prochazka and Onelio Jorge Cardoso, and again a Czech director of photography and editor, this time sharing credits with Cubans. The story concerned the different paths taken after the victory of the Revolution by two friends who had fought the dicatorship together, one of whom now found that his personal interests were challenged by the new social order. Finally, Mikhail Kalatozov (director of *The Cranes Are Flying*) directed *Soy Cuba* ('I Am Cuba') with a script by Yevgeni Yevtushenko and Enrique Pineda Barnet, and a Russian director of photography and editor. This was a film of four episodes showing different aspects of life in Cuba before the Revolution. It was the most ambitious of these co-productions, and ICAIC knew enough about Soviet production practices with their lengthy and leisurely shooting schedules to prevail upon their comrades to bring their own transport and equipment, so as not to tie up ICAIC's limited facilities and halt their other productions; by informal arrangement the equipment was then left behind in Cuba when they finished.[5] None of these films was very successful.

The Czech film grafted its plot on to a superficial and picturesque vision of the Carnaval in Havana; the German one was a miscalculated action movie; and the Soviet effort was a kind of 'delirium for the camera' from an impossibly baroque screenplay – the description is Ulive's, but no-one in Cuba thinks much of these films today either. The truth is that while it made sense for ICAIC to undertake these co-productions for both artistic and material reasons, the foreign visitors didn't do their homework properly – even Yevtushenko, who was especially enthusiastic. Still, even he was unable to get beneath the skin and go beyond the traveller's image of the island which Soviet revolutionary poetry inherited from Mayakovsky's visit in the 20s.

The truth is that the visiting film-makers were no better equipped to respond to the expressive needs of the Cuban Revolution than the engineers of their countries to the need for projectors to be used in a tropical climate. This was the kind of problem that cropped up continually with the aid that Cuba received from the socialist countries. Many were the disruptions caused by the wrench which the country's fixed productive forces underwent as the US blockade took effect, and technicians and engineers of another breed stepped into the breach. ICAIC's experience was entirely typical. Most of the cinemas were in terrible condition, the projection gear was old and decrepit and the previous managers had relied on the readily available supply of spare parts. As US trade investigators had reported years before, most of the equipment was purchased second-hand in the first place. Now it urgently needed maintenance and replacement. The Institute conducted a technical survey and discovered that they had inherited seventy different types of projector – a real nightmare. They made a count of the most common types and sent samples of the basic set of spare parts to their East European partners so that they could make moulds from them and stave off disaster. They found, when the new parts arrived and were installed, that they were not correctly engineered for tropical conditions, and they buckled in the heat.

It is true, of course, that these co-productions may also have served a political purpose by helping to take the edge off sectarian criticisms of ICAIC. Fidel himself directly addressed the problem of sectarianism in the strongest terms in the Spring of 1962, when he declared in a television broadcast that 'the suppression of ideas was a myopic, sectarian, stupid and warped conception of Marxism that could change the Revolution into a tyranny. And that is not revolution!' The occasion was his denunciation of the behaviour of Anibal Escalante and others working through the Organisaciones Revolucionarias Integradas (Integrated Revolutionary Organisations – ORI) which had been set up in 1961 with the object of integrating the old Communist Party, the 26th July Movement and the Directorio Revolucionario (the group which carried out the attack pictured in the first episode of *Historias de la revolución*).

García Espinosa has described the behaviour of the sectarians vividly: their dogmatism, their rigidity in the face of the problem of creating socialism, their rejection of the principle of armed struggle by the national liberation movements in Latin America. These failings, he said, became well known. They also, he continues, had the effect of undermining the militancy which came from comradeship, the process of discussion with those who were still without direction, and the attempt to stick to principles and avoid personal attacks. They made popular participation, he said, almost impossible. They had an absolute distrust of artists and intellectuals, whom they regarded as an irremediable evil which they hoped would go away with time, to be controlled by means of sops and small concessions. They placed their faith in training up new generations, replacing their own tutelage for the inspiration of the revolutionary process itself. They attacked cultural policies which, through mobilising this inspiration, aimed to raise the level of ideological struggle against inherited cultural tendencies and trends.[6]

ICAIC levelled serious arguments against sectarian ideas as they affected cultural politics, beginning with an address by Alfredo Guevara to the First National Cultural Congress in which he criticised the orthodox positions of the National Council for Culture (CNC) under Edith García Buchacha. His point of departure was Fidel's 'Words to the Intellectuals' and the claim that art could not exist in Cuba outside the Revolution, which was itself a creative phenomenon of the highest order and the only possible source of artistic innovation. He insisted, however, that the endeavour of the artist was autonomous. For example, it has educational values but its purpose is not educational. ICAIC therefore believed that 'if a "revolutionary" message is required of the creator of a work of art, in the same way as of a political speech or a philosophical essay, then only one thing will be accomplished: the spiritual assassination of the creator, the asphyxiation of art in an oxygen tent.' In the light of the short fiction films they were producing, he was obviously here defending the need for a space in which the young directors could freely experiment in order to find their feet.

He did more than defend however. He launched a critique of populism. Artists were being confused, he said, by 'theoretical propaganda and pseudo-cultural phraseology' which tried to persuade them that the way to reach the superior level of the people was to reduce the substance of the work of art. Such falsely proletarian ideas could only breed the crudest propaganda and demagogy, and then a primitive kind of art would invade the most inappropriate places, which working people would either overvalue or ridicule. 'This mechanical concept of the working masses' rise to culture will thus produce not the elevation of the intellectual level but its debasement and disintegration. This is the origin of the wave of bad taste which is washing over the country and which is no way inherent in socialist development.' The problem was a set of erroneous, facile and routine ideas to be found within the cultural organisations, including the National Council of Culture, the Union of Writers and Artists (UNEAC) and ICAIC itself. 'Up to now these organisations have not known how to say "No!" publicly and openly to this ridiculous cartel, to the absurd murals which have invaded workplaces and centres of social and cultural life, to the useless papering of each wall, column and window, many times to the concealment or deterioration of true national momuments and sites, simply in order to meet numerical goals rather than for the sake of political effectiveness.'[7]

As chance would have it, ICAIC was given an opportunity to take up battle not just with images on screens but also on the streets as well. The haphazard process of confiscation and nationalisation gave them possession of a commercial graphics studio for making silk-screen posters. Saúl Yelín, son of an immigrant Jewish family and one of the most imaginative of ICAIC's production staff, immediately saw the possibility of ICAIC going to work to produce its own cinema posters. It would be possible in this way to invade the streets and link the battle against commercial art and the aesthetic trash of the Hollywood poster with the struggle against the cartel of bad taste. They would not only put their posters up outside the cinemas but would erect poster stands all over the city, in squares and on corners. To design the posters they would call on individual artists who, individualistic or not, wanted to be part of the process but didn't know how, because they had too much integrity for the methods of the cartel.

In this way ICAIC became the midwife of an unprecedented artistic explosion, and the Cuban revolutionary poster was born. Painters who until then must have wondered what their fate would be, perhaps because their style was abstract and avant-garde, were now drawn into the cultural process without having to compromise their aesthetic ideals. As a Latin American observer, Nestor García Canclini, has written:

Artists used to painting canvases who move into this new form of production have to subordinate, but not necessarily abandon, their taste, emotional states and desires to the collective message which is to be transmitted. Good poster art, such as the Cuban or the Polish, doesn't demand that the artist renounces personal style or experimentation, because the message becomes more effective when, instead of being direct and singular, it exhibits a certain tension between affirmation and suggestion, and the clarity the message must have for its reception, and the economy, condensation and ambiguities which provoke the interest of the receiver. What the good poster requires is that the personal and formal search should be at the service of the object of communication. Instead of the narcissistic complacency over individual language that belongs to easel painting, the poster and the mural bring participation in the decoration of the urban landscape, and in the formation of popular taste and imagination.[8]

The new poster style rapidly began to drive the cartel out of business. From a formal point of view, it was sometimes reminiscent of the revolutionary Soviet poster before the institution of socialist realism. It not only introduced colourful new images, it had a playful typographical style, a direct response to the popular experience of the literacy campaign of 1961. As UNESCO was able to confirm, the campaign, in the space of a year, reduced an illiteracy rate running in the countryside at anything up to 43%, to the level of three or four per cent which is normal in developed countries. The creative effects of the campaign in expanding the print market and stimulating cultural consumption were contagious, and the new poster expressed this in the animation it seemed to impart to the written word, using imaginative plastic design combined with the utmost economy of means. The style was quickly taken up by other organisations with a need for imaginative propaganda, and gave a good number of artists much needed economic employment. It also provided them with spiritual sustenance, linking them with the revolutionary process through their own productivity. This process brought their aesthetic ideas closer to the popular viewer so that they could return to the creation of more formal works without having to retreat into isolation. The effect which all this had on the cultural image of the Revolution is neatly captured in a story told by Ernesto Cardenal in the diary of his Cuban visit in 1970. The painter Portocarrero showed him a photograph of the large ceramic mural of his in the presidential palace. 'He told me that some delegates from Russia or one of the Eastern European countries at a reception asked Fidel, with a certain tone of sarcasm, "And what does this mean?" (meaning "and what does this have to do with the Revolution?"). Fidel replied, "Nothing, it doesn't mean anything. It's just some crazy thing painted for some people who like crazy things of this kind, by a crazy person who was commissioned by the crazy men who made this Revolution".'[9] Certainly, by all accounts, Fidel is no connoisseur of art; but he is also reported to have said to someone who demanded an end to abstract painting (Khrushchev had just publicly condemned it): 'The enemy is imperialism, not abstract art.'[10]

The debate was soon taken up with energy. Julio García Espinosa formulated a number of urgent questions on aesthetic matters in an article in *La Gaceta de Cuba*, the publication of the Union of Writers and Artists, in April 1963. The film-makers then met for three days' discussion in July and published their conclusions as a document in the *Gaceta* in August. The *Gaceta* was the successor to *Lunes de Revolucion*. It did not achieve the same circulation but it was not the 'run of the mill' publication lacking in originality claimed by K.S. Karol.[11] The same issue that carried this document also included articles on James Joyce's *Ulysses*, on Braque, and the art of collage (the latter by Clement Greenberg); and an announcement that the Union's library had acquired 600 musical scores, including contemporary works by Stockhausen, Webern, Berg, Schoenberg, Bartok, Boulez, Eisler, Nono, Birtwistle, Haubenstock-Ramati, Shostakovich, Pousseur, Messiaen and others.

The film-makers' manifesto had twenty-nine signatories. Not quite everyone,

Posters: *Un retablo para Romeo y Julieta/El extraño caso de Rachel K*
   *La ultima cena/ The circus*

Posters: *79 primaveras/El tigre saltó...*
*Maputo: meridiano novo/Sulkari*

but the overwhelming majority. It was a forthright document which declared that while it was both the right and the duty of the state to promote cultural development, aesthetic tendencies and ideas are always in a state of conflict with each other and it is mistaken to try to impose solutions. Moreover, the relationship between bourgeois and proletarian culture is not exclusively antagonistic (as Lenin had pointed out) and 'the obvious fact that a liberal bourgeois like Thomas Mann is a better writer than Marxist-Leninist Dmitir Furmanov shows that a specifically aesthetic criterion exists which cannot be reduced to the ideological position of the writers.' Art cannot be reduced to its external determinants and formal categories have no class character. Therefore it is to be concluded that in the battle between aesthetic ideas, suppression on the grounds that certain forms have an undesirable class character restricts the evolution of art by restricting the struggle between the ideas themselves.

Theoretically the argument is not without contradictions, so that when it was reprinted in *Cine Cubano* a couple of months later, Alfredo Guevara pointed out that the editors of the magazine had certain reservations about it, but they did subscribe to its conclusions and gave full support to its signatories' moral intentions.[12] For the manifesto had given rise to heated debate. Edith García Buchacha wrote a reply in the *Gaceta*, other articles appeared in *Cuba socialista* and the Communist Party newspaper *Hoy*, and the film-makers were invited to a debate at the University of Havana. In November, the *Gaceta* published responses by T.G. Alea and García Espinosa.[13] They both emphasised that the document had achieved it purpose by stimulating all this discussion. Alea said he didn't agree with every one of its points but with its antidogmatic spirit, and he criticised certain professors who insisted the real enemy was idealism, not dogmatism, because (they said) at least the dogmatists were on the right side. To the professors, the artists were suffering from the 'original sin' of belonging to the bourgeoisie. But as the writer Lisandro Otero had pointed out, said Alea, so did Marx, Engels and Lenin.

García Espinosa, on the role of the Party, admitted that their reaction to the threat which the dogmatists represented had been too mechanical. But he went on to discuss the artist's relationship to the audience in a way that completely exposed the dogmatists' populist myths. The issue has been poorly represented in previous accounts of these episodes. The dogmatists, says Michèle Firk, in a passage which Ulive quotes as if it summed it all up perfectly well, tell the film-makers, 'The Revolution has generously given you the chance to make films. What have you given in return?' The film-maker answers, 'The Revolution has only fulfilled its duty; I am an artist.' The dogmatists say, 'Go to the people.' The artist responds, 'Let the people come to me.'[14] But this is not a very intelligent way to represent the argument and has little to do with García Espinosa'a position. Until now, he said, the only thing that has been insisted on is that the artist should have more contact with the people and its problems. This is correct but it isn't enough. The people also need to have more contact with art *and with the problems of the artist*. The public is neither a monster nor an ignorant mass, as the reactionary and the decadent artist both see it, but nor is it a new species which has to be fed only with predigested foods, as the dogmatists seem to believe. It is capable of errors of judgment. It can be misled, for example, into accepting a concept of productivity in art which it is false and mechanical to attempt to apply.

This example, casually introduced, is cardinal. It puts the issue firmly in the most rigorous Marxist terms: the question is about the production and consumption of art, and in particular about the labour process of the artistic worker. The Mexican philosopher Adolfo Sánchez Vásquez has examined this question in an essay entitled 'Art as Concrete Labour', where he shows that the quantification of aesthetic labour by means of its reduction to the same criteria as regular labour under normal conditions of production is of no use in evaluating the work of the artist. Why? Because the value of a work of art is determined by qualitative, not quantitative characteristics. To apply a common quantitative denominator to artistic production can only lead in practice to a standardisation of aesthetic creation, the mechanical reproduction of repetitive formulae which are totally incompatible with the creative character of the imagination.[15] This is precisely what Alfredo Guevara had spoken out against at the 1962 Cultural Congress. The disquiet of the film-makers with the dogmatism of the sectarians was thus rather different from that of the liberals of the *Lunes* group, and went far beyond abstract notions of creative inspiration and freedom, just as it also went beyond a simple attack on socialist realism as a stylistic norm. The ICAIC critique of socialist realism was not just that it constituted a culturally alien style, but that it resulted from inadequate conceptualisation of the conditions of production in art.

For ICAIC this was a practical, not a theoretical issue. But in Cuban revolutionary praxis, the two were very close, and the issue was part of a theoretical debate on the nature of labour in a socialist society, a debate which invigorated the Cuban Revolution and is closely linked with the name of Che Guevara. So the film-makers thought hard about their labour process, and the question of how the film crew should be organised in a socialist society, in order to overcome the alienation of the capitalist mode of film production, and to release not just individual, but also collective creativity. Julio García Espinosa spoke about this in a particularly appropriate place – the Chilean cultural magazine *Primer Plano* in 1972.[16] ICAIC's advantage, he said, was having the endorsement of a revolution, that is, of knowing that they were working not for an exploiter but for the country. It was helpful to them that they were mostly young and new to the medium, although there were also a few older people, mostly technicians, accustomed to capitalist relations of production, with its overtime payments and the rest. Overtime was one of the first problems they tackled, because it induced people to work slowly to earn more money, and thereby damaged the collective. They instituted instead a system of bonus payments for completing the work schedule (*plan de trabajo*). This indeed fostered a more collective attitude towards material reward. But it was only the first stage, because the next was the debate about moral incentives which Che stimulated.

Collective discussion produced concrete improvements to the labour process. For example, they discussed the case of the director who used time arbitrarily, who came along and asked the construction department for a wall to be built for the next day's shoot, and after they worked all night, he used only a small part of it in the shots he devised. So to find more effective and economical methods of working, ICAIC tried to develop a method of participation. They defended the prerogatives of creative imagination, but required discipline in its application. The result was to help overcome the problems of divided labour, because it also required the members of the different departments in the film crew to relate their specialisms to parallel problems in other departments, which in regular capitalist film production are often kept separate.

To meet the principles of collective participation, ICAIC evolved a managerial system in which, while decisions are made by a directorate who have various collective and individual responsibilities, these decisions are based on collective discussion. In 1983, the year after Julio García Espinosa succeeded Alfredo Guevara as head of ICAIC, one of the directorate, Jorge Fraga, for some years head of production, explained to a group of visitors from Britain some of the ways collective discussion in the Institute works: 'We don't plan anything without first having a collective debate with the directors, cameramen and everyone else involved. We base our planning on their consensus. If we are increasing production, notwithstanding the kind of restrictions we have, it's because in the last year we've made an agreement to make cheaper films in order to do more.'[17] In the same way, the pursuit of related themes in a series of films by different directors over the same period, like those on the hundred years of struggle which were made in the late 60s, are the result not of some kind of directive but of collective discussion, and the consensual feeling that there is more to be gained by making films which support each other than by films which in their choice of theme remain isolated.

Individually, the selection of films is based on treatments, or scripts in the case of fiction, submitted by directors (or for first films, which are always documentaries, by members belonging to other grades) to the head of the appropriate department. Ideas are discussed, and advisers may be called in, who are drawn from among the directors or scriptwriters with most experience. Among the benefits of this system, directors are always at work and earning their salaries, a necessary provision when resources are limited and only a few films can be shot at the same time. This way, you are either working on your own script, on the basis of an agreed proposal, or else you are working with someone else on theirs. Each project goes through several stages, from synopsis to treatment to script, which aids the process of planning and organisation. It also helps to stimulate discussion, Fraga said, because there's no cutting away at final results, which is the role of a censor: 'If you work in the process from the start you're more constructive, you're part of it, trying to stimulate and seek solutions.'[18] Alea has also spoken of the importance of the role of the adviser in this process. Trying to explain why the North American film critic Andrew Sarris was way off the mark in certain comments he'd made, he told Julianne Burton: 'For me, this work is just as important as my own personal achievements. I firmly believe in our collective work. In order not to appear saintly, like some extraterrestrial being removed from all personal interest, let me explain: in order to satisfy my individual needs as a director, I need the existence of Cuban cinema. In order to discover my own concerns, I need the existence of the whole Cuban film movement. Otherwise, my work might appear as a kind of "accident" within a certain artistic tendency. Under such circumstances, one might enjoy a certain degree of recognition, but without really achieving the level of personal realization to which you aspire. This isn't a question of personal success, but rather of the conviction that you're giving all you can in an environment where everyone, without exception, has the same possibility.'[19]

Behind the introduction of a system of participation in ICAIC, there lies an undogmatic analysis of the relations of production in the film industry. Fraga again:

> Well, as everybody knows, cinema is a collective art. Even in Hollywood it's a collective art, and this is based on a division of labour. So the main question is how this collective is organised and how the individualities play within this collective. We don't have a norm to determine the way that the individuals and the collective are interlinked. It is different with different directors and different people, but in general terms there is a consensus, and the consensus is that art is a very personal process, whether it is an individual or a collective art, and the collective spirit and discussion involved in the various stages of film production cannot replace the role of the personality. We are collectivists because we think that the growth of the personality needs a basic requirement: a collective sense of responsibility . . .

ICAIC combined collective discussion with improvisation. It had to compete with numerous other organisations for scarce resources. The national building and construction programme, for instance, did not allow ICAIC as many new cinemas as they would have liked. They would quietly deliver additional architectural plans, however, in the hope that someone else would miss the deadline. Their initiatives didn't always succeed. On one occasion, in need of specialist technicians, Alfredo Guevara enlisted the help of his brother, a psychology professor, to carry out an investigation to find the year's best technical graduates. They were invited to join ICAIC but failed to turn up. It turned out that the list had fallen into the hands of Fidel, who commended his friend's initiative in organising the investigation but told him, 'I'm sorry, you can't have these people, we haven't got such highly qualified applicants for the sugar industry, we need them there!'[20] It was typical of the way Fidel intervened in questions of the allocation of resources, human and material, about which there are many stories. (His detractors use them as evidence of dictatorial behaviour.)

A major part of ICAIC's work during this period, however, to which resources were systematically devoted, was the organisation of a new Cinemateca, which began in 1961 under Hector García Mesa. Of the old one, nothing remained but the files with its programme leaflets in them. The new Cinemateca was intended, from the outset, to be much more than an archive of Cuban and world cinema, with its own auditorium. Its activities were to extend throughout the island. It was to establish film theatres in other cities where the Havana programmes could also be presented, it was to be responsible for the mobile cinema units, and it was to service and advise the film clubs. It was to succour an active film culture, from which eventually new film-makers would emerge, just as the generation of ICAIC's founders had emerged from the film club movement of the 50s.

In Havana, the Cinemateca took charge of programming the new cinema which was attached to ICAIC's headquarters – an office block in the bourgeois district of Vedado, originally occupied by dentists and doctors. The Institute started out occupying the building's fifth floor but soon took over the rest, remodelled the auditorium next door, and later overflowed into other neighbouring buildings. The Cinemateca opened its doors in 1961 with a season of Soviet classics of the 20s to the 40s, provided by their Soviet counterpart Gosfilmofond, the first time such a comprehensive retrospective had ever been shown in Cuba. There followed other national cinema seasons, from Czechoslovakia, Germany, France and Italy, as well as a world cinema retrospective supplied by the International Federation of Film Societies.

It was an immense task the Cinemateca faced, to generate popular comprehension and preference for a completely different kind of film than audiences were used to. It was compounded by the switch which inevitably occurred when the USA imposed its blockade, and the familiar Hollywood product was replaced by a sudden influx of films from the USSR and the other socialist countries. There was to begin with no great liking for them. For one thing, when these countries first began to send their films to Cuba there were no effective arrangements for their selection. No one in Cuba knew enough about the cinema of these countries to be able to make such a selection, nor did anyone in these countries know very much about Cuba and Cuban audiences. Films were sent – and they had to be shown, because new films were at a premium – that were clearly inappropriate. Perhaps it was not a rich period for socialist cinema and too many poor films got through, but they were mostly disliked because they were too different. How should an audience brought up under the narrowest Hollywood tutelage be able to respond spontaneously to films from such different cultures, with such distinct styles and symbolic systems?

ICAIC did its best to leaven the diet with films from non-socialist Europe, where cinema in the 60s was undergoing a true renaissance. Not that these European films were by any means always easier of access, but ICAIC believed passionately in aesthetic pluralism, in the conviction that the only way for audiences to become more discerning was by having the opportunity and encouragement to see as many different kinds of film as possible. The results of this exhibition policy was renewed attack from sectarian quarters.

Early in 1964 the US trade journal *Variety* gloated ungrammatically:

*'La Dolce Vita' Stirs Tain't Wholesome*
Several years late, Federico Fellini's *La Dolce Vita* is stirring a number of lively debates in Castro's Cuba and adding immeasurably to the artistic excitement in that tight (control) little island. According to a report from Havana, by Maurice Halperin, published in the Jan. 9 issue of the *National Guardian* [a small-circulation left wing weekly that has always been sympathetic to the Cuban Revolution] the Fellini pic started an 'ideological brawl' when *Hoy*, the official organ of the United Party of the Socialist Revolution, editorialised that the pic could not be considered wholesome entertainment for the Cuban working class.

Immediately, 10 directors of the official Cinema Institute jumped to the film's defence in the newspaper *Revolución*. They charged that *Hoy*'s position was like that of the Catholic Church (Ed. note: In the US, the Roman Catholic Legion of Decency gave the Fellini film a 'separate classification' meaning 'morally unobjectionable for adults, with reservations') and like the 'Hollywood Hays Code'. *Hoy*'s position, reported Halperin further, 'was pronounced a "deformation of Marxist-Leninist philosophy".'

No one in Cuba, he goes on, denies the need for the state to control the production or purchase of films because of the lack of foreign exchange. 'The problem is the criteria by which the films to be bought or produced are selected, and in the socialist world, value judgments can be poles apart, as in the case of China or Poland or in different periods of Soviet cinema history . . .

The current movie flare up is part of a general and continuing debate on art and society in which nearly all of the artists and writers who embraced the revolution had always had free access to the competing aesthetic currents of the whole world.'

Halperin reports that the entire Cuban movie scene began perking in 1963 'after a year of movie drought during which people lined up to see beat-up American films pulled out of the archives while Bulgarian, Czech and Chinese features played in empty houses.'

Last year films began coming into Cuba from Italy, France, Japan, Britain, Spain, Argentina and Mexico. 'For the sophisticated moviegoer 1963 was undoubtedly a banner year in Havana. In addition to *La Dolce Vita*, films which were released included Buñuel's *Viridiana* and *The Exterminating Angel*, Wajda's *Ashes and Diamonds*, Kurosawa's *The Brave One* and Richardson's *The Loneliness of the Long Distance Runner*.'[21]

The original piece in *Hoy* was by a senior ranking Communist Blas Roca in his regular ideological question-and-answer column.[22] The ICAIC directors referred to by *Variety* replied in *Revolución*, where they compared Roca's position to the Hays Code and the Catholic List. Alfredo Guevara wrote his own withering reply in *Hoy* itself. 'To men like you,' he wrote, 'the public is made up of babies in need of a wet-nurse who will feed them with ideological pap, highly sterilised, and cooked in accordance with the recipes of socialist realism.'[23] K.S. Karol comments on the episode in a footnote: 'Alfredo Guevara's use of such strong language could only mean that he enjoyed the support of Fidel Castro, his old university friend.'[24] But there's nothing fishy in this: anyone can draw this conclusion from what Fidel said in the 'Words to the Intellectuals'; only Blas Roca hadn't done so.

All along, ICAIC encouraged the development of every strand of promise it discovered, an attitude that entailed the Institute's tolerance towards aesthetic risk, experiment and failure which Alfredo Guevara publicly argued for. The growing pains were only expectable. For a short period they were numerous, and the films mentioned earlier by Canel and Villaverde were not the only casualties. However both these directors went on, like others who failed in some of their attempts, to be entrusted with full length feature films. (Eduardo Manet, for example, whose first feature project in 1961 hadn't even reached shooting.) Few of these pictures were successful. Ulive modestly omits any reference in his article to his own feature, *Cronica cubana* ('Cuban Chronicle'), made in 1963, a story that attempted to show the changes that the construction of a new society involves, which the commentators Torres and Pérez Estremera describe as simplistic. *El otro Cristobal* ('The Other Christopher'), directed in the same year by the Frenchman Armand Gatti, they describe as a pretentious satire on Latin American dictatorships suffering too much from a European vision of its theme.[25]

This film was never given a release in Cuba, though it was shown in France with modest success. Eduardo Manet made *Transito* ('Traffic') in 1964; Ulive describes it as 'a poor imitation of the insouciance of Godard's early films'. Manet's second feature, *Un día en el solar* ('A Day in the Tenement', 1965), he calls 'a hybrid whose least disappointing moments revealed a fruitless attempt to imitate the musical comedies of Stanley Donen' – the film added dialogue and songs to a ballet by Cuba's leading choreographer, Alberto Alonso. Fausto Canel also made two features. The first, *Desarraigo* ('Uprooted', 1965), concerns an Argentinian engineer who comes to Cuba with the intention of incorporating himself into the work of constructing the new society, but his romantic and touristic idea of the Revolution impedes him. Its treatment, says Ulive, was 'hasty, superficial, pseudo-modern' and the film was a fiasco. Canel's second attempt, *Papeles son papeles* ('Paper is Paper', 1966), a comedy on the theme of dollar smuggling by counter-revolutionaries during the early years of the Revolution, was not much better. Jorge Fraga also made two features, following the episode he contributed to *Cuba 58*. *En días como estos* ('In Days Like These', 1964) was based on a novel about the life of voluntary teachers in the countryside and the effects of the experience on a girl of bourgeois extraction. He followed this in 1965 with a theatrical adaptation, *El robo* ('The Robbery'), dealing with a provincial petty bourgeois family during the period of Batista's dictatorship.

Fraga himself considers neither of these films to merit attention.[26] The first of them was pretty aggressively representative of a stylistic modernity inspired by new European 'art' films that many critics found hard to take. García Espinosa later mentioned the film as an example of the pugnacity of the young directors 'who were trying to find an equivalent in the cinema of the modernity which the Revolution signified politically'. Raúl Molina in the *Gaceta de Cuba* compared it unfavourably with the two documentaries on closely related themes which Fraga had made previously, *La montaña nos une* ('The Mountains Unite Us') and *Me hice maestro* ('I Became a Teacher'). The feature was too schematic, he said, in comparison with the power of observation in the documentaries.[27] The criticism is highly significant.

The most unfortunate case was that of Villaverde's *El mar* ('The Sea'). The script, says Ulive, could have been made to work in the hands of a self-confident director, but the film had to be aborted at the last moment when it only remained to make the show print: a costly mistake which was also 'the most drastic measure taken against any film in the entire history of Cuba cinema'. Villaverde, he says, was thrown into deep personal crisis, and shortly afterwards left Cuba with no intention of returning.

Villaverde was neither the first (that was Nestor Almendros) nor the last director to leave ICAIC and Cuba. Canel, Alberto Roldan, Robert Fandiño, the cinematographer Ramon Suárez, Manet, have all left. (Almendros has been by far the most successful of them, though as a cinematographer not a director.) They all made films that were not exhibited. But they were not the only ones, and others, including José Massip, Jesus Díaz and Manuel Octavio Gómez, chose to remain (or rather, it didn't cross their minds to go). Díaz and Gómez both had films that were stopped in the course of production during the late 60s because, like other Institutes, ICAIC's budget was cut during the diversion of resources to the battle for a ten million ton sugar harvest in 1970. These directors did not lose faith in the Revolution because they failed personally or were asked to sacrifice personal projects.

Both Massip and Gómez made promising feature debuts in these years, with *La decisión* ('The Decision', 1965) and *La salación* ('The Saltings', 1966) respectively. Both films possess considerable fluidity though the control of the director is in neither case complete. Curiously, they suggest as models not the French New Wave but the English. At any rate, in spite of the different luminosity of the air south of the Straits of Florida and north of the English Channel, their black-and-white photography by Jorge Haydu and Jorge Herrerra respectively is reminiscent of films like *Loneliness of the Long Distance Runner* and *A Taste of Honey*. Moreover in both the narrative style is rather less florid than in the new French films, more calmly paced, as in the English, and the acting quieter. Both films also have this in common, that they centre upon young couples whose partners come from different social classes, with the consequent disapproval of both their families.

*La decisión*, which is set shortly before the Revolution, opens in a classroom at the University of Santiago de Cuba during a lecture on classical Greek society, a subject ironically contrasted with the tensions and political differences among the students. Daysi Granados makes her screen debut as Maria, an artistically rather than intellectually inclined daughter of a bourgeois family which disapproves of her liaison with Pablo, the best student in the class and a mulatto from a poor background, the nephew of a slave – 'the son of a son without a father' as he describes himself. Their relationship is an awkward one, due to Pablo's pride – the pride of someone who knows that the social order is refusing to give him his due: his colour bars him from getting the university teaching post his academic achievements qualify him for. Pablo is his mother's favourite, and has an uneasy relationship with his brother, who works in the factory managed by Maria's father, where he is active in the struggle for union recognition. In spite of his experience of racial discrimination, Pablo cannot accept his brother's militancy and the argument for revolutionary violence. Through these and other contrasts, the narrative traces a series of structural oppositions – between black and white, worker and student, bourgeois and working class, male and female, struggle and fatalism, mother and daughter/mother and son, high culture and popular culture – by means of cross-cutting between different levels of the plot in different scenes of action. Probably the thing is too schematic, but it comes to a fine heady climax with the contrast between the popular Carnaval and the masked ball of high society which Pablo gatecrashes in disguise, till his identity is discovered and he is forced to flee. Carnaval in Santiago is Cuba's Mardi Gras, but it also carries political associations as the day of the attack on the Moncada barracks in Santiago in 1953, after which the 26th July Movement is named, chosen by Fidel in the first place because on this day the whole population is busy singing and dancing in the streets (or high society masked balls). It here becomes an effective symbol for the popular forces which alone are capable of guaranteeing justice.

*La salación* deals with a pair of young lovers in the early years of the Revolution harassed by the prejudices of bourgeois morality on the one hand, working-class pride on the other. The girl's is a petty bourgeois family not unlike that of *Cuba baila*, the boy's is working class. He is reluctant to get married because with his father dead he has to keep his mother and two younger brothers on a mechanic's wage. Visually stylish, a particularly memorable sequence shows the couple meeting in a large North American style house that stands abandoned by its former owners. Evocative photography follows them entering as the rain pours down outside. Thunder and echoing footsteps intensify the atmosphere. The couple are drawn into this cavernous Freudian space where they seek refuge in order to make love, but which makes them feel distinctively uncomfortable at the same time. The tension they feel is at the heart of the film: the way in which the heritage of the physical environment, shaped by the social relations of the past, interferes with the realisation of desire, and in the most immediate ways. Like García Espinosa in *Cuba baila*, Manuel Octavio Gómez has a keen sense of the social significance of different spaces. This large empty house is contrasted with the crowded environment of the family apartment where the couple have to retreat on to the tiny balcony to gain even a minimal amount of privacy, while behind them the family argues over the volume of the radio and TV sets different people have on in different rooms. This observation of social space – and the mapping on to it of the relationships among the family members, including mothers, cousins, aunts – lifts the rather coy love story out of the dissociation from social reality in which the cinematic genres generally leave such couples. The film shows how the personal preoccupations of young lovers do not disappear in a revolution, and what the social problems of the country look like from their point of view. It has its limitations as a first feature, its style is borrowed rather than thought out, but the intelligence of its social observation combined with its personal concerns is sufficient indication of the breadth of sympathies which ICAIC was cultivating. It is also a memorable film for another screen debut: that of Idalia Anreus in the role of the boy's mother.

## References

1. Alfredo Guevara, 'Realidades y perspectivas de un nuevo cine', *Cine Cubano* No.1.
2. Conversation with Sergio Giral, Havana, January 1980.
3. Conversation with Solás, Havana, January 1980.
4. T.G. Alea, '12 notas...', cit.
5. Conversation with Alfredo Guevara, Havana, September 1978; see also remarks by J.G. Espinosa in Augusto M. Torres and Manuel Perez Estremera, 'Breve historia del cine cubano', *Hablemos de cine* (Peru) No.69, reprinted in the same authors' *Nuevo Cine Latinoamericano*, Editorial Anagrama, Barcelona (no date).
6. Julio García Espinosa, *Cine Cubano* No. 54-5 (cit.), p.12.
7. Quoted in Ulive, op.cit.
8. García Canclini, op.cit., p.196.
9. Ernesto Cardenal, *En Cuba*, Ediciones Era, Mexico 1977, p.164.
10. Interview with Claude Julien, *Le Monde* 22 March 1963.
11. K.S. Karol, *Guerrillas in Power*, Jonathan Cape, 1971, p.241. Karol, a left wing critic of the Cuban Revolution, was heavily criticised by the Cubans when his book was first published in France. As far as its discussion of cultural affairs is concerned, it is certainly in places inaccurate.
12. Alfredo Guevara, 'Sobre un debate entre cineastas cubanos', *Cine Cubano* No.14-15.
13. T.G. Alea, 'Notas sobre una discusión de un documento sobre una discusión (de otro documento)', and J.G. Espinosa, 'Galgos y Podencos', both in *La Gaceta de Cuba* No.29, 5 November 1963.
14. Ulive and Firk, op.cit.
15. Adolfo Sánchez Vásquez, *Art and Society, Essays in Marxist Aesthetics*, Merlin Press, 1973.
16. Julio García Espinosa, 'Antecendentes para un estudio del cine cubano', interview in *Primer Plano*, Ediciones Universitarias de Valparaiso, Vol.1 No.2, Autumn 1972.
17. 'Discussion with Jorge Fraga Recorded in Havana', *Undercut* No.12, Summer 1984, pp.7-14.
18. Ibid.

19. Julianne Burton, Interview with Alea, *Cineaste* Vol. VIII No.1.
20. Conversation with Alfredo Guevara, Havana, September 1978.
21. *Variety*, 12 February 1964.
22. 12 December 1963.
23. 17 December 1963.
24. Karol, op.cit., p.394.
25. Torres and Perez Estremera, op.cit.
26. Conversation with J. Fraga, Havana, January 1980.
27. Raúl Molina, 'En días como aquellas', *La Gaceta de Cuba* No.50, April-May 1966.

# 9

# THE DOCUMENTARY IN THE REVOLUTION

*Affinities and disaffinities with cinéma vérité – Joris Ivens in Cuba – The evolving philosophy of Cuban documentary*

The historical moment of the Cuban Revolution was also, by coincidence, a period of aesthetic revolution in documentary cinema. Within the space of a few years, sixteen millimetre, previously regarded as a substandard format like 8mm or half-inch video today, was relaunched. Technical developments, inspired by the needs of space technology as well as television, stimulated the production of high quality 16mm cameras light enough to be raised on the shoulder and in due course equipped with fast lenses and film stocks which reduced or even eliminated the need for lighting. They ran quietly and could be matched with portable tape recorders fitted with improved microphones, directional if need be, on which a synchronous soundtrack could be recorded by a sound recordist as mobile as the camera operator – though until the improvement of the system they moved around together, since they were linked by cords. The result was that documentarists who had previously been forced to shoot with bulky 35mm equipment completely unsuitable for flexible filming away from a studio or prepared location felt as if reborn. New-style documentary film-makers sprang up on both sides of the Atlantic. Thus the terms *cinéma vérité* and direct cinema were born.

The concepts and practices of documentary go back to three developments of the 1920s: the appearance of a small film avant-garde in certain countries of Europe; the work of a maverick film-maker of Irish descent in North America, Robert Flaherty; and the creation of a revolutionary film industry in Soviet Russia which included the agit-prop of Dziga Vertov and the comrades of the Kino-Train. There was also, at least as far as non-communist cinema was concerned, a catalyst in the person of a nonconformist Scottish intellectual who went to study the emerging mass communication society in the United States. It was he who gave the term 'documentary' its currency when he saw Flaherty's first film and wrote in its praise that it had the force of a living document. His name was John Grierson.

Within the group that he created in England upon returning from the States, Grierson argued for a concept of the form as didactic and social rather than poetic and individual, within which the image was to be employed for its status as plain authentic record of the actual. This aesthetic was based on a thoroughly empiricist philosophy which closely corresponded to certain practices of journalism. Though this is not how he put it himself, Grierson wanted the documentarist to regard the non-fictional image as an authentic document of social reality (to be filmed as artistically as you like but with appropriate discretion) in rather the same way that journalists take documents like parliamentary reports or the sworn statements of witnesses as authoritative and unimpeachable versions of events. For the journalist actually to believe the authority of such documents, however, is plainly naive, and will sometimes cause problems. On similar grounds, the aesthetic which treats the authenticity of the film image uncritically can be called naive realism.

During the Second World War the rather special conditions of official sponsorship allowed a few gifted propagandists, like Humphrey Jennings in Britain, to contribute some artistic development to the form. After the war, the ideals which inspired the first flowering of the social documentary seemed to dissolve (though they find another location in neorealism) and the best documentaries in the post-war years mostly took the shape of individual poetic essays by directors like Franju and Resnais – a form in which non-fictional images provide the substrate for a more or less literary kind of reflection and self-expression. For the rest, the documentary became a merely utilitarian form serving various dominant ideological interests, including educational purposes conceived in a rather mechanical fashion. The exceptions, like Joris Ivens – of whom more below – are very few. As Karel Reisz described one typical prestige product of the genre from the 50s:

> *Song of the Clouds* has some distinguished names on its credits and, the scientific film apart, represents the norm of our documentary industry. From the film-maker's point of view this is particularly disturbing because the film represents the almost complete abdication of the creator in the film, the director. A film of this kind is planned in terms of the facts it will have to present; it is conceived in committee; it has a commentary written by another hand, which tries to give the images a weight they do not have. Under these conditions, the director's function becomes that of a technician.[1]

At the time he wrote this, Karel Reisz was a member of a new documentary movement which anticipated the appearance of *cinéma vérité* in a number of ways, the movement known as Free Cinema – the style of which the defenders of *P.M.* in Cuba in 1961 saw their *cause célèbre* as an example. Free Cinema was originally a handful of young British film-makers of liberal disposition including Lindsay Anderson and Tony Richardson, the same generation as the so-called Angry Young Men, who subsequently became leading figures in British new wave cinema in the 60s, and whose approach to cinema was originally made through film criticism – like that of several French New Wave directors and some of the Cubans too. They presented a number of films together under this banner in London between 1956 and 1959. Stylistically the films were rather diffuse, but they had enough in common to make the group name workable. Although the name was invented largely to attract publicity, it signalled a certain attitude of humanist commitment and sense of artistic responsibility that was real enough, and it quickly caught on among film critics and aficionados. No one in similar circles in Cuba denied that Free Cinema was an important idea. On the contrary, it was regarded as an idea to be discussed and analysed, with arguments for and against its various features. Alea wrote about Free Cinema in an article in *Cine Cubano* at the end of 1960 – before *P.M.* appeared.[2] The same issue of the journal announced the impending visit to Cuba by Tony Richardson, who at that time had just graduated to features where he caused a flurry with his radical techniques, fresh sense of style and challengingly honest content. The Cubans saw Richardson as a representative of the same spirit of aesthetic renewal that was also to be found in the post-war cinema of several other European countries (the Free Cinema programmes at London's National Film Theatre had themselves included two devoted to Poland and France) and he was one of many foreign visitors invited by ICAIC to exchange ideas and, in some more trusted cases, to work with them.

Alea's article was a polemic directed against accepting Free Cinema uncritically. One of the best assessments of Free Cinema made by anyone, its historical significance lies primarily in its implications for the whole constellation of issues about documentary which ICAIC was then debating, in which they went beyond the approach of liberal humanist commitment. Free Cinema, he began, had been translated into Spanish as *cine espontaneo* – spontaneous cinema. This was not, he observed, a literal translation. However it was appropriate enough in the Cuban context, where film-makers no longer found themselves opposing an unfree cinema compromised by its economic and political connections. Free Cinema was obviously important because it was by definition anti-conformist. Its origins lay with a group of young film-makers faced with obstacles to their freedom of expression erected by the commercial institution of cinema: the demand for scripts, actors, lights, make-up, planned camera movements, special effects and all the other ingredients of the 'proper' movie. The Free Cinema group had offered up, in a spirit of opposition, simple fragments of daily reality, modest film essays on things close to common experience. They wanted to use film as a witness of this reality, a testimonial that brought a living document to the screen.

But Free Cinema is only one way of doing this, warned Alea. It was a certain style, characterised by great mobility and agility, in which the film-maker took up position as a spectator and filmed fragments of reality spontaneously, as it unfolded, and without interfering in its unfolding. Afterwards the material took shape in the editing. Its strength was in the way the film thus 'liberated itself not only from various economic and political obstacles, but also largely from the dead weight which the normal processes of film production have to suffer.' If, he said, a certain degree of technical perfection has to be sacrificed to achieve this, what is returned to the audience by way of the invitation to engage with what is on the screen, is more important.

Here Alea is one of the first to express what soon became one of ICAIC's foremost criteria: the conviction that a film-maker's sensitivity to the audience is more important than the achievement of technical mastery, since without it the greatest mastery is pointless. This is a different emphasis from the Free Cinema directors themselves, who were more concerned with the personal artistic aspirations of the individual director. Alea was unquestionably in favour of spontaneity and the rewards of the feeling of creative freedom, but he thought that this in itself was not enough. You must not, he said, as a film-maker, let spontaneity allow you to forget that you're there behind a camera taking up the position of an artist or creator, and that every process of creation implies the modification of the elements it employs, which in the way that this is done gives it the film-maker's individual stamp. Not that this is anything the Free Cinema directors would have denied. On the contrary, this individual stamp was what they were aiming for. But when cultural attitudes are translated from the great metropolis to the artists' cafés of peripheral capitals, their character changes. And what was important to emphasise in Havana at that moment was that artistic creation presupposes, as Alea put it, an attitude in the face of reality which is not impartial. Artistic creation involves judgment, and 'all attempts to portray reality while avoiding judgment on it, are dud. Sometimes this leads to half-truths, which can be more immoral than a complete lie.' Hence Alea's conclusion – prophetic of the problem about *P.M.* – that 'one shouldn't think that Free Cinema is the new cinema . . . Free Cinema is only a new step in a particular direction, of great value but with great dangers.'

Although its example was still alive, Free Cinema as an historical phenomenon was already over when Alea wrote these lines. It was superseded by *cinéma vérité* and direct cinema, which in certain ways it anticipated. These movements began more or less simultaneously on both sides of the Atlantic. In France, a highly skilled camera engineer called André Coutant introduced the enthnographic film-maker Jean Rouch to a camera that had been developed for use in military space satellites for purposes of surveillance by the Paris company Eclair, for which Coutant worked. Coutant knew that Rouch would find more liberating uses for it, especially since it could be paired with one of the new portable tape recorders which could be swung on the shoulder. Rouch had spent ten years making remarkable documentaries in a hand-held camera style he had evolved for himself, but he had been limited by the impossibility of shooting them with synchronous sound because available sound equipment, designed to meet studio needs, restricted the mobility of the camera. You also needed a truck and crew to shoot sound on location. Even if this had been possible in ethnographic settings, for Rouch it defeated the purpose of making a film at all, since to show anything ethnographically authentic you had to be able to shoot *around* your subject and not do what they did in studios: move things around in a way that suited the camera (and the lights and the microphones). The new equipment allowed the development of a distinct and appropriate camera style, which is a necessary feature of direct cinema, just as the elaboration of a new sense of screen space was a necessary part of neorealism. Clearly the two things are not unrelated.

In the United States the English-born Richard Leacock felt a similar frustration to Rouch's. Leacock mistrusted what he called the 'controlled' film, the film that recreated what a director thought a situation should be even in documentary, either because of the impossibility of shooting it as it was, or because a director like Flaherty (he had worked as Flaherty's cameraman on *Louisiana Story* in 1948) had a penchant, even a flair for it. And it's true: this practice had come largely to negate the original idea of documentary.

It was said that the new style fetishised the camera, in the form of the unsteadiness of hand-held shooting, the jerky zooms and going-in-and-out-of-focus which became its trade mark – 'wobblyscope', as the older generation of film cameramen in British television called it (they were all men). The truth is, of course, that it was in the studios that the camera was treated like a fetish, a veritable idol, everything laid at its feet and arranged for its convenience. Yet a certain fetishisation did take place in direct cinema. At the start, you got wobblyscope because cameramen were having to relearn their craft and to begin with they were still clumsy. Then some of them began to cultivate the effects of inexperienced hand-held shooting for their own sake, because you could feel the activity of the person behind the camera in them, moving around within the same space that the image within the viewfinder is part of. But as the skills of direct filming were extended, the persistence of such features arguably became an unnecessary affectation.

Leacock has spoken, however, of how he became fascinated with effects that arose when the situations he was filming in got out of control. He began to find bits in the resulting film which he thought extraordinarily interesting: 'Not because they were clever or chic or anything, but because they were true. They presented you with data to try and figure out what the hell was really going on.'[3] This recalls something Walter Benjamin explained about cinema. Film, he said,

> has enriched our perception with methods which can be illustrated by those of Freudian theory. Fifty years ago, a slip of the tongue passed more or less unnoticed. Only exceptionally may such a slip have revealed dimensions of depth in a conversation which had seemed to be taking its course on the surface. Since *The Psychopathology of Everyday Life* things have changed. This book isolated and made analysable things which had heretofore floated along unnoticed in the broad stream of perception. For the entire spectrum of optical, and now also of acoustical, perception, the film has brought about a similar deepening of apperception. It is only an obverse of this fact that behaviour items shown in a movie can be analysed much more precisely and from more points of view than those presented in paintings or on the stage.[4]

To aim to work up this process of apperception has pretty clear political implications, whether the film-maker sees them or not. For Rouch this took on a particular form. His academic background schooled him in both philosophical and instrinsic problems about observation. He knew the observer had an effect on the observed which could never be wholly eliminated, and which was more and other than what was registered by camera wobbles. For Rouch, the whole problematic of making the film had to become a central subject for it.

The film which gave the term *cinéma vérité* its currency is the film which gave paradigmatic expression to this concern. Rouch used the term, a translation of Dziga Vertov's *kino-pravda*, 'film truth', in the subtitle of *Chronique d'un été*, which he made in 1960 with the sociologist Edgar Morin and the French-Canadian cameraman Michel Brault. Ninety minutes long, the film is a study of 'the strange tribe that lives in Paris'. What emerges, however, is rather different from the kind of thing Vertov meant. *Chronique d'un été* is not so much a dynamic dialectical visual enquiry as an unscripted psychodrama enacted by real persons which is called into play by the camera itself. The film proceeds in a strange way to create its own reality, which only exists because it is the result of the film-makers' activity, the reality of a situation which the camera provokes but which isn't conventional fiction. At the end, Morin and Rouch are seen pacing the halls of the Paris anthropology museum, the *Musée de l'Homme*, questioning themselves about the rights and wrongs of probing someone's emotional crisis, or whether another's account of wartime deportation was not perhaps dramatised for the camera. At the door of the museum Rouch asks Morin what he thinks. He replies, 'I think we're in trouble.' The films ends.

Why they were in trouble emerges from the contradiction in the appeal they made to Vertov. Vertov had not regarded even the most directly filmed scene as in itself cinematic truth. Like the other early Soviet film-makers he had emphasised the importance of montage, which he interpreted not simply as a process of cutting apart and putting back together, but as a fundamental principle of film art which operates on several levels: it applies to the selection of the theme; to its execution; and then to the actual editing of the film. He declared that it is not enough 'to show bits of truth on the screen, separate frames of truth', but that 'these frames must be thematically organised so that the whole is also truth'.[5]

For the new documentarists, however, editing was a necessary evil, to be minimised not only through the greater fluidity of the camera but also by respecting the order of events as filmed, on the grounds that any other order would be 'subjective'. 'In the discourse surrounding direct cinema,' as one commentator puts it, 'editing (montage) is cast as the villain of cinema's quest for the holy grail – regarded as a distortion, a formalist cul-de-sac.'[6] The Cubans were highly suspicious of such dogma. They did not at the time of the Revolution know the work of Vertov, but they quickly rediscovered his principles. Perhaps this is not surprising. Their own explanation is that these principles come from the creative and dialectical application of Marxist thinking to cinema within the context and process of a revolution. This is surely how Alea arrived at the view he expressed in his Free Cinema article, that since reality is forever changing it presents an infinite number of aspects with their own multiple antecedents, which must somehow be taken into account. Such thinking is also entirely congruent with criticisms which came to be made of *cinéma vérité* by independent Marxist thinkers in Europe, like the remarks which Lucien Goldmann directed at *Chronique d'un été*: as a sociological piece of work, he explained, *Chronique d'un été* has serious limitations, though it did, he commented, go far enough in its chosen method to imply 'a justified criticism of the very large number of imaginative works which lose all contact with reality while at the same time posing as realist'. However,

the root of Morin and Rouch's preoccupations was precisely to avoid the arbitrary, to grasp actual reality, to get the truth. But precisely at this point, we fear that they have come up against a major methodological difficulty which was long since pointed out in the methodological works of Hegel and Marx: when it's a question of human realities, the truth is never immediate, and anything which is immediate remains abstract and, for that very reason, stained by inexactitude as long as it is not inserted into the whole by a number of more or less large and complex mediations.[7]

The film is really a kind group therapy, its characters entering into its unconventional fiction in the name of a special kind of truth, with the self-consciousness of a very particular cultural and intellectual world. This is where it gets the idea of self-reference from, like the incorporation of the responses of its self-searching participants. Who were they, then? One was a young student who began a few years later to get deeply involved in the Cuban Revolution and the liberation struggles of Latin America, who in the film is just called 'Régis'. In 1967, imprisoned in Bolivia as an associate of Che Guevara, Régis Debray recorded his memory of those days: 'With the academic year measuring out our seasons and weeks,' he wrote in his *Prison Writings*,

we could stroll around the streets of the Latin Quarter with nothing to worry about except ourselves and our salvation ... we roamed about the Sorbonne in groups, as we met to found a magazine, or work out a manifesto, or drink a beer ... we were the hopeless prey of eroticism, little in-groups, literary journalism and the *cinémathèque* ... We also learnt, for we were good pupils, that the sirens of ideological error are always singing, on the cinema screen, in novels and in the street, and that few scholars are wise enough to close their ears fully to them. So, to save us from ourselves, we were taught to mistrust our own credulity and our enthusiasms, and to lay in a supply of ear-plugs as a protection.[8]

The very achievement of *Chronique d'un été* in communicating this world – from the professors' point of view – also made it a completely unlikely model for the critical but enthusiastic cinema which the Cubans needed, with or without the appropriate gear.

The preoccupations of Jean Rouch were also remote from the concerns of the Anglo-Saxon North Americans. The year afer *Chronique d'un été*, Leacock, D.A. Pennebaker and Albert Maysles went off to find out what was going on in Cuba, the first of many film-makers from the metropolis to do so. But they too got into trouble, and the film they made shows how easily ideological compromise was able to swallow up the new principles. *Yanki No!* allowed people abroad to hear Fidel Castro speaking for the first time, but bowing to the demands of television for which it was made, it overlaid a commentary which undid much of what the film-makers intended: over shots of people on their way to a rally, the narrator intones 'Now the Revolution is going to stage a show'; and about Fidel: 'Fidel Castro, who looks like a raving madman to North Americans, is seen by Latin Americans as a sort of messiah. Now you will see him at his messianic best.'

In fairness, Leacock was both an old Communist and a member of the Fair Play for Cuba movement that sprang up in 1959 within the emerging New Left in the United States. (The left-wing journalist K.S. Karol shared a table with him at the 'Fair Play for Cuba' meeting on the eve of Fidel's UN address in 1960, where they met Fidel and the rest of the Cuban delegation.[9] Cartier-Bresson was there and took photographs.) But the film is caught up by the limitations of the radical liberal ideology which dominated this movement, and which led the film-makers to compromise in the interests of getting the film on to television. This is not to say they necessarily knew what the effect would be – it was early days for such endeavours – but such experiences taught them to hate television.[10]

It was a Frenchman, Chris Marker, who made the film the Cubans themselves regarded at the time as the best documentary about the Revolution: *Cuba Si!*. The title alone spells out the difference from Leacock's film. Where the North Americans aimed to shock their audience into realising the way Washington policies were estranging what was previously thought to be a docile country, Marker identified completely with the Cubans and made a celebratory film. 'Shot rapidly in January 1961,' he wrote in the preface to the published script, 'during the first period of alert (you know – at the time when the majority of French papers were hooting over Fidel's paranoia in imagining himself threatened with invasion), it aims at communicating, if not the experience, at least the vibrations, the rhythms of a revolution that will one day perhaps be held to be the decisive moment of a whole era of contemporary history.'[11] Even pretty severe critics of *cinéma vérité* have admired this film – which was banned in France – for its poetic qualities. But then Marker was not one to restrict himself by purist notions of film art. Already in *Letter from Siberia* he had incorporated newsreel and travelogue footage, still photos and even animated cartoons. At one point in *Cuba Si!*, in a scene of Fidel speaking, he inserts shots from an old Robin Hood movie – a more affectionate and more filmic way of commenting on Fidel as a living legend than the heavy-handed commentary of *Yanki No!*. Montage effects like these are entirely alien to the aesthetics of purists (each in his different way) such as Rouch or Leacock. But they are soon to become a characteristic feature of Cuban documentary, especially in the work of Santiago Alvarez.

Cuba became a subject of great interest to practitioners of the new documentary because the whole circumstance of the Revolution made a great deal much more directly available to the camera than was normal elsewhere. And because it was a symbol of the throwing off of shackles which was part of the spirit of the new documentary too. For the Cubans themselves, however, it was not primarily a matter of style or technique. Alfredo Guevara wrote in *Cine Cubano* in 1960, a couple of months before Alea's Free Cinema article, about a process of discovery that began with two films by Julio García Espinosa, *Sexto aniversario* ('Sixth Anniversary') and *Un año de libertad* ('A Year of Liberty').[12] Both of them, because of the speed of change of events, had to be re-elaborated during editing. The second, said Guevara, was the more difficult to make, because it used newsreel and archive footage which was very poor in narrative quality. But by reworking it they found a narrative method for the film which took them away from the bare chronology of the old propaganda material they were using. This way they managed to construct a certain historical understanding of the events portrayed. They made their minimal resources work. How had this been possible? asked Guevara. Expertise at the editing table? The use they made of dissolves and shock cuts? No, it was the conception of events which they'd had to get right, in order to give the editing technique direction – in this case, the technique of montage.

Guevara's attitude here is the twin of Alea's and implies the same criticisms of direct cinema. This way of treating material is strictly anathema in direct cinema, not simply because of the prohibition on interfering, but because direct cinema avoids the use of found material. Guevara believes, however, that you need a critical conception of events to make a film, the kind that is summoned when you rework material, looking for a way to turn it inside out to find what was previously hidden within it. This makes you realise that appearances are liable to be both truthful and deceptive *at the same time*; and that therefore the only guarantee of cinematic truth lies beyond the lens. Better to violate aesthetic theories, felt the Cubans, in order to make the subject more intelligible, because truth is always served by its more effective communication, and communication is part of the political purpose of the film.

What is common to the approaches of Cuban documentary and direct cinema, *cinéma vérité*, is the aim of liberating documentary from the conventions of commercial film, such as insistent but insensitive background music, swish editing based on misplaced codes of fictional narrative, the alienation and paternalism of the commentary (not that the early ICAIC documentaries entirely avoid these ills); and the conviction that reality is not so elusive that it cannot be induced to show itself. Crucially, there was also the aim of returning documentary to the centre of attention in cinema – in which by the end of the 60s the Cubans had succeeded as no other cinema has done, with feature-length documentaries becoming regular fare in Cuban cinemas. But the way the Cubans arrived at this position strongly suggests that even if they had had the same technical resources as in the metropolis, they would still not have developed a documentary cinema substantially different from the one they did. They had good reasons for rejecting dogmatic or extreme versions of any style or aesthetic. Rouch's way of thinking was unappealing to them because with him, under the guise of objective investigation, there lurked a certain individualistic subjectivism. Rouch once expressed the notion that the best result of further technical advance would be to let the film-maker work completely alone; but this dream of realising what the French critic Astruc called the *caméra-stylo* ('camera-pen') amounts to little more than saddling the film-maker with the traditional role of the author. In Cuba the whole problem was how to break down the isolation of the author, not how to bring the film-maker to approximate to it. What does this isolation have to do with revolutionary politics and ICAIC's concern to foster collective consciousness?

Or take the idea of the camera obtruding as little as possible. Here the Cubans saw a failure in dialectical reasoning. They also suspected the need for subterfuge. They were not themselves primarily interested in people forgetting the presence of the camera in order to see them 'as they really were' (even if the results could be very interesting): they wanted people to accept the presence of the camera and of the film-makers, in order that they should open up and share their experience, through them, with others. What this needed was not better technology to make films with, but better conscience in making them.

Among the pioneers of direct cinema, those the Cubans would have found most sympathetic were the French Canadians. For their situation as members of a national minority living under the cultural as well as the political hegemony of the Anglo-Saxon-Nordic empire was the closest to the situation the Cubans were beginning to leave behind. 'When we try to find out what the problems of our culture mean,' said Gilles Groulx, 'we become aware that our uneasiness is not artistic but social: we might call it the attempt to express the man born in this country.'[13] This could be a Cuban speaking.

The fact is that ICAIC was far more disposed to learn about documentary from the veteran socialist film-maker Joris Ivens. 'There is nothing surprising about Ivens' presence in Cuba,' said *Cine Cubano* in November 1960 (the issue before Alea's Free Cinema piece) of Ivens' visit earlier that year. 'Wherever there's a country struggling for its freedom, a people trying to liquidate the old structures and forge a sane and healthy future where man can find and reclaim his dignity, Ivens will be present. And as a creator, not a tourist.'[14] Ivens, whose principal films had been prohibited in West Germany, France and Italy, who had filmed in Spain during the Civil War, in China during the war against the Japanese invader, who had voiced a cry of alarm over the Dutch Government's intentions against the young Indonesian Republic at the end of the Second World War and thus become an undesirable in his native country, Ivens represented an ideal the Cubans could readily identify with – the participant witness who wielded the camera with the precision of a rifle. They invited him not just to make a film about the Revolution but also, as he modestly describes it himself, to impart his experience of making films under difficult conditions.[15]

Though Ivens began immediately upon arrival to give talks and hold discussions with his hosts on the theory and practice of militant cinema, it was primarily through making a pair of films with Cuban crews that his pedagogic flair took effect. The idea for the first, *Carnet de viaje* ('Travel Notebook'), arose from discussion in the first few days of his visit about the problem of how a foreign film-maker, however proven a militant, could possibly film 'The Revolution' when he had only just arrived. (Ivens had been to Cuba once before, in 1937, with Hemingway, one of his collaborators on the Spanish Civil War film, but for present purposes that didn't count.) The idea for the film was that in order to get to know the Revolution he would have to see what was going on in different places around the island; the trip would become the itinerary of the film. The simplest of ideas, only a master like Ivens could bring it off.

The second film, *Cuba pueblo armado* ('Cuba, A People Armed') was made in response to a request by Fidel, whom Ivens met on his second evening in Havana. When Ivens and his crew reached the region of Escambray in the centre of the island, Fidel called to ask if they could interrupt the shooting of the film that was in progress in order to make a film of the People's Militia there, who were engaged in an offensive against counter-revolutionary bands. Fidel explained, said Ivens, that the operation could have been carried out rather more quickly by the Rebel Army but it had purposely been given to the Militia. The Militia commander in the area was not too keen on having to cope with a film crew and it fell to their production manager, Saúl Yelín, to deal with the problem. Yelín, who subsequently became until his death in 1977 what Ivens affectionately called ICAIC's foreign minister, asked the commander to call Havana. Next day his attitude had changed completely – not because he had been given some order from on high but because it had been explained to him why Ivens had been asked to make such a film. He went up to Ivens saying 'Why didn't you tell me you filmed the wars in Spain and China?'

On his second visit to Cuba the following year, while he worked at ICAIC as an adviser and assessor, helping to sort out the teething problems of the new Institute, he was again called on because of his experience in filming military conflict to carry out a special task. He was approached by Osmani Cienfuegos (brother of Camilo) to undertake the training of military cameramen. With the knowledge that an invasion was due, the Cubans realised the importance of being able to film such an eventuality. They also realised it was a task beyond the capacity of ICAIC, though ICAIC would obviously contribute. A remote hacienda previously belonging to an uncle of Batista's was chosen as the site of the school, which was naturally placed under tight military security: Ivens went there in secret (it was said he'd gone elsewhere in Latin America). Faced with the problem of training 50 or 60 students, some peasants, some workers, very few of them with even an amateur photographer's knowledge, Ivens asked for six months. Impossible, said Fidel, we need you to do the job in a month: 'You'll see, our people work day and night.' But Ivens managed to get a concession from him and they agreed upon two.

The real difficulty was how to teach without cameras. Ivens got hold of an old Eyemo from ICAIC and found a carpenter among the students who undertook to make models of it out of wood; these were weighted so as to give the feel of the real thing. He conducted exercises with these models, and in the absence of real film to show results, each student had to recount to the others the pictures he had pretendedly taken. Ivens explained to them the way he had filmed in the Spanish Civil War and the students constructed a model of the battle in question and worked out how the filming could have been improved. One result was that the Rebel Army thus re-entered the arena of Cuban cinema. In subsequent years the Cuban armed forces have not only made their own instructional films but have also made a significant contribution to Cuban documentary in collaboration with ICAIC in the shape of a number of front-line reports on liberation struggles in Africa.

Ivens spoke to *Cine Cubano* at the end of his first visit about what he had seen in Cuba. It is not difficult to see why his approach was readily appreciated:

Among the men and women who represent the Cuban Revolution you can see the desire to manifest clearly the dignity and meaning of the idea they're defending . . . I saw this example of dignity – and it impressed me – not only in the struggle of defence but also in places of work. In co-operatives, in industrial centres, you noticed the decision which the whole people put into constructing their own destiny. If I can be allowed to offer young Cuban film-makers any advice, I would say that this represents the best filmic lesson for them. They should forget about the problems of technique and style. They will acquire these things with time. The important thing for now is to let life into the studios and not become bureaucrats of the camera. Film quickly and as directly as possible everything that's going on. To accumulate burning hot direct material can be considered the best way to get to a cinema with national characteristics. [16]

Direct filming comes into this not as a normative stylistic principle – Ivens says don't worry about questions of style – but as a way of making the film-maker answerable to the ideals of the Revolution as they are lived out by those around them. As ICAIC developed, this idea – though doubtless Ivens wasn't its only source – became the linchpin of its system of apprenticeship in which all directors in ICAIC up to the present have been required to serve in either documentary or newsreel work.

One of the members of Ivens' film crew in Cuba wrote a diary of the filming for *Cine Cubano*. The first thing Ivens taught them was how to look afresh at their own countryside. The Cuban countryside is a great problem for the cinematographer, wrote José Massip:

This green which is so beautiful to the human eye is not so to the mechanical eye of the photographic lens. With black-and-white film, the different shades of green are lost in a dark and undifferentiated mass. This means, for example, that if the dramatic quality of an action is accentuated in nature by the countryside behind it, this emphasis will be considerably reduced on the screen.

The solution to this problem probably consists in finding an appropriate relationship between the landscape and the sky. Cuba's sky could be the salvation of its countryside. Ivens could not remember a sky to compare with it. Its astonishingly rich plasticity comes not only from its marvellous shade of blue but above all from the extraordinarily varied shapes of its clouds. The sky, wisely included in the composition, can cancel the betrayal of the green.[17]

Massip goes on to recount lessons Ivens taught in how to photograph things so as to suggest the process of change; the importance of using the bottom third of the frame, the 'forgotten area' in the pictorial composition of the film image; how to capture special aspects, moments and relationships in a scene. The camera-man Ramón Suárez added a note which mentioned among other things the importance Ivens placed on faces. Here Ivens was passing on a lesson he himself had learnt from Russian workers when he first visited the Soviet Union in 1930. When he showed them his avant-garde film *Rain*, 'It seemed to them', he wrote in his autobiography,

> that I had fallen in love with reflections and textures. They said *Rain* showed too little of human reactions and concentrated too much on objects. One challenging remark was – 'Why are you afraid of faces? If you could look at a face with the same frankness with which you look at a raindrop you would be wonderful.' This reaction made a deeper impression on me than when audiences compared the lighting and composition in *Rain* with that in Dutch genre painting.[18]

Still, from what he taught the Cubans, Ivens had clearly not allowed himself to forget that lighting and composition were of primary importance, only as means not ends. In a third article, Jorge Fraga noted how Ivens did not follow a rigid work schedule but instead often filmed intuitively, grasping passing moments. He re-enacted things only if it was necessary not to lose a shot or because it was the only way to get the image in question, and then he always did it in the simplest way possible. Fraga also noted Ivens' constant awareness that the 'phrases' of montage, the 'expressive moulds' of film language, are historically conditioned aesthetic categories, and that he preferred spontaneity to irrupt into the frame rather than adhering to classical rules of composition; and that he kept his camera almost always in movement.

These reports in *Cine Cubano* were one of the means adopted in ICAIC to transmit the lessons learnt by those chosen to work with Ivens to the others. A later issue of the magazine includes a transcript of a round-table discussion on Ivens' work which was another such means. ICAIC organised itself from the outset to provide an environment of a kind to facilitate the collective assimilation of experience. This work is carried on at two levels, for *Cine Cubano* and the Cinemateca reach the broad aficionado public, while there are also internal publications and ICAIC's in-house cine-debates, in which all their own productions and selected foreign films are discussed among a range of production workers – directors, producers, editors, camera people, etc. The oral history of ICAIC is alive in these debates, and more, for just as *Cine Cubano* is a journal not only of Cuban cinema but of the whole New Latin American Cinema movement, so too other Latin American film-makers, both visitors and exiles to whom ICAIC has given a home, take their places in these debates as respected comrades. Even the visiting film critic researching the history of Cuban cinema is invited to participate in the debate, which is conducted at a high and wide-ranging level, without neglect of detail and without shunning either polemic or stringent criticism. These debates, which date right back to the early years, have helped to forge the sense of collectivity in ICAIC and provide a means of mutual instruction.

Many of Ivens' practical lessons were by these means pretty rapidly and effectively disseminated but it is also clear that the most important lessons ICAIC drew from Ivens were human rather than technical. The human content of Ivens' example has been well summed up by Tom Waugh in an excellent account of the veteran film-maker's two Cuban films. He mentions the filming of a conversation between two militiamen guarding a bridge which appears in *Cuba pueblo armado*:

> At the time of the shoot, the crew were struck not only by Ivens' instinctual recognition of a good scene and of 'natural actors' but also of the way in which he was able to make the two subjects feel comfortable and trustful with regard to the camera... His... secret for bringing out the 'natural actors' in such subjects was his authentic respect for them, his involvement with them as human beings rather than as subjects.

To this effect, Jorge Fraga remembered a heated argument between Ivens and a peasant that he at first found shocking because of the obvious social disadvantage of the latter. But he suddenly realized that it was rather a total absence of paternalism and sentimentality that was responsible for Ivens' attitude, his assumption of the peasant's equality despite social and cultural barriers. Ivens' attitude was essential to the active collaboration between artist and subject in his work, which the Cubans greatly admired, a clear challenge for Havana intellectuals such as Fraga and Massip. The triumph of Ivens' approach came when he attempted to persuade captured counter-revolutionaries to re-enact their night-time surrender... The prisoners, no doubt bewildered by the Communists' generous treatment, consented and can be seen in the film emerging from the jungle, hands above their heads.[19]

*Historia de una batalla*, ('Story of a Battle'), by a director who had no direct

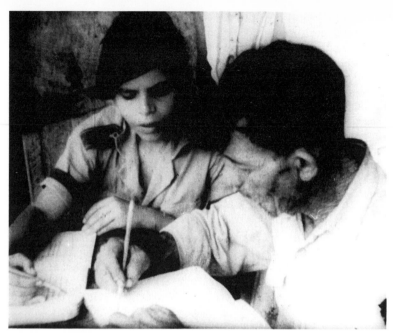
*Historia de una batalla*

contact with Ivens, Manuel Octavio Gómez, shows how widespread his influence was and how much he helped ICAIC find its feet. The battle in Gómez's film is the literacy campaign. The metaphor of the title is not an invention of the film but is taken from the campaign itself, for the sheer scale of the undertaking – to eliminate in a matter of months an illiteracy rate that at its highest in the countryside was anything up to 43% – required a quasi-military form of organisation; though not, as we can see from the film, one that was particularly militaristic.

The political import of the campaign was established at the outset when a young volunteer teacher was assassinated by counter-revolutionaries. A few days later Castro announced that schools would close on April 15th and 'an army of 100,000 literacy workers' aged 13 and over would set out to live, work and learn with the poor and humble of the land. It is the image of these children leaving for the countryside in their brigades (while adult literacy workers took on the job in the cities) that opens the film and sets the tone. The film concentrates on the role of the children not only because it was their participation that provided the most graphic possibilities but also because the experience which challenged them was the very stuff of revolutionary social change. The encounter of city children, mostly middle class, with peasant life and values would be a learning experience for them as well, far beyond the immediate purpose of the campaign. It was a challenge too to their parents to let their children – girls as well as boys – leave the safety and comfort of their homes to spend weeks and months with strangers in possibly dangerous circumstances. Indeed towards the end of the campaign there were further assassinations of *brigadistas* (brigade members) by counter-revolutionaries, to which Fidel replied by declaring that the revolutionary response to the attempt to sow terror among the families of the *brigadistas* was to refuse to call home a single one of them. But this was only the most dramatic of the dangers. The scenes in the film of mothers tearful as their children depart evoke their trepidation as they steel themselves to let the Revolution shatter the *mores* of the past. In fact, it was through participation in the campaign that a whole generation of children was able to join the revolutionary process with which they so eagerly wanted to identify. Richard Fagen calls the experience 'a revolutionary rite of passage, their first opportunity to prove that they were fully-fledged revolutionaries'.[20]

UNESCO was impressed when it made an independent evaluation of the success of the campaign the following year. (The illiteracy rate had been reduced to the level of a metropolitan country.) This film, however, is not an empirically evaluative report. The campaign was a testing ground for many of the ideas which were later to be incorporated into the revolutionary style of governance through mass participation, and it became an essential step in a process of civic education which brought about not only literacy but political awareness, a deeper understanding of national problems, a new concept of citizenship and its rights and responsibilities, a new willingness to work for the transformation of the old society. The film is a celebration of all this, which through celebrating it becomes part of it. Hence the interweaving in the film of mass demonstrations, the speech by Che Guevara at the UN, and the events of the Bay of Pigs, images which are presented not as background but as the expression of the play of social forces among which the Literacy Campaign is another.

The Peruvian critic Mario Tejada, observing that the early ICAIC documentary directors lacked sufficient dominion over filmic language to match the magnitude of the subjects they filmed, singles out this film (together with *Muerte al invasor*, 'Death to the Invader', a report on the Bay of Pigs by Alea and Alvarez) for achieving an epic quality.[21] Yet at the same time Gómez personalises his subject in the manner that was taught by Ivens, by picking out individually significant details within the overall scene in front of the camera. It isn't just the generalised anxiety of mothers as their children depart, and the joy of the reunion when they return, but the particular woman searching a parade of *brigadistas* for her child somewhere in the middle of it, or the camera following a *brigadista* home to film the doorstep embrace. The influence of Ivens is also to be felt in the lyrical-poetic commentary. Ivens has made this kind of commentary into something of a fine art, in films like *La Seine a recontré Paris* (1957) which employs a poem by Jacques Prévert, or *A Valparaiso* (1963) with its commentary by Chris Marker.

The rapid expansion of ICAIC's documentary output, from four films in 1959 to twenty-one the following year and forty in 1965, makes it a hopeless task, because of the sheer volume of production involved, to attempt to survey these films individually without looking for a way to categorise them. Inspection of the catalogue with this aim yields half a dozen or so main thematic categories, some with internal subdivisions. The two largest groups are:

first, films on the revolutionary process, including mobilisations, struggle against the counter-revolution, social transformations, political subjects proper and the history of the Revolution;

second, didactic films: this covers an enormous range of topics, from artificial respiration to the domestic flea, the origins of the human species, surgical operations, genetics, agricultural methods, hygiene, machine maintenance, etc. These are followed by:

third, another large group of films dealing with cultural and artistic subjects: music and ballet, architecture, painting, handicrafts, etc.;

a fourth group comprising social history and the observation of Cuban character and social life, subjects that are frequently related to the third group;

fifth, a group of films related to the first category, which treat of the revolutionary critique of capitalism and imperialism, of international solidarity and the principles of internationalism, including coverage of liberation wars;

sixth, a group of films on the subject of women;

and seventh, sport.

A group of students in Havana, using ICAIC's own Cuban-asssembled computer, have analysed the Institute's documentary output over the years 1959 to 82. Their findings were reported by Mario Piedra in *Cine Cubano*[22]. Using thirty-three thematic categories divided into nine broad groups, they found, for example, that documentaries on working-class themes, the largest group, represented 24.27% of the output, those on 'artistic culture', 20.38%. The problem with this kind of approach is that it neither takes account of the stylistic variety of the films, nor does it have any way of dealing with films which belong to more than one thematic category. A film like José Massip's *Historia de un ballet* ('Story of a Ballet', 1962) is a film about artistic culture but it has significant overtones of social history. Nor is it just a matter of viewing the film and deciding which is the correct emphasis. It is partly a conceptual problem. Is an instructional film on prenatal care, like *Atención prenatal* ('Prenatal Care') directed by Sara Gómez in 1972, to be classified as a didactic film or under the heading of women?

There is another consideration too: the themes which are less often treated are not necessarily less important. Films themselves are of different weight. A major film on a given subject may have more effect than half a dozen films with more modest intent – though also, a wholly successful modest film might go further than a botched major one. Both things have occurred in Cuba. Films dealing directly with the need to promote the equality of women and advance their position have been relatively few, but several have been substantial films which in their moment received considerable attention, like Octavio Cortazár's *Con las mujeres cubanas* ('With Cuban Women', 1974). At the same time, one of the most significant Cuban documentaries of all, not because it attracted attention immediately but because its reputation and influence developed over a period of years, is a six-minute montage experiment made by Santiago Alvarez in 1965, called *Now*.

And then there is the question of what a didactic film actually is. There is a sense in which, within a set of terms referring to subject areas, the category is anomalous, for it delimits not so much subject as treatment. In fact it is an umbrella term which covers a completely diverse range of subjects and refers to the functional purpose of the film. It really belongs, as a category, to a different set of terms altogether, the set which identifies rather than subject, the intention with which the film is made. There is indeed a set of terms of this kind available, it doesn't have to be invented. It does not provide a systematic scheme of classification any more than do subject headings, but it represents the way documentary is thought of in Latin America itself, because it arises directly from the conditions under which film-makers at the receiving end of imperialism have to operate. These terms, of which didactic cinema (*cine didáctico*) is one, are far more aesthetically compelling than what has been suggested so far. Other categories include:

*cine testimonio* – the testimonial film;

*cine denuncia* – the film of denunciation;

*cine encuesta* – the film of inquiry, investigative documentary;

*cine rescate* – the film of historical recovery;

*cine celebrativo* – celebrational cinema;

*cine ensayo* – the film essay;

*cine reportaje* – reportage, not quite the same as investigative film but overlapping with it;

and above all *cine militante* or *combate* – the militant film or film of combat *par excellence*.

This list is not exhaustive or definitive and there is no single source from which it is drawn. They are only the most frequently used of a series of terms which occur across the whole range of Cuban and radical Latin American film writings, that is to say the writings which belong to the same movement as the films themselves, which express its preoccupations and objectives. They can be found in film journals from several countries, including Peru, Venezuela, Chile and Mexico as well as Cuba: *Hablemos de Cine*, *Cine al Día*, *Primer Plano*, *Octubre* and *Cine Cubano* respectively, to cite only the most important of them. The distinctive feature of all the terms listed is precisely their intentional character. They indicate a variety of purposes: to teach, to offer testimony, to denounce, to investigate, to bring history alive, to celebrate revolutionary achievement, to provide space for reflection, to report, to express solidarity, to militate for a cause. These are all needs of revolutionary struggle, both before and after the conquest of power (which only goes to show that the conquest of power doesn't divide things into before and after in the clearcut way that is often supposed, in the mass media, in the careless thinking of daily life, and in what Sartre called 'lazy Marxism'). The only difference is that after the conquest of power the conditions qualitatively change.

Quite likely all of this is what an unsympathetic critic from the metropolis would call propaganda. But then you have to understand not what propaganda is supposed to be, but what it is capable of becoming. Bourgeois ideologies have always equated propaganda with mere rhetoric, the selective use of evidence to persuade, or – as a Cambridge professor once put it – 'a branch of the art of lying which consists in very nearly deceiving your friends while not quite deceiving your enemies'. The purposes of propaganda are usually considered incompatible with what is supposed to be didactic and vice versa – as if the contents of formal education were sacrosanct, indubitable and objectively true. Every revolutionary aesthetic finds this a false and mendacious antinomy. There is a tradition in revolutionary aesthetics which takes the classical concept of rhetoric as the practical art of persuasion much more seriously. (It is not for using rhetoric that advertising, commercial propaganda, is to be condemned, but for the *way* it is used, and to what ends.) Propaganda is the creative use of demonstration and example to teach revolutionary principles, and of dialectical argument to mobilise intelligence towards self-liberation (and if it isn't, it won't be effective for revolutionary purposes). It seeks, and when it hits its target it gets, an active not a passive response from the spectator. Revolutionary cinema, according to the Argentinian film-makers Fernando Solanas and Octavio Getino, 'does not illustrate, document or establish a situation passively; it attempts instead to intervene in that situation as a way of providing impetus towards its correction'. This is one of the central assertions of the essay they wrote about the experience of making the epic *La hora de los hornos* ('The Hour of the Furnaces') in the mid-60s, which they called *Hacia un tercer cine* ('Towards a Third Cinema').[23] There is obviously a didactic element in this, but there is a difference: the aim of teaching is not immediately to inspire action, but to impart the means for the acquisition of more and better knowledge upon which action may be premised. Accordingly there is a difference in revolutionary aesthetics too, from the practical point of view, between the propaganda and the didactic film.

*La hora de los hornos* is a film from a radical Peronist position from which the Cubans were politically distant, but the essay in which Solanas and Getino analysed the functions of revolutionary cinema represents a stage of thinking within the new cinema of Latin America as a movement which bears strong relationship to where the Cubans had reached in their own development. At an earlier stage, ten years earlier, when another Argentinian, Fernando Birri, set up the film school at the University of Santa Fe, he had based the idea of the kind of cinema he was aiming for on two main sources: Italian neorealism, and the idea of the social documentary associated with John Grierson (whose teaching has sometimes had a more radical effect in underdeveloped countries, anyway in the long term, than in the country where it was born). These, however, are precedents conventionally dominated by a naive realist aesthetic, and it's not surprising to find a few years later a Colombian film-maker, Jorge Silva, saying in an interview in the magazine *Ojo al cine*: 'At the inception of the militant film movement, it was said that the essential thing was simply to capture reality and nothing more, and to make reality manifest. Afterwards this formulation began to seem insufficient.'[24]

However it was not as if Birri or anyone else involved meant these paradigms to be accepted uncritically – after all, these models were still European. The way Birri saw it, to apply the humanistic ideas behind neorealism and the social documentary to the context of underdevelopment immediately gave them a dialectical edge. In an interview in *Cine Cubano* in 1963, he explained the function of the documentary in Latin America by means of a play on the word 'underdevelopment' – in Spanish, *subdesarrollo*. In opposition to the false images of Latin American commercial cinema, documentary was called to present an image of reality, as it was and could not in all conscience otherwise be shown. It was thus to bear critical witness and show that it was a sub-reality (*sub-realidad*), that is to say, a reality suppressed and full of misfortune. In doing this, says Birri, '*it denies it*. It disowns it, judges it, criticises it, dissects it: because it shows things as they irrefutably are, not as we would like them to be (or how they would have us, in good or bad faith, believe that they are).' At the same time, 'As a balance to this function of negation, realist cinema fulfils another, one of affirming the positive values in the society: the values of the people, their reserves of strength, their labours, their joys, their struggles, their dreams.' The same values, in fact, that Brecht saw in the working people. Hence the motivation and the consequence of the social documentary, says Birri, is knowledge of reality and the grasp of awareness of it – *toma de conciencia* in Spanish, *prise de conscience* in French. What Brecht wanted his theatre to be. Birri summarises: 'Problematic. The change: from sub-life to life.' In practical terms: 'To place oneself in front of the reality with a camera and film this reality, film it critically, film underdevelopment with a popular optic.' Otherwise, you get a cinema which becomes the accomplice of underdevelopment, which is to say, a sub-cinema (*sub-cine*, like *subdesarrollo*).[25]

This is not just a play upon words. Birri's thinking is informed by both the philosophy and the theology of liberation in Latin America, with their emphasis upon the process of *concientización*, particularly in the work of the Brazilian educationalist Paulo Freire. Freire's philosophical arguments draw both on Hegelian philosophy and existentialism as well as on radical Christianity, but he is thoroughly materialist in his understanding of social reality; what he proposes is a philosophy of praxis. He argues that self-knowledge is only possible because human beings are able to gain objective distance from the world in which they live, and 'only beings who can reflect upon the fact that they are determined are capable of freeing themselves'.[26] In consequence they become capable of acting upon the world to transform it, and through understanding the significance of human action upon objective reality, consciousness takes on a critical and dialectical form. It is never, says Freire, 'a mere reflection of, but reflection upon, material reality'. In the same way, Birri wants to say that the documentary film is the production of images which are not a simple reflection of reality, but become in the act of the film a reflection upon it – first by the film-makers and then for the audience. This is clearly not the position of a naive realist. But it's not the position of a simple idealist either. It can best be called *critical realism*.

A film may thus break through the *culture of silence* – Freire's term for the condition of ignorance, political powerlessness, lack of means of expression, backwardness, misery, dehumanisation, of the popular masses. It can promote the recognition of the condition in which the people live, and the way they are conditioned, and can sometimes even seem to give them their voice. In this way it succours *concientización*, which is only viable, says Freire, 'because human consciousness, although conditioned, can recognise that it is conditioned'. Hence the possibility of popular consciousness whose emergence is at least, if not an overcoming of the culture of silence, the entry of the masses into the historical process.

The power elite of the ruling classes are extremely sensitive to this. Their own form of consciousness develops to try and keep pace. There is always an intimate relationship between the ruler and the ruled (as in Hegel between master and slave). 'In a structure of domination, the silence of the popular masses would not exist but for the power elites who silence them; nor would there be a power elite without the masses,' says Freire. 'Just as there is a moment of surprise among the masses when they begin to see what they did not see before, there is a corresponding surprise among the elites in power when they find themselves unmasked by the masses.'

The conscientious documentarist is bound to serve as a witness in this process of twofold unveiling, as Freire calls it, which provokes anxieties in both the masses and the power elite, and in doing so the very idea of the social documentary is transformed. For in this transitional process, says Freire, contradictions come to the surface, and increasingly provoke conflict. The masses become anxious to overcome the silence in which they seem always to have existed, the elites become more and more anxious to maintain the status quo. As the lines of conflict become more sharply etched, the contradictions of dependency come into focus, and 'groups of intellectuals and students, who themselves belong to the privileged elite, seek to become engaged in social reality', critically rejecting imported schema and prefabricated solutions. 'The arts gradually cease to be the mere expression of the easy life of the affluent bourgeoisie and begin to find their inspiration in the hard life of the people. Poets begin to write about more than their lost loves, and even the theme of lost love becomes less maudlin, more objective and lyrical. They speak now of the field hand and the worker not as abstract and metaphysical concepts, but as concrete people with concrete lives.' Since the middle 50s, film-makers have been in the forefront of this process in Latin America, beginning with the social documentary and moving on to explore a whole range of militant modes of film-making.

Take the idea of *cine testimonio*, testimonial cinema. In fact there are two distinct strands to this idea. One of them is well represented by the Mexican documentarist Eduardo Maldonado, founder in 1969 of a group which took the term itself as its name: Grupo Cine Testimonio. *Cine testimonio* according to Maldonado is concerned to put cinema at the service of social groups which lack access to the means of mass communication, in order to make their point of view public. In the process, he says, the film collaborates in the *concientización* of the group concerned. At the same time, the film-makers' awareness is directed towards the process of the film. The process of shooting becomes one of investigation and discovery which reaches, he believes, its final and highest stage in the editing. The film thus embodies 'the aesthetic approach to *concientización*'.[27]

The other strand to the idea of *cine testimonio* comes from a literary source and is particularly strong in Cuba. The earliest paradigms are found in the *literatura de campaña*, the 'campaign literature' of the nineteenth-century Cuban wars of independence: the memoirs, chronicles and diaries of Máximo Gómez, Céspedes, and others including Martí himself. They are the accounts of participants writing in the heat of the events, with economy of style and aware of their necessarily partial but privileged perspective. These are the same imperatives that Che Guevara followed in his accounts of the Cuban revolutionary war in the 50s and the Bolivian campaign of the 60s in which he died. A striking thing about all these writings is that they always remain extremely personal. Hence, as the Cuban documentarist Víctor Casaus observes, the elegance and melancholy of Céspedes, the outrage and violent jottings of Gómez, the brilliance of Martí.[28]

In Cuba, he continues, this literature was the origin of a genre that took shape in the 30s, in the new and imaginative journalism of Pablo de la Torriente Brau (who died fighting in the Spanish Civil War) and Raul Róa (a historian who became one of the Revolution's distinguished elder figures). Pablo de la Torriente Brau's *Presidio modelo* ('Model Penitentiary'), dealing with his experience as a political prisoner, was an antecedent of testimonial writings by authors throughout Latin America, like the Argentinian Rodolfo Walsh, the Salvadorean Roque Dalton, the Uruguayan Eduardo Galeano. In Cuba itself, the genre has further flowered since the Revolution, and has produced four distinct sub-genres. The first is the journalistic report or chronicle such as César Leante's *Con las milicias* ('With the Militias'). Second are the accounts of their own experiences by non-professional writers, like Rafael del Pino's *Amanecer en Girón* ('Dawn in Giron') – the author was a Cuban pilot during the invasion of the Bay of Pigs. Third, works like Miguel Barnet's *Biografía de un cimarrón* ('Biography of a Runaway Slave'), in which the author transcribes, as an anthropologist, the oral testimony of a man more than 100 years old concerning the experiences of his youth. Lastly, there are works like *Girón en la memoria* ('Giron in the Memory'), by Víctor Casaus himself, which uses a film-like montage technique to bring together a variety of materials, including interviews, documents and press reports, around a particular theme.

These or works like them have served ICAIC directly for several documentary films, but film-makers have also developed their own testimonial sub-genres, says Casaus. The ICAIC newsreel is the first of these because its character as a week-by-week chronicle is not a simple piecemeal record of the events but under the guidance of Santiago Alvarez has become their interpretative analysis. It is obviously essential to the idea of the testimonial that it convey a sense of lived history. This means, in cinema, that the camera is not to be a passive witness. The newsreel has learnt how to insert itself, so to speak, into the events it deals with by breaking the inherited conventional structure of the newsreel form and converting itself into a laboratory for the development of filmic language. This influenced the whole field of documentary, with its already obvious affinities to testimonial literature. However, it is not, says Casaus, a matter of simply translating the written word into the filmic image or, as sometimes happens, using a first-person voice-over to narrate, and the evolution of documentary technique adequate to the re-creation of the literary genre in cinematic terms was not accomplished overnight. The vast majority of the documentaries of the early years of the Revolution, Casaus observes, are today forgotten – the proof that their method did not succeed in transforming the immediate reality into an enduring expression. This was not, according to Casaus, simply because of the inexperience of the film-makers, but rather because of an underestimation of documentary, and consequently the persistence of techniques imported from the fiction film. The films which have survived are the ones which approached the documentary form creatively. In these films, says Casaus, a paradigmatic series of principles can be distinguished. Firstly, rapid and flexible filming of unfolding reality without subjecting it to a pre-planned narrative *mise-en-scène*; second, the choice of themes – the literacy campaign, military actions in defence of the Revolution, the sugar harvest, cultural processses like the mobile cinema – these are all subjects of important documentaries; third, the employment of an audacious and intuitive style of montage, of which the outstanding exponent is Santiago Alvarez; and lastly, the use of directly filmed interviews both for the narrative functions they are able to fulfil and because they provide the means of bringing popular speech to the screen. This was the last of Casaus's four principles actually to be incoporated into the Cuban documentary since the technical capacity for direct sound filming was what the Cubans to begin with lacked.

This essay by Casaus is a piece of reflective analysis of what the testimonial film had already become at the time he wrote it. The ideas behind the didactic film, on the other hand, were actively developed by ICAIC at the same time they were experimenting in the genre itself, for it is a form which acquires particular importance when a revolution achieves power. Since militant film-makers are no longer forced to work in clandestinity or semi-clandestinity, the emphasis of their art changes, the tasks for which their films are intended qualitatively shift their focus, and nowhere is this more marked than in the scope which now opens up for a didactic cinema. As Pastor Vega explained in an article dating from 1970 entitled 'Didactic Cinema and Tactics', when ICAIC set up a didactic films department in 1960, dealing with a whole range of scientific and technical subjects, not all the necessary conditions for such a project existed, 'but it wasn't possible to wait for them... the demands of a revolution which alters the dynamic of history in all its dimensions, leaves no alternative.'[29] ICAIC recognised that it was necessary to create a whole new batch of film-makers without having the time to give them proper training in the shape either of lengthy apprenticeship or more formally in a film school. The films were needed. They would have to learn on the job by jumping in at the deep end. But because of this the didactic film had to become didactic in more than one way. A film on a scientific or technical subject intended to contribute to the training of the technical cadres which the Revolution needed, would also serve the training of the cadres within ICAIC itself.

A film might be needed, for example, on gasteroenteritis. In a similar way to Solanas and Getino's concept of militant cinema, such a documentary is conceived as an intervention into a given reality with the object of modifying it by enabling people to transform it – in this case, by learning how to combat the disease. In order to accomplish this the film has to become a learning experience for the film-maker first, before it can be so for the audience. In this way both become involved in a life-and-death struggle, for in under-developed countries gasteroenteritis is a killer. What the film-maker has to learn takes on a double aspect – there is the subject on which the film is to be made, and at the same time, learning how to make this kind of film. Formally speaking these are two separate functions, but in the circumstances they get completely intertwined. *Cine didactico* then becomes a paradigm for new ways of thinking about film, and again, the original idea of the social documentary is transformed.

The new tasks of the social documentary become the essential training ground in Cuban cinema because the film-maker has to learn to treat reality by engaging with the people the film is for. *Cine didactico* teaches that the value of communication is of paramount concern because the film would achieve nothing if it did not succeed in its primary function, which is instruction (in the broadest sense). This theme is taken up in a paper presented jointly to the National Congress of Culture and Education in 1971 by Jorge Fraga, Estrella Pantin and Julio García Espinosa, 'Towards a Definition of the Didactic Documentary'. The mood at the time of this Congress – four years after Che's death in Bolivia, a year after the Battle for the Ten Million had not quite reached its target for a ten million ton sugar harvest, and Fidel had made rigorous self-criticism – this is a very different mood from the first few years. Euphoria has now given way to pragmatic realism. The joint authors therefore begin by offering to this extremely workmanlike Congress for its consideration the old utilitarian definition of the didactic documentary as an instrument for use by a teacher in front of a class, and proceed to demonstrate the inadequacy of this concept. ICAIC's first didactic films eleven years previously, they say, even those which were not intended to be used as teaching aids, corresponded too much to the functional criteria this model required. 'They were illustrations for a learning situation; it didn't matter whether that situation was real or potential.'[30] This is true. Despite some notable exceptions, those early films had often been somewhat over-deliberate in their style. Flexibility and fluidity take time to learn.

But after a decade, they said, it was time to be critical. Their first concern was that the didactic film conceived this way does not provide the maximum educational efficiency even in the classroom it is intended for, as long as it remains utilitarian and takes the form of exposition of the teacher as its model and example. This is to constrain the medium unnecessarily. Film is an expensive means of cultural communication. It is impossible to make as many films as are needed. Is it legitimate to limit the scope of the films that do get made, when they could be angled to a broader synthesis of functions? Because the synthesis of functions is precisely the method of cinema.

The ICAIC team then proceeded to reconstruct for the Congress the idea of the didactic documentary according to the preoccupations which had been animating their work over the course of the whole decade. Their line of argument is itself eminently didactic. Much of what they say is philosophically grounded in the analysis of commodity fetishism and alienation, which says something about the style of Marxist thinking which had developed at ICAIC, but it is equally significant that they appeal, as professional communicators speaking to a large audience that is made up of both professionals and aficionados at all levels of culture and education in the country, to more popular concepts and ideas. This does not mean talking down, however, for in Cuba even popular ideas are a long way from being the lowest common denominators of the populism of the capitalist democracies. They first take note of the heritage of cultural imperialism. They remind their listeners of the low level of industrial development in the country, consequently of the low level of science and technology, and the inadequacy of the means of communication endowed by neocolonialism. They observe that it is no coincidence that in these conditions serious forms of cultural alienation to be found in the metropolis, such as gambling, lotteries and astrology, make deep and extensive inroads into the consciousness of people in underdeveloped countries. This produces a way of thinking that perceives things only in a dissociated way, only as results, without grasping the processes that create them. Underdeveloped thinking comes to be ruled by a sense of contingency and fatalism, which hearkens back to the magical (but the magical now shorn of most of its previous cultural legitimacy). 'After twelve years of revolution', they say, 'we still find examples of this way of thinking even in our own communications media, mostly modelled after the tendency to exalt results and omit the process which led up to those results.' But cinema possesses the very qualities needed not only to communicate knowledge and skills effectively, but also to educate for a rational, concrete and dialectical way of thinking. Why? Because it is capable of reproducing reality in motion and therefore of demonstrating processes, and further, because it is capable of revealing relationships between items that come from the most dissimilar conditions of time and place. The utilitarian conception of the didactic documentary narrows down this field of potential (like, we can add, any kind of aesthetic prescriptivism, including that of the direct cinema purists). What is more, the result is a dry and boring genre that is sterile and quite ahistorical. Capitalist cinema conventionally deals with the problem of the genre's dryness by adding enticements to the treatment of the film, the way that pills are sugarcoated – a technique known from advertising as 'the snare'. Advertising 'appeals to stimuli which have nothing to do with the nature of the product in order to create more demand for it or stimulate the consumer's interest: sex, desire for recognition and prestige, fear of feelings of inferiority – anything apart from concrete demonstration of the actual properties of the object.' This mentality, which thinks only in terms of selling, becomes all-pervasive, and everything, including ideas and feelings, is reduced to bundles of exchange-values. To fall in with all this was obviously hardly acceptable. The didactic documentary, they said, must break once and for all with this retrogressive tradition, it must link with the urgency of its subjects and themes. The formal techniques employed 'must be derived from the theme and put at its service. It's the old moral demand for unity between form and content.'

Pastor Vega's account of the didactic film has exactly the same moral emphasis, and his arguments are similarly built on historical materialist analysis. The socio-economic transformation created by the Revolution, he explains, has propelled the newly literate peasant from the middle ages into the second half of the twentieth century, to become an operator of tractors and agricultural machinery. This accelerated passage through multiple stages of development which the sudden acquisition of the products of modern science and technology involves, requires a qualitative leap in the process of mass education. In these circumstances the mass communications media acquire the most important functions as levers in the country's development through their catalytic action. The didactic film must be transformed accordingly, throwing off the moulds of the form as it originated in the developed countries and going in search of a new originality which arises from the very different pattern of development of the Revolution. The film-maker must acquire new perspectives and go for a different filmic language than the archetypes of the documentary tradition. The didactic film must be seen as a new aesthetic category, in which the artist and the pedagogue meet – although this only happens if certain imperatives are observed. For the work of the artist and the pedagogue, aesthetic production and teaching, are not identical activities, and in the didactic film certain requirements of both must be met. This disjuncture disappears, however, when immature ideological prejudices which paralyse mental processes are no longer sustainable; as they cannot be, because 'all living thought is anti-mechanistic'.

Many of the principles evolved in the course of development of the social documentary in the new Latin American cinema, and especially in Cuba, have strong parallels with positions that have been taken up within radical film practices in Europe and North America over the same period. The Venezuelan critic Raúl Beceyro is effectively speaking for both when he writes that 'one of the initial tasks of "new cinemas" all over the world has been to destroy certain norms of grammatical construction... A cinema which aspires to establish new ties with the spectators or which intends to modify the role which spectators assign themselves, could not continue to use the formal structures [of what preceded].'[31] But in certain respects the radical film cultures of the metropolis and of Latin America think rather differently.

Both would agree about naive realism. As the French art critic Pierre Francastel had already written in 1951:

> What appears on the screen, which our sensibility works on, is not reality but a sign. The great error which has regularly been committed is to embark upon the study of film as if the spectacle of cinema placed us in a double of reality. It should never be forgotten that film is constituted by images, that is to say, objects which are fragmentary, limited and fleeting, like all objects. What materialises on the screen is neither reality, nor the image conceived in the brain of the film-maker, nor the image which forms itself in our own brain, but a sign in the proper sense of the term.[32]

But what *is* a sign in the proper sense of the term? This is where the trouble begins. Following Saussure, the founder of modern linguistics, as interpreted by structuralists of various disciplines, a strong current within the new radical film theory in the metropolis has come to regard the sign as a very peculiar kind of symbol. As the North American Marxist critic Fredric Jameson has written:

> The philosophical suggestion behind all this is that it is not so much the individual word or sentence [or image in the case of film] that 'stands for' or 'reflects' the individual object or event in the real world, but rather that the entire system of signs... lies parallel to reality itself; that it is the totality of systematic language, in other words, which is analogous to whatever organised structures exist in the world of reality, and that our understanding proceeds from one whole or Gestalt to the other, rather than on a one-to-one basis. But, of course, it is enough to present the problem in these terms, for the whole notion of reality itself to become suddenly problematical.[33]

It becomes problematical, however, in quite a different way from the reality of underdevelopment.

The whole concept of truth is different. Truth, in the structuralist system, says Professor Jameson, becomes a somewhat redundant idea, as it must do when there is nothing to which it can be unproblematically referred. An image in a film, therefore, is not to be thought of as truthful because it pictures something real which at least visually corresponds to it, even though the automatic mechanism of the camera would lead us to believe that there must indeed be some element of truth in this. Instead, it is said to yield meaning only because it stands in a certain relationship to the other images through which it is, so to speak, refracted. The trouble is that the result of this way of thinking in aesthetic practice is often a thin and rigid formalism.

In any radical film practice in the underdeveloped world, truth is far more immediate and material than this. Nor is it a question of the accuracy or fullness of fit of the image to what it pictures, which everyone knows can never be anything like complete. More importantly, it lies in the relationship with the audience, in the film's mode of address, because the meaning of what is shown depends on the viewer's position. This has also been of great concern to radical film theory in the metropolis. The new Latin American film-makers, however, have been worried less about the way the filmic discourse positions the spectator, and rather more whether it recognises where the spectator is already. This arguably requires a more conscientious political attitude on the part of the film-maker.

The biggest difference is in the practice of cultural politics, or more precisely, the cultural-political field within which the film-maker intervenes. In the metropolis, there is little to stop the film, the film 'text', the 'discourses' of cinema, from becoming dissociated objects in themselves. Whereas for the new cinema in Latin America 'the film-maker becomes more and more involved in the process of the masses' and 'the film must become an auxiliary part of this whole formative process'.[34] This is a dialectical affair which promotes a very different attitude towards both the idea and the criteria of truth. Not because the masses are seen as depositaries of truth in the mechanistic manner of lazy Marxism, but because the film-maker is involved in a process of *concientización* in which truth undergoes re-definition. The philosophy of liberation holds this to be an inherent potential of underdevelopment.

## References

1. Quoted in Alan Lovell and Jim Hillier, *Studies in Documentary*, Secker and Warburg, Cinema One Series No.21, 1972, p.138.
2. T.G. Alea, 'Free Cinema', *Cine Cubano* No.4.
3. Quoted in Louis Marcorelles, *Living Cinema*, tr. Quigley, Allen and Unwin, 1973, p.47.
4. Walter Benjamin, 'The Work of Art in the Age of Mechanical Reproduction' in *Illuminations*, Schocken Books, New York 1969 pp.232-3.
5. Vertov, 'Writings', *Film Culture* No.25, 1962, pp.55,57.
6. Mick Eaton ed., *Anthropology – Reality – Cinema, The Films of Jean Rouch*, BFI, 1979, p.42.
7. Goldmann, 'Thoughts on *Chronique d'un été*' in Eaton, op.cit., p.66.
8. Régis Debray, *Prison Writings*, Penguin, 1975, pp.176-9.
9. See Karol, op.cit., p.7.
10. Conversation with Leacock, Paris, April 1980.
11. *L'avant scène du cinéma* No.6, 1961.
12. 'Revisando nuestro trabajo', *Cine Cubano* No.2, p.14.
13. Quoted in Marcorelles, op.cit., p.19.
14. 'Joris Ivens en Cuba', *Cine Cubano* No.3, p.21.
15. This and other details following, conversation with Joris Ivens, Paris, Spring 1980.
16. *Cine Cubano* No.3, p.22.
17. José Massip, 'Cronicas de un viaje, Una lección de cine', *Cine Cubano* No.3, p.24.
18. Joris Ivens, *The Camera and I*, Seven Seas Publishers, Berlin 1969, pp.56-7.
19. Tom Waugh, 'Joris Ivens' work in Cuba', *Jump Cut* No.22, p.28.

20. See Richard Fagen, *The Transformation of Political Culture in Cuba*, Stanford University Press, 1969, p.62.
21. Mario Tejada, 'Introducción al cine documental cubano', *Hablamos de Cine* (Peru) No.64, p.30.
22. Mario Piedra, 'El documental cubano a mil caracteres por minuto', *Cine Cubano* No.108, 1984.
23. Fernando Solanas and Octavio Getino, 'Hacia un tercer cine', *Tricontinental* No.13, October 1969, translated in Michael Chanan ed., *Twenty-five Years of the New Latin American Cinema*, BFI/Channel 4, 1983.
24. Interview with Jorge Silva and Marta Rodríguez by Andres Caicedo and Luis Ospina, *Ojo al cine* No.1, 1974.
25. 'Cine y subdesarrollo, entrevista a Fernando Birri', *Cine Cubano* No.42/3/4, 1963.
26. Paulo Freire, *Cultural Action for Freedom*, Penguin, 1972 p.52ff.
27. Interview with Eduardo Maldonado by Andrés de Luna and Susana Charand, *Otro Cine* No.6, 1976.
28. Víctor Casaus, 'El genero testimonio en el cine cubano', paper presented to seminar on the New Cinema and Literature, 2nd Havana Festival, 1980, in *Cine Cubano* No.101, 1982.
29. Pastor Vega, 'El documental didáctico y la táctica', *Pensamiento Crítico* No.42, 1970, p.99.
30. Fraga, Pantin, García Espinosa, 'El cine didáctico', *Cine Cubano* No.69/70, trans. as 'Towards a Definition of the Didactic Documentary' in *Latin American Film Makers and the Third Cinema*, Zuzana Pick ed., Carleton University Film Studies Program, 1978, p.200.
31. Raúl Beceyro, *Cine y politica*, Dirección General de Cultura, Caracas 1976, p.27.
32. Pierre Francastel, 'Espace et Illusion', *Revue Internationale de Filmologie* (Deuxiéme Année No.5) tome II, 1951.
33. Fredric Jameson, *The Prison-House of Language*, Princeton, 1972, pp.32-3.
34. Interview with Jorge Silva and Marta Rodríguez, cit.

# 10
# THE REVOLUTION IN THE DOCUMENTARY

*Mainly on the work of Santiago Alvarez*

We have seen how it came about that a generation of film-makers emerged in Cuba in the early 60s who were not only committed to the Revolution but also to the task of revolutionising cinema. The very naiveté of the film culture they inherited became an elemental factor in their development. Through the *concientización* which the encounter with the popular audience brought about, they found themselves questioning their own naiveté, and thus became involved in questioning the production of the image. Because of the sense of urgency which the Revolution imparted, they had to do this not so much theoretically as practically. Only this would correspond to the demands of revolutionary politics; it became a priority in the programme ICAIC adopted. As Alfredo Guevara later explained: 'In the beginning we faced the dilemma of either teaching or doing. We lacked time for artistic introspection and decided on making films at once, without wasting time on theory. We began from scratch and filming became our school.'[1] And yet, as we have also seen, the school which the Revolution itself constituted impelled the film-makers into theoretical reflection on the nature of their practice, and even in the early years the level of theoretical discussion in ICAIC was not at all undeveloped.

With the priority of practice went a commitment to documentary. Everywhere in Latin America where film-makers had become active, the concern for documentary was a concern to produce images that questioned reality. The critical realism which fuelled the new Latin American cinema was both an outgrowth and a transformation of the tradition of the social documentary. In Cuba, the problem of creating an authentic popular film culture within the Revolution in place of the heritage of cultural colonisation expressed itself in the question of how to overcome the distance of the screen from the streets which lay outside the cinemas. The key to the solution was to take the naive relationship of the audience to the screen and build on it, transforming it in the process into a collective re-evaluation of the nature, content and status of the image – a process which was to yield some extraordinary films within only a few years.

A couple of documentaries which appeared in 1965 can be seen in historical retrospect to give clear notice of something new in Cuban cinema. The two films are *Hombres del cañaveral* ('Men of Sugar') directed by Pastor Vega, and *Now*, directed by Santiago Alvarez.

*Now* is a film to a song – which had been banned in the United States where it came from – sung by the black singer Lena Horne, a militant call to the black oppressed which employs the rousing tune of the Ashkenazi-Israeli dance song 'Hava Nagila'. Upon this soundtrack Alvarez constructs a powerful collage on racial discrimination in the USA which he had observed during a visit many years before the Revolution, on a trip from Florida, through the Deep South and up to New York.[2] The images in the film's pre-title sequence are of racist incidents in California in August 1965 followed by a photograph of President Johnson meeting with a group of blacks under the leadership of Martin Luther King (whom Alvarez was to eulogise in film three years later after his assassination); a juxtaposition which establishes the film's tone of sceptical irony. This short film essay is impressive not only for the resourcefulness with which it uses its found materials, including pirated newsreel, but also for the syncopation of the editing, which intensifies the insistence of the song and leads up to its militant ending better than it would have done by slavishly following the music's surface beat.

Alvarez's film acquired within a few years the reputation of being a work of great and forceful originality. The impression made by Pastor Vega's *Hombres del cañaveral* was hardly comparable. It is difficult to judge, but the feeling of the present author is that this is because stylistically the film is somewhat self-effacing, the very opposite of Alvarez's bombshell. But it is certainly a film of considerable originality which gives it more than historical interest. The historical context, however, is crucial to its proper assessment: it is a product of the ideological debate led by Che Guevara in the mid-60s about the moral qualities of work in revolutionary society.

It was Che who, to begin with, propelled the Cuban economy towards central direction and control. At the same time, however, he rejected mechanical and over-schematic explanations of the economic forces involved. Some have said that Che was too idealist, or at any rate too voluntaristic, but the Revolution was attempting to transform the forces of production and Che wished to see the process of socialist economic development operate as a force for the creation of a new morality, which would itself feed and strengthen the transition to socialism. Accordingly he argued for moral as opposed to material incentives in the struggle to relieve the island's almost unrelieved monocultural dependency on sugar.

The first few years of the Revolution saw a large migration of labour from agriculture to urban industrial and service employment, in line with the attempt to break this dependency by rapid economic diversification. The expansion of the urban sector was relatively easy because of a large pool of un- or under-utilised resources which included labour. Unemployment in 1958 had been officially rated at 17%[3] – a figure which disguised the truth about rural employment since so many of those who worked in the sugar harvest actually worked only a few months in the year. The rest was known as *tiempo muerto* – 'dead time'. Urban expansion was partly designed to take up this hidden, seasonal unemployment, but it left a problematic reduction in the labour force available for the harvest. The solution ultimately lay in the development of agricultural technology, but because of the difficulties of designing harvesters suitable for the crop, the terrain and the climate, this was a matter for the future. Meanwhile there was need of a system of temporary redeployment of urban labour to agricultural production during the harvest. As Bertram Silverman has explained:

> The type of labour required was the most menial and unskilled. Material incentives would have had to be unusually high to induce urban labour into these occupations. Moreover, the use of wage differentials made little sense because the transfer was frequently of workers from more skilled and productive activities to less skilled . . .[4]

In such circumstances, the idea of mobilising labour through moral incentives was perfectly logical, though there were also certain contradictions which did not escape attention. The moral incentive, if it is to operate truly, cannot be manipulated from above. It must be generated and sensed within the populace. This, says Silverman, is why many Cubans came to ask, with characteristic directness, 'How can you plan voluntary work? Is this not a contradiction in terms?' Abroad, people didn't even ask; the mass media in the metropolis simply pooh-poohed the whole idea, scorning it as one more case of Communist manipulation of the population.

Clearly this was an area where the social documentary had a crucial role to play, as potentially one of the most effective forms in which to militate for moral aims without losing sight of reality – at least if an appropriate new political language could be found. *Hombres del cañaveral* is indeed far from strident agit-prop and the political tract. It's the study of a brigade of voluntary workers from the city at work in the sugar harvest, with no commentary, and a meticulously observational camera. It opens, like *Now*, with an encapsulating juxtaposition: an electric light display spelling out 'Vivan la Paz y el Socialismo' (Long live Peace and Socialism) followed by an image of someone being shot that immediately calls to mind the sacrifice upon which the Revolution is founded. Then come a set of intertitles which inform us that the film was made with the collaboration of one of the urban voluntary work brigades; that the brigade in question, 'Africa Libre' (Free Africa), held first place in the *Emulación Nacional*, the national emulation league table; but this was not the reason why the film-makers had chosen this group as their subjects (though maybe it *was* the reason after all), the real reason was (and then one by one come titles and portrait shots): The Cook; The Driver; The Cane-cutters; The Chief; and all of them. The film is a record of a day and night in the life of the brigade.

In the course of the film's seventeen minutes we see the men at work, with images of their factory in the city cut in to remind us where they've come from; we see them receiving letters from home; see them getting medical attention, washing off the sweat of the fields, and playing cards. They play music and listen to the radio. The style in which all these scenes is presented is curiously reminiscent of some of the wartime films of Humphrey Jennings; in other words, the product of the accumulated experience over more than ten years of the British social documentary. Though Jennings was of course unknown in Cuba, many of the narrative devices in Pastor Vega's film are similar to those of the British documentary, including the simple 'day in the life' narrative structure; though the music in the film gives it, at the same time, a rather different hue. In one respect, however, the film goes beyond the classic social documentary style, and that is in the use of expressionist devices to communicate identification with the feelings of the subjects. The film is one of the very few Cuban documentaries ever to make direct self-reference to the artifice of film-making. The workers have come back from the fields, cleaned up and started to relax. Suddenly the mood is interrupted by a camera slate and the call of 'action' and we are in the middle of a lesson in maths. Eagerly attentive as they are, the men find it difficult to keep up their concentration, and through a series of changing lens effects the screen embodies their weariness.

There is also an affinity between *Hombres del cañaveral* and a film which Santiago Alvarez directed two years earlier in 1963, *Ciclón* ('Hurricane'). *Ciclón* was a newsreel special of twenty-two minutes (double the usual length) using footage shot by a long list of cameramen belonging to ICAIC, the Armed Forces and Cuban television, who recorded the devastation occasioned by Hurricane Flora in the provinces of Camagüey and Oriente, and the subsequent rescue work and clearing-up operations, which were personally directed in the field by Fidel. The film is an example of how far the ICAIC newsreel, under Alvarez's direction, had already come in the space of only four years in the creation of a new concept of the newsreel form. As Alvarez explained in an interview:

A newsreel is essentially a product which provides information. That's clear, but it isn't all. And even though that may be its principal characteristic, this is no reason either to neglect it or to turn it into a social chronicle of socialism, following the usual linear sequence of unconnected news items. My concern has not been to separate out the news, but to join things up in such a way that they pass before the spectator as a complete entity, with a single line of argument. This concern produces a structure that aims at unity. Because of this, many people regard our newsreel as documentary.[5]

In *Ciclón*, this aim is achieved in a quite exemplary manner, not only because the film does entirely without commentary but nevertheless succeeds in constructing the clearest narrative line, but also because of the way it makes an exemplary political statement. The necessarily unplanned actuality material assembled from the multitude of cameramen in different places at the same time has, added to it, only some graphics indicating the path of the hurricane across the island. These graphics are integrated with the images to produce a political statement: at one point, we see the blades of a helicopter revolving in the same direction as the animated hurricane in the preceding graphic, so that across the cut, the helicopter becomes a symbol of command over the forces of nature in response to natural disaster. This, rather than the heroic images of Fidel, is the centre of gravity in the film. Fidel, anyway, doesn't look heroic so much as business-like. Like *Hombres del cañaveral*, the style of the film is also self-effacing, and it was not immediately picked out as innovatory. All the same, it is a film which shows remarkable mastery over what is arguably the most fundamental of the skills of film-making, namely, narration with mute images, here juxtaposed only with music and effects.

A year after *Now*, Alvarez made another significant advance. If *Ciclón* is a pure example of reportage, *cine reportaje*, he now extended this to produce a piece of *cine cronica*, or documentary chronicle. *Cerro Pelado* takes its title from the name of the boat which carried the Cuban sports team to the Tenth Central American and Caribbean Games which in 1966 were held in San Juan, Puerto Rico, where, being a US colony, the North Americans attempted to prevent Cuban participation. By now, Alvarez has developed the basic characteristics of his style. The film is constructed in the form of a chronological visual narration of the events, with minimal verbal commentary, interspersed with sections using montage and captions to expound the political background to the events. The whole is knitted together with music which is used in place of both commentary and direct sound, not just to fill space on the soundtrack but to narrate the film. In order to achieve this, Alvarez not only employs humour in his choice of musical items but also draws on music's own iconography. Shots of the 'Training Centre for Cuba Counter-revolutionaries' in Puerto Rico (as a caption descibes it), for example, are juxtaposed with the fast passage from Rossini's *William Tell* Overture, which naturally recalls the use of this same piece as the title music of the television western *Lone Ranger* series. Alvarez thus calls up the stereotypes of the idiom of cultural imperialism only to invert them, and present the counter-revolutionaries as imitation cowboys; an image at once satirical and deflating, which at the same time condemns the way these people see themselves, modelled on the propaganda myths of the USA.

To say that Alvarez uses music to narrate is therefore to say that he uses the cultural associations of his chosen music (its iconography) to orient the viewer's frame of reference. What he is doing is to politicise the representation through aesthetic means that are at once highly articulate but non-discursive. This, for Alvarez, is a central resource of political documentary, because it is a way of mobilising popular intelligence, which is not merely unformed by discursive intellect but, for this very reason, lies in danger of suffocation by the tricks of conventional commentary.

Various sections of the film are titled with chapter headings. 'This is the boat' is followed by scenes on board of the team dancing on deck. 'This is the enemy' leads into shots of warfare, and is repeated on the right hand side of a divided screen, superimposed over a sequence of newspaper front pages, with moving images continuing screen left, to form a most complex montage between both simultaneous and successive images. The dancing on deck is replaced by the athletes warming up, cut with humour and grace to the music of 'El Manisero' ('The Peanut Vendor' – a Cuban song, composed by Moises Simons, and not, as many people think, North American). Shots of riflemen practising are cross-cut with the ever-present menace of aircraft circling overhead as the boat approaches its destination, which in turn give way to images of warfare in Vietnam and a newsreel interview with a captured USAF pilot.

Another chapter heading introduces 'The site of the Games – Puerto Rico, "freely associated" Yanqui Colony', and captions inform us of significant statistics, interposed with images of Puerto Rican life and conditions. Within this framework these images, which critics pretending to omniscience would regard as hackneyed, fully recover their eloquence. Then comes the response of the Cuban athletes to the coastguards' refusal to admit the boat – the Declaration of the Cerro Pelado: 'The rights of Cuba are not negotiable' – which forces the North Americans to uphold the Olympic Regulations which govern the Games. After a section on crude North American attempts at psychological warfare, the film ends with a light-hearted portrayal of Cuban victories on the field and Fidel greeting the returning athletes.

In 1965, the same year as *Now*, Alvarez had already made another piece of *cine solidaridad*, a nine-minute report entitled *Solidaridad Cuba y Vietnam* ('Cuba-Vietnam Solidarity'). This was the first of many films to come on the struggle of the peoples in South East Asia. Two years later, following *Cerro Pelado*, Alvarez turned to Vietnam again to produce an eighteen-minute compilation film under the title *Escalada del chantaje* ('Escalation of Blackmail'), a report on increasing US aggression there. Then came his first trip to South East Asia and *La guerra olvidada* ('The Forgotten War'), a documentary report from Laos in which Alvarez employs avant-garde music by the Cuban Leo Brouwer and the Italian Communist composer Luigi Nono. The film is subtitled 'Filmic Fragments'. Apart from war footage and narrative captions at the beginning to summarise the history of Laos, Alvarez simply, and once more without commentary, shows us scenes of the activities of the Patriotic Front. Many of these scenes are taken in the caves which served for refuge and protection. In addition to such activities as newspaper printing, schooling, the manufacture of medicines and a hospital, we also see the projection of a film of Laotian dramatic dance. This is perhaps a veiled reference to the artifice of film. At any rate it has the effect of placing quotation marks around the doubly filmed, doubly projected image, thus emphasising how difficult it is to reach to the heart of a reality beyond one's direct experience. Through its very restraint, the film becomes a moving call upon the viewer's ignorance. It is also a model of what can be made under the most limited conditions, while refusing to engage either in the sensationalising tactics of the capitalist media or falling into the trap of pretending, even for laudable propaganda purposes, that the film is more than it is – an assembly of visual fragments.

Pastor Vega also made another significant film in 1967, *Canción del turista* ('Song of the Tourist'). This film is in colour and 'scope, one of the first Cuban films to use such resources, and at no more than fifteen minutes, it is a paradigm of *cine ensayo*, the film essay. The subject is the contrast between underdevelopment and revolution. The titles come up over a dancing girl in scanty costume gyrating in the style of the 50s to soundtrack music composed by Carlos Fariñas, with pressing rhythms and electronic noises that produce a menacing effect. The image here is in sepia and, still in sepia, cuts to a river and the countryside. The rhythm stops, leaving electronic noises over a series of images of underdevelopment. There is a shot of children dancing, and of a boy tapping out the rhythm on an upturned metal basin. Colour begins to creep in very slowly as we watch a singer, in synchronous sound, singing about a world without love or money, in the style of a traditional ballad. Now come stills of Fidel and then shots of Fidel in action on a podium, followed by panoramic views of the demonstration he is addressing. Colour continues to grow through images of industry and agriculture, women tractor drivers, the mechanisation of cane-cutting, new housing, new roads. Here the images are given an extra dimension, that of a wide-angle lens. The succession of images is again narrated by the music, keeping the film constantly free from every demagogic trace. We catch a glimpse of a couple kissing in the fields ('even the theme of love becomes more objective, more lyrical') and then there is traditional dancing and images of conviviality, entertainment and sports; children doing physical training; a ballet studio. The film concludes with images of a solitary child leading back to further images of underdevelopment. A previous image of Fidel reappears and the frame closes in on a girl standing behind him. A title appears: *SIN FIN* – 'Without End'. Not underdevelopment, that is, but the struggle against it. Song of the Tourist? The title is clearly ironic.

There is another even shorter film made a year earlier which shows the same lucid use of montage. The portrait of a North American soldier fighting in Vietnam, *La muerte de J.J. Jones* ('The Death of J.J. Jones') is the work of a young black director who had spent part of his youth in New York, returning to Cuba with the victory of the Revolution – the same who made the experimental fictional short *La jaula*: Sergio Giral. Here there is no specially composed music, but a soundtrack put together against the black-and-white image on the editing bench to create a kind of *musique concrète* in a highly satirical key. 'I am a soldier of the US army in Vietnam,' the film begins. 'We fight Communism because Communism wants to deny people Coca Cola.' It proceeds by deconstructing – that is, dissecting and dismembering – the imagery of consumer society, the mass media, the movies, comics, he-men of the Mr Universe type, the army, racism and advertising. A patriotic army advertisement is montaged with a film clip of new recruits being inducted by a sergeant who, between spitting, addresses the recruits: 'You guys are going to hate the day you met me. As far as I'm concerned, you're NOT HUMAN BEINGS.' The images are assembled from an ad hoc range of sources, mostly culled from the products of the North American publicity machine which sells the

'American way of life'. They are images of a kind by which Latin America is engulfed (the very phrase 'American way of life' is regularly used by Latin American writers on media and cultural imperialism in English, in quotation marks, to indicate this ubiquitousness).

After the induction the film comes to images of training and fighting, intercut with shots of Tarzan. Scenes of Vietnam itself are accompanied by the Hallelujah Chorus – 'For the Lord God omnipotent reigneth'. Images of German Nazism and the modern us Nazi party are introduced. The film concludes with an infamous quotation from Hitler: 'For the good of our country we need a war every ten or fifteen years.'

The play of montage on which these films are carried is clearly and immediately reminiscent of the role which montage played in Soviet cinema in the latter part of the 20s. In the work of Alvarez himself as well as a number of other examples, it comes close to Dziga Vertov. The affinity is there because the two cinemas were animated by the same qualities of revolutionary thought, intelligence and imagination. 'Art is not a mirror which reflects the historical struggle, but a weapon of that struggle,' Vertov declared. 'Cinema,' Alvarez proclaimed, 'is not an extension of revolutionary action. Cinema is and must be revolutionary action in itself.' 'We are here,' says Vertov, 'to serve a specific class – workers and peasants – we are here to show the world as it is and to explain the bourgeois structure of the world to the workers.' 'One can only be a revolutionary artist,' according to Alvarez, 'by being with the people and by communicating with them.'[6] The two cinemas centre on the same definition of cinema as a revolutionary weapon, as a medium of communication, as a dialectical medium in which montage and the process of editing is the means of synthesis. And they both prioritise the need to offer in the film an interpretative vision according to the goals of revolutionary society.

But the Cuban montage style also reflects a purely practical problem – the lack of sufficient material and resources. 'The North Americans,' says Alvarez, 'blockade us, so forcing us to improvise. For instance, the greatest inspiration in the photo-collage of American magazines in my films is the American government who have prevented me getting hold of live material.' 'Perhaps,' as Miguel Orodea observes about this, 'this is why there isn't a theory that holds Alvarez's work together and why he doesn't seem interested in elaborating one.'[7] This indeed is something which distinguishes Alvarez from other Cuban film-makers. Alea, García Espinosa, Alfredo Guevara, Pastor Vega, Massip, Fraga and many others have engaged in theoretical reflection. Alvarez does not seem to have the same intellectual cast of mind, or even a bent for criticism. He expresses himself best in conversation. His written pieces are few and short and originally produced for meetings and conferences, in a terse kind of political shorthand. 'Technical advances,' Orodea explains, 'have allowed Alvarez to experiment on a much bigger scale than Vertov could have aimed at, in the use of techniques of rostrum animation, optical re-filming, sound, colour, etc. Alvarez's visual resources vary from the use of photographic material from *Playboy* and the whole of the North American press, to extracts from Hollywood movies, Soviet classics, scientific documentaries, archive footage and television images, newspaper headlines and animated titles, put together in counterpoint with the most eclectic range of music.' Some of this is at this point still to come, but the point Orodea is making is already apparent: it is difficult to speak of Alvarez's style if by style is meant anything like the conscious pursuit of a set of rationalised aesthetic aims. His style, says Orodea, 'consists in adapting to the needs of the moment and using everything at his disposal. It is a style of constant evolution and change. The only constantly dominant criterion in his cinema is support for the Revolution and the anti-imperialist offensive.' As Alvarez himself puts it, 'My style is the style of hatred for imperialism.'[8] He describes himself as 'a product of "accelerated underdevelopment"':

The Revolution made me a film director. I learnt the job fondly handling millions of feet of film. I was enabled to fulfill very old dreams, from the time of Nuestro Tiempo, when we had a film club and the aspiration to create a Cuban cinema that would be part of a different kind of society. I was restless, like every good mother's son, who goes to the cinema a lot but cannot express his restlessness. Now that I can, I do.[9]

It was not only his restlessness that he expressed. Born in Havana in 1919, Alvarez is the son of immigrant parents from Spain; his father, who earned his living as a corner shopkeeper and later a grocer's supplier, was arrested for anarchist activities when Santiago was about five or six years old. For a couple of years while he was in prison, the family had to struggle hard to survive. At the age of fifteen, Alvarez started working, as a compositor's apprentice. Before long he was participating in strikes organised by the Union of Graphic Arts. As his political involvement grew he also decided to get himself an education. He went to night school, where he found himself setting up a students' association.[10] From these beginnings he carried forward with him a powerful sense of struggle, from which, as his creative mastery flowered in the 60s, he drew deep poetic feeling.

The film in which this poetry is first maturely expressed is *Hanoi martes 13* ('Hanoi Tuesday 13th' – the equivalent, in Latin America, of Friday 13th), filmed in North Vietnam on the same trip as the Laos 'filmic fragments'. One of Alvarez's indisputable masterpieces, this is a film of the greatest sensitivity, made with the greatest integrity and constructed with the greatest economy of means, with memorable music by Leo Brouwer.

At the beginning and the end of the film, colour is used briefly for paintings and engravings by Vietnamese artists which testify to the richness of Vietnamese cultural traditions. They accompany at the beginning a striking text about the inhabitants of South East Asia by José Martí, from a children's book he wrote called *La edad de oro* ('The Golden Age'), which speaks of the culture of the Anamites and their age-old struggle for freedom. This opening is abruptly interrupted by an explosive montage that portrays the grotesque birth of a monster in Texas in 1908 – none other than Lyndon Baines Johnson, who is treated to a rapid and satirical biography. The Vietnamese images resume peacefully, in black-and-white, with a visual account of their methods of fishing and agriculture. This paradigmatic structure of interruption and resumption is followed through the length of the film. Work in the fields in interrupted by the flight overhead of attacking aeroplanes (the film takes its title from the date of this attack, at 2.50 p.m. on 13 December 1966, shortly after Alvarez and his crew had arrived in Hanoi, and while they were out filming), and the workers in the field discard their ploughs and take up their guns.

These shots are unimpeachable actuality. Alvarez filmed them because he was there already filming when the attack began, and he had his wits about him. The film's title sequence, after the Johnson montage, has told us where and when: now we discover what. Because of the way Alvarez constructs the narrative, to give this information in a commentary would be redundant. And yet the scenes are not particularly dramatic, as they would be if this were conventional reportage. Alvarez knows they don't need to be, especially if the rest of the material in which they are embedded is also filmed and edited in such a way that they too give up their information visually and without commentary.

As the workers resume, Alvarez inserts a title, not only so as to avoid breaking the mood of visual attention with a commentator's voice, but also the better to make his words speak for the Vietnamese rather than the film-makers: 'We turn anger into energy.' Subsequently we move to Hanoi and gradually begin to pick out from among the many activities the film observes, shots which show the artisanal process of production of strange large concrete drums. Sunk into the pavements and open spaces, they each have a lid and turn out to be air-raid shelters, just big enough for one or two people. To an educated European viewer, these drums are reminiscent of nothing so much as the dustbins or mounds of earth in which characters in the plays of Samuel Beckett become immobilised, so much so that one would be forced to regard this connotation as obligatory if this were a European film. But here they become symbols of something which, though oppressive, signals primarily defiant tenacity (which in a sense they do in Beckett too).

Although in this film the means are of the simplest, the editing is exceedingly subtle. True, it has a certain looseness, but the result is that the narrative line is spun out in such a way that it becomes anything but linear. It unfolds more like continuous counterpoint, which also gives you time to reflect upon the images and their rhythms. Brouwer's music encourages this, with the result that the film informs in a manner not just different, but positively alien to what documentary orthodoxy expects. Film by film, Alvarez is turning the whole mode of documentary cinema inside out.

The score for this film is one of the finest that Brouwer has written. The style has nothing to do with conventional film music, but belongs rather with isolated examples of the idiom of the contemporary concert hall brought to the screen; like, say, the music Hanns Eisler wrote in 1940 for Joris Ivens' *Rain* of 1929, in which the relationship of music to image transcends conventional associations, the two become much more independent of each other than normal, and the music far more plastic than usual. Brouwer uses a small group of instruments with contrasting tone colours, and freely juxtaposes echoes of traditional Vietnamese music, which, however, he neither merely imitates nor pastiches, together with a variety of modernist effects in a continuously unfolding texture. What is even more remarkable are the circumstances under which this score was written. The job had to be done, he has recalled, in record time, 'and I even had to compose by telephone.' Alvarez called him, he explained, and over the phone described the succession of shots with their timings. But this, he adds, was just the way films got made in Cuba. Instead of the usual successive stages, with the music coming almost last, everything got done practically at the same time.[11] To go by the comments of other collaborators of Alvarez, this atmosphere of creative improvisation was particularly strong in the newsreel department, which Alvarez directed, not merely for the expectable reasons but because Alvarez encourages this way of working.

In *Hasta la victoria siempre* ('Always Until Victory'), also made in 1967, Alvarez virtually reinvents *cine denuncia*, the film of denunciation, in a twenty-minute newsreel put together in the space of 48 hours non-stop work in response to the traumatic news of the death of Che Guevara in Bolivia. It was made not to be shown in cinemas but, at Fidel's request, to be projected at a mass demonstration in the Plaza de la Revolución in Havana preceding Fidel's eulogy for el Che. Only the intense co-operation of Alvarez and his team made this possible. The triumph of the film is that even working at such speed Alvarez produces a poetic and far from simple aesthetic construction, though the film is understandably very rough at the seams and edges. Beginning with a prologue which employs stills to portray the misery of life in Bolivia and signal the presence there of US imperialism, the film uses fragments of archive footage of el Che during the guerrilla war in Cuba, and then after the Revolution cutting cane with others in the fields, to exemplify his creed of revolutionary selflessness, and it concludes with grainy, poorly focused but riveting images of two of Che's last public speeches, at the UN in December 1964, and the Non-Aligned Conference of 1965.

Che had been involved since the Revolution, and especially after 1962, in an extended theoretical debate on the transition to socialism, in which his own always clearly argued position had not always been accepted. Outside Cuba, too, his theory of guerrilla struggle around a *foco* ('focus') was hotly argued, and the disagreements were only highlighted by his death. Fidel would not allow such blemishes on Che's character, whom he called 'the most extraordinary of our revolutionary comrades' and 'our revolutionary movement's most experienced and able leader'. Repudiating attempts 'now after his heroic and glorious death... to deny the truth or value of his concepts, his guerrilla theories,' he asked what was so strange about the fact that he died in combat? What was stranger was that he did not do so 'on one of the innumerable occasions when he risked his life during our revolutionary struggle'. He then went on to endorse the essential element in the example that Che had left behind him in Cuba: 'he had a boundless faith in moral values, in human conscience . . . he saw moral resources, with absolute clarity, as the fundamental lever in the construction of communism . . .'[12] The film is a perfect preparation for Fidel's eulogy. The excerpts from Che's speeches emphasise his anti-imperialist resolution, which he articulates in a characteristically blunt and direct fashion, in simple but forceful and graphic language. It is not that Fidel told Alvarez what he was going to say or what to put in the film – there was no time for that and in any case Fidel was not inclined to such artistic collaboration. He once told the Soviet documentarist Roman Karmen who asked what he would like them to film, 'Unfortunately I understand nothing about the art of film, so I refrain from giving advice.'[13] It was rather that Fidel had seen the closeness of Alvarez's thought to his own. And from now on, the relationship between Alvarez and Fidel is to grow closer.

*Hasta la victoria siempre* has left a curiously tangible imprint in the popular culture of contemporary Cuba. For his soundtrack music Alvarez uses a piece by Pérez Prado, a Cuban composer who had once been associated with one of the most popular of Cuban singers, Beny Moré. Pérez Prado had left Cuba for the United States, where he devised the transformation of Cuban dance rhythm known as cha-cha-cha, which took Tin Pan Alley by storm in the 50s – one of a succession of Latin American dance rhythms with which the music industry in the United States periodically injects itself. Carried to US shores by the process of migration, the culture industry there pulls them out and reprocesses them, and then churns them out in sterilized, safe and predigested form, which of course it re-exports. The piece which Alvarez uses here is a syrupy arrangement which on first hearing sounds oddly inappropriate to a European ear inclined to reject – like Adorno and Eisler in their book on composing for the cinema – the devices of musical commercialism. A first reaction, then, is how can Alvarez be so tasteless as to use this kind of music? The piece, however, is actually a version by Pérez Prado of a work by the Brazilian Heitor Villa-Lobos, composer of the nationalist bourgeoisie, one of the few Latin American composers of art music with the originality and expertise to have commanded a reputation in Europe; and it turns out that Alvarez is doing some re-arranging of his own. By using this music Alvarez is, as it were, reclaiming it. This, at any rate, is what it must now seem, for to this day the piece is indissolubly fused in Cuban popular consciousness with Che's memory, and is regularly played on the radio and at gigs on the anniversary of his death.

A year later, in 1968, Alvarez produced his most biting piece of anti-imperialist satire yet, *LBJ*, which has deservedly become one of his best-known shorts. Running eighteen minutes, it is a stunning piece of visual and musical montage made entirely of found materials (except for titles), which achieves a pitch of satirical denunciation which Alvarez seems to have reserved especially for Lyndon Baines Johnson.

The film is in three main sections with a prologue and an epilogue. These

*LBJ*: Johnson

sections correspond to the three letters of Johnson's initials, which are used to stand for Luther, Bob and John (or Jack): Martin Luther King and the two Kennedys. It is a bold play on the strange coincidence that the corpses of these three men littered Johnson's ascent. Alvarez is not actually accusing Johnson of these assassinations, though he steers pretty close to libel, so to speak. However, this is not the point. There is no commentary, no direct verbal statement, and accusations by unsympathetic critics that the film is nothing but the expression of Marxist hysteria about conspiracy are simply philistine. What Alvarez is doing is to portray Johnson's presidency as the culmination of a whole history of socio-political corruption, not of individuals – the matter of individual presidential corruption was to come with Johnson's successor – but of the 'American way of life' itself. As Stuart Hood has put it, the film is 'a deadly and accurately aimed attack on a political system in which assassination had become an accustomed weapon and the circumstances of the killings veiled in misinformation and mystery.'[14]

The core of the satire is the image, culled from a North American newspaper cartoon, of Johnson as the incarnation of the Texan cowboy on his bucking bronco. Alvarez doubles this up with Johnson as a medieval knight in armour astride his mount, and reinforces his line of attack with clips from two types of Hollywood movie – westerns and the historical adventure. Movies of this kind are very familiar in Cuban cinemas, and Cubans, like other audiences, are still ingenuously attached to them to one degree or another. These clips are in 'scope, and in refilming them on the optical camera the film-makers have not used an anamorphic lens to unsqueeze the image – because the Cubans didn't have the appropriate lens for this particular piece of equipment. But the effect conforms entirely with the aim of the film, it puts quotation marks round the clips, as if to foreground the iconographic dimension of Hollywood mythology. And by applying this mythology to Johnson, Alvarez symbolises one of the ideological functions of the 'popular culture' of the market place.

The entire fabric of the film is woven out of allusions and connotations of this kind, combined in a crisscrossing montage of fine political wit. In the sequence portraying the assassination of J.F.K., for example, the picture cross-cuts a still photo of the President's car in the fateful Dallas cavalcade, showing the scene supposedly from the assassin's point of view, gun-sights superimposed, with a shot not of a rifleman but of a medieval archer aiming a crossbow. A moment

*LBJ*: Martin Luther King/Stokely Carmichael

later, Johnson taking over the White House is captured by a photograph of Kennedy's rocking chair being carried away by the removal men.

As the Cuban critic Manuel Lopez Oliva put it, in the Havana newspaper *El Mundo* at the time the film appeared, Johnson becomes 'an X-ray caricature of the North American "hero".' The image is multiplied and distorted so that 'each aspect – the initials of the name, the face, the grin, Johnson's little fancies' – like his pet dogs – 'his hands – come to amplify the subject's fleeting attributes, turning them into symbolic allusions which fill out the representation of the death-laden acronym.'[15] This review captured the significance of the film in its moment very well. It appeared to many people in Cuba at the time as a too-personalised poetic, which broke away from Alvarez's preceding and, as it were, more classical style. It *is* highly personalised, says Lopez Oliva, but not for that reason inferior. Several of Alvarez's films anticipated *LBJ*, like three which had gained international awards – *Ciclón*, *Now* and *Hanoi martes 13*. They had used the same type of montage to create a new expressive dimension quite capable of carrying a narrative, even though the images employed were the most diverse and sometimes even contradictory. There were some recent newsreels too, he says, especially a report on springtime sowing, where again, traditional poetics were mixed with a poetic logic of the photographic image that is taken direct from life; in other words, a kind of fusion of the individual language of the artist with the aesthetic logic of the camera, in which the primary connotation of the image is public and anonymous.

What Lopez Oliva is arguing for, in the Cuban context, is the recognition of an expressive need in Alvarez's idiom: in political terms, that both authority and popular opinion should reaffirm the artist's autonomy of style, which Fidel had recognised in the 'Words to the Intellectuals' of 1961. By the late 60s, the debate about the application of the principles had, if anything, intensified, and Lopez Oliva's review is densely argued. Alvarez occupied a cetrifugal position as the head of the newsreel department and it fell to him to be, as Lopez Oliva puts it, the first film-maker in Cuba 'to get to the point of entirely banishing classical rhetoric from the lens'. To be sure, the result was a 'pretty personal expressive stucture', but because of the way Alvarez and his team worked, it was also collective. People around ICAIC knew that. It also constituted a 'lucid collage assembly of ideas, in which historical, ideological and didactic elements were all imaginatively deployed'. In Alvarez, Lopez Oliva concludes, art, documentary and politics coalesce into an organic unity inseparable from the very film strip itself, which becomes wholly and positively suggestive from start to finish. There is no question but that the Cubans found in *LBJ* a paradigmatic expression of the defiance with which they responded to the loss of Che Guevara.


Alvarez forced the pace, but there are also other significant films of these years to be noted. In 1964, there was the first documentary by Sara Gómez, *Ire a Santiago* ('I'm Going to Santiago') – we shall look at all of Sara Gómez's films separately later on. Cuban and Latin American critics have singled out several others, including *El Ring*, a short on boxing by Oscar Valdéz (1966), and Alejandro Saderman's *Hombres de Mal Tiempo* ('Men of Bad Times', 1968), which the Peruvian Juan M. Bullitta has described as 'a film about the good memory of a group of veterans from Cuba's independence struggles' and hence a fine example of *cine rescate*.[16] Then there was Octavio Cortazár's *Por primera vez* from 1967, and a year later another film of his, an inquiry into the hold still exercised on various sectors of the population by the religious beliefs of underdevelopment, a piece of *cine encuesta* called *Acerca de un personaje que unos llaman San Lázaro y otros llaman Babalú* ('About a Personality Some Call San Lazaro and Others Babalú', 1968). In *El ring*, Bullitta finds a demonstration of the advantages of the compact dialectical montage of the 'classic structuralist methodology' of the documentary. The film is a portrait of the world of boxing under several aspects. It juxtaposes sequences of training and interviews with both a trainer and a retired fighter from the time of Cuba's most famous boxer, Chocolatín, contrasting what the sport used to be like with what it has now become, with the commercialism removed. Saderman's film Bullitta singles out for its avoidance of the frenetic and over-audacious uses of the camera which, he says, constitute one of the notorious weaknesses of Cuban cinema. For us, the most significant of these films is the last, but that will be in another context later on.

There are also two films made in 1968 by José Massip. In *Madina-Boe*, Massip reported from the liberation struggle in Portuguese Guinea, as Alvarez did from South-East Asia, but using a distinct approach. Massip brings to the screen a close identification with African culture which is one of the constant features of his work. There is an affinity with Pastor Vega's *Hombres del cañaveral* in the way, using captions but no commentary, he selects individuals from the group in the guerrilla band he is filming for individual portraits: Braima, the hunter, who performs ancestral rites before going out hunting; Indrissa, who is a Builder of Canoes; Kalunda d'Acosta, a Football Player; and Fode, the Poet. He then develops the report through parallel scenes at the camp and at a guerrilla hospital base, where a doctor from Portugal is one of the personnel, a white man whose anti-fascist commitment leads him to give his services to the liberation struggle. The sense of actuality is intensified by the use, a couple of times, of a simple intertitle, 'At this very moment', to mark the cross-cutting between the hospital and the camp in the scrub, where the guerrillas are preparing for an attack

Fidel: *La nueva escuela*/ *Y el cielo fue tomado por asalto*

against enemy positions in the village of Madina where some of them come from. Scenes of Braima the hunter have prepared us for the rites and rituals which the fighters observe before setting out, and the film ends with shots from behind the guerrilla lines as they go into the attack; these are built up by the special effects department back in the studios into the battle it had not proved possible to film, and the sounds of battle crossfade into children singing, over still images of children's faces. Like *La guerra olvidada*, *Hanoi martes 13* and the two films by Pastor Vega, this is a film in which revolutionary urgency is expressed reflectively, and with a strong feeling of human empathy.

Massip's *Nuestro olimpiada en la Habana* ('Our Olympiad in Havana'), on the other hand, is a film of idiosyncratic Cuban humour, down to the allusion in the title to Graham Greene's novel. The Olympiad in question is the international chess tournament which Havana hosted in 1968. The film is a simple nineteen-minute montage of the preparations for the tournament; the interest taken by quite large numbers of ordinary Cubans; the tournament games of the grand masters – here the camera picks out facial expressions and little unconscious nervous ticks and gestures as they concentrate; and the scene in the open air in which one of the grand masters performs his trick of playing simultaneous games against all-comers, one of whom, of course, is Fidel. The shots of Fidel in this film are perhaps the most original that had yet been seen of him in Cuban cinema. They conform to none of the common images of Fidel in the old photos and newsreels as a young lawyer and then a guerrilla commandante, or those of the Revolution in power where he becomes an orator and a TV star, the embodiment of Cuban pride and defiance. Here, following the glimpses we have had of so many different styles of concentration among players at the chess board, Fidel is suddenly seen as just another of them, both familiar and unfamiliar at the same time. It might well be said that in this way Massip humanises Fidel's image, except that it is not as if it were not already human.

In subsequent years, the image of Fidel on the screen is to undergo considerable elaboration, above all, but not exclusively, in the work of Alvarez, who becomes something like his poet laureate. On three occasions Alvarez travelled with Fidel on foreign trips which he chronicled in films of length: *De America soy hijo y a ella me debo* ('Born of the Americas') of 1972, the film of Fidel's visit to Chile, is by far the longest, 195 minutes in the full version; but . . . *Y el cielo fue tomado por asalto* ('. . . And Heaven Was Taken by Storm') –

Fidel: *Mi hermano Fidel/Viva la republica*

Fidel's East European and African tour of 1972, and *El octubre de todos* ('Everyone's October', 1977), of the second African tour, run 128 and 80 minutes respectively. As Stuart Hood reflected, after a retrospective of Alvarez's work in London in 1980, we are not used to lengthy documentaries like this with their easy pace and 'a certain discursive quality which can be deceptively innocent'; especially *De America soy hijo...*, 'loose-jointed but powerful in its cumulative effect and its insistent contextualisation of the Chilean situation'.[17] They offer, nonetheless, a rich collection of glimpses of Fidel in a large variety of circumstances, both formal and informal. As an orator, Fidel comes across in these films as both jurist and actor: he commands his part as an actor like Olivier in a Shakespeare play delivering a monologue to a gripped theatre. There is no denying that Fidel greeting crowds and crowds greeting Fidel can become repetitive, but such images are frequently offset by moments of individual interaction, like an exchange he has with a working woman at a rally in Chile, or by the habit Alvarez has of leaving in the bits which many an impatient editor would wish to leave on the cutting room floor ('untidy moments', as Stuart Hood calls them), Fidel fidgeting with the microphones on the podium in front of him, for instance. To these one must add the manner of his interaction with the gathered crowds, in both individual shots and whole sequences, like a scene in which he plays bastketball with students in Poland and which gave the lie to rumours in the capitalist media of a heart attack. They all add up to the image of a man who is in fact, like the film star, larger than life.

This is tempered, however, by two other appearances he makes, in Alvarez's *Mi hermano Fidel* ('My Brother Fidel') of 1977, and a sequence in Jorge Fraga's 1973 feature-length documentary *La nueva escuela* ('The New School'). In both these films, though in rather different circumstances, we observe Fidel in direct personal interaction with ordinary Cubans. The first is a short in which he interviews an old man who, as a child, met José Martí himself, when he landed in Cuba in 1895 to enter the War against Spain; the second is a report on Cuba's new educational system. Adjectives to describe Fidel's manner in these films trip off the tongue: spontaneous, warm, intimate, uninhibited, humorous. We recognise a kind of behaviour quite untypical of political leaders which, however, in the advertisements of US presidential campaigns, is quite calculatedly staged.

How can we be sure that in Fidel's case it is everything that it seems to be? There is a significant piece of evidence in each of these two films, in one case in the language, in the other in the image. Fidel's closeness to the people he meets is generally to be remarked in the mutual use of *tú*, the ordinary singular 'you' in Spanish, instead of the more polite *Usted*. Except that in *Mi hermano Fidel* Fidel throughout addresses the old man, who fails to recognise him because of his poor eyesight, as *Usted*, as a mark of respect. The evidence of the camera is equally subtle. Fidel tends fairly frequently to look at the camera (and there is no attempt to cut these shots out; in *Mi hermano Fidel* they even become a visual leitmotif). When he does so, we feel the same searching eyes with which we observe him to listen to the old man and others with whom we see him engaged in conversation. We get the impression that he behaves towards the camera just as if it were another person. I have heard it remarked that people who treat cameras like people tend to treat people like cameras, but in Fidel's case the quip misfires, because we can see nothing calculating in these looks, only the signs of curiosity and attention. And the gift of entering into the moment, like the way, in *La nueva escuela*, he joins in with the schoolchildren in games of baseball, volleyball and table tennis. It is perfectly evident from this last mentioned sequence that Fidel is a man with a highly competitive spirit, he likes to win – he was a prominent sportsman in his schooldays – he enjoys his stardom. It is also evident that there's a strong paternalistic element in his relationship to the children. But there is also something else which comes across very strongly in this sequence, which is also strong in *De America soy hijo...*, namely an easy familiarity, and a total absence of fear in these encounters by ordinary people with the leader.

A revolutionary cinema committed to the demystification of its medium is sooner or later bound to confront the question of the image of the hero and the revolutionary leader in all its aspects. The first to explore the image of heroism was García Espinosa in *El joven rebelde*, which created an anti-militarist paradigm. The idea of heroism was to be actively deconstructed in the early 70s by Manuel Herrera in his major documentary *Girón*. At the moment when Alvarez made *Hasta la victoria siempre* in 1967, something different was required. The film's very function was to eulogise the heroic revolutionary martyr, and the quality of Alvarez's creativity produced a way of doing this at once original and innovatory, and also as vibrant with revolutionary fervour as the oratory which served as its model. The poetry of the film partly comes from the way the screen is given over to reproductions of Che's image. This succession of images of differing quality creates an effect of deconstruction of the image, which also comes from the insistence in the way they are refilmed upon their material quality as reproductions, signifiers of what is absent. Which is to say that Alvarez does not engage in this exercise for its own sake, but for its metaphorical significance, the sense of loss in the photographic imprints a man has left behind conjuring up his presence in the hour of his death. To make people realise this is all that is left of him – his captors have secreted his body away – but it's enough because it's everything: his living example. (The theme was taken up again some years later by the Chilean film maker exiled in Cuba, Pedro Chaskel, using the appearance of Che's image on placards and posters in newsreel footage of student demonstrations around the world in the late 60s to make a film of great beauty and poetry, *Un foto recorre al mundo* – 'A Photograph Traverses the World', 1981.)

In the very same year, however, as the film by Alvarez, there appeared a film which treated the question of the image of the martyred revolutionary hero to an exhaustive and very different investigation, perhaps the most substantial it has ever had in documentary form. The product of three years' research and production, and the biggest documentary project at that time mounted by ICAIC, *David*, directed by Enrique Pineda Barnet, is a film of 135 minutes on the subject of Frank Pais, a leader of the 26th July Movement in Oriente province who was captured and killed on the streets of Santiago de Cuba in 1957, after an informer had told the police where he was hiding. His murder sparked off a wave of unrest and Santiago was a city in mourning when he was buried the next day in a 26th July Movement uniform with the rank of colonel.[18] 'David' was Frank Pais's *nombre de guerra*, his clandestine name.

What they did not want to do was simply make an outsize biography. They wanted 'not just to study the character of a hero but also to break the schema of the hero as a universal and infallible example. To fight the idea of the *guapo* and the *comecandela*'[19] – Latin American slang words for 'tough-guy'. They wanted, he says, to break the fetishism of such images, demystify, too, the 'dogmatic and melodramatic schematisation of certain radio and television programmes, which present young people with unachievable models of superhuman heroes'. They wanted a film which would promote discussion about this, which therefore had to maintain a position of marked protest against the formulae and ritual of the stereotype, without forgetting that the traditional relation of the spectator to the screen, the ambience of cinema, the immediacy of the image and ease of emotional identification with it, all conspired against them. This in turn they took to mean that they had to find for the film a form that was neither horizontally nor chronologically linear, but which developed a dynamic series of contradictions that would expand along the length of the film, without, however, reaching the normal closure of a passive and conservative dramaturgical method.

Method was the problem they felt themselves facing. This problem they sought to resolve by assembling, along with all their material, ideas from a wide range of sources in both cinema and theatre which might serve as paradigms for the endeavour. They found them in Jean Rouch and Edgar Morin, in Chris Marker, and in the Danish documentarist Theodor Christensen, who made a film on women, *Ellas* ('They' – feminine) with ICAIC in 1964; in Ivens, Kadar and Klos, Rosi, Godard, Visconti, even Preminger, as well as Brecht, Piscator and Stanislavski.[20]

The theatrical paradigms held a special interest for Pineda Barnet. Here he saw a solution, a reply to the conspiracy of cinema to maintain the passivity of the spectator, in the idea of using the dialectical permutation of the epic and dramatic elements of the narrative to transcend the level of anecdote. The results of this approach can be seen in the opening section of the film. At the very start, a sense of pending investigation of a mystery is communicated by shots in which the camera tracks up on objects surrounded by darkness, followed by sections of interviews from which emerges the shape of a shadowy figure to whom is attributed the words, 'Nobody understands me. I'm tired of so many things. I want to go and meet other people.' Some interviewees say that Frank was a church-going person – and a Presbyterian, not a Catholic – others that he was a man of action. A caption gives us a date: 10 March 1952. The film signals this as a time of disorder and topsy-turvydom in the form of a film clip, a musical with the singer singing in the broken English accent of a Latin American, with Spanish subtitles. An archive montage of the period ends with demonstrations at the University of Havana. Whereupon we see a blackboard, with a text written on it, from Marx's 'Theses on Feuerbach', about Feuerbach's failure to understand the social relations within which the individual lives.

For Desiderio Blanco, writing in the Peruvian film journal *Hablemos de Cine*, *David* is an example of *cine encuesta* incoporating the procedures both of direct cinema and classical montage, which creates a coherent universe around its absent subject more effectively than Jean Rouch created the world of *Chronique d'un été*. The film, to be truthful, is overlong, but it is another early example in Cuban cinema of a new idiom, which in Spanish might be called *cine desmontaje* – what we know in the radical independent film movements of the metropolis as post-Brechtian deconstruction.

Experience especially in Europe has shown that this kind of cinema tends to inordinate length. It has also shown that while aiming to activate the audience, very often it becomes paradoxically unassertive and passive. It is therefore not surprising to find José Massip, in expressing the general response to the film in a review in *Cine Cubano*, saying:

I do not think that *David*, aesthetically speaking, can be considered an accomplished piece of work. Its principal defect is the passivity of its structure and even more so, its language. However, this passivity is a result of the film's great virtue, which makes it the most important in our feature-length cinema at the moment: its audacious and intense approach to the revolutionary reality of Cuba. This paradox of passivity-audacity, a true example of the law of the unity of contraries, which makes up the most characteristic facet of *David* as a work, is nothing other than the expression of a contradiction between form and content.[21]

The film indeed left its audiences disoriented. Some remember that they came out of the cinemas disconcerted and a bit frustrated – they had not been given the emotional charge they had come to find in the films of Alvarez, they had not been made to cry and laugh (in this respect the film did not exactly live up to its Brechtian model either). But a little later, it happened that people began to talk about the personality of Frank Pais. Whatever its deficiencies, *David* made a strong impression, and Massip prophetically declared that it initiated a new stage in the Cuban feature-length film.

In 1969, Alvarez made a film which re-created *cine militante: Despegue a las 18.00* ('Take off at 18.00'). Slow dance music and images of blood pulsating through veins, then phrases and words appearing on the screen one by one and advancing towards the viewer: YOU ARE GOING TO SEE / A FILM THAT IS / DIDACTIC / INFORMATIVE / POLITICAL / AND... / PAMPHLETEERING... / ABOUT A PEOPLE / IN REVOLUTION / ANXIOUS... / DESPERATE... / TO FIND A WAY OUT OF / AN AGONISING / HERITAGE... / UNDERDEVELOPMENT. The words give way to a picture of a thatched roof and the camera zooms out to reveal a large barn being pulled down. Another title appears, the words inscribed within a circle: IF WE WERE BLOCKADED / COMPLETELY / WHAT WOULD WE DO? The camera zooms into the dot of the question mark. STOP PRODUCTION? / FOLD OUR ARMS? The image changes to an old map of the Antilles with drawings of sailing ships covering the sea – an icon of colonialism. The music changes to a Cuban *danzón* (traditional urban popular dance music) and the credits roll. (The music is again by Leo Brouwer.)

The credits end and the image cuts to a sign outside a shoe shop. The camera pans along a queue of people as the music passes into a minor key, like a blues. Then there's another queue, this time people waiting for bread. Street sounds are mixed in, and the frame freezes on a face. Faces and hands are seen in slow motion. Close-up of an old woman; again the frame freezes, and a caption is superimposed: NO HAY – 'There isn't any'. The caption repeats itself several times, intercut with a woman gesturing with her forefinger as if to reiterate the caption. More special optical effects: the picture jumps from one freeze frame to another of the woman's gesture and grimace. The effect is repeated with another, as if in conversational reply. Strange whistling sounds in the music interpret what they are saying. An old couple shrug their shoulders and the same caption appears again: NO HAY. Then without warning another image altogether: the eagle being toppled from the monument erected in Havana by the USA in the early years of the Republic, a symbolic piece of newsreel from the first years of the Revolution, a repudiation of servility to the USA. Then a strange engraving of a Chinaman lying horizontal, his clothing covered with images of various animals and objects. The captions now spell out what there isn't any of: THERE ISN'T ANY ILLITERACY – THERE ISN'Y ANY PROSTITU- TION – THERE ISN'T ANY UNEMPLOYMENT – THERE AREN'T ANY DESTITUTES – THERE AREN'T ANY HOMELESS – THERE ARE NO LOTTERIES – THERE'S NO POLIO – THERE'S NO MALARIA.

These opening moments of *Despegue a las 18.00* demonstrate what happens when Alvarez applies the virtuosity he has developed to the full in *LBJ* to the mobilisation of workers in Oriente province in April 1968, a trial run for the kind

*Despegue a las 18.00*

of mobilisations that were being planned for the whole country in the battle to increase agricultural production and especially the production of sugar cane. Turning from the enemy back to the Revolution, Alvarez's restlessness takes on new energy. He first calls his audience to attention, and then teases them, almost unfairly ('If we were completely blockaded...' – as if they were not blockaded!) He coaxes and cajoles the audience with images of the daily reality of the effects of the blockade – the ration queues. It is not presented as reportage or news – everyone knows this already. Nor are these images any apology for hardship, they are the very reality of it. With his expressionist stretching of the image, Alvarez means his audience to re-experience in their cinema seats the grind of their daily lives, in order to launch from here into a piece of emblazoning agitational propaganda which reinvents the whole idea of propaganda and agitation. Not for nothing has Alvarez commented on the inventiveness of advertising techniques. But rejecting the ways, if not all the means, of advertising, his wish is not to replace the propaganda of the market place with some kind of socialist equivalent. He wants to engage the audience on their own territory.

Only the fainthearted will blench at the parallel the film draws between mobilisation for production and mobilisation for war. The film analyses the strategy (to which, as an agitational work, it also belongs itself) needed to engage in a battle. When Fidel in a speech talks of the demanding opportunity the Revolution has created for Cuba, which asks people to work like animals so that they need no longer work like animals, and he compares this with the misery that continues in the rest of the continent, the film takes in images of Bolivia, Brazil, Guatemala. Fidel's voice gives way to a song by Silvio Rodríguez, one of the 'Nueva Trova', the Cuban New Song Movement, which takes up a theme from Fidel: 'Four thousand a minute, five million a day, two thousand million a year, ten thousand million the century, for every thousand who overflow the earth one of them dies, a thousand dollars a death, four times a minute, this is life. Sharks' teeth have never come cheap...' This comes from the Second Declaration of Havana, presented by Fidel for popular ratification at a mass meeting in Havana on 4 February 1962, and like the First Declaration, an answer to the anti-Cuban pronouncements of the OAS, in this case at its meeting at Punta del Este a few days earlier.

*Despegue a las 18.00* is not one of the films by which Alvarez is known abroad. It is a film directed so specifically to an internal need that outside Cuba the

*Despegue a las 18.00*

context is lacking to grasp it properly, though it is obviously a *tour de force* anyway. In the same year, however, Alvarez, now at the height of his creative powers, produced another work which has justly been internationally appreciated. *79 primaveras* ('79 Springs') is an incomparably poetic tribute to Ho Chi Minh. A film of twenty-five minutes, the title refers to the Vietnamese leader's age at the time of his death. Its form is that of a biographical resumé of the principal dates in Ho Chi Minh's political life. The decorative titles which announce these dates are interspersed among archive footage and other intertitles, inscribed with lines of poetry elegiacally assembled. Again the opening is beautifully constructed: first there are slow motion shots of flowers opening, then a shot of bombs dropping almost gracefully through the sky. Then the screen goes blank and we hear the human cry of a singer. After the first credit a negative image of the young Ho Chi Minh appears, which transforms itself into a positive image and then dissolves into close-ups. Because these close-ups are re-filmed they have become somewhat grainy – by now a familiar effect in Alvarez's language, which gives a gain in the plasticity of the image and reminds you of its material nature. We see Ho Chi Minh aging, the image returns to the negative, the screen turns a brilliant white, and the titles resume.

At the end of the credits, which incorporate moving pictures of the Vietnamese leader, we come to a close-up of him sitting in the open air at his typewriter. A title: 'They tied my legs with a rope', followed by a shot of him washing his feet. Another: 'And they tied my arms', followed by a close-up of his hands rolling a cigarette. 'I gave my life to my people', and a shot of Ho at a house in the jungle. An army band playing at his funeral. The simplicity of it.

When the biographical resumé reaches the victory of Dien Bien Phu, the film begins to shift gear. The Internationale is heard and we see the faces of international communist leaders at the funeral. We cut to a popular Cuban singer: 'The era is giving birth to a heart, it is dying of pain and can stand no more...', and her audience of cheerful Vietnamese children. The scene is violently interrupted by bombs and the devastation of napalm. Over horrific images of children's burned faces and bodies the music becomes violent and discordant. A title declares: THEY BEGAN TO KILL IN ORDER TO WIN. Then, in slow motion, one of the most infamous images of the Vietnam War, a couple of North American soldiers beating a Vietnamese who has collapsed on the ground: we see feet and hands and the rifle butts of his attackers, but not their faces. Then:

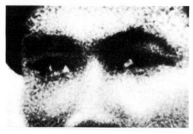

*79 primaveras*

AND NOW THEY KILL BECAUSE THEY CANNOT WIN. No-one has ever commented on Vietnam with greater economy or dignity.

The portrayal of the war continues with shots of anti-war demonstrators in the USA with placards which unequivocally establish a universalising message: VIETNAM, WATTS, IT'S THE SAME STRUGGLE; AVENGE CHE and FUCK THE DRAFT. Then another of the most notorious media images of Vietnam, a pair of GIs taking souvenir snapshots of their victims on the battlefield, to which Alvarez appends another piece of poetry by Ho Chi Minh – and in these lines the film knits its imagery together:

> Without the glacial winter, without grief and death,
> Who can appreciate your glory, Spring?
> The pains which temper my spirit are a crucible
> And they forge my heart in pure steel.

At this point many a film-maker would have been content to conclude. Not Alvarez, who has the nerve, or better, the cheek, to proceed with more scenes of the funeral, set to the music of Iron Butterfly. This is not simply a grand aesthetic gesture. The film was made in a period when, once again, sectarians were vocal, condemning the importation of music from the metropolis and those who were influenced by it – one of those they attacked was Silvio Rodríguez. Alvarez defies them, picking one of Silvio's songs for *Despegue...*, making solidarity with the North American music of popular protest in *79 primaveras*.

And then comes the *coup de grâce*. A new title appears: DON'T LET DISUNITY IN THE SOCIALIST CAMP DARKEN THE FUTURE. Using animation, the title is torn apart into little pieces which slide off the edges of the frame to leave the screen blank. The music disappears. A gunshot announces a split-screen, multi-image sequence of war footage, freeze frames, scratches, sprocket holes, flashes, guns, planes, bombs, sounds of battle with electric keyboard noises on the soundtrack, in which brutal reality bursts through the limits of its portrayal on celluloid in an unrelenting and terrifying assault that ends in the annihilation of a freeze frame, which burns up before our eyes leaving a blank white screen. And then? The torn pieces of the title reappear and join up again. The picture cuts to rockets firing, to the accompaniment of energising music by Bach, bursts of gunfire flash across the screen, the flowers reappear,

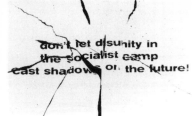

*79 primaveras*

and a final title appears: THE YANQUIS DEFEATED WE WILL CON-
STRUCT A FATHERLAND TEN TIMES MORE BEAUTIFUL.

After seeing this film, Alvarez's revolutionary aesthetic comes into the clearest
focus. Having banished classical rhetoric in *LBJ* – an achievement dependent on
its prior mastery – and having invented agitational propaganda anew in
*Despegue...*, he now explodes the cinematic image itself. Yet this is something
very much more than theoretical deconstruction. For one thing, what he does is
not theorised, it is the product of the aesthetic logic he has been working out from
one film to the next, it answers to expressive, not theoretical needs. Alvarez
cannot be called a deconstructionist film-maker, though in his practice he seems
to know more about deconstruction than the most eloquent theorist. He is,
stylistically, something of an expressionist, almost the spiritual descendent of the
expressionists of the first decades of the twentieth century whose revolutionary
aesthetics thrust art into the modern world. But with this difference, that in
Alvarez the temper of the individual and of the collective coincide. His idiom is
deeply personal, like that of any major artist of integrity, but at the same time it is
a completely public form of utterance, cleansed of the shit of individualism. In
Alvarez, the individual is fully submerged in history.

The result is that Alvarez also knows better than many of us who live in the
belly of the monster, the truth about the cinema and its place within the military-
industrial culture of imperialism: that everything we hate about it, its lies, its
arrogance, its preachments about what is popular and the childish mental age it
projects upon its audience, its pornographic pandering to the caprice of the
market place, all this belongs to the same stable as the soldiers who shoot their
victims with guns and then with Kodaks. Nevertheless, everything we hate
about the screen to which we entrust our dreams is redeemable, but only on
condition that there be openly displayed in the oppositional film what the films of
the enemy try to hide: their political provenance. The most experimental
techniques can then be freely explored without sacrificing communicability;
indeed the opposite. But there's a corollary: if these techniques are used, as they
are by many avant-garde film-makers, without marrying them to a clear political
purpose, nothing at all can be gained. On the contrary, such films can only
reinforce the breakdown of communication which they pretend to expose.

# References

1. See Hans Ehrmann, 'Cuba's Films', *Variety* 26 April 67.
2. Conversation with Santiago Alvarez, Havana, January 1980.
3. Quoted in B. Silverman ed., *Man and Socialism in Cuba*, Atheneum, New York 1971, p.17.
4. *Ibid*. p.7.
5. 'Santiago Alvarez habla de su cine', *Hablemos de Cine* (Peru) No.54, p.39.
6. Quoted in Miguel Orodea, 'Alvarez and Vertov' in *Santiago Alvarez*, ed. M. Chanan, BFI Dossier No.2, 1980.
7. *Ibid*.
8. Conversation with Alvarez.
9. *Hablemos de Cine*, op.cit.
10. Conversation with Alvarez.
11. Brouwer speaking in *New Cinema of Latin America II – The Long Road*, dir. Michael Chanan, 1983
12. Speech of 18 October 1967 in Che Guevara, *Reminiscences of the Cuban Revolutionary War*, Penguin, 1969.
13. Roman Karmen, *No pasaran!*, Editorial Progreso, Moscow 1976, p.368.
14. 'Murder on the Way', *New Statesman* 18 April 1980.
15. Manuel Lopez Oliva, 'Imagenes de LBJ', *El Mundo*, 13 December 1968.
16. In *Hablemos de Cine* No.54.
17. Hood, op.cit..
18. See Bonachea and Valdes, cit., p.141.
19. 'David: Metodo o Actitud?', *Hablemos de Cine* No.54.
20. *Ibid*.
21. 'David es el comienzo', *Cine Cubano* No.45/6, 1967.

# 11
# THE CURRENT OF EXPERIMENTALISM

From La muerte de un burocrata to Las aventuras de Juan Quin
Quin and the Cultural Congress of 1968

For the Cuban fictional film, the three years which Enrique Pineda Barnet spent in making *David* were transitional years. From the years 1966 and 67 there are four films of significance: Tomás Gutiérrez Alea's *La muerte de un burocrata* ('The Death of a Bureaucrat', 1966); Humberto Solás' *Manuela* (1966); *Tulipa* (1967) directed by Manuel Octavio Gómez; and *Las aventuras de Juan Quin Quin* ('The Adventures of Juan Quin Quin', 1967) by Julio García Espinosa. All are full length and black-and-white, except for *Manuela* which is only forty minutes, and was originally intended as part of a three-episode film by different directors but was judged to merit release on its own. In both *Manuela* and *Tulipa* the title role is that of a woman and the film is a drama. The other two are comedies.

*La muerte de un burocrata* is about a country which has made a revolution and decided to become socialist and therefore insists that its bureaucrats provide equal treatment for all, including the dead: a corpse gets itself unburied for the sake of bureaucracy, and then finds that bureaucracy won't let it be buried again. The country where these events take place is a hilarious mixture of revolutionary Cuba and the Hollywood land of comedy.

The story is very simple and ingenious. A man dies and his family buries him. Afterwards they are asked for his *carnet laboral* (labour card) for the bureaucratic process to take its course, but unfortunately they buried it with him as a mark of honour – he had been considered a model worker. To recover the card, they dig up the body in the dead of night. Unable immediately to rebury it because the cemetery keeper has been scared and sent for the police, they take it away and return next day to bury it afresh. The bureaucrat in charge refuses them permission to do this on the grounds that they have nothing to show that the body is not where it is supposed to be – in the ground. They need a certificate of exhumation. The film pursues the efforts of the corpse's nephew to get one. When he finally has it and returns to the cemetery, the same official, following the same logic, still does not let him rebury the corpse because he takes the certificate as an order to exhume it. Whereupon the exasperated nephew, who has already been chased through an office building by a throng of pursuers, and

*La muerte de un burocrata*

has balanced precariously on a parapet above the crowds, even hanging from a clock like Harold Lloyd, loses patience and strangles the bureaucrat. For this misdeed he is taken away in a straitjacket while the film ends with the bureaucrat's funeral.

Alea discovered after making the film that the seminal idea had a counterpart in reality, when a woman left a screening of the film in tears, because her husband had, as in the film, been buried with his *carnet laboral*.[1] In the film, the story has been elaborated to provide innumerable opportunities to parody Hollywood comedy. Whether or not Hitchcock's *The Trouble With Harry* of 1955 was part of its inspiration, Alea borrows liberally from practically the whole Hollywood comedy tradition, with especially pungent plagiarism of Chaplin, Keaton, Laurel and Hardy, and Harold Lloyd, as well as references to Jerry Lewis and Marilyn Monroe. It is almost as if Alea felt a need to exorcise the Hollywood comedy, although since the great tradition of film comedy is itself subversive of genre, this is not a cinema that needs to be repudiated in the same way as the rest of Hollywood.

There are other comic strands to the film as well, especially a streak of black humour about death which struck some Cuban critics as Mexican in character, though Alea himself considered it rather more Spanish.[2] Either way, there are certainly echoes of Buñuel, in small surrealist touches like the driver of the hearse with a plastic skeleton hanging in the cab, or the dog during the fight in the cemetery who runs off with a bone. Black humour is also the home key of several entire scenes which turn on the consequences that everyday problems may create for an unburied corpse. Since, for example, the family is forced to keep the corpse at home, neighbours pool their ice to keep it fresh; but ice, like other commodities in blockaded Cuba, is in short supply, and vultures circle overhead.[3]

The Cuban critics found the acts of homage to the masters of comedy truly delightful. They also found the film – not surprisingly – somewhat Kafkaesque.[4] As Alea was about to depart with the film to the Karlovy Vary Film Festival in Czechoslovakia (where it shared the Special Jury Prize with *La Vie de Crateau* by the French director Jean-Paul Rappenneau), he was asked if, perfectly lucid as it was for the Cubans, the film would be found intelligible there. 'Indeed yes,' he replied, not mincing words, 'the bureaucracy thing is very old. It was not invented but inherited, and in some cases enlarged, by the socialist countries, where it seems like an oppressive stage that has to be passed through. I think the mechanisms of bureaucracy as they're shown here can be understood anywhere.'[5] In Cuba itself the film was praised precisely for its implaccable criticism of bureaucracy, and the very high political level it demonstrated in achieving this.

But there's another target in *La muerte de un burocrata* too. According to Alea himself, 'It's a satire on rhetoric and the stereotype in art.'[6] Indeed this is how the film begins, with an animation sequence in which the uncle whose death sparks the story off is killed when he falls into a machine he has made to manufacture busts of José Martí. This machine looks as if it's been patched together in a fashion only to be expected in a country where, as Ruby Rich observes, 'parts are unavailable due to the blockade and remedies left entirely to individual ingenuity.'[7] It is also reminiscent of the contraptions of the 'nutty professor' Jerry Lewis, and also reminded one Cuban critic of the machines in Chaplin's *Modern Times*.[8] 'We started,' Alea explained, 'with the busts of Martí because they were the order of the day – that's what I was criticising. I went out and took a hundred photos of "Martí corners" – the spots where the busts had been installed. Many looked cold and formal, official, a ritualistic gesture. Others, in the popular districts, were often primitively done and suggested veneration, of the same kind as popular altars to the saints. These had an authentic popular character which isn't shown in the film.'[9] But this exclusion corresponds with the satire's target, for the film is a weapon in the continuing ideological battle not just against bureaucracy but also against the influence of the bureaucrats in art. The relevance of this kind of satire four years after Fidel's criticism of the political sectarians is evidence of how difficult it is to uproot uncritical thinking in relation to art and culture. Nor was this aspect of the film lost on people. The critic Bernardo Callejas, the one who saw the Martí bust machine as an echo of *Modern Times*, thought this very appropriate because it is 'a satire on those who by dint of mechanistic thinking cut themselves off from the thought of great men, turning them into hollow symbols. The Martiesque is not to be found in the repetitive bust, but in the recovery of the Apostle from absurd mystification.'

Callejas ended his review of Alea's film by announcing the premiere of another new Cuban film of interest: Solás' *Manuela*. Manuela is a guerrilla, a *guajira*, a peasant woman, who demonstrates that the qualities needed to be a rebel soldier are not a monopoly of men but belong to every true Cuban. The film portrays her apprenticeship as a fighter in much the same terms as *El joven rebelde* – a process of learning to overcome the ignorance of illiteracy and to call for justice rather than revenge. At the beginning, when Batista's army razes the village where Manuela comes from, and her mother is murdered, she seeks vengeance by attacking a drunken soldier; by the end, she has become an advocate of revolutionary discipline. The plot also revolves, however, around a relationship she develops with another fighter, Mejicano, a handsome guitar player. The growth of this relationship is gently observed; she teases him, for example, for his ineptitude at washing clothes. But we never really stray far from the principal theme. After an attack on a village, Manuela joins the villagers in calling for the informer to be lynched and it is Mejicano who tells her, no, the man must be tried. Still, in between the duties of the struggle, they speculate about marrying when it is all over – though here again it falls to Mejicano to tell her how different things will then be (as we shall later learn when the same pair of actors meet again in the last part of Solás' next film, *Lucía*). In the end, Manuela is fatally wounded in combat and this time Mejicano loses his self-control, and it is she who has to remind him with her dying breath to put aside thought of personal vengeance. The message of the film could hardly be clearer.

There is a certain justice in the criticism of the film by a group of Venezuelan critics, that if *Manuela* had been made five years earlier it would have been perfect, but for 1966 it suffers from a certain lack of ideological depth, and in its moral insistence remains somewhat sentimental.[10] The image of the woman fighter is still romantic and idealised, and even in its anti-heroism it makes no innovations. The dialogue is bare, deficient, though not, as far as it goes, incompetent, and the result is that all but Manuela herself remain secondary and incomplete characters, even Mejicano. What most impressed people at the time, however, was the power and assurance of the film's visual style, which is evident from the very first moments, in the judicious lensing and framing and the careful pacing, and above all in the controlled use of the hand-held camera. The music, by Tony Taño, similarly alternates between expressionism and lyricism. Compared with, say, *Historias de la Revolución*, *Manuela* shows the distance travelled in the stylistic evolution of Cuban cinema in only a few years. Studio and studio lighting have been abandoned and dress and make-up have become more naturalistic too, even if the stylisation of character remains. But then Solás was only twenty-three at the time he made this film; even so his characters already look less like the visual stereotypes of the earlier film. In the final analysis, the strength of *Manuela* lies in Solás having found himself an extraordinary actress, Adela Legrá, a *campesina* with no previous acting experience, to play opposite the young actor Adolfo Llauradó. At the same time, the film represented for Solás a return to public themes after the experimental shorts he had been making for a couple of years, in contrast to which, he told an interviewer, *Manuela* represented *cine rescate*, a recovery of national rather than personal values.[11]

While *Manuela* is not exactly a feminist film, *Tulipa*, a circus story of the 30s or

Adolfo Llauradó and Adela Legrá in *Manuela*

40s, is in this respect far more striking. Idalia Anreus, who has become over the years the doyenne of Cuban screen actresses, plays the title role, an aging stripper in a side-act in the circus of Ruperto & Sobrino (Rupert & Nephew) who befriends a new recruit. Beba, played by Daysi Granados, has been enticed to join the circus as a 'dancer' by the junior partner in the business, Cheo the nephew, and she's an eager recruit, for the circus seems to her a way of escaping from home, which offers her no future. But she grows quickly disillusioned when she discovers what kind of act Tulipa performs and realises that she is being groomed to take her place. 'If it wasn't you,' Tulipa tells her, 'they'd find someone else. I've been expecting this for some time. Go on, drink. If you're going to enter show business you've got to get used to it. Don't look at me like that. You're staying, and that's it. And that's the first thing you have to learn: to sleep alone. I've been sleeping alone so long I'm practically a señorita.'

The film is based on a stage work which Manuel Octavio Gómez saw in the early 60s, by Manuel Roguera Saumell, who then collaborated on the script. The itinerant circus which is pictured here was a popular form of entertainment in the countryside – the early film distributors Santos y Artiga were also circus pro-prietors – and hence the film was predictably popular with peasant audiences. It was readily understood as an allegory of the conditions of the time, a microcosm of the pseudo-republic with its portrait gallery of the whole range of circus types; including the owner who abandons it all when some more profitable enterprise comes his way. 'The film is full of social critique,' wrote one reviewer, and 'the profiles of the exploited circus personnel, from the bumpkin who raises the curtains to the variety star, via the master-of-ceremonies, are completely faithful.'[12] Cheo, in the words of another, 'incorporates all the primitive machismo of the Cuban man before the Revolution, his violence, his spiritual weakness.'[13] For this second reviewer, 'Tulipa is confronted by Beba in whom she sees her own youth and at the same time a rival.' There is also the Bearded Woman Tomasa, in whom the actress Teté Vergara shows 'the gentleness of the woman forced to live such a role because poverty obliges her, but who has not been contaminated.' The film is thus a study of struggle by individuals in the pseudo-republic to live an authentic life, but it also goes further and becomes an examination – unique in Cuban cinema at the time – of the particular modes of exploitation which were forced upon these women, who stand for all women in the pseudo-republic, and the solidarity they create between themselves in order to survive. For in spite of the threat which Beba represents towards Tulipa, Tulipa not only, like Tomasa, retains her dignity, but the friendship which both the older women extend to Beba is the most positive human value in this world.

At the same time, the male characters are not mere cyphers. On the contrary, *Tulipa* is perhaps generally the best acted Cuban film up to the moment it was made. This also extends to the crowd scenes, and the honesty with which the contradictions of circus entertainment are presented – the portrayal of the sexism of the circus, for instance, which is located here quite specifically as a deformation of a kind that arises in the typical social relations of both the production and consumption of popular entertainment to be found in the pseudo-republic. In the scene which first reveals Tulipa's act, the camera mainly holds back, at first

Idalia Anreus in *Tulipa*

because it is looking at the scene from Beba's point of view; but this camera position fulfils other functions too. It distances the spectator of the film from the spectacle, discouraging voyeurism and guarding our respect for Tulipa, revealing instead the way the spectacle is designed not to satisfy but merely to titillate. Finally, through the empathy the film produces for the three women, it also becomes an allegory on the frustrations forced upon *any* artist in the circumstances. By using these women as the vehicle of this allegory, Gómez marks the changing consciousness of the artist within the Revolution in some important respects.

In a way, *Tulipa* stands half way between Alea's *La muerte de un burócrata* and García Espinosa's *Las aventuras de Juan Quin Quin*, Cuban cinema's first fully accomplished experimental feature film, and significantly a comedy. This is a film which was conceived in direct relation to the problem of a growing crisis in communication, in which experimentation seemed to be becoming more and more urgent. Before the Revolution, García Espinosa explained in 1969, cinema entertainment was regarded by many people as escapism, but now the film-makers could not afford to think that way. However, a crisis of communication had developed because the serious film-maker could hardly continue to employ the traditional concept of art, a concept premised upon a split between 'serious' and 'popular' in which the artist was left isolated in a self-protective cocoon of elitism. The Revolution had made the need for such self-protection an anachronism (as Fidel had argued in the 'Words to the Intellectuals'). But simply to try and exchange elitism for populism was equally unacceptable. An entirely new mode of addressing the audience was needed, combining entertainment with the critique of the old forms of entertainment. This, for García Espinosa, was connected with another challenge, that of learning how to avoid the tendency of the Revolution to treat itself too solemnly: 'Which is not to say that the processes of the Revolution are not dramatic; they are very serious, but they don't have to be treated in a formalist way, which is when stupidity begins.'[14] *Juan Quin Quin* was an attempt to confront these problems.

Like *Tulipa*, *Las aventuras de Juan Quin Quin* was based on a recent literary work, in this case a novel by Samuel Feijóo entitled *Juan Quin Quin en Pueblo Mocho*. It was a novel in many ways suited to the task in hand, evoking the popular Hispanic tradition of the picaresque, in which the romantic hero is replaced by the rascal who lives off his wits. Yet in spite of the typically episodic structure of the picaresque novel, it had, they felt, for their purposes, too linear a structure:[15] a pair of peasant woodcutters, Juan and his friend, pass through a series of adventures which spur them to a *toma de conciencia*, a moment of enlightenment, that leads them to take up arms against an intractable reality. The original adaptation proposed a familiar world in which the picaresque aspect appeared as a cross between a western and a classical adventure. This treatment was rejected, partly on grounds of length, and they began to rework it, both eliminating characters and combining them. In the process, they discovered a way of giving it a highly original non-linear structure.

The film begins with a brief sequence which shows Juan Quin Quin at war, burning canefields and being cornered by soldiers commanded by a caricature mayor. This immediately gives way to Juan Quin Quin in times of peace, in which our hero advances from being a rather too worldly acolyte in the service of a self-righteous priest, to becoming a bullfighter. But then we see him at war again, among a band of fighters trying to break an encirclement by the enemy; Juan's friend Jachero escapes to try and bring help but meets with unexpected and gratuitous death – though since the narrative is not linear, this does not stop him reappearing during the rest of the film. Next, it is revealed how our hero met his sweetheart Teresa – while appearing in a circus act as Jesus on the cross; and also how he begins to rebel against the established order, which he confronts in the shape of the manager of a sugar mill and his North American paymaster. In the final section, we learn how Juan and his comrades form a small guerrilla band.

Not only is the narrative structure thus shaken apart and reassembled in an apparently haphazard way, but in the process, each different sequence has come to be treated as if it belonged to a different kind of film. Juan's adventures thus become, as Anna Marie Taylor has observed in an article in *Jump Cut*, a series of escapades through different cinematic genres.[16] The film begins like a 'scope western; there are parodies of the war movie and the detective picture with its wealthy oriental villain, and always there's the handsome hero, the beautiful heroine, and the excitement of adventure. The parody even moves outside cinema proper: Jachero meets his untimely end in a skit on the *fotonovela*, or photo-novel (a cross between the comic-book and the magazine love-story in which drawings are replaced by photographs staged to look like film stills; a cheap printed format which first appeared just after the Second World War in Italy and then found its true market in Latin America).[17] The 'elaborate inappropriateness', as Anna Marie Taylor puts it, 'of the parodies in *Juan Quin Quin*, succeeds in effectively calling attention to the artificiality and formulaic quality of the cinematic codes at work in each case... Distanciation effects used in the film's long series of adventures require the viewer to be constantly aware of cinematic illusion as patterned convention.'

There are other purposes in this treatment too. As well as 'demonstrating to the spectator that this is a film and not reality,' as García Espinosa himself puts it, there was also the problem of how 'to ridicule a number of typical elements of the adventure film without being led to satirize our own reality.'[18] So the film foregrounds the trickery of editing and special effects in order to frustrate narrative expectation, to subvert narrative logic, and to satirise genre by means of exaggeration. A lion turns miraculously into a bull; character types from one genre interpose themselves in another; Juan jumps off a roof to land ever so conveniently on his horse. At the same time, there are interpolations on the nature of underdevelopment. Among captions which come up like chapter headings, like 'Juan Quin Quin in Peacetime', 'How Juan Quin Quin met Teresa' and so forth, are a couple which break the framework: 'Here we could insert a number of scenes of daily life in Latin America' and 'We could equally show any one of the useless meetings of the United Nations'.

Enrique Santiesteban in *Las aventuras de Juan Quin Quin*

For Anna Marie Taylor, there is, however, an area of the reality of under-development which the film still evades: 'Juan's handsome demeanor and cool, understated, Hollywood-style acting... hardly confront, let alone undercut... audience identification, even with a comic hero... the women are still dressed and act as exploited sex objects and García Espinosa's intent to satirize such roles cannot compensate for his more or less straight reproduction of these sexist codes.' And it is perfectly true that in this respect *Juan Quin Quin* is less advanced than *Tulipa*.

However, the film's treatment of the idea of the hero has other complexities. The problem as García Espinosa saw it was the antagonism that exists between the dramatic idea of the positive hero (who is finally, he observes, less interesting than the 'baddies') and the superficiality of the hero in the adventure genre. They belong to different aesthetic traditions. He wanted not to combine them, elide the one into the other, but to expose the contradiction; not an easy thing, since 'questioning genre isn't a pure, clean, abstract matter'[19] (which Anna Marie Taylor's criticism of course confirms). The problem revolved around the concept of the *toma de conciencia*, the hero's moment of enlightenment, when the truth is revealed and his duty becomes clear. In both cinema and literature this moment is always carefully constructed, and is central to the ideological function of the work. It normally comes after the hero has suffered a series of defeats and disillusioning experiences – which the mechanisms of the genre are designed to provide – and is given the force of a psychological breakthrough. Indeed, the entire genre philosophy of the good, the bad and the ugly is based on an hypostatised psychology – a notion, that is, of psychological types and processes as causes instead of effects. In this way, the realities of social history and class struggle drop out of the picture; instead of the hero's *concientización*, a process of critical reflection on the world which surrounds him, genre cinema treats the hero to a sudden moment of revelation, not unlike the decongestion of accumulated tension which Enrique Colina and Daniel Díaz Torres speak of in their analysis of the Latin American melodrama.

The scene in which this comes to the surface is at the end of the film's penultimate section, where Juan is being inspected by the North American paymaster of the sugar mill like a piece of livestock. A caption interrupts the image, inscribed with a ridiculous sentence from a play well known in Cuba and Latin America, *Don Juan Tenorio*, written by a Spanish romantic poet, José Zorrilla, in 1844. It reads: *Llamé al cielo y no me oyó* ('I called upon heaven and it did not hear me'). Our hero has lost his patience. He lunges at everyone in sight, and jumping through the window, departs to join the struggle. A second caption drives the message home: *y pues sus puertas me cierro* ('and it closed its doors against me'); after which it only remains for a third caption to state: *etc. etc.* The rationale behind the choice of these lines is really quite simple: it clinches the preceding religious satire – from Juan the acolyte to Juan on the cross. For the film is militantly atheistic. The sequence concludes with a transitional caption to the final section, quoting Fidel: 'There is always armed struggle, but sometimes they're the ones with the arms, and it's necessary that we have arms too.' Evidently, this includes films.

*La primera carga al machete*

The experimentalism of *Juan Quin Quin* is an expression of currents already found in various documentaries by Santiago Alvarez and the example of Pineda Barnet's *David*. It also anticipated a series of major fiction films of 1968 and 69: Jorge Fraga's *La odisea de General José* ('The Odyssey of General José'), Alea's *Memorias del subdesarrollo* ('Memories of Underdevelopment'), *Lucía* of Humberto Solás, and *La primera carga al machete* ('The First Machete Charge') by Manuel Octavio Gómez; as well as others that came later, like José Massip's *Paginas del diario de José Martí* ('Pages from the Diary of José Martí') and another film by Alea, *Una pelea cubana contra los demonios* ('A Cuban Battle Against the Demons'), both dating from 1971. The sheer exuberance of all these films fuels an attack on stable and established filmic vision which has very few precedents in the history of cinema. The attack takes shape most strikingly, but by no means exclusively, in the matter of camera style and cutting, especially in the first part of *Lucía*, in *Una pelea cubana . . .* or in sections of the film by Massip. In *La primera carga al machete*, Jorge Herrera's hand-held camera combines with high contrast black-and-white photography in a swirling battle scene which takes place in a forest, in which the battle consequently becomes an abstract image of pure energy which reveals a high degree of tolerance for controlled visual chaos, or, to put it more positively, for Gestalt-free form. According to the teachings of Gestalt Theory, the artist is primarily concerned with organising perception into stable forms according to the laws of unity, segregation and balance, which reveal harmony and order, and stigmatise discord and disorder. Ironically, this theory was being elaborated at the very same moment that the modernist movement was engaged in dramatically changing the rules, breaking down the traditional surface structures of art to reveal complex relationships that refuse to be caught in the stable and neat grid of orderly perception. Instead (as the psychoanalyst Anton Ehrenzweig has explained) 'incompatible outlines and surfaces permeate and try to crowd themselves into the same point in time and space.'[20] In this way, traditional artistic languages, especially those of the plastic arts and music, were revolutionised; similar experiments in the disruption of the rational surface followed in every other art form. In cinema, however, this kind of avant-gardism found itself restricted to the margins by the aesthetic intolerance of big money; or in the Soviet Union, after the experimentation of the 20s, by the orthodoxy of socialist realism. The fears which motivated this refusal of filmic experimentalism were not just of the destruction of the naturalistic illusion and the realism effect, but of the rupture of the exemplary nature of narrative. And indeed the subversion of traditional narrative is another major feature of this extraordinary period in revolutionary Cuban cinema, which made a lot of otherwise good-natured people very uncomfortable.

This experimentalism was by no means limited to cinema. There was an experimental current alive around this moment in other art forms too. Indeed in painting it was the tradition – and it was already a few years since Fidel had said . . . 'Our fight is with the imperialists, not with abstract painters'. In literature, there are various examples; 1967, for instance, saw the publication by the writer Pablo Armando Fernández – once assistant editor of *Lunes* – of his best-known novel, *Los niños se despiden* ('The Children Say Goodbye'), which received a Casa de las Americas prize the following year. As one foreign commentator has recently said of it: 'With its kaleidoscopic treatment of time, its promiscuous blend of the rhetorics of dream and technology, its characters that merge and separate, its disembodied voices, *Los niños se despiden* is a modern classic.'[21] Other less spectacular kinds of literary experiment can be found in testimonial literature like Miguel Barnet's *Biografía de un cimarrón* ('Biography of a Runaway Slave') of 1968, where the author, recording as an anthropologist the memories of a man of 108 years of age, has turned them into a unique first-person literary narrative of the experience of slavery, escape, and participation in the Cuban Wars of Independence, the whole redolent of the cultural heritage, including their roots in African religion, of the Cuban slave in the nineteenth century.

In music, too, there was more than one kind of experimentation going on. Indeed, nothing symbolises the spirit of the moment better than an orchestral work in an advanced avant-garde style which Leo Brouwer wrote for a modern music festival in Colombia, called *La tradición se rompe... pero cuesta trabajo*, 'Tradition is breakable, but it's hard work'. But it was also hard work breaking the hold of the contemporary musical environment. Music was probably, except for cinema, the area of cultural production most deeply affected by the processes of cultural imperialism and the unstoppable invasion of the products of the culture industry of the metropolis. In 1967, a Joseph Klapper of CBS told a Congressional Committee in Washington inquiring into 'Modern Communications and Foreign Policy', that 'the broadcasting of popular music is not likely to have any immediate effect on the audience's political attitude, but this kind of communication nevertheless provides a sort of entryway of Western ideas and Western concepts, even though these concepts may not be explicitly and completely stated at any one particular moment in the communication.'[22] Certainly the Miami radio stations which poured their ephemera into Cuba threatened to wreak havoc on popular musical sensibility, and in 1968, in an excess of revolutionary fervour of the moment, a ban was issued against rock music on Cuban radio and television. The year was one of great revolutionary upheaval. Fidel had launched a campaign to eliminate petty profiteering, which swept away the remnants of private trading such as stalls, bars, shops and private servicing; some of it was illegal and among its effects there was hoarding. A war was declared on 'indulgence, selfishness, individualism, parasitism, vice'. In the course of events, the cabarets – there were dozens and dozens of them across the country – were closed, and many musicians found themselves without the usual places to play. For the younger ones, experimenting with new styles, there were real problems.

Those at ICAIC, amongst others, felt that the ban on rock music was misconceived, because it failed to comprehend the complexities of the problem. For one thing, the moment was one of rejuvenation of popular music in the metropolis itself, with groups and singers like the Beatles, Bob Dylan and many others.

Leo Brouwer (photograph by the author)

Much of the most interesting of this music was known in Cuba not from the transmissions of US radio stations, from which a lot of it was excluded, nor even from records, which were very difficult to get hold of, but from the circulation of cassettes, which were just beginning to become available. Many people in Cuba found this music appealing not only for its musical originality but also for its voice of protest, against the war in Vietnam and the inhuman and aggressive society which was conducting it; and a group of young musicians emerged who began to take up the various styles of this music. ICAIC, which until that time had mainly worked with classically trained musicians, responded to the situation with the creation of the Grupo Sonora Experimental, the Experimental Sound Group, which brought the best of the young popular musicians together – including Pablo Milanés, Silvio Rodríguez, Noel Nicola – alongside instrumentalists like Leo Brouwer, Sergio Vitier and Emilio Salvador. There were two workshops formed, one devoted to instrumental music and the other to the transformation of popular song; and it was out of this initiative that the 'Nueva Trova', the New Song movement, was born. A distinct and important ingredient was the discovery of a different popular music of the moment in Brazil – which came about, according to Alfredo Guevara, partly through clandestine contacts with Brazilian revolutionaries.[23] With its Afro-Brazilian provenance and the closeness to Cuban culture of its rhythmic and melodic subtleties, the Cubans immediately understood its mobilising power.

There were, at this time, a couple of cultural events of the greatest importance which also gave expression to the militant desire for an experimental aesthetic. In July 1967 the Cuban government invited to Havana the modernist *Salon de Mai* from Paris, an exhibition of European avant-garde painting and sculpture, and a good number of writers and artists with it. Then, at the beginning of 1968 came the momentous Havana Cultural Congress on the theme of 'The Intellectual and the Liberation Struggle of the Peoples of the Third World', which brought together about five hundred revolutionary and progressive artists and intellectuals from as many as seventy countries in a great act of affirmation. They were, in the words of the Mexican Alonso Aguilar, 'intellectuals in the broadest Gramscian sense': 'poets and dramatists, physicists and doctors, actors and economists; old party militants and young people just entering the revolutionary struggle; blacks and whites; Europeans, Asians, Africans, delegates from Vietnam, India, Mexico, Algeria and Laos.'[24]*

The atmosphere of the Congress is vividly conveyed by Andrew Salkey, in his book-length account *Havana Journal*. Participants joined one of five working parties on different aspects of the problems of culture, underdevelopment, national independence, and the mass media. Salkey joined the group discussing intellectual responsibility in the underdeveloped world and gives a very detailed report of its sessions. The Cuban Federico Alvarez read the opening paper, on the theme that 'One kind of man is dying and a new kind is being born, and the intellectual must assist in his birth':

Alvarez suggested that we must own up to Julio Cortázar's dictum: '*Every intellectual belongs to the Third World!*'

In reply, C.L.R.[James] objected to one of Alvarez's statements which included the fact that Albert Schweitzer had contributed to the emancipation and development of the Third World. C.L.R. also proposed that all intellectuals, those from the developed world and those from the underdeveloped, should be firmly discouraged, and in fact abolished as a force.

Salon dead still. Consternation. Bewildered, silent delegates everywhere.

Alvarez disagreed vehemently. He counter-proposed by saying that the Third World has the right to make use of the finest intellectual energy and benefits which it can pluck from the developed world. He said that the Third

---

* Participants from Britain, who numbered twenty-three, included Arnold Wesker, Nathaniel Tarn, David Mercer, Adrian Mitchell, Ralph Milliband, Eric Hobsbawm, David Cooper, Irving Teitelbaum. Bertrand Russell, like Sartre and Ernst Fischer, sent a message of support. The US delegation included Jules Feiffer, David Dellinger, Barbara Dane and Irwin Silber. Amongst others from Europe – including sixty-six from France, twenty-seven from Spain and twenty-five from Italy – there were Michel Leiris, Jorge Semprun, Hans Magnus Enzensberger, Rossana Rossanda. From Latin America and the Caribbean, apart from the host country, there were seventy-five. The Antillans included C.L.R. James, Aimé Cesaire, John La Rose, Andrew Salkey, René Depestre; the continental Latins, Mario Benedetti, Julio Cortázar, Adolfo Sanchez Vasquez, etc. etc.

World does have to depend on the help, cultural development, technology, wealth, good will, troubled conscience and proved sincerity of the few countries of its choosing in the developed world. It is vitally important, he advised, that the Third World learned to pick and choose with great care and with enlightened self-interest.

Julio Cortázar of Argentina explained, succinctly, that the ivory tower intellectual is dead.[25]

Thus the Congress proceeded through its eight days, with the Cubans presiding over the thorniest sessions and acting as peacemakers with great skill and tact.

C.L.R. James' call for the disappearance of the intellectual may have struck his audience as shocking because it seemed out of step with what might be called the tone of revolutionary existentialism of the Latin American intellectual which dominated the intellectual style of the Congress. The concept of the intellectual with which this philosophy operated was well articulated by the Uruguayan writer Mario Benedetti.[26] To begin with, the intellectual is seen as a non-conforming social critic, a witness with an implacable memory. The type stands opposed to another familiar kind of Latin American, the man of action (a term which is not exactly sexist, for the type itself is a male type, a *machista* category – though Benedetti can be criticised for not making this clear). The motivation of the man of action, whether political *caudillo* or entrepreneur, army officer or advertising agent, is 'the search for a dynamic style in his way of life'. Most of them, however, says Benedetti, 'are the typical exponents of a dissolute conformism before the most abject exigencies of the empire. To such a man of action, the intellectual begins to acquire a certain ignominious reputation as the passive observer, or the static being.' But in fact, within the revolution, the intellectual may fulfil a new kind of activity: the anthropologist, the linguist or the ethnologist, for example, may play a decisive role in providing the guerrilla with real knowledge of the population in which a *foco* is to be established. (One can also think of the role of the revolutionary priest in a number of revolutionary movements across Latin America.)

Also, of course, it falls to intellectuals to become guardians of truth. If this is a somewhat unfashionable idea for post-war generations in Europe, it was nevertheless a European, Régis Debray, who said, as quoted by Benedetti: 'Militant is also he who in his own intellectual work ideologically combats the class enemy, he who in his work as an artist roots out the privilege of beauty from the ruling class.' Explains Benedetti: 'The truth is that neither beauty nor art is to be blamed for having been monopolised for centuries by the social strata which had easy access to culture. At the same time as it liberates the soil and the subsoil, the Revolution also tends to put an end to the latifundists of culture, to restore to the people its well-earned right of having access to beauty, of ascending to good taste, of producing its own art.'

Finally, the intellectual becomes, within the revolution, its vigilant conscience, its imaginative interpreter and its critic. But this word 'critic' is problematic, too ambiguous. There is a crucial difference from bourgeois society, where the critic, to be more than either apologist or mere journalist and reviewer, is forced to take up an antagonistic stance. In revolutionary Cuba, such a stance was by now liable to seem sectarian and divisive – and this was something which worried not the functionaries with their own sectarian susceptibilities but other intellectuals, with a better grasp of the movement of history. Alea's film of the same year as the Congress, *Memorias del subdesarrollo*, with its incapacitated and unfulfilled writer as its anti-hero, and its self-enclosed round-table discussion of intellectuals and artists, is very much about this struggle for redefinition by the intellectual, the struggle to pass successfully through the *desgarramiento*, the 'rupture', which was spoken of by Roque Dalton and Roberto Fernández Retamar.[27]

Still, it is clear enough what Benedetti envisages as the role of the intellectual within the revolution. The dichotomy between the intellectual and the man of action is not to find its solution in the intellectual becoming the amanuensis of the revolutionary, a coarse puppet of the kind the bourgeois media love to ridicule. '"We must not create wage-earners, docile to official thought", Che Guevara warned us,' says Benedetti. Nevertheless, the intellectual is to take on a certain role, like that of the technician, the teacher, or even the athlete: a person with particular skills all of which are needed in the effort to create a new kind of human being, a job just like any other.

Not that this really contradicts C.L.R. James, it's only a less shocking way of putting things. For James is not talking of the intellectual abdicating responsibilities but rather of a kind of self-propelled dissolution of the intellectual's privileges – which is also what ought to happen in Benedetti's scheme of things. Besides, what James has to say about the Caribbean intellectual is very relevant. The West Indian intellectual for James means such names as Marcus Garvey, George Padmore, Frantz Fanon; Bellay, Dumas pére, Leconte de Lisle, José de Heredia, St-John Perse, Aimé Cesaire; the West Indian novelists, including Alejo Carpentier and Wilson Harris; 'and the American revolutionary leader Stokely Carmichael who was born in Trinidad'. In the brief discussion paper he presented to the Congress, which Salkey quotes in full, he explains:

This unprecedented role of West Indian intellectuals is due to the fact that the population of an underdeveloped area uses highly developed modern languages and, although many of us live at a level little above that of slavery, the structure of life is essentially European . . . That situation has produced this tremendous body of intellectuals both in politics and in literature whose climax has been attained in the Cuba Revolution, embodied, for our purposes, in the work and personality of Fidel Castro . . . The Cuban Revolution tells us that the remarkable contributions which the West Indian type of intellectual has made to the emancipation of Africa and to the development of Western civilization have now come to an end. This unprecedented capacity for creative contributions to civilizations must not now be primarily applied abroad, as formerly in regard to Africa, or to the development of French or

British literature; but it is in the application of this capacity to the life of the Americas that the West Indian intellectual will find the necessary elements for the development of culture in the underdeveloped countries, and this must not be forgotten in the developed countries as well.

There were, however, many difficulties which got in the way of the greater understanding of the conditions of underdevelopment by the artist of the metropolis. The whole historical situation seemed to go against it, as the Mexican philospher Adolfo Sánchez Vásquez explained.[28] There is a powerful link, the philospher argued, between revolutionary idealism and aesthetic experiment. Artistic creation has long revealed a tendency towards rupture and innovation whenever creative possibilities have fallen into decadence and been exhausted. An artistic vanguard arises in opposition to the dominant aesthetic order, in order to ensure the continuity of innovation and creative movement. The notion of a decadent avant-garde is in this sense a contradiction in terms: there is, in fact, a definite incompatibility in capitalist society between the artistic vanguard and the social decadence which surrounds it. But the manner in which an artist responds to this situation, and to the nature of the ideological machinery which is brought into action against the avant-garde, is crucial. There are several historical phases which can be distinguished. Surrealism, for instance, marks the limits of protest of an artistic vanguard which, not wishing to accept such conditions, attempts to draw closer to the political vanguard. (Doubtless Sánchez Vásquez is thinking here of the Manifesto *Towards Revolutionary Art* written by his compatriot, the muralist Diego Rivera, with the French surrealist André Breton, and Trotsky as their collaborator.) The ruling echelons, however, discovering that artistic revolutions do not really endanger the body politic, learn to modify their initial hostility towards the avant-garde. The rebellious artist is no longer proscribed, but tempted instead, and provisions are made for the avant-garde's incorporation – but only on condition that it remain isolated from the broad populace. (This, one may add, is not too difficult, since the institutions of art, the galleries and museums, the dealers and auctioneers, have already isolated High Art, allowing access only through a protective and myth-making grid which removes it from living experience.) If the artist gives in, artistic rebellion is contained by social conformism, and becomes the accomplice of the bourgeois order.

It would be false, says Sánchez Vásquez, to reply to these conditions with utopianism or voluntarism. Artistic revolutions *cannot* change society. But nor should the endeavour be put aside or renounced in favour of a search for lost communication by means of simplification or vulgarisation. This way the vanguard can only negate itself. To remain true to the drives that produce artistic revolutions, the artist is obliged to find ways of relating his or her work to the diverse currents of struggle for social transformation; in fact the artist's revolutionary needs are double: to dissolve the illusion that aesthetic revolution can be self-sufficient, and to show that political and social conformism are incompatible with artistic creativity. Unfortunately, orthodox Marxist-Leninist politics, both within and beyond the socialist camp, has contributed to the split through a failure to think through properly the categories of 'progressive' and 'reactionary', and through a failure of imagination concerning the possible meeting between aesthetics and politics. (Here one might add: in spite of the successful work of Rivera, of Eisenstein, and Vertov, of John Heartfield, Bertolt Brecht and Kurt Weill, and quite a few more.) Bourgeois ideologies have been able to exploit this situation by encouraging the avant-gardes to try and preserve themselves from contagion by politics. With the result that many artists close their eyes to the real significance and magnitude of the modernist revolution, and turn instead to formalist and decadent preoccupations (whereupon they cease to be a real avant-garde at all).

If this scheme sounds over-simplified, we need only remember that Latin American society allows many fewer subtleties, the characteristics of the social formation are more starkly and clearly seen – in the same way that the very sight of rich and poor is starkly contrasted in cities where mansions are overshadowed by shanty towns, and poverty invades every street. And in this kind of world, the Cuban Revolution had brought about, said Sánchez Vásquez, the timid beginnings of a profound change, for it created the first real experience in Latin America of a revolution in an underdeveloped country, where the springs of popular culture have not yet been alienated to anything like the degree of their alienation and destruction in the metropolis. The Revolution opened up a field of action for the artist and intellectual, a potential influence in the creation of new cultural values of a kind no longer within reach in the metropolis – not in the same way that the artist and intellectual had a formative influence a century and more ago. For Sánchez Vásquez, the Cuban Revolution was not only a creative act in itself, it also established the conditions for art to become a social birthright, through creating a new base from which the dichotomies and antinomies of bourgeois society could be overcome.

It also, he believes, showed that vital questions of art such as freedom of expression are *political* problems which require of the artist a revolutionary political commitment – but again, of a kind that does not imply a servile relationsip to politics. Clearly the function of the artistic vanguard changes. In the first place, the sudden acceleration which the Revolution engenders places many traditional values in crisis through the exertion of a new reality which demands novel forms of expression. At the same time, the inertia of traditional forms intervenes, and to attack this resistance, a new spirit of experimentalism is also needed. Inevitably there are problems. The new reality creates a new audience which is still naive because only newly literate. The artistic vanguard therefore begins to split into two again: there are some who remain attached to experiment for experiment's sake, and take advantage of the revolutionary principles which vouchsafe stylistic freedom; others, however, look to the application of a critical consciousness for the creation of new forms, in which the traditions of the avant-garde can be preserved, only modified by the demands of the new audience.

This whole argument is clearly allied to the position at ICAIC. It also finds force in the connection to be found between this upsurge of experimentalism in Cuba in the late 60s and the wider political events of the period, in particular the intensification of international struggle. For the difference between the two avant-gardes – and not only in Cuba – or between what perhaps should be called the traditional avant-garde and a new political-artistic vanguard, is nowhere more clearly to be seen than in the response of the latter to international events, which is usually entirely lacking in the former. There can rarely be found in history as direct an artistic expression of political affairs – on the contrary, such connections are usually indirect and often delayed. But the 1960s were an exceptional decade, exploding in 1968 into months of intense and violent agitation, protest, confrontation and rebelliousness right across the globe. In Europe, there were many intellectuals who solemnly declared their decision to commit suicide as a class. In Cuba, in April 1967, the revolutionary body OSPAAAL (Organisation for Solidarity Among the Peoples of Africa, Asia and Latin America) published the text of a message from Che Guevara calling upon Latin American revolutionaries to declare their solidarity with Vietnam, and to create 'two, three, many Vietnams' in their own continent.[25] Four months later the Latin American Solidarity Organisation, OLAS, held a widely publicised conference in Havana, which declared the political, economic and social unity of Latin America to be far more significant than the political divisions and antagonisms in the continent.

Cuba had been gripped with an intense spirit of internationalism ever since Che had departed the island in 1965 'for new fields of battle', as Fidel informed the people. Fidel, after Che's departure, gave continued support to his ideas and their moral emphasis. It was in any case a constant element in Fidel's own thinking that 'the duty of a revolutionary is to make a revolution'[30] and that revolutionaries are not to be distinguished by adherence to scholarly principles but rather 'the best textbook in matters of revolution [is] the revolutionary process itself'.[31] There were plenty, and not only on the right, who accused the Cubans of the invention of a new revolutionary dogma of guerrilla struggle, when Che was killed in Bolivia. The Cultural Congress had already been called when the event took place, and when the intellectuals gathered in Havana, the spirit of defiance was high. Fulfilling expectation, Fidel took the opportunity in his address to the closing session – which some interpreted as a defiant reply to critics – to praise the assembled company for the way the intellectuals had carried Che's banner to the rest of the world after his death, when politicians and political organisations of the left had failed to respond. And to the delight of the audience, he repeated his conviction that 'Marxism needs to develop, to break away from a certain rigidity, to interpret today's reality from an objective, scientific viewpoint, to conduct itself as a revolutionary force and not as a pseudo-revolutionary church.'[32] The debates didn't cease after this, any more than after the 'Words to the Intellectuals'. A series of articles appeared in *Verde Olivo*, the journal of the Cuban armed forces, directed against refractory intellectuals. There was even, among some of them (if they hadn't left), a stiffening of attitude that was to cause further trouble. But at ICAIC, the euphoria of experimentalism was in full flood.

# References

1. Conversation with T.G. Alea, Havana, June 1984.
2. *Ibid.*
3. Cf. B. Ruby Rich, 'Madcap comedy Cuban style', *Jump Cut* No.22.
4. See Bernardo Callejas, 'La muerte de un burocrata', *Granma* 28 July 1966, and Desiderio Navarro, 'La muerte de un burocrata', *Adelante* (Camagüey), 23 August 1966.
5. In Rodríguez Aleman, op.cit.
6. Conversation with T.G. Alea, Havana, January 1980.
7. B. Ruby Rich, op.cit.
8. Callejas, op.cit.
9. Conversation with Alea, Havana, January 1980.
10. 'Resultados de una discusión', cit.
11. Pablo Martínez, 'Entrevista con Humberto Solás', *Hablemos de Cine* (Peru) No.54.
12. *Vanguardia* (Santa Clara), 26 December 1967.
13. *Verde Olivo*, 1 October 1967.
14. 'Julio García Espinosa en dos tiempos', *Hablemos de Cine* No.54.
15. See Julio García Espinosa, 'A proposito de Aventuras de Juan Quin Quin', *Cine y Revolución en Cuba*, Editorial Fontamara, Barcelona 1975, pp.157-160.
16. Anna Marie Taylor, 'Imperfect Cinema, Brecht and *The Adventures of Juan Quin Quin'*, *Jump Cut* No.20.
17. See 'Fotonovelas: la realidad entre paréntesis', in Michèle Mattelart, *La cultura de la opresión femenina*, Ediciones Era, Mexico 1977; also Fellini's first solo film as director, *Lo Sceicco Bianco*.
18. García Espinosa, 1975, op.cit.
19. Conversation with Julio García Espinosa, Havana, January 1980.
20. In Hogg ed., *Psychology and the Visual Arts*, Penguin, 1969, p.114; see also A. Ehrenzweig, *The Psychoanalysis of Artistic Vision and Hearing*, Routledge and Kegan Paul, 1953, especially Ch. II.
21. Bell Gale Chevigny, 'Running the Blockade: Six Cuban Writers', *Socialist Review* No.59, 1981, p.92.
22. Quoted in Herbert Schiller, *Mass Communications and American Empire*, Beacon Press, Boston 1971, p.106.
23. Conversation with Alfredo Guevara, Havana, January 1980.
24. Alonso Aguilar, 'The Intellectuals and the Revolution', *Monthly Review* Vol.19 No.10, March 1968.
25. Andrew Salkey, *Havana Journal*, Penguin, 1971, p.110.
26. Salkey, op.cit., p.118ff.
27. See *El intellectual y la sociedad*, cit.
28. 'Vanguardia artistica y vanguardia politica' in *Literatura y arte nuevo en Cuba*, Editorial Laia, Barcelona 1977.
29. Che Guevara, 'Socialism and Man in Cuba' and other works, Instituto del Libro, 1968.
30. Second Declaration of Havana, 4 February 1962, in *Fidel Castro Speaks*, Penguin, 1972, p.127.
31. Speech of 28th September 1967, *Granma Weekly Review* 8 October 1967.
32. Speech of 12 January 1968, *Granma Weekly Review* 21 January 1968.

# 12
# FOUR FILMS

*La odisea de General José, Lucía, Memorias del subdesarollo, La primera carga al machete*

Of the fiction films released by ICAIC in 1968, the most closely related to the figure of Che Guevara himself is Jorge Fraga's *La odisea de General José*. Premiered at the end of February, it was one of the first of a group of films around the theme of the hundred years struggle, which also included *Lucía* and *La primera carga al machete*, the short fiction *El desertor* ('The Deserter') by Manuel Pérez, and two documentaries, Saderman's *Hombres del mal tiempo* and *1868-1968* by Bernabé Hernandez. These films were more than a celebration of the anniversary of the start of the Cuban Wars of Independence: they constituted an extended essay in *cine rescate*, the recovery of history from the suppression, distortion and falsification to which it had been subjected by bourgeois ideology. As Manuel Octavio Gómez expressed it, they were films that corresponded to an historical necessity to discover the sources of Cuban nationhood, and the continuity between the birth of the independence struggle and the final achievement of national liberation with the victory of the Revolution.[1]

Internationalism is a theme which repeats itself in several of these films. In *General José*, José Maceo and his brother Antonio are Dominicans, not Cubans; nor were they the only foreigners to take part in the Cuban struggle at one stage or another. The same is true of Che Guevara himself of course, an Argentinian who was engaged in his last internationalist endeavour in Bolivia at the same time this film was being shot. The film is based on an incident recounted in a letter by another independence leader, Máximo Gómez,[2] and further informed by a careful study of Gómez's Campaign Diary. The incident in question occurred in 1895, when José and Antonio landed in Oriente province with some twenty comrades, to join the freedom fighters engaged in the new campaign against the Spanish which had just been launched. A few days after the landing, the group is surprised by an enemy ambush from which they only just manage to escape, becoming dispersed in the process. José seeks refuge with two or three others in the mountain forests where the film opens, hiding behind trees, using the undergrowth for camouflage, to escape the Spanish soldiers pursuing them.[3]

The identification of the camera with the pursued permeates and pervades the entire film, but without any of the tricks which genre cinema plays in such situations. Suspense is an alien posture to this film. The bond between the camera and the subject is of a completely different order. After an exemplary scene in which the General shares with a compañero an edible snail plucked from a bush, the group is once more attacked; he himself makes an escape by jumping a precipice, but his companions are either killed or captured. The camera now indissolubly attached to a single man, it transfixes him and becomes a wholly objective scrutineer of his struggle against nature to survive. The intensity which the film takes on in this portrayal invokes memories of King Lear shorn of all pretence in the face of the tempest, or invites comparison with Kurosawa's *Dersu Uzala* and the solitary individual battling for survival against the full force of nature's might in the Siberian winter: here it's a tropical forest. For the Cubans, there was also shortly to be a more immediate source of comparison. 'We had walked a kilometre,' wrote Che Guevara in his Bolivian diary (entry for 16 June 1967):

> when we saw the men of the vanguard on the other side. Pancho had found the ford and had crossed it while exploring. We crossed with the icy water up to our waists and with some current – without mishap. We arrived at the Rosita an hour later, where we noticed some old footprints, apparently the army's. We then became aware that the Rosita was deeper than we had foreseen and that there are no traces of the trail marked on the map. We walked for an hour in the icy water and then decided to camp so as to take advantage of the *palmito*

*La odisea de General José*

*de totai* [edible top of the palm tree, usually considered a delicacy] and to try and find a beehive that Miguel had seen while exploring yesterday; we did not find it, and ate only *mote* [dried corn kernels boiled without salt] and *palmito* with lard. There is still food for tomorrow and the day after (*mote*). We walked for three kilometres down the Rosita and another three down the Rio Grande. Height: 610 metres.[4]

Miguel Benavides turns in a carefully measured performance as the General, holding the screen alone for a large part of the film, displaying as he confronts the hostile environment the steel will and tenacity that Fidel recalled in Che. When a cold wind begins to blow he starts to perform a weird kind of dance, running backwards and forwards and beating his arms across his chest to keep warm; when it starts raining he crouches down to keep his bag and rifle covered. In all of this, the most memorable aspect of the film, the camera is the actor's most intimate partner, counterpointed by the chatter of the forest on the soundtrack, until, hungry and fevered, Maceo begins to hallucinate and meets a corpse. The moment is one of highly charged ambiguity: is this his tormented imagining or the real remains of another fleeing *guerrillero?* The Peruvian critic Nelson García Miranda finds this the first occasion in Cuban cinema in which the movement from the conscious to the unconscious – attempted by several directors – is accomplished with the same conviction as in – his example is – Mizoguchi's *Ugetsu monogatari.*[5] Humberto Solas will achieve something similar even more effectively in the first part of *Lucía.*

In *Lucía*, Humberto Solás has interpreted the theme of the hundred years' struggle in an entirely novel way to create an epic in three separate episodes: each centres around a woman called Lucía and takes place in a different period of Cuban history, corresponding to the three stages of colonialism, neocolonialism and socialist revolution; the three episodes also present us with Lucías of different social classes. In the first, the year is 1895, approaching the climax of the Wars of Independence, the milieu is that of the landed creole aristocracy. The second episode takes place in 1933 at the moment of the abortive revolution in which the dictator Machado was overthrown; this time Lucía is a member of the bourgeoisie. Finally the Revolution, 196-, and Lucía is a rural peasant girl, a member of a new agricultural collective.

A love story provides the basic plot for each episode: the first is tragic, the second melodramatic, the third a comedy. The first and last are of a richness that can only be called Shakespearian. This, and the film's length (160 minutes) make it by far the most ambitious movie that ICAIC had yet attempted, and the most expensive. Solás chose to make women his principal protagonists, as in *Manuela*, because, he explained, 'The woman's role always lays bare the contradictions of a period and makes them explicit... *Lucía* is not a film about women; it's a film about society. But within that society, I chose the most vulnerable character, the one who is most transparently affected at any given moment by contradictions and changes.'[6] This, he says, has nothing to do with feminism *per se*. Nonetheless, the final episode is directly concerned with 'the problem of *machismo*... which undermines a woman's chances of self-fulfilment and at the same time feeds a whole subculture of underdevelopment.'

On another occasion, Solás explained the germination of the film. 'I began to prepare *Lucía* rapidly following the premiere of *Manuela*. The present group of stories is not what originally appeared in the first project. Only the first remains. The second and third (those concerning the Republic and the Revolution) were not accepted. In truth, it was a very different film from the present one. And I'm really happy that the project as a whole was not approved. Neither of the rejected stories has ceased to interest me: a satire on the Republic seen through a couple trying to find a place to make love one day in Santiago de Cuba, and a dramatic story on the difficulties of a pair of lovers (him married, her single) who work in the same firm. But with the passage of time, I feel that the stories that have been substituted for these give the film a much richer and more harmonious structure.'[7] Aesthetically, the most interesting thing about the alteration is that not only have the stories been changed but the positions of the melodramatic and the humorous episodes have been swapped around. At the same time, the changes are a positive result of the production system at ICAIC, where scripts are able to evolve through criticism, which unsympathetic commentators describe as regimentation and censorship.

'Lucía 1895' begins – like the other episodes – with a paradigmatic shot that presents the historical period in a dominant aspect; in this case a town square framed to show its colonial architecture weighing down upon the inhabitants. We are introduced to the daughters of the aristocracy, lavishly dressed and parasoled, living a life of opulence, leisure, gossip and superficiality. Several of the many accounts of the film – *Lucía* has been written about more than any other Cuban film except *Memorias del subdesarrollo* – emphasise the European appearance of this group 'with its imported furniture, sculptures, photographs and drapes' and 'the envy displayed towards the new Parisian husband and hat of a returning acquaintance'.[8] Lucía herself, according to the most substantial of these accounts, by the North American critic Stephen Kovacs, is 'a spinster who stands at that delicate age where she is still capable of falling in love but is already on the road to settling in to a carefully circumscribed world of maidenhood... her company consists only of her family and of other women of her class... while her friends bubble with excitement at afternoon tea parties, she remains sedate, smiling, accommodating.'[9] Playing the part, Raquel Revuelta, one of Cuba's leading stage actresses, displays in Kovacs' eyes the linear features of a classic Spanish profile. For the Peruvian critic Isaac León Frias, the similarity of her appearance to that of Dolores del Río or María Felix is not accidental, for we are in the world of 1940s Mexican melodrama crossed with Emily Bronte's *Wuthering Heights*.[10] Solás himself has mentioned the influence of the novels of Flaubert.[11]

Suddenly, in stark contrast to the comforts of the aristocratic setting, there is

'Lucia 1895': Idalia Anreus as Fernandina

a cut to a cart full of bloody, ragged bodies of soldiers making its way through the streets, and the character of Fernandina – a bravura performance by Idalia Anreus as the mad nun whose story parallels Lucía's as Gloucester's does King Lear's. The tale of her brutal rape by Spanish soldiers which drove her mad is told with morbid excitement by one of Lucía's companions, and we see it on the screen in surrealistic, overexposed shots, which Anna Marie Taylor describes as a 'dream-like allegory, the rape of Cuba by Spain'.[12]

As a virgin approaching middle age, anxiously hoping for a man to appear to complete her social existence, Lucía's life changes when she meets Rafael, a Spanish dandy who professes love to her. The last flower of an effete and doomed colonial culture, explains another commentator on the film, Peter Biskind, Lucía breaks away into the only alternative available to a woman of her class and time: 'She abandons herself to a grand passion, to a myth of self-fulfilment... which is as derivative in its way of a bygone Byronism as the finery of her class is imitative of Paris fashions.'[13] Her happiness is shattered, however, by the rumour that Rafael is a married man. She goes to meet him at an abandoned sugar mill – an ambiguous location: Kovacs calls it 'a desolate monastery', a Venezuelan critic 'a small abandoned fort'.[14] As Kovacs describes the scene, Rafael 'tries to insist on his love for her. The genteel mood of courtship is past. He looks darker, more menacing, desperate, as he chases her amidst sombre stone walls. He throws himself upon her, attempting to possess her at once. His energy spent, he retreats into a corner, like a beaten animal, sobbing in the dark. Lucía herself has changed: her dishevelled clothes and her hair in disarray indicate that she has come closer than ever before to her own sexuality . . . she approaches resolutely, tears his shirt and embraces him.' Several critics have found this an extraordinary scene, but too extended. For the Venezuelans, the way the camera hugs the walls with Lucía as she retreats before Rafael – the subjective camera in full flood again – is an image of beauty as long as its signification is fresh, but once exhausted it becomes precious. For Daniel Díaz Torres, the scene is 'one of the most beautifully achieved moments of all, containing an almost perfect blending of the sentimental and the visual, or of the sentimental-aesthetic – some other ambiguous term might do just as well,' but again it should have been shorter.[15] What is certainly true is that there is something very uncomfortable about this scene. Biskind remarks that 'in the fragile world of colonial Cuba, far from Europe, [Lucía's] gestures of passion become a strained and unnatural parody of borrowed forms, a feverish mimicry of Continental literary romances.' This could also be said of the very style of the film, except that it is perfectly deliberate in its feverish mimicry of the grand style of directors like Visconti or Fellini.

Lucía's passion is shattered, however, in a collision with historical reality (as Biskind neatly puts it). Gradually the political conflict that surrounds them inserts itself. As a guest at her house, Rafael purports to have no interest in taking sides in the war, while she, on the other hand, is a tacit supporter of the revolutionaries through her love for her brother Felipe, who is organising guerrillas on the family plantation. When Rafael entreats her to take him to the estate, the full political drama unfolds. As they approach their destination, the Spanish cavalry suddenly emerges to wage battle on the guerrillas. As Rafael

'Lucia 1895': Raquel Revuelta

dumps her in the middle of the Spanish troops he has led to the site, Lucía realises that he has been using her to accomplish his task as a Spanish agent. The battle claims her brother as a victim and, back in the city, driven mad with shame and sorrow, she finds Rafael, dressed in Spanish uniform, and publicly stabs him to death. The critics are generally agreed that this is not just a murder for revenge, but the execution of the oppressor.

Solás has acknowledged Visconti as an influence; the critics concur. Biskind pins the model down to *Senso*, the tale of a high-born Italian woman compromised by a desperate passion for an Austrian officer which leads her to betray her patriotic cousin and her country during the war of Italian unification (though in Solás, Lucía is more the victim than Visconti's Livia, more a pawn of forces beyond her comprehension). But if, says Biskind, the affair between the lovers is 'orchestrated to a score of sighs, flutters, fixed stares and throbbing music characteristic of the later, operatic Visconti', for the trip to the plantation – lush, mist-shrouded tropical rain-forest – Solás has adopted the look of Kurosawa; while the stark landscape of battle he finds reminiscent of Has's *Saragossa Manuscript*: 'In fact, this entire section of Lucía is strongly flavoured with a feverish romanticism characteristic of the Polish school in some of its wilder moments.' This is not such an unlikely comparison: the Cuban critic Puri Faget refers to the influence of the Polish director Jerzy Kawalerowicz's *Mother Joan of the Angels*, a film which seems to have made a deep impression in Cuba.[16] One thing is certain. *Lucía* is just the kind of film which inspires critics to the heights of speculation about its sources and influences. The names of Buñuel, Godard, Antonioni, Resnais and Bergman have all been mentioned. For Díaz Torres, the battle recalls the extraordinary battle sequence in Orson Welles' *Chimes at Midnight*. Solás himself outdoes his critics by bringing in Pasolini as well. He also mentions the Brazilian Cinema Novo directors, and Faget believes that Glauber Rocha's concept of the Aesthetics of Violence is more important than the Italian or Polish influences. Cinema Novo, Rocha wrote, 'teaches that the aesthetics of violence are revolutionary rather than primitive. The moment of violence is the moment when the coloniser becomes aware of the existence of the colonised. Only when he is confronted with violence can the coloniser understand, through horror, the strength of the culture he exploits.'[17]

As for the role of Fernandina, there is a crucial moment half way through the tale, when Lucía decides to ride off with Rafael, when their paths cross. She steps out onto the street and immediately Fernandina throws herself on her, pleading with her not to go. They meet again at the end, after Lucía has executed her lover, Fernandina following her as she is led away. Lucía is a daughter of the upper classes with fine Castilian features; Fernandina a *mestiza* with dark skin and the hooked nose of her ancestors. Lucía we first meet surrounded by her friends in a tranquil environment, and situated within a stationary framing, Fernandina we encounter crazed and alone in the streets, pictured with a jerking shifting hand-held camera. This scheme of binary oppositions is every bit as poetic and resonant as it would be in a Shakespeare play. The coming together of these two women at the end, Kovacs observes, produces 'not only a moment of human recognition and solidarity, but a confluence of mythical forces as well'.

These mythical forces find their most luminous symbolic expression in the battle scene, which for Kovacs is 'one of the most striking ever to appear on the screen. Naked black men ride out on horses to meet the Spanish cavalry: they are man and horse combined, human flesh joined to animal, modern centaurs bringing horror to the uniformed Spanish...' The image is not invented by Solás. A troop like this rode in the Wars of Independence at night, naked because it made their black bodies almost invisible. With the cry they let out as they rode into battle, they had a terrifying effect on the enemy.[18] That image, says Kovacs, 'seems so modern, yet its modernity is merely an affirmation of its mythic, timeless verity.' At first, he says,

we are aware only of the massive, choreographed battle scenes in the manner of Hollywood and Soviet spectaculars. Soon the men are on the ground and we recognize the hand-to-hand combat implanted in our memories by countless fist-fights in Western saloons. Then suddenly a new sensation overtakes us as we experience the physical agitation of the hand-held camera running after the soldiers. The unwritten but strictly observed rule requiring a relatively stable image on the screen is flung to the past as our eyes ricochet off one body, then another, our balance upset, our senses jerked to attention. Yes, the hand-held camera has been used before by New Wave directors, but they sought to create a casual, personal – at the most extreme – disjointed style. Solás, on the other hand, infuses the image with a kinetic tension unknown to his Parisian predecessors, almost as if the storm of the battle engulfed the camera in one of its powerful waves. Even in its agitated state the camera responds to his command to focus in close-up, if only momentarily, upon distorted faces, distended limbs. [This is where *Chimes at Midnight* is evoked.] He used the hand-held camera and extreme close-up before, when he wanted to depict the rape of Fernandina and her harassment on the streets, and he uses them again in the final scene of Lucía's revenge and emotional collapse.

This technique of hand-held close-ups keeps recurring, Kovacs speculates, because it faithfully expresses both individual anguish and mass violence, two succeeding stages in the struggle against oppression.

The cameraman who accomplished this, one of the most creative cinematographers not only in Cuba but throughout Latin America, was Jorge Herrera. From now on, the increasingly fluid use of the hand-held camera will recur in a good number of Cuban films, reaching its apogee in the work of its most sensitive and creative practitioner, Mario García Joya (Mayito), in the films of T.G. Alea in the 70s. Indeed, Mayito built his own blimps – the sound-proof casing which masks the noise of the camera motor from the microphone – specially designed to make it easier to carry the weight of a fully loaded 35mm movie camera. The aesthetic effects of the technique will vary, of course, and the associations and connotations of the style will not remain fixed. What Solás and Herrera achieve in *Lucía* is not to provide the language of Cuban cinema with new terms of vocabulary, but the elaboration, in flinging the rule of the relatively stable image away, of a startling new tone of voice, an uncompromising new accent. Manuel Octavio Gómez and Herrera in *La primera carga al machete* and Alea and Mayito in *Una pelea cubana contra los demonios* ('A Cuban Battle Against the Demons', 1971), will adapt this new accent to their own expressive needs. Both of them also exceptional films, a number of critics have found them physically straining to watch. Indeed they strain at the very fabric of vision, pressing against the limits of visual comprehension as they wrench at traditional patterns of perception in giving birth to the new.

After the heightened bravura of 'Lucía 1895', 'Lucía 1933' is more controlled and gentler on the eyes. It is also the most personal of the three stories. In 'Lucía 1933', Solás explained in the *Jump Cut* interview,

> I'm reflecting a family experience, particularly the story of my father – a man who participated in the insurrection against the dictatorship of Gerardo Machado. He didn't die a violent death then, as the character Aldo does, but he 'died' as a vital human being – a sort of death by frustration. When I was born, I was surrounded by all those ghosts, by a failed revolution, by a man whose course in life was interrupted by this collective failure.
>
> That segment of the film grows in part out of the need to express this experience which, though not directly mine, touched me deeply. The fact that I joined the revolutionary insurrection against Batista when I was very young, given my lack of ideological orientation at the time and the spontaneous nature of my actions, must have had a lot to do with my desire to resume my father's interrupted trajectory.

Where 'Lucía 1895' is Europeanised, 'Lucía 1933' is already closer to North American culture, and belongs to the commercial middle class. The establishing shot, however, which opens the episode (like the colonial town square previously) is this time of a factory interior, the camera looking down towards its women workers with Lucía among them, and the story is then told in flashback. The flashback begins with Lucía and her imposing mother arriving by ferry at one of the offshore keys for a vacation in their summer house away from the city. (We later find out that they have been sent there early in the season by Lucía's father to allow him more time with his mistress in Havana.) Lucía observes the clandestine arrival, after a gun battle in the streets of Havana, of the wounded Aldo, and she becomes involved with him. Kovacs observes that the contrast between the spacious summer house and Aldo's single room succinctly spells out the contrast of life-styles which Lucía now begins to cross. Her mother posing in front of an ornate mirror is contrasted with Lucía in long shot sitting up in bed in Aldo's bare room. Their love is very gentle. Aldo confesses, 'You are my first love; I'm not sorry to say, you're my first woman.' Obviously he is her first love too.

The mirror shot of her mother is particularly significant. There have already been mirror shots in 'Lucía 1895', especially a shot of Lucía preparing herself to

'Lucia 1933'

meet Rafael, with the camera watching the mirror image over her shoulder so that the social stereotype of her mirrored self is at the centre of attention. The image of the mother in 1933, however, is shown from a camera position that is quite clearly her daughter's point-of-view. According to the detailed visual analysis in a second essay on the film by John Mraz, this shot captures 'the neocolonial deformities of Cuban culture [which] are expressed in her imitation of Jean Harlow'.[19] Then, 'after seeing her mother serve as a model of colonised femininity, Lucía enters the room and is forced by her mother to sit in front of the mirror in order to be moulded into the same alienated patterns'. The different relationship mother and daughter each has to her mirror image is given expression in the different composition of the two shots, in particular the way the segmented reflection of the daughter cuts across the film frame. It is clearly to escape from this alienation that Lucía joins Aldo; the equality of their relationship is based on this knowledge she already has of the nature of the world she comes from. With him, she is able to learn about the world she has been guarded from.

Back in Havana, Lucía goes to work. And while the menfolk carry out an ambush on a bunch of policemen enjoying a rehearsal for a 'girlie show', Lucía is organising the women in the factory. Parallel editing between the two compares and contrasts the two modes of exploitation of women in the pseudo-republic, the rampantly sexified as opposed to the artificially demure, as Lucía also discovers that mirrors can be put to new purposes: for scrawling political slogans on them with lipstick.

There are demonstrations on the streets in which the women participate, which are violently suppressed. Still, Machado falls. The Revolution, however, is abortive and produces no fundamental change. What transpires is well described by Mraz in his earlier article: 'The disillusionment of Lucía and Aldo with the new situation contrasts sharply with the opportunism shown by their counterparts and former co-revolutionaries, Antonio and Flora. While the latter move quickly to ensure themselves an advantageous position in the regime, Aldo and Lucía remain true to the ideas that guided them in the struggle against Machado. Sickened by the decadence and debauchery which characterize the new political arrangements... Aldo returns to terrorist activity. He is killed and Lucía is left alone, as indeed the superficiality of the relationship with Flora, her only friend, had shown her to be almost throughout...' It almost goes without saying that there is also a mirror shot of Flora and Lucía together: it shows Lucía's face and Flora's back and Flora's mirror image between them.

For Peter Biskind, Aldo, 'with his troubled student's face, his straw hat and tommy gun, is a militant Michael Corleone, a tupamaro of the thirties'. And it is true, Aldo is given a highly romantic image, the most idealised in the whole film; the odd mixture of Biskind's references shows that this is one of the film's weakest elements. He operates, Biskind continues, 'in a seemingly isolated guerrilla band without apparent contact with the other such groups we assume must exist'; and thus, with the virtues and limitations of the bourgeois urban revolutionary, he gets gunned down amid what another commentator calls 'the general political chaos of the street fighting of the time'.

Like the first Lucía, the second Lucía goes through dramatic changes brought about by personal and historical circumstances. But her liberation as a woman is inevitably constrained. Biskind again: 'It is Aldo who talks, fights and dies; it is Lucía who sticks loyally to him ("I'll follow you; I'm your wife, Aldo"), carries his baby, and endures, alone, after his death.' Anna Marie Taylor notices that 'several cuts to the figure of Lucía, pregnant and alone in their room in Havana during Aldo's long absences, dramatize the marginality of women to the events of this period. Even her political involvement at the factory can be seen as merely an adjunct to Aldo's activities. Nevertheless,' she concludes, 'the moments of solidarity among the women of the factory show more promise for the future than do Aldo's individualistic and ultimately nihilistic acts.' There is a lot to be said for this reading of the episode, though it ends nonetheless in a mood of desolation.

There are various symbolic moments in this episode too, especially in the music. In the first episode, the composer, Leo Brouwer, uses a theme from Schumann to create a musical icon of the period. In the second, the dominant mood is conveyed by the use of themes from Chopin and Dvorak, and he also uses 'Poor Butterfly' to depict the American penetration of Cuba in the scene of a debauched victory party. This is like the way Alvarez uses music. Overall, the style of the episode remains quiet and muted. Biskind likens it to Truffaut's *Jules et Jim* and Franju's *Thérèse* in its employment of slow, deliberate pans, tracks and zooms. On the other hand, another writer, Michael Myerson, finds in its muted tones a pastiche suggestive of Hollywood of the period portrayed, and Mraz agrees with this, speaking (in his earlier article) of 'long, slow, soft shots in which foreground focus and lighting are used to convey a "portrait image" closely resembling that of Hollywood productions during the golden age'.[20]

The Peruvian critic Isaac León Frias finds 'Lucía 1933' close to Hollywood models of the 30s such as Cukor or Kazan. Among the Cubans critics, Elena Díaz likes the sobriety of the episode, which she thinks the most mature of the three. The ending, however, she finds stereotyped. Evidently the inadequacies in the portrayal of Aldo's character become too much for her. But it is a minor deficiency, she believes, commending the accuracy of observation of the women in the tobacco factory, the demeanour of women in a certain way imitating men, which was characteristic, she says, of (Cuban) feminism in the 30s.

In the final episode, Solás emerges, as Kovacs felicitously puts it, from the haunted past, and steps into the sunshine of the present. He also moves out of the close and seething city of 1933 to the brilliant light of the Cuban countryside, for 'Lucía 196-' is set in a new agricultural co-operative. It opens with an early morning shot of two peasant women chatting on a roadside as a noisy truckload of their fellow workers comes to pick them up. We find ourselves immediately in a highly particularised scene as the truck stops outside a row of small houses. The driver honks the horn and says 'Let's see how long it takes her today. Since she's got a boyfriend we have to wake her up in the morning!' The boisterous characteristics of a fast-paced farcical comedy are thus immediately established, and never let up. There's an enormous sense of exhilaration in this last episode, exuberance and optimism. This is also carried by the music, which employs the traditional 'Guantanamera' (its roots, according to Alejo Carpentier, are Spanish 16th century), to which Brouwer gives a brilliant and jazzy orchestration not unlike the Leonard Bernstein of *West Side Story* – though the Mexican composers Chávez and Revueltas are present in this music too – and to which Joseito Fernández, on the soundtrack, sings humorous and moralistic verses the way he did on the radio in the 30s.

Adela Legrá (of *Manuela*) as Lucia 196– emerges to join the women on the truck, and they all talk animatedly about changing social mores as she tells the compañeras that her new boyfriend, Tomás (Adolfo Llaurado from *Manuela*), doesn't want to let her work after their marriage. We meet him waiting for Lucía after work as the first of the 'Guantanamera' verses is heard:

> My divine country girl, girl from Guantánamo,
> The country is a source of innumerable riches…
> Men and women alike must gather its bounty.

The sequence stands in for their wedding, which we hear about in the next scene from two old peasant women. 'He spends the whole day on top of her,' says one, 'he doesn't even let her up for air.' This is what the other calls the 'steamroller treatment'. Tomás is shown through their joking as oversexed – and from a women's, not a men's, point of view. Then the film moves from the public

234

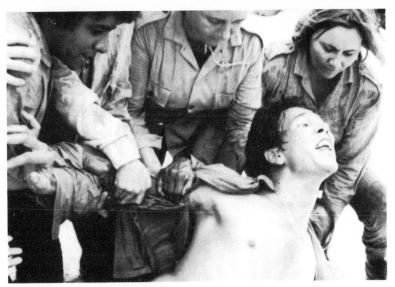

'Lucía 196-': Adolfo Llauradó

world in which it began into the private interior space of the married couple, where we now see them playfully running around the house, Lucía hiding, Tomás seeking, till they end up on the bed, Lucía shrieking (as the published script describes it) both delighted and terrified.[21] The entire scene inevitably recalls Lucía 1895 with Rafael in the abandoned outhouse of the sugar mill.

The couple are then summoned to a birthday party at the community centre. The scene is crowded and eventful, in the greatest contrast to the party in 'Lucía 1933'. Lucía discusses with an older woman from the truck, Angelina, Tomás's refusal to let her go to work. Lucía seeks from her sisterly advice: 'He says that the Revo... that *he's* the Revolution! I love him a lot, Angelina, what am I going to do?' We catch a glimpse of a group of foreigners – evidently Russians or East Europeans – whose appearance is so distinctive that they create quite a stir among the campesinos. Some critics have made rather too much of this, supposing it to be a deliberate jibe. But although bemused and, when one of these women attempts to dance like a Cuban, amused as well, it is not as if the community finds them alien. The symbolic significance of their presence is not, as Mraz thought in the first of his articles, to compare Soviet penetration in the 60s with European and North American penetration previously, as if they were equivalents; but something much less devious, an icon of the modernity of the new era, of the entry of Cuba into the twentieth century, for which the Soviet Revolution is still the supreme symbol.

Their appearance is in any case brief. A moment later, Tomás, consumed by clearly irrational jealousy, picks a fight with someone who is dancing with Lucía

235

while he talks with Flavio, Angelina's husband. Immediately we are back with the couple in their small house, Tomás, possessed, nailing the windows shut to turn the house into a prison, shouting at Lucía: 'What did you expect? That you could go around dancing to crazy music with every pair of balls that comes along? I want you to obey me, you hear? That's what you're my wife for!' For the second time comes the 'Guantanamera' commentary: 'The scourge of jealousy... causes a ton of grief... such behaviour in our new life/Today is out of place.' The interpolation of the song is more Brechtian than Shakespearian, but the unfolding of the story is very much like Shakespearian comedy – one that deals with the public and private lives of a warring couple.

The community breaches Tomás's defences by means of the literacy campaign. Tomás is of course intensely suspicious of the young teacher ascribed to Lucía, but in the end Lucía's education must take its course. To cut a long and subtly narrated story short, Lucía finally escapes from the house leaving Tomás a note which reads 'I'm going. I'm not a slave.' She moves in with Angelina. When Tomás comes searching her out on the salt flats where she is working, her compañeras energetically restrain him. He has been weakened, 'morally destroyed' as Joseito Fernandez sings, 'a laughing stock... a product of that jealousy which comes of poor imagination'. As the film closes, Tomás and Lucía are still fighting, but the final image is that of a little girl who laughs at them and then goes off, as if turning away towards the future.

The camerawork in 'Lucía 196-' is mostly in a rough and fluid, hand-held eye-level mid-shot with a good proportion of close-ups which, as Anna Marie Taylor has noticed, brings the viewer into intimate contact with the people of this small country community. Mraz, in his second article, observes that there is also a recall of the mirror shots of the previous episodes, in which Lucía is seen making up, but this time flinching from the mirror image for its reflection of behaviour so obviously inappropriate. The shot in question comes just as Joseito Fernández is singing 'But such behaviour/ Today is out of place.' It combines with the sung commentary to create a perfect instance of Brechtian cinema – an effect of distanciation combined with the gesture of an actor stepping out of one role and into another. This is contrasted with Tomás at the mirror too – proudly preening himself. It makes a powerful critique of *machismo*.


In *Memorias del subdesarrollo* the Cuban intelligentsia, the artistic and intellectual community Fidel spoke to in the 'Words to the Intellectuals', confronts itself. It discovers itself in the act of breaking down the vocabulary of its own existence. Tomás Gutiérrez Alea's film, based on a novel by Edmundo Desnoes, is an exercise in the fragmentation and dissociation of imagery and representation, as the pre-revolutionary world is dismembered while the cultural shapes of the new have not yet emerged. Of all Cuban films of the 60s it is in certain ways the closest to the ethos of the metropolitan intellectual, a film which portrays the subjective condition of its central character, a kind of intellectual anti-hero in a state of paralysed perceptiveness. But although metropolitan critics have compared this film to Antonioni, and its lead actor Sergio Corrieri to the young Mastroianni, seeing the film as a portrayal of middle-class angst in the midst of a vapid society, there is none of Antonioni's nihilism here and, as Michael Myerson has said, 'revolutionary Cuba is not capitalist Italy, and the milieu in which Corrieri's Sergio operates (or rather, cannot operate) is far different from that pictured by Antonioni.'[22]

Sergio is neither a revolutionary nor a counter-revolutionary. He would like to be a writer, which he perceives as a vocation outside the realms of the political imperative. Before the Revolution he owned a furniture store, which his father gave him to set him up in business. Now he lives off the payments made to him by the state as an allowance for the confiscation of his property as a landlord, for he also owned a block of flats in the well-appointed Havana district of Vedado, one of the city's tallest buildings, at the top of which he now lives alone. His wife, from whom he is divorced, left with his parents for the United States during 1961 in the mass exodus of the bourgeoisie. This is the point in Sergio's tale of woe at which the film opens.

Except for the title sequence, that is. The titles are superimposed over a night-time carnaval scene filmed from within the midst of a dancing, jostling crowd by a hand-held camera. A disturbance takes place, we catch a glimpse of a body lying amid the feet on the ground in a pool of blood, then lifted up and carried away through the throng. The last credit appears and the picture cuts to the airport, where we discover Sergio, in a different crowd, with his wife and parents, making their farewells. As the images of the title sequence recede into the antechamber of our attention, they leave behind the feel of enigma, an unresolved tension which pervades everything that proceeds to unfold (until eventually, much later in the film, the scene is repeated, only from a different point of view); while the cut to the airport establishes a paradigm for the oblique montage and narrative style of the film, which sets up many an enigma as it unfolds through the surprise juxtaposition of some new scene of contrasting aspect. One of the modes the film adopts for its fragmentation of imagery and representation, this is of course a characteristic form of expression of the modernist aesthetic.

The look in Sergio's eyes as he separates himself from the parting embrace of his family shapes another paradigm which will be constantly evoked throughout the film. It is the look of distanciation, which is immediately reinforced here by the not quite invisible wall of plate glass – visible only in the reflections cast upon it – which separates the travellers from their homeland as they go through the partition into the departure lounge, a wall of silence which the camera places us alternately on either side of.

On the balcony of his flat after returning from the airport, Sergio surveys the scene below him through a telescope, obviously a habitual occupation since the telescope is mounted on the parapet, and at the same time a metaphorical extension of the distant look in Sergio's eyes, because the telescope fragments, breaking vision up into an infinity of rounded images each of which is a separate little scene in itself. What Sergio does not seem able to discover as his story unfolds, but which the film itself exemplifies as it does so, is the synthesis of perception through creative montage. This is not so much an interpretation of the film as a statement of its method. In a set of working notes on the film the director explains: Sergio is a person unable to enter into the new reality which the Revolution forces upon him, which is so much vaster than his previous world. Why then did he not leave too? Because 'for him everything has come either too early or too late and he is incapable of making decisions.' Yet 'through this personage who in almost all respects we are inclined to reject, we can discover new aspects of the reality which surrounds us. Sometimes through him, sometimes by contrast. His attitude as a spectator with a minimum of lucidity keeps the critical spirit awake in us... the confrontation of his own world with the "documentary" world which we show (the world of our subjectivity, not his) becomes rich in suggestion.'[23]

They accordingly set out, says Alea, with the basic intention of making a kind of documentary about a man who ended up alone, and the idea that the vision of reality offered by documentary inserts would strike against the subjective vision of the protagonist. Direct documentary filming, bits of newsreel, photographs, recordings of speeches, filming in the streets with a hidden camera, these were the resources that would be brought to bear. Some things in the novel would be dropped, new sequences introduced, Sergio's voice-over would speak its testimony, but the film's open and 'seemingly disarticulated' language would give the effect of a plastic montage more than a literary narration. The multiplicity of means would make the idiom of the film not only more open but also richer in its signifiers. Ultimately the intention was not to reflect reality but to detect a problem, not to soften reality but to bring it alive, even aggressively, even, so to speak, to disturb the peace. Not, one should add, that things in Cuba were exactly peaceful at that moment: there was great revolutionary energy and ideological struggle going on. But there were always people, says Alea, who thought certain things would look after themselves, and these were the same people who tended to believe themselves depositaries of the revolutionary bequest, who spoke of the people as a promising child and tried to tell others how this child should be spoken to. These people the film, among other things, proposed to aggravate and provoke.

Surveying what he can see of Havana from his balcony, Sergio's voice is heard over the images speaking to himself: 'Everything remains the same,' he says, seeing lovers by the swimming pool of an adjacent hotel; 'Cuba free and independent', over scenes of defence preparations, 'who would have thought that this can happen?' And over a shot of the plinth from which the imperial eagle of the United States has been removed (one of the established icons of Cuban cinema – the scene of the demonstration in which it was pulled down crops up in several ICAIC documentaries) he wonders, 'Where is the dove that Picasso was going to send?' adding that 'it's very comfortable being a communist millionaire in Paris'. Loaded with the ambiguity of innuendo, these are significant words, which spell out several things about the person who speaks them: the European axis of his thinking, his sense of frustration, his feelings of passive belligerence towards the world, his resentment. No, he's not an attractive character.

Especially as he goes on to enact his own unattractiveness to himself in a grotesque orgy of self-abuse. He rummages through the belongings his wife Laura has been forced to leave behind, trying on her furs and manhandling, so to speak, the icons of her femininity – a powder puff, pearls, lipstick. Twisting the lipstick up and down obviously seems a classic Freudian symbol, and Alea is not the kind of director to overlook this. On the contrary, he means to advise us of Sergio's phallocentricity, which the film will develop. And for once, because of corresponding symbols in the film concerning vision – like the telescope – the film itself licenses the finding of the relationship which psychoanalytic film theory posits between phallocentrism and the camera.

Sergio then sits down with the lipstick in front of a mirror and proceeds to doodle with it. If the image reminds us of 'Lucía 1933', it should also be observed how differently the same idea is used here. Sergio scribbles on the mirror not so much to interfere with its hated reflection, but rather more narcissistically, like an artist putting the finishing touches to a self-portrait. Finally he takes one of Laura's stockings and pulls it over his head, distorting his features, as he listens to a tape recording he made of a conversation in which he and Laura are arguing, first about a movie they have seen, then, as he taunts her, about herself and what he calls her 'struggle between elegance

*Memorias del subdesarrollo*: Sergio Corrieri

*Memorias del subdesarrollo*: Sergio Corrieri

and vulgarity', her use, to disguise her vulgar origins, of all the commodities women are offered to construct their image with. 'You get more attractive each day,' Sergio mocks her, 'you're more artificial, I don't like natural beauty.' At the climax of the row he tells her he has recorded the whole thing on tape, 'everything, word for word, it'll be fun later on, when you hear it.'

The nature of Sergio's attitude towards women is developed out on the streets of Havana where he scrutinises them. He enters a bookshop, where the shelves are stocked with the classic works of Marxism, cheap editions of novels, and clearly situated behind his shoulder, drawing our attention away from his observing eye, a book called *The Hero of Our Times*. Voice-over he is saying, 'Here women look into your eyes as if they want to be touched by your look. That only happens here.' Out on the streets again, Sergio passes a bust of Martí – Alea has not forgotten, as a good modernist artist, to allude to himself – with an inscription, *Nuestro vino es agrio, pero es nuestro vino* ('Our wine is sour, but it's our wine'). But Sergio evidently does not share the feeling of combativity which surrounds him.

A title appears, the single word *Pablo*, and the film changes pace as we cut to Sergio driving with a friend along the Malecón, Havana's sea-front drive. Over a flashback to the two men with their wives at a nightclub, Pablo spills out his cynicism – 'I never got involved with politics, I have a clear conscience' – but Sergio is completely uninterested. More than uninterested. Something in him is incensed by his erstwhile friend's insensitivity, and as he stares ahead of him (the absent look in his eyes we've seen before) the picture cuts to a montage of stills of scenes of poverty in Latin America, as he muses: 'He says the only thing a Cuban can't stand is hunger. All the starvation we've gone through since the Spanish came! In Latin America four children die every minute due to illnesses caused by malnutrition . . .' The statistic comes from the Second Declaration of Havana. A moment later, up in Pablo's apartment, the conversation turns to the subject of the prisoners captured at the Bay of Pigs, a topic Sergio introduces to taunt Pablo. In a most extraordinary and spectacular event, 40 of these prisoners were interrogated by a panel of journalists before a packed audience in a Havana theatre just a few days after their defeat. The whole event, which lasted four days, was televised, published verbatim in the press and later in book form. The sequence begins with a newsreel of the invasion and the captured mercenaries being marched along hands on head. A title appears: *The Truth of the Group is in the Murderer*. Sergio, reading from the book, narrates: 'We found beneath the military organisation of the invaders an order in their social duties that summarises the division of the moral and social functions of the bourgeoisie: priest, businessman, official, philosopher, politician, torturer, and the innumerable sons of good families . . .' Alea's procedure here in putting Sergio's voice-over to work like a newsreel commentator is a bold one, which allows the film to elaborate the sense of social anatomy through which Sergio himself is refracted. One of the prisoners on trial declares, like Pablo, that he's not a political person. A moment later, Sergio's voice-over appears to be holding a dialogue with another. We surmise that Sergio understands perfectly well what these claims about being non-political amount to. At the end of the sequence he comments that 'in none of the cases considered was there a recovery of the true dialectical relationship between individual and group'; we are left reflecting not only that this is true of his own situation, but that he knows it.

Another title, *Noemí*, introduces us to the girl who cleans his apartment (played by Eslinda Nuñez of 'Lucía 1933'), about whom he fantasises vividly. Then another title, *Elena* comes up and we're on La Rampa, Havana's nightlife strip of yore. Elena (played by Daysi Granados) is a pretty Havana girl whom he spies and picks up. His opening words, 'You have beautiful knees, do you want to have dinner with me?', are spoken with the self-assurance of a man of social advantage who knows that women find him attractive, especially since he is taller and his features are more European than most Cuban men. His whole demeanour hides his internal angst.

The film enters a new phase, for each new name title also brings a new theme. Elena is waiting, she tells Sergio, for someone from ICAIC about a possible job, but he hasn't turned up. Sergio tells her, as they eat dinner, that he has a friend who is a director there, and then asks her why she wants to be an actress. 'Because,' she says, 'I'm tired of always being the same. That way I can be someone else without people thinking I'm crazy. I want,' she adds, speaking the words like a line she's learned, 'to unfold my personality.' She thus enters the film and Sergio's life like his shadow, his double, another lens through which his own identity crisis is refracted; which he himself undoubtedly recognises since he is too intelligent not to see it, and which he decides to humour: 'But all those characters are like scratched records...' No one by this stage in the film will be wholly surprised when this scene cuts to a montage of clips of scenes from movies. But Alea still has plenty of surprises up his sleeve and the clips arrest us by repeating themslves – images of couples in the clasp of love-making, of a woman stepping into a shower, of a stripper. Abruptly the images stop and lights go up and we are in a viewing theatre. Sergio, sitting next to Elena, turns to someone behind them and asks 'Where did you get them?' This is evidently his friend the director. In fact it's Alea, though as a character in his own film he remains unnamed. 'They showed up one day,' he replies, 'they're the cuts Batista's censors made, they said they were offensive to morals and good breeding.' 'What are you going to do with them?' asks Sergio. The director explains that he's going to put them into a film, 'it'll be a collage with a little bit of everything'. Obviously it's the film we're watching. 'Will they release it?' asks Sergio. The scene is a kind of conceit, but it is much more than a clever way of suggesting, as a number of metropolitan critics thought, that the new regime was not as mindless as its predecessors.

Actually the scene is a step in the translation of the novel to the screen. The adaptation of the novel involves certain problems, because the whole thing is a conceit: it is written in the first person by a character with the ambition to be a writer who has the same name as the author of the novel. This is a kind of play upon the identity of the author which is another typical trait of modernism. In the work of a Borges, for example, such conceits are used to set up metaphysical conundrums about the human condition. Here the purpose is to capture, in the spider's web of language, certain elusive aspects of the identity crisis of the artist within the revolutionary process, the problem of the *desgarramiento*, the ideological rupture with the past. But how can you translate the novel's first person to the screen? There is no direct or logical equivalent in film of the persona of the first person narrator in literature except a voice on the soundtrack, which is not the same. As an analogue of the writer's pen the camera is impersonal, it cannot say 'I', it always says 'there is', 'here is'. This is why the film-makers chose to oppose the camera to the pen as instruments through which to record the world, by contrasting Sergio's subjectivity with the documentary quality of the camera image. In fact the film invites us alternately to identify the camera with Sergio and to separate them, and it does this in odd and irregular ways, like making his voice the commentary to a piece of newsreel.

Sergio takes Elena back to his apartment. She is awkward and embarrassed. Sergio tries to win her over by giving her some of his wife's discarded clothing to try on. A classic game of seduction takes place, filmed with a nervous hand-held camera, as she alternately lures him on and repulses him until he forcefully pins her down on the bed and she gives in to him. Afterwards she cries, protests that he has ruined her, and leaves. With Sergio alone again, the camera pans around the room until it lands on Sergio together with Laura, in the middle of the argument on the tape-recording we heard earlier.

Pablo is leaving. Sergio goes to see him off at the airport. His departure occasions in Sergio another bout of self-reflection, in which a certain self-honesty is mixed up with his self-delusion. 'Although it may destroy me,' he says, 'this Revolution is my revenge against the stupid Cuban bourgeoisie. Against idiots like Pablo... everything I don't want to be.' The trouble is not only that he has forgotten how his wife left Cuba to escape him as much as the Revolution, but that he has also conflated the personal and the political without properly understanding either. His only solution is to try and hold himself apart, even though he knows what it costs him to do so: 'I keep my mind clear. It's a disagreeable clarity, empty. I know what's happening to me but I can't avoid it.' In a flashback to his childhood, he associates his present self-paralysis with the subjugation of the schoolboy to the power of the priests at his Catholic school, which taught him the relationship, he says, between Justice and Power. But the flashback is paired with another, his induction into the mysteries of sex in a whorehouse, and as the image cuts back to the present, with Sergio reflecting upon Elena and his discovery that she wasn't as 'complex and interesting' as he first thought, it's not so certain that he really understood the relationship between Justice and Power after all, at least in so far as it concerns the power men wield over women. That he has power over Elena he is perfectly aware, but he conceives of himself wielding it benevolently as he decides to educate her. As they visit an art gallery his voice-over explains, 'I always try to live like a European, and Elena forces me to feel underdeveloped at every step.'

The sequence which follows is not in the original version of the novel, only in the rewrite Desnoes produced after collaborating on the film. Julianne Burton records that in the view of Desnoes, Alea 'betrayed' the novel, but in a creative and illuminating way, objectivising a world that was still abstract in the book and giving it social density; the interpolation of this new sequence goes even further, expanding the commentary on the social role of the artist. It is also another step in transposing the novel to the screen. Following a title, *A Tropical Adventure*, we find ourselves in Ernest Hemingway's house near Havana which is now the Hemingway Museum. Sergio has taken Elena there in the interests of her education. She is predictably unimpressed ('Is this where Mr Way used to live? I don't see anything so special. Books and dead animals...') and she quickly becomes bored, wandering off and posing for photographs for some foreign tourists. Sergio hides from her and watches as she gives up searching and hitches a ride back to town. There is much more to the sequence, however, which is a long one, than Sergio ditching Elena. It amounts to a disquisition on the social and historical relations of the writer and is in many ways the pivot of the entire film, the confluence of Sergio's most objective reflections on the topic and the analysis of the film-makers, in which, by uniting the two, the film-makers at once pay not uncritical homage to the tradition of the writer as the embodiment of social conscience and reflect upon the revolutionary transformation which this conscience must now undergo. The sequence begins with the commentary of the museum guide, about whom we learn from Sergio's voice-over: 'Hemingway found him when he was a little boy playing in the streets... He moulded him to his needs. The faithful servant and the great lord. The colonialist and Gunga

243

Din. Hemingway must have been unbearable.' The guide, however, describes him as a good man, a humane man, a war correspondent in the Spanish Civil War who joined the International Brigade, by implication a friend of the Revolution even though not a revolutionary himself. It is clear, nevertheless, that he was not only a good writer, he was a rich one too. As Sergio explains: 'This was his refuge, his tower, his island in the tropics... Boots for hunting in Africa, American furniture, Spanish photographs, magazines and books in English, a bullfight poster. Cuba never really interested him. Here he could find refuge, entertain his friends, write in English, and fish in the Gulf Stream.' But if we conclude that he came here to solve his problems, we are not slow to think of his last problem, whose solution he found elsewhere, at his Idaho ranch. (It was after his suicide that his wife gave his Cuban house to the Revolution.)

From Sergio's commentary upon the commentary of the guide, two things emerge. One is the question of 'official' museum versions of culture; this belongs to the critique the film directs towards the paternalists within the Revolution. But secondly, from the position of the sequence within the unfolding argument of the film, it becomes symbolic of the inevitable death, indeed the necessary spiritual suicide, of the old kind of writer in the face of the new society. And yet although Sergio realises this perfectly well, he's unable to tear himself away from the relics in the museum in the same way that he cannot kick over the traces within himself of the anachronistic social model which Hemingway represents.

The problem is not only Sergio's. Another screen title announces: *Round Table – Literature and Underdevelopment*. Like the guide at the Hemingway Museum, the participants are real people: the Haitian poet René Depestre, the Italian novelist Gianni Toti, the Argentinian novelist David Viñas and, significantly, the author of *Memorias del subdesarrollo*, the novel – Edmundo Desnoes. The panel discusses the topic while Sergio, in the audience, tries to follow the argument but like everyone else becomes restless. When the discussion is thrown open, someone requests permission to speak in English. He is the North American playwright Jack Gelber, author of the foreword to the English edition of Desnoes' novel. 'Why is it,' he asks, 'that if the Cuban Revolution is a total revolution, they have to resort to an archaic form of discussion such as a round table and treat us to an impotent discussion of issues that I'm well informed about and most of the public here is well informed about, when there could be another more revolutionary way to reach an audience like this?' The picture cuts away to a long shot of Sergio walking the streets again. The camera zooms in very slowly towards him, into bigger and bigger close-up until finally the image loses focus and he disappears into a blur, while his voice-over reflects: 'I don't understand. The American was right. Words devour words and they leave you in the clouds... How does one get rid of underdevelopment? It marks everything. What are you doing there, Sergio? You have nothing to do with them. You're alone... You're nothing, you're dead. Now it begins, Sergio, your final destruction.'

Another title, *Hanna*, another flashback, girls emerging from a school. Hanna was a Jewish refugee from Hitler, they were going to get married but her parents took her off to New York; she had all the poise he finds lacking in his other women, especially Elena who, back in the present, is waiting for him outside his flat. He avoids her, but then it turns out she's told her family he's ruined her. They demand that he marries her and when he refuses they decide to press charges against him for rape. Is this then to be his final undoing? He fully expects so, and as the courtroom scene unfolds, so do we. But the court finds the charges against him unproven. He is left to wonder: 'It was a happy ending, as they say. For once justice triumphed. But was it really like that? There is something that leaves me in a bad position. I've seen too much to be innocent. They have too much darkness inside their heads to be guilty...'

The closing section of the film shows Sergio's ultimate self-paralysis as the city around him engages in defence preparations during the unfolding of the so-called Cuban missile crisis. If the confrontation between the United States and the Soviet Union in October 1962 over the placing of Soviet missiles in Cuba was experienced throughout the world as a moment of reckoning, the place it occupies within collective and individual memory in Cuba itself is saturated with peculiar significance. It was another of the experiences of the Revolution's early years which played a definitive role in forging social cohesion and bonding the island's unity, like the experiences of the Literacy Campaign and the invasion of the Bay of Pigs. In the popular experience, the way people remember it, it was a moment in which individual fears were submerged in the collective, and national consciousness took on a peculiarly tangible form, as of a people which finds itself condemned to an historical test in the defence of self-determination. A junior member of ICAIC, in his early teens at the time, remembered in a conversation with the present author the sensation of knowing they were targets for a kind of attack which no-one, if it came, would be able to escape, and which therefore called up a unique shared resoluteness. The sensation gripped them with special intensity because while the world was holding its breath because of Cuba, the Cubans themselves were powerless. As Sergio puts it, in his final voice-over, sandwiched between speeches on television by Kennedy and by Fidel, 'And if it started right now? It's no use protesting. I'll die like the rest. This island is a trap. We're very small, and too poor. It's an expensive dignity.'

I believe it must have been this last sequence as much as anything which was responsible for the initial misreading of the film which occurred in the metropolis, where a number of critics were so suprised to find a Cuban picture handling the theme of bourgeois alienation that they failed to perceive the critique which it levelled not merely at Sergio but by implication at anyone identifying too closely with him. These critics, insensible to the nature of Sergio's narcissism but narcissistically sharing his all-consuming sense of resentment, instead felt flattered at seeing such an accurate portrayal of their own reflection. And the epilogue is constructed with such understatement that it must have allowed them to identify completely with his own sentiments in the face of the threat of nuclear annihilation. Since they could hardly, as alienated intellectuals, conceive of any other sentiment in the face of the missile crisis – for example, that national dignity is not negotiable – so they imagined that the film was meant to be critical of the political process that led up to it. They assumed that the director of such a film could only be a fellow spirit, that he couldn't possibly be an enthusiastic supporter of such a state as they took Cuba to be. They saw the film's critique of underdevelopment as a criticism of the stupidity of the common people, as if individuals and not the social heritage were responsible. Many critics, to be sure, escape these strictures. Vincent Canby, for instance, who cited Antonioni in order to contrast the Italian and the Cuban.[24] But if there was a Vincent Canby there was also an Andrew Sarris, who as President of the US National Society of Film Critics, tried to turn Alea into a dissident of the type the capitalist media love to find in the Soviet Union.[25]

That was when the US State Department refused to grant Alea a visa to attend the Society's awards ceremony at which he was due to receive a special prize for the film. This was not the first time a Cuban film-maker had been refused a US visa. The same thing happened a short while earlier in 1972, to a delegation from ICAIC intending to visit the USA for a Cuban film festival planned by an independent distributor, ADF (American Documentary Films), in New York and other cities. Not only were they refused visas but anti-Castro emigré terrorist groups threatened violence if the festival were allowed to go ahead, and there were indeed attacks on the Olympia Theatre in New York where the films were to be shown. But the biggest attack on the festival was that of the US Government, which seized one of the films from the cinema and raided the ADF offices, thus bringing the festival to a halt. The grounds the government used for these actions were that the films had been illegally imported. As Michael Myerson has explained: 'A meeting between a Festival spokesman and Stanley Sommerfield, Acting Head of Foreign Assets Control in Washington, was straight out of *Catch-22*. Sure, said Sommerfield, the government exempts the news media and universities from the Cuban embargo statutes because news gathering and a body of scholar-ship are in the national interest. But no, he continued, in answer to a question, it would not be in the national interest if the population as a whole had direct access to the materials instead of having selected elites act as middlemen in deciphering them...'[26] Protests were made, of course, on both occasions, and they involved a large number of distinguished persons. When the ICAIC delegation were refused their visas at the very same moment Nixon was visiting China, Senator Fulbright asked why the US Government should consider four Cuban film-makers a security threat and not Mao Tse-tung and the People's Republic. When Alea was banned he declared in Congress: 'I find it passing strange that the Treasury Department would be so terrified of the impact of Cuban films on the American people, while the State Department is encouraging such exchanges with the Soviet Union.'[27] *Washington Post* columnist Nicholas von Hoffman, criticising the aforementioned Treasury offi-cial, pointed to a more insidious anomaly: 'Go every morning to your hutch in the Treasury Department, Mr Sommerfield,' he wrote, 'drink your coffee, read your paper, and daily bring a full measure of aggravation into the lives of people who don't yet know your name. Keep out the movies... The rest of the Treasury

Department will let the heroin flow in.'[28]

ADF was forced by these attacks into bankruptcy, though *Memorias del subdesarrollo* was finally able to open commercially in New York in May 1973, to be selected early in 1974 by the *New York Times* as one of the year's ten best movies. The same newspaper, when Alea's visa was refused, again criticised the ridiculous behaviour of the officials and declared it irrational to treat the offer of a prize to a film as a subversive act.[29] The Cubans took the whole affair stoically. It did not escape their attention that these responses didn't all square up. As Alea made plain in the declaration he sent to be read at the awards ceremony, the Cubans were not surprised by any of it, for the film itself, the subject of the whole to-do, reflected the aggressions directed by the US Government against the Cubans from the beginning, including the blockade, the disinformation and the gamut of actions intended to impede contact between the two peoples, which kept the North Americans in a state of ignorance about Cuba and what was really going on there.[30] It was precisely this kind of ignorance which allowed Andrew Sarris to utter his misinterpretation of Alea's position. As the Cuban director put it when Julianne Burton asked him for his comments on Sarris: 'His lack of information was such that one suspects a kind of tendentious ignorance, if such a thing is possible. It's hard to know in such cases where ignorance leaves off and stupidity or malice begins.'[31]

In Cuba itself, *Memorias*, because of its sophistication of style, proved a difficult film for many of the audience. But Alea recalled later that it produced the very positive effect of sending many people back to the cinema to see it a second and even a third time.[32] Here was evidence that ICAIC's policies were really beginning to bite.

From *Memorias del subdesarrollo* on, the interpenetration of fiction and documentary becomes a distinctive preoccupation in a number of Cuban films. In particular, it is next pursued with great originality and virtuosity, a year after *Memorias*, by Manuel Octavio Gómez in *La primera carga al machete*. A shortish film of eighty-four minutes in black-and-white and using a wide screen, *La primera carga* is another of the films on the theme of the hundred years' war. It deals with the events which opened the war against the Spanish in 1868 when independence fighters under the generalship of the Dominican Máximo Gómez began the rebellion in the east of the island, where they succeeded in taking the important city of Bayamo. The Spanish Captain General sends two strong columns of the colonial army to recapture Bayamo and put down the rebellion. The rebels force one of the columns to retreat by means not of direct confrontation but of a strategy of deception, while the second column is destroyed at the very entrance to Bayamo by the attack after which the film is named.

Gómez said that he found the historical movie, the grandiloquent kind of film the term is usually identified with, insupportable, and for this reason a documentary method seemed to him the logical way to approach the subject. But how exactly to apply this to an historical subject? 'From the beginning we set about trying to give the idea that we were developing the story as if it were being filmed at that very moment, as if it had been possible at that time to use a camera and recorder to collect the facts.'[33] They applied this idea visually by using high contrast photography to give the impression of very early film stock. This is combined with a hand-held camera and direct sound (which Alea had used extensively for the first time in Cuba in *Memorias*). At the same time the film employs a number of documentary procedures, especially the interview carried out in the manner of television reportage, interviewee on camera speaking to an interviewer off-screen. There is also a discussion among a patriotic group commenting on the events, who begin by introducing themselves to camera one by one; and a sequence in which an agitator, a kind of accomplice of the camera, accosts people in a public square in Havana and obliges them to give their opinions about the independence issue, until Spanish soldiers appear on the scene to break up the disturbance which has thus been created. Other interviewees, at the scene of battle, include Spanish soldiers who have survived the machete charge and describe the terror of having to face such a deadly weapon; Spanish functionaries – including both the island's Governor and the commander of the troops; patriotic inhabitants of Bayamo, victims of Spanish repression; and rebel soldiers. The documentary techniques allow considerable fluidity in the structuring of the film. Indeed the film opens after the machete charge, with Spanish soldiers who have survived it and the patriots discussing its significance, before going back to reconstruct the events, by way of a documentary sequence on the machete itself, its origins and uses, which is thus presented as a character in the film in its own right, so to speak. Finally, the film is punctuated by the figure of a singer (Pablo Milanés), a roving troubador who sings a ballad that provides a further commentary on the events.

The net result of these techniques is not so much to transport the viewer of the film into the past as to bring the past into the present. This is the very opposite of the conventional historical movie, which aims, in its crassest examples, through creating an illusion of distant times to provide a vehicle of escapism. Such films misconstrue the past in order to shore up the present status quo through the back-projection, as it were, of the supposedly universal and eternal values of the dominant bourgeois ideology. This film, as the Venezuelan critics put it, changes the habitual perspective of such historiography, and thereby displays the continuity of struggle between past and present with incomparable urgency. One indication of this is the parallel the film-makers found to emerge while they were making the film between the figure of Máximo Gómez and that of Che Guevara, which they had not originally thought of. At the same time this transportation of the past achieves, once again, distinctly Brechtian results, for as the Venezuelan critics also observe, the mummification of the past in the scholarly texts is substituted by a form of representation which eliminates conventional emotional identification with the characters in the drama, and stimulates instead a process of reflection which inserts the contemporary viewer into the problematic of the past just as much as it inserts the heritage of the past into the problematic of the present.

If this film had been made for British television it would doubtless have been called a drama-documentary in the manner of Peter Watkins' not dissimilar *Culloden*. For Latin American critics it's an example both of *cine rescate*, the recovery of history, and of the application of *cine encuesta*, the film of enquiry, to an historical subject. This again is to place the emphasis on the film's affinity with documentary. It is more than affinity, really: the entire conception of the film is that of documentary; with the consequence that while *Lucía*, with which it shares a great deal stylistically, especially in the way the camera is used, remains firmly within the fictional mode, *La primera carga* does not. On the contrary, it represents a high point in the attack upon conventional narrative with which several Cuban film-makers now engaged, and which is one of the themes behind Julio García Espinosa's concept of imperfect cinema.

## References

1. 'Entrevista con Jorge Fraga con la participación de Manuel Octavio Gómez', *Hablemos de Cine* No.54.
2. Letter to his wife of 27 July 1896.
3. Cf. Nestor García Miranda, 'La odisea del General José de Jorge Fraga', *Hablemos de Cine* No.54.
4. *The Bolivian Diaries of Che Guevara*, Betrand Russell Peace Foundation, undated, p.136.
5. García Miranda, op.cit.
6. Marta Alvear, Interview with Humberto Solás, *Jump Cut* No.19.
7. Teresa Fernández Coca, Interview with Humberto Solás, *Granma* 23 October 1968.
8. Anna Marie Taylor, 'Lucia', *Film Quarterly* Vol.28 No.2, Winter 1974/5; John Mraz, 'Lucia: History and Film in Revolutionary Cuba', *Film and History* Vol.5 No.1, 1975.
9. Steven Kovacs, 'Lucia: Style and Meaning in Revolutionary Film', *Monthly Review* Vol.27 No.2, 1975, p.34.
10. Isaac León Frias, 'Lucia', *Hablemos de Cine* No.54.
11. Fernández Coca interview, cit.
12. Anna Marie Taylor, op.cit.
13. Peter Biskind, 'Lucia – Struggles with History', *Jump Cut* No.2, 1974.
14. 'Resultados de una discusión...', cit.
15. Daniel Díaz Torres, 'Lucia', *Granma Weekly Review* 20 October 1968.
16. Puri Faget, 'Lucía, un punto de partida', *El Mundo* (Havana) 15 October 1968.
17. Glauber Rocha, 'The Aesthetics of Violence' in *Revista Civilizaçao Brasileira* No.3, 1965, translated in *Twenty-five Years of the New Latin American Cinema*, ed. Michael Chanan, BFI/Channel 4, 1983.
18. See Manuel Octavio Gómez in 'Entrevista con Jorge Fraga...', cit.
19. John Mraz, 'Lucia: Visual Style and Historical Portrayal', *Jump Cut* No.19.
20. Michael Myerson, ed., *Memories of Underdevelopment, The Revolutionary Films of Cuba*, Grossman, New York 1973, p.118.
21. *Ibid.*
22. *Ibid.*, p.43.
23. Tomás Gutiérrez Alea, 'Memorias del subdesarrollo, notas de trabajo', *Hablemos de Cine* No.54.
24. See citation of Canby's review in *Granma*, 'Elogian críticos norteamericanos filme cubano', 13 June 1973.

25. See Julianne Burton, Interview with Alea, *Cineaste* Vol.VIII No.1, p.59.
26. Myerson, op.cit., p.34.
27. *Ibid.*, p.36.
28. *Ibid.*, pp.34-5.
29. See Pastor Vega, 'Medida torpe y arbitraria de los imperialistas yanquis', *Granma* 22 January 1974.
30. *Ibid.*
31. Burton interview, cit.
32. Conversation with Alea, Havana, January 1980.
33. Interview with M.O. Gómez, *Hablemos de Cine* No.54.

# 13

# IMPERFECT CINEMA AND THE SEVENTIES

*Julio García Espinosa's essay – more from Alvarez –*
*Afrocubanism and syncretism – Caliban and the slavery films*

It was at the end of the 60s, arising from the experience of *Juan Quin Quin*, that García Espinosa wrote the essay, *Por un cine imperfecto* ('For an Imperfect Cinema'), a polemical reflection on the whole practice of revolutionary film, which is not only a powerful credo for Cuban cinema but one of the major theoretical statements defining the scope of the New Cinema of Latin America.[1] Much misunderstood, the essay starts off as a warning against the technical perfection which after ten years now began to lie within the reach of the Cuban film-makers. Its argument, however, is more widely applicable, and its implications for revolutionary film practice outside Cuba were the subject of heated debate. The thesis is not that technical and artistic perfection necessarily prevent a film being politically effective – that would be absurd – but that in the underdeveloped world these cannot be aims in themselves. Not only because to attempt to match the production values of the big commercial movie is a waste of resources, but also because in the commercial cinema of the metropolis these values become irredeemably superficial, the beautifully controlled surface becomes a way of lulling the audience into passive consumption. This is contrary to the needs of an authentically modern cinema which seeks to engage with its audience by imaginatively inserting itself and them into social reality, to film the world around it without make-up, to make the kind of film which remains incomplete without an actively responsive audience taking it up. This sense of incompleteness without the audience is part of what García Espinosa means by imperfection. Fifteen years after the original essay, García Espinosa admits that the term 'imperfect' was confusing, and explains it this way: art is essentially (or traditionally) 'a disinterested activity, but if we're in a phase when we have to express interests, then let's do it openly and not continue to camouflage it. And therefore, if art is substantially a disinterested activity and we're obliged to do it in an interested way, it becomes an imperfect art. In essence, this is how I used the word imperfect. And this... isn't just an ethical matter, but also aesthetic.'[2] Sara Gómez, the director in the early 70s of *De cierta manera*, summed up imperfect cinema in her own way in the same year as García Espinosa's essay, when she said in an interview about her work as a documentarist, 'Cinema, for us, is inevitably partial, determined by a *toma de conciencia*, the result of a definite attitude in the face of the problems which confront us, of the necessity of decolonising ourselves politically and ideologically, and of breaking with traditional values, be they economic, ethical or aesthetic...'[3]

On the face of it, the concept of imperfect cinema has a number of similarities with ideas that have been developed within radical film culture in the metropolis over the last fifteen years, which often invoke the name of Brecht, are theoretically based in the intellectual techniques of structuralism, and are concerned with the business of deconstruction. For instance, speaking of the production of the news in the media, it is necessary, according to García Espinosa, 'above all to show the process which generates the problems... to submit it to judgment without pronouncing the verdict', so as to enable the audience to evaluate it for themselves instead of passively submitting to the commentator's analysis, permeated as it is with a priori assumptions which block the viewer's intelligence. There are differences, however. For one thing, imperfect cinema is less dogmatic and sectarian than you frequently find within radical film culture in the metropolis, about how to achieve its aims: 'It can use whatever genre or all genres. It can use cinema as a pluralistic art form, or as a specialised form of expression. These questions are indifferent to it, since they do not represent its real problems or alternatives, still less its real goals. These are not the battles or polemics it is interested in sparking.' The core of imperfect cinema is the call that García Espinosa shares with other key polemicists of third world struggle, like Fanon and Freire, for cultural decolonisation. It therefore asks for something much more than deconstruction, which instead it subsumes as one of its possible methods; and this also gives it a critical stance towards the radical cinema of the metropolis.

It is also more visionary. There is, says García Espinosa, a dangerous trap, a contradiction, liable to beset even the most revolutionary artist as long as resources and opportunity remain scarce. In ideal conditions, where the means of production were equally available, this would be not only socially just but would also liberate artistic culture: it would mean 'the possibility of recovering, without any kind of complex or guilt feeling, the true meaning of artistic activity', namely, 'that art is not work and that the artist is not in the strict sense a worker'. Here, it must be said, the hard-headed Cuban revolutionary seems every bit as idealist as the student on the barricades in Paris in 1968. Except that he does not fall for thinking that this utopian state of affairs is just around the corner. He therefore sees that, until such time, there remains a difficulty: 'The feeling that this is so, and the impossibility of translating it into practice, constitutes the agony and at the same time the pharisaism of all contemporary art.' What is needed in this situation, says García Espinosa, is not so much a new cultural policy as a new poetics, based on an openly partisan belief in the Revolution as itself the highest expression of culture, because its purpose is to rescue artistic activity from being just a fragment of the wider human culture. When that has happened, he says, the old idea of art as a disinterested activity will again be possible. But for any such thing to come about, what is needed is, paradoxically, a poetics 'whose true goal will be to commit suicide, to disappear as such' (curious echo of C.L.R. James at the 1968 Cultural Congress); and to achieve this, the artist must resolutely turn outwards, to the demands of the revolutionary process, the demands of the construction of a new culture. 'The Revolution has liberated us as an artistic sector. It is only logical that we contribute to the liberation of the private means of artistic production.' To do this, the way García Espinosa means it, is to challenge, of course, precisely those complexes and guilt feelings which constitute the agony of contemporary art, whose effect has been to turn the artist's individual neurosis into the central subject of his or her work: but 'the narcissistic posture has nothing to do with those who struggle'.

Born of the disquiet which produced *Las aventuras de Juan Quin Quin*, García Espinosa tried to develop some the ideas of imperfect cinema in practice in a feature-length documentary about Vietnam, *Tercer mundo, tercera guerra mundial* ('Third World, Third World War'). The film was shot during the period following the cease-fire at the end of March 1968. Its purpose is on the one hand to analyse the policies and strategies of the United States in the conduct of the war, and on the other to demonstrate the essential creativity of the response of North Vietnam. Its manner is both didactic and demonstrative. It employs a range of documentary devices, techniques and styles to show up Washington's behaviour, contrasting the inhumanity of the North American war machine with the very simple but very real humanity of the Vietnamese peasants forced to take up armed struggle in order to survive. Among key scenes are those of a carpenter experimenting with an unexploded 'anti-personnel' bomb to find out how it works; peasants learning to shoot down enemy aircraft with mere rifles; and above all an encounter in which the Cuban crew hand their camera over to a Vietnamese girl of eighteen so she can then direct a short sequence of the film herself; García Espinosa had argued in his essay for a cinema that would among other things demystify itself. The rough-edged but hard-headed manner in which this film delivers its analysis ensures that these lyrical moments do not get lost in sentimentalism or romanticism. García Espinosa's thesis is that the third world = third world war = anti-colonial war = war against an imperialist enemy which can only be vanquished on condition that the inhuman machinery of its warfare is countered by the simple human resourcefulness and creativity which is all the third world has to fight with.

*Tercer guerra, tercer guerra mundial* remains an imperfect example of imperfect cinema. More successful, in the view of the present author, is a subsequent film, *Son o no son*, an untranslatable pun on 'To be or not to be' (*son* means 'they are' and is also a type of song): a satirical critique of the weakness of the Cubans for the kind of nightclub entertainment which might charitably be described as in poor taste. Filmed largely at the world-famous Tropicana in Havana, García Espinosa however regards the film as unsatisfactory, and it has not yet been completed. Unfortunately it is now unlikely he will be able to do so, since he has become the new head of ICAIC and hasn't the time to spare. But the film deserves to be seen.

The theme of internationalism in *Tercer guerra, tercer guerra mundial* is pursued by ICAIC in a long series of major documentaries during the 70s: in the same year comes Alvarez's *Piedra sobre piedra* ('Stone Upon Stone') about Peru, and in 1972 his film of Fidel's tour of Chile, *De America soy hijo*... Pastor Vega follows his *Viva la Republica* of 1972 with a film on Panama, *La quinta frontera* ('The Fifth Frontier') in 1974. Alvarez returns to Vietnam to produce *Abril de Vietnam* ('April in Vietnam') in 1975, and in 1976 come two films on Angola, José Massip's *Angola, victoria de la esperanza* ('Angola, Victory of Hope'), and *La guerra en Angola* ('The War in Angola') by Miguel Fleitas, made in co-operation with the Film Department of the Cuban Armed Forces.

*Piedra sobre piedra*, in the country where it was shot, was a controversial film. Some Peruvian critics felt it was awkwardly structured. The first half was too general, and the second half, which reported the devastation of the Peruvian earthquake of 31 May 1970, was too disconnected. According to Isaac León Frias, Alvarez was proposing an equation between the 60 seconds of the earthquake and the earthquake of underdevelopment that lasted 365 days a year; to which Juan M. Bullitta responded that if you were not already familiar with Alvarez's style, or were not familiar with the political concepts he dealt in, then it did not come across very clearly. Behind these doubts was the key question about what stance the film adopted towards the country's new military regime, headed by Velasco Alvarado, which claimed to be revolutionary, held anti-imperialist attitudes, enacted an agrarian reform, reopened diplomatic relations with Cuba, but declared that it was neither capitalist nor communist itself.[4]

Alvarez himself had provoked these doubts by his oddball approach to the subject. Faced with the problem of being an official film-maker, in other words, the difficulties of what to film and what not to film and of who, the atheistic Cuban chose to structure the entire documentary, all seventy minutes, round an interview with an army chaplain. In the circumstances, this was an astute thing to do. You are faced with the problem of representing to an audience most of which has never been abroad, a picture of a co-lingual country which you yourself have never visited before. Captain García was working-class. 'As a boy I worked as an agricultural labourer,' he tells the interviewer. He became a priest, he explains, and then joined the army, because he felt too distant from the people he preached to. At the end of the film, when we watch him talking with a crowd of people, trying to win over his listeners, some of whom display a noticeable degree of recalcitrance, to believe in Velasco's goodwill, we see him clearly as one of the radicals of the junior officer ranks in the Peruvian army whose backing Velasco depended on, but who were more radical than the leader, for this Velasco was no Fidel. Nevertheless, the chaplain – who does not actually look like one – sees the army, with its obligatory military service, as a school available to the abandoned classes for their betterment. There was a lot that a Cuban audience could identify with in such a character, for various and even contradictory reasons: the familiarity of his way of speaking, and a certain attitude towards the army as a body which got things done; but also the oddity of seeing this in a priest for the people of a country where religion was weak. This was like a signal to the Cubans to remember that revolutionaries could well be religious. In this respect, it is a film prophetic of the growing militancy of the radical priesthood throughout Latin America since the Cuban Revolution, from the actions of individual priests like Camilo Torres, through the theology of liberation, to the integral role of popular religion in the revolutionary movements of Central America in the 80s.

The following year, 1971, Alvarez made the first of three films about Chile, *¿Como, por que y para que se asesina un general?* ('How, Why and Wherefore is a General Assassinated?'). This is an extended newsreel of thirty-six minutes on the assassination of General René Schneider on 22 October 1970, with which the right wing attempted, with CIA backing, to destabilise the Popular Unity Government of Salvador Allende at the very outset, two days before the Chilean parliament was due to ratify his electoral victory. The last of the group is a shorter extended newsreel, fifteen minutes, Alvarez's response to Popular Unity's overthrow three years later, *El tigre saltó y mató, pero morira...morira* ('The tiger leaps and kills but it will die... it will die'). As entirely unorthodox a newsreel as such a title suggests, the film is named after a phrase of Martí's; its sound is that of three Chilean songs sung by Victor Jara, who died among the numberless victims of the coup who passed through Santiago's football stadium; the tragedy and horror is expressed to this accompaniment in a varied montage of visuals combined in chunks from a number of sources, including evocative animated titles. Very rapidly made, it incorporates sections of material lifted bodily from the second of Alvarez's films on Chile, *De America soy hijo... y a ella me debo* ('Born of the Americas...'), a title drawn, again, from the writings of Martí.

Subtitled 'Film Record of a journey which transcends seas and mountains and unites the Sierra Maestra in the Antilles with the Andean Sierra in the South', this is a chronicle, running three hours and a quarter in its full version, of Fidel's visit to Chile at the end of 1971: Alvarez at the height of his powers deliberately laying down a challenge to the habits and theories of commercial cinema – as he himself announced to the Cuban press in an interview for the film's launching.[5]

Alvarez takes his strategy for holding a film of such length together from a unique source: Fidel's speeches. A growing influence on Alvarez's film-making, they are paradigmatic in various respects. First, Alvarez derives the paradigmatic structure of the film from the speeches Fidel made during the trip. He uses them to provide entry points to sequences which narrate a key series of moments and aspects of Latin American history, contrasting them with critical features of the experience of the Cuban Revolution. The film alternates between reportage, which is gently paced, full of relaxed observation of Fidel's encounters with the people of Chile as well as picturesque images of the country, even of a meeting between Fidel and a llama, and the interpolated sequences with their maps and engravings and animated textual graphics, which are sometimes even accompanied by a different spoken text. The result of the whole procedure, which is described by Stuart Hood as 'deceptively loose-jointed but powerful in its cumulative effect',[6] is exactly, from the point of view of rhetoric, that of Fidel's style of speaking. To examine the published texts of these speeches shows why: while his form of argument owes everything to his legal training, the listener is guided also by a series of metaphors and images, often aphoristically expressed, which Alvarez translates on to the screen through his instinct for montage.

From an economic point of view, 1970 in Cuba was a year of trial. The attempt during the 60s to diversify production and lessen the country's dependence on sugar was less than successful. There was a certain distance between hopes and realities. Economically the Revolution had not yet succeeded in breaking the vicious circle of underdevelopment, despite Che Guevara's energetic optimism. How could industrial development be achieved in a small island under a blockade, cut off from the continent which forms its natural geographical and economic sphere? The emphasis on industrial development left a falling sugar harvest and a reduction in foreign earnings, exacerbated by the fact that most of the sugar produced went to the Soviet Union, which, even though it paid preferential prices, did so mostly in non-convertible currency and was unable to satisfy the variety of Cuba's developmental needs. The year known as the Year of the Decisive Effort, 1969, was to be devoted to the reinvigoration of agricultural and especially sugar production. The aim was a ten million ton sugar harvest in 1970. The media in all their forms – newspapers, radio, television, cinema, posters – and the political organisations, the trade unions, the Committees for the Defence of the Revolution, were all enlisted to mobilise the people for the effort. Resources were diverted, and their diversion caused privations. ICAIC's production programme was reduced: in 1970, twenty-four documentaries, only one short fiction film of half-an-hour, and one animation. Even fewer documentaries were made in 1971, as the limited resources were diverted to make up for the lack of new fiction. Five new fiction films were produced, one of them a half-hour short, one of them a ballet film; the other three were Massip's *Paginas del diario de José Martí* ('Pages from the Diary of José Martí'), *Los días de agua* ('Days of Water') of Manuel Octavio Gómez, and Alea's *Una pelea cubana contra los demonios* ('A Cuban Struggle Against The Demons') – all of them (as we shall see) very considerable achievements which significantly develop the thematics of Cuban cinema.

In the event, the 1970 harvest fell somewhat short of the target at 8.5m tons, and Fidel made a momentous speech of self-criticism; and yet it was still the largest ever sugar harvest in Cuba's history, and 18% higher than the previous largest.[7] Nevertheless, the mood was less than celebratory, and there was a change from 1968 sufficiently great to be difficult to understand from the perspective of the European intellectuals who had gathered in Havana in that year. Then, in 1971, unfortunate events concerning the poet Heberto Padilla made matters worse: when his arrest and detention for twenty-eight days produced an international protest; signatories who included visitors to the

Cultural Congress in 1968 interpreted the incident as a betrayal of the principles Fidel had so clearly enunciated.

There is no denying that Padilla was a marked man, for he had attacked the respectable revolutionary writer Lisandro Otero and defended a book by Guillermo Cabrera Infante, who had finally parted company with his country with a certain amount of self-publicity in 1965. In 68, Padilla had won the prize of the international jury of the Casa de las Americas competition with a book of poems provocatively entitled *Fuera del juego* ('Out of the Game'). Some of these poems were sceptical about the Soviet Union and others expressed disenchantment with things in Cuba. They had a cyncial tone to them, and it is easy to see why they produced offence. They were attacked in the armed forces' journal *Verde Olivo*, and when the book was published it carried an introduction by the artists' and writers' union in the form of a disclaimer; Padilla lost his job at the Party newspaper *Granma* (hardly surprising). He did not, however, want to leave his country, like the sorry rump of the liberals who departed one by one during the late 60s. (Among them were the film-makers Fausto Canel, Alberto Roldan, Roberto Fandiño and Fernando Villaverde; some of these self-exiles brought into the circles of Cuban sympathisers abroad attitudes and responses that contrasted sharply and unfavourably with those of political exiles from Chile and Argentina in the 70s.) What happened in 1971 has been recorded by the Chilean writer Jorge Edwards, who served in Cuba as chargé d'affairs when diplomatic relations between the two countries were restored with Allende. Edwards, a Chilean liberal intellectual who kept company with Padilla, is not a sympathetic observer of the Cuban process, but he recounts the cause of the arrest as a consequence of the poet's unstable mental condition. Padilla was behaving, Edwards writes, in a somewhat paranoid fashion, carrying the manuscript of a novel around with him wherever he went; he was 'over-excited . . . half-crazed', full of 'indiscretion and egomania': 'The truth is that Padilla was very fond of hinting at the existence of mysterious links between him and some secret powers. He had given me to understand on more than one occasion that he managed to stay successfully afloat thanks to the conflicting currents inside the Government. These hints, which were figments of his passion for inventing myths, would be accompanied by bellows of self-satisfied laughter.'[8] These are the sad facts. Padilla was detained, and doubtless had to confront an angry Fidel. Then he was released and made self-criticism (not a procedure to appeal to the foreign critics) at a meeting at the artists' and writers' union. The 'affair' was marginal to ICAIC. The collective methods of work at the Film Institute served to save the film-makers from the lingering effects among the writers of isolation from the collective which writing as a profession is prone to suffer. The Cubans themselves have never played on the incident, and were sorely disillusioned by the unfriendly and aggressive reactions form Europe.

As for ICAIC in the period of these events, all three of the fiction films released

*Paginas del diario de José Martí*

in 1971 in one way or another develop the ideas behind 'imperfect cinema'. Massip's *Paginas del diario de José Martí* uses almost every imaginable resource, fictional, documentary, realist, surrealist, ballet, cantata, theatrical, to create a mobile tapestry that moves impressionistically through the events which the diary obliquely narrates. It opens with a spoken delivery of the film credits by a chorus of simultaneous and overlapping voices, which very much sets the tone for the film's idiosyncratic form of narration. Images pass rapidly. An old man carrying a naked baby enters a group of peasants singing unaccompanied in prayer. Ballet dancers mime a fertility rite. Period engravings of scenes from the late nineteenth century appear. The voices evoke a time 'a hundred years ago [when] the nation was born in war'. Colour is used expressionistically, with filtered reds and greens, as the voice of an old man remembers Martí stopping at his house just after his clandestine return to Cuba's shores. The film proceeds in episodic fashion, through scenes of peasants at work, and of Martí and Máximo Gómez preparing their campaign, and the violence and brutality of raids by Spanish soldiers in the countryside, always interspersed with the voice of the diary, until we come to the day of battle and the death of the Apostle from a stray bullet, shown in mute sepia accompanied by an avant-garde orchestral score by the composer Roberto Valera; a reflective epilogue concludes the film with images of Martí in a mural in an artist's studio. A truly hallucinatory film.

*Una pelea cubana contra los demonios* is the furthest back Cuban cinema has gone in historical reconstruction, a film about priests and pirates and demons at the time of the Spanish Inquisition, based on a work of the same name by the cultural anthropologist Fernando Ortiz, a leading figure of the rebellious intellectual generation of the 20s. It enacts a documented story of the year 1672 (given as 1659 in the film) in which the priest of a coastal township, fuelled by religious fanaticism, attempts to remove the entire community to an interior site, out of reach of pirates and heretics – the latter a euphemism for Protestant privateers trading illegally along the coast. He has to contend, not surprisingly, with the opposition of practically all of the landowners he is seeking to prevail over, among them the distinctive figure of Juan Contreras, hedonist, sceptic, and a bitter ideological enemy of the church. Against Contreras and his ilk, Padre Manuel (marvellously acted by José Rodríguez) calls upon the same methods which the Inquisition uses against the fearful forces of witchcraft and black magic, superstition and demons, which it everywhere sees, of course, in the pagan religion of the illiterate. In order to enlist the support of the authorities from Havana, he concocts a testimony about calamities that have overtaken the community, in which he claims to have exorcised hundreds of evil spirits. The authorities order the community to remove itself to another site, though some of the townspeople refuse to leave.

This is a film which in its narrative style refuses all conventions of genre, and again Alea refuses us the chance to identify in the familiar way with a positive hero. The first of Alea's films to be photographed by Mario García Joya, who has collaborated on all his subsequent films, the fluid camera style involves long takes with an almost constantly moving hand-held camera which allows few of the syntactical devices of genre film language – point-of-view shots, reaction shots, strategic close-ups – by which such identification is normally established. (In general, of course, it is not a question of these devices being totally eliminated, but of their not being used in the form of the articulated system of orthodox

*Una pelea cubana contra los demonios*

259

narrative découpage.) Instead, Alea creates the loaded atmosphere of a world half real and half mythical, of brazen individuals and collective hysteria. The film's extraordinary visual fluidity, together with its striking black-and-white photography, leads it to depart from the straightforward narration of historical facts, but it also turns the film into a corrective interpretation of history, a study of the social and economic forces of seventeenth-century Cuba, with their demons both spiritual and physical: the theology of the Inquisition, and the smugglers and pirates who came in the wake of the Spanish colonists.

The film is rich in the parallels and oppositions contained in its metaphors and symbols, especially those which are built around the similarities and contrasts, visual and symbolic, between the rituals and ceremonies of the Church and the shamanism of the slaves. This is a tendency towards the structural organisation of symbolic language to be found in several Cuban films, especially *Lucía* by Humberto Solás and *De cierta manera* of Sara Gómez. A raid by pirates, who pillage and rape, is followed with an attack by invisible predators: during a hellfire sermon, a woman is seized with convulsions – her body twisting as if once again struggling against the rapist's attack. The preaching priest himself seems to be possessed, the camera moving in on him in close-up, as he cries out that the devil is always among them, chaos rules over them. It is the island's economic and political structure which is in chaos. Sugar exports are threatened by smugglers who prey on shipping and then undercut the market price, while desperate slaves commit suicide to escape their misery, in the hope that their bodies will return with their souls to Africa.

Among the landowning class, contradictions are personified by the contrast between the sceptical Contreras and Padre Manuel's ally Evaristo. To try to dissuade their work force from abandoning them, Contreras warns the people of the town against Padre Manuel's promise to lead his followers to a land free of demons; while Evaristo advises the authorities from Havana of the impending arrival of a smugglers' ship, with which Contreras is involved in doing business. But if we see in the figure of Contreras elements of a critique of the Church, he is also refracted by his position outside not one, but two religious systems. The other, which he is voyeuristically drawn to, leads him to visit a shaman woman who lives in a cave and goes into a trance in which she speaks of the river of native blood to come. Her voice is heard over a blank screen while tachistoscopic images flit by, a frame or two at a time – the faces of Martí, Fidel, el Che. He understands from her vision that the rebellion of the people is inevitable.

*Los días de agua*, scripted by Manual Octavio Gómez with Bernabé Hernández and Julio García Espinosa, is about the same themes in more recent times, a story of the political manipulation of religious hysteria in the 1930s, based on real events in the province of Piñar del Rio in 1936. A local woman, Antoñica Izquierdo, has become known as a saintly healer. Long processions of the sick come to her house to receive the healing she administers with holy waters. With them comes a journalist after a story, and an opportunist business man who sets up food stalls. The place becomes both a sanctuary and a fair. The local doctors, drug stores and priests, seeing their interests threatened, conspire to get rid of the

*Los días de agua*

healer and her followers. There is a death among the sick, and Antoñica is accused of murder. A lawyer seeking the governorship of the province comes to her defence and wins her freedom, his consequent popularity winning him election. Once in power, he decides that her activities now hurt his interests. The army mounts an attack, Antoñica tries to defend herself with holy water, while amongst her followers, violence provokes them to respond with violence. But this open act of rebellion is doomed before it begins, for the journalist has been right about one thing: 'What a waste of power! What a stupid woman! People believe in her and she doesn't know how to lead them!'

On one level the film is about who pays the costs of sickness in a sick society. Antoñica declares her powers a free gift, an act of social rebellion against the cartel of the priests and medics. But she also declares that there are diseases which cannot be seen. Like *Una pelea cubana...*, this narrative is offered not in the form of a cold and considered historical reconstruction, but in the shape of an hallucinatory allegory. The story is told inside out, as it were, and from a series of different angles, like a written narrative which shifts the point of view of the narration between the different characters: Antoñica herself, the journalist, the opportunist, the fanatic, the politician Navarro, the priest, the municipal sanitation officer, the chief of the rural guard. The film is particularly memorable for the manner in which the various episodes are plastically expressed in the treatment of colour, from the early sequence which narrates the origins of Antoñica's powers – a vision in which the Virgin saves her child – where colour is rendered dreamlike through underexposure, to the wild activity of the scene of the rebellion, which the hand-held camera pictures from within as a participant, with the result that the surface smoothness of orthodox colour photography is broken up, not unlike the rupture of the image in the battle scene of *La primera carga*...

These two films about religious and magical beliefs, and the hierarchy of repression which is built upon them, share important features with a number of the most distinctive Brazilian films of the previous decade, belonging not to the neorealist tendency pioneered by Nelson Pereira dos Santos, but to the very different stylistic impulses, much more baroque and emotional, identified with Glauber Rocha and dubbed with the term 'tropicalism'. Thematically these films include *Ganga Zumba* of 1963 by Carlos Diegues, about the search of escaping slaves for the mythical black kingdom of their kind; but the main paradigms are *Deus e o diablo na terra del sol* ('Black God, White Devil' – literally 'God and the Devil in the Land of the Sun', 1963) and Rocha's *Antonio das Mortes* (1968). Rocha's world is one in which emblematic characters perform stylised actions in a dream-like amalgamation of history and legend, epic and lyric. For Rocha, the mysticism of popular religion in the Brazilian North-East is a fusion of Catholicism and the motifs of African religion transplanted with the slave trade, which produces the authentic voice of the people of these lands, the expression of a permanent spirit of rebellion against constant oppression, a rejection and refusal of the condition in which they have had been condemned to live for centuries. The Cuban films are less schematic, less formalist, but the style is in many respects, visually and in other ways, closely similar. Fundamentally, they have the same feel for that process, known as syncretism, by which the religious symbols not merely of different but of clashing cultures are conjoined. In a key scene in *Los días de agua*, two religious processions, one Christian, the other Yoruba, meet and fuse: a paradigmatic rendering of the simultaneous presence in the syncretistic culture, in its practices and its products, of symbolic elements from historically separate origins, which have been brought into confrontation and have interpenetrated.

Several documentaries on themes of religion and syncretism were made during the 60s, including two films by Bernabé Hernández on the Abakuá religious society and aboriginal culture in 1963 (*Abakuá* and *Cultura Aborigen*). Octavio Cortázar, after making *Por primera vez*, investigated the question of syncretism in a twenty-minute documentary from 1968 with the intriguing title *Acerca de un personaje que unos llaman San Lázaro y otros llaman Babalú* ('About a character some people call St. Lazarus and others call Babalú'). The object of investigation is an annual religious saint's day celebration in which the worshippers approach the shrine crawling on their knees to give thanks or to pray for recuperation from illness. Interspersed with the scenes of the pilgrimage and festivities are a series of interviews with both participants and commentators, either specialists or just people in the streets. It emerges that there is considerable confusion about who this Lazarus is. A Catholic priest maintains that he is a separate person from the Lazarus raised from the dead, a lay leader of the procession holds the opposite. (Cortázar playfully intercuts an old film clip of the

Raising of Lazarus.) The provenance of the icons of Lazarus to be found in Cuban churches is traced – three of these images come from different parts of the Christian world and suggest different associations. But whichever, Lazarus has an alter ego in Babalú, the African god with whom he shares a number of characteristics, most importantly his healing powers. There is some disagreement, too, between people who hold these beliefs incompatible with the Revolution, and others who consider them harmless enough. And there is also the analysis of the cultural historian who sees the phenomenon as a paradigm of syncretism, for Lazarus and Babalú are not separate, the one identified with the other merely for convenience, they are one and the same, Christian and African at the same time, or in short, Afrocuban.

Another area where Cuban film-makers have drawn attention to a closely similar phenomenon is music. A number of documentaries from the late 60s on, dealing with different aspects of Cuban popular music, have celebrated its diversity and riches, showing that much of it is a result of syncretistic processes. *Y . . . tenemos sabor* ('And . . . We've Got Taste', 1968) by Sara Gómez, who was a trained musician, is a guide to its exotic range of percussion instruments – claves, spoons, maracas, bongos, the güiro (made from gourds), cowbells, horse's jawbone and so on – and their origins, some primitive, some mixed (mulatto).

Musicologists have shown that the evolution of musical forms is also a long and complicated affair. The *habañera*, for example – like the one Bizet included in *Carmen* – can be traced back to the early English country dance and the French *contredanse*, transmitted largely through the Spanish *contradanza*. However, while Cuba was a Spanish colony, it also received French musical influences more directly, as a neighbour of Sainte Domingue (Haiti) and French Louisiana. Havana itself was a point at which many cultural influences coalesced, carried by sailors and their passengers across the seas. It was a city of sojourn for long-distance travellers, like the emigrants to Veracruz in Mexico who left a dance on their way through known in Havana as the *chuchumbá*, which was banned by the Tribunal of the Sacred Inquisition for the indecency of its forms and rhythms. This is a constant theme, and all sorts of excuses will do. In 1809, the journal *Aviso de la Habana* condemned the French *contredanse* simply on the grounds of its national origins: 'Why have we not disposed of the waltz and the contradanza, those always indecent fabrications introduced to us by the diabolical French? They are diametrically opposed in their essence to Christianity. Lascivious gestures and an impudent vulgarity are their constituents, which, from the fatigue and the heat with which the body suffers, provoke concupiscence . . .'[9] But music defies edict, and the dance continued to evolve, crossing backwards and forwards from Cuba to Spain and back to Latin America, to produce the inimitable lilt of the *habañera*, which got its name in Spain; and the *danzón*, as the Cubans called their own version; and in Buenos Aires, the tango (which when it took New York by storm in the 1920s was again subjected to pious protests).

As with instruments and dances, so with song forms, which are often particularly reponsive to social and political currents. *¿De donde son los cantantes...?* ('Where do the singers come from?', dir. Luis Felipe Bernaza, 1976), recalls the career of the Trio Matamoros, three brothers from Oriente who started playing together in 1925, singing serenades under balconies at night. They based their music on a version of a traditional song form called the *son* (as in García Espinosa's *Son o no son*) which took shape, the commentary tells us, in the Sierra Maestra in the last years of the nineteenth century, among singers who were engaged in the independence struggles and composed satirical verses against the Spanish and North Americans alike. The style took a couple of decades to reach Havana where, like the equally satirical *decimas*, it enjoyed great popularity during the so-called 'golden period' of Cuban music in the 30s – the decade following the arrival of RCA Victor and Columbia and the stimulus they gave to commercial music production in Cuba.

The film celebrates the survival in this music of certain authentic popular values – those which E.P. Thompson describes as the Brechtian values of irony in the face of moralism and the tenacity of self-preservation – in the midst of all the commercialism, when singers were promoted under such tags as *el tenor de la voz de seda*, 'the tenor with the voice of silk', and *la estrella de la canción*, 'the star of the song' (female). Cinema itself, of course, with the coming of sound, contributed to the process, a succession of films from different countries helping to create fashions and crazes – tap-dancing after *Piccolino*, tangos with *Boliche*, both in 1935; Spanish music with *Nobleza baturra* and *Morena clara* in 1936 and 37; Mexican music with *Alla en el Rancho Grande* and *Jalisco nunca pierde* in 1937. But not all the music documentaries of the 70s are equally successful in dealing with the problems of this history. *Que buena canta Ud.* ('How Well You Sing', dir. Sergio Giral, 1973) is a homage to the singer Beny Moré, which interweaves memorabilia and interviews with his family and colleagues, but says very little about the manner of his commercial promotion – he was one of the biggest of Cuban musical stars, whose records captured markets throughout Central America and the northern shores of South America, the hinterland of the Cuban commercial music business. 'Vox pop' interviews, which generally follow the line 'Beny is dead but he lives; his music is neither old nor modern', testify to his genuine popularity, but their effect, when the film is viewed outside its original context as obituary, is to leave an otherwise highly delightful film with an excessively populist evaluation of the music. Yes, his music is very vibrant, but all those pre-revolutionary film clips of him, where do *they* come from? There is rather little in this film of the approach of imperfect cinema, no questioning of the construction of the imagery, or of the ideological uses of its musical clothing, no interrogation of the mythology of 'popular' music (of which Colina and Díaz Torres wrote, speaking of the use of music in the melodrama and the musical comedy of the time: 'the melodic motifs of tangos, rancheros and boleros fulfil a double function: they enhance the spectacle, channelling it towards the popular classes, and they serve, in their own right, to reduce the essential content of the film to that of contagious tunes.'[10])

One of these films, however, from the late 70s, *La rumba*, directed by Oscar Valdés with a script by Julio García Espinosa, confronts the question head on. The opening images are of two contrasting snatches of dance. 'For the people of Cuba,' says a narrator over the first, 'this is a commercial manifestation of the rumba, a commodity, and false'. 'This,' continues the voice over the second, 'is an authentic rumba. But there are still lots of Cubans who don't feel it belongs to them. The rumba is one of this people's most legitimate artistic creations. What is the prejudice they hold against it?' In the course of forty-five minutes the film proceeds to trace its historical origins. The word itself comes from Spain, where it was not originally the name of a dance, but described a certain kind of woman, who lives what is called a 'happy life', a certain kind of frivolity; in other words, the very name of the dance involves a prejudice. This is amplified later in the film: such a prejudice is typically machista, and the rumba has developed an erotic narrative version, danced by a couple, which evolved from African fertility ritual and enacts the possession of the woman by the man. What happened was that a Spanish word gave a name and an identity to a dance and a rhythm whose origins were completely African (and in which the eroticism doubtless had different cultural meanings). To confirm this thesis, we learn that there were musical clubs in Cuba, particularly among the petty bourgeoisie, which for respectability's sake never danced the rumba, but took to the *danzón* instead.

Another film which deals directly with the African roots of a large part of Cuba's musical heritage is *Miriam Makeba*, a portrait of the African singer by Juan Carlos Tabío, made during her tour of Cuba in 1973. There is a sequence in which she and her band meet with a group of Cuban musicians and compare notes. Makeba's is by no means the purest of African song; she has adopted harmonies and other elements which are of modern Western origin and originally alien to the African idiom. Nor, as she tells her hosts, is she a 'learned musician'. But listening and watching attentively with growing delight to black Cuban drummers, she declares that 'If Cuban drummers play, unless they start singing in Spanish, I can't tell whether they're Cuban or African!'

Of these films, only the one by Sara Gómez is filmically remarkable in any special way. The others are all more or less conventional in their various uses of commentary, interviews, historical footage and the filming of historical relics. The first impression which *Y... tenemos sabor* makes on the viewer is the way its jagged and syncopated cutting captures and expresses the rhythms of the music it is describing. It is also an excellent example of imperfect cinema. Towards the end of the film, the musician showing us the instruments remarks, 'But we don't *need* all these instruments, we can just as well make music with bits of iron and sticks.' 'This,' Tomás Gutiérrez Alea remarks, 'was Sarita's attitude to making films.'[11]

There is another musical documentary, however, *Hablando del punto cubano* ('Speaking of Typical Cuban Music', dir. Octavio Cortazár, 1972), which is an altogether exceptional film, the effect of a truly delightful paradox built in to its commentary, which is sung instead of spoken. The word 'punto' in the title cannot really be rendered into English; it refers to the art of the verbal improvisa-

*Hablando del punto cubano: the 'controversia'*

tion in song form, either by an individual singer or by a pair of singers engaged in what is called a *controversia*, or controversy. Again we are given historical information: the *punto* has a Spanish heritage. It became an art of itinerant *campesino* singers, who in this way carried news and comment around the countryside. But instead of dying out, a new generation of professional campesino musicians grew up in the 30s with the opportunities provided by the radio. Later, many of these artistes suffered eclipse, but one of them is featured through the length of the film, the incomparable Joseito Fernández. His is a name inseparable in Cuba from one of the Cuban songs best known internationally, *Guantanamera*. The form in which it's known abroad, appropriately enough set to verses by José Martí, is only a recent adaptation, popularised in the early 60s in solidarity with the Cuban Revolution by the North American folk protest singer Pete Seeger, who learnt it from a student. According to Alejo Carpentier, the tune of the song's opening phrases is none other than the old Spanish romance 'Gerineldo', preserved through the centuries by the most authentic peasant singers.[12] In the 30s, it became Joseito Fernández's theme tune, when he had a weekly radio programme and used it to improvise a popular commentary on politics and current events. Here in this film it turns up in a new guise: this is its commentary.

The whole film plays on the paradox of using film, whose personae are not physically present to the audience but only projected, and can therefore have been manipulated any this way and that, to portray an improvised art form. In fact it takes the bull by the horns. 'Lots of people,' sings Joseito, 'would like to know if this stuff's improvised or not'; and there is a spontaneous discussion – one of those discussions which is provoked by bringing a group of people round a camera and asking them certain questions – among a group of workers outside a bus factory, arguing about the kind of artistry involved in the practice of the punto. One speaker accuses another of credulity at the idea that a *controversia* is really improvised. The singers, he says, have so much practice and preparation that it isn't really improvisation, it is virtually prepared, they don't really have to improvise because they've got it all stored up in their heads. It clearly, however, looks very different from that in the example of a *controversia* we see on camera. Cleverly, the camera operator has kept the camera trained part of the time on the

*Hablando del punto cubano: the 'controversia'*

singer in the pair who is not at that moment singing, and the editor has left the shot to pan backwards and forwards without cutting so we know they have not cheated: the look of concentration on the silent singer's listening face reveals all: the moment, listening to his rival, when he slowly tilts his head and breaks into a broad and very special smile of anticipation, as he discovers how to couch his reply. Other singers show similar evidence – it is impossible not to recall the passage of Walter Benjamin's where he talks about the way film makes it possible to analyse minutiae of behaviour which were previously too fleeting sometimes even to be noticed. And carrying it all along, the masterly Joseito himself, a graceful, thin, tall moustachioed figure, who wanders through gates, gardens and down streets, a floating presence, teasing us with his improvised singing commentary, challenging us, it seems, to challenge him over it, knowing of course we cannot, and even if we could, it would have to be on his terms, and he would win.

Afrocuban or tropicalist, the style which succeeds in communicating the syncretism of Latin American music and religion plastically or dramatically is itself an expression of syncretism, almost by definition. This requires some explanation. The term syncretism means two different things in Latin America and in Europe. In Latin America, where it is a much more familiar concept among educated people than in Europe, it comes from the discourse of anthropology; in Europe, it belongs to specialist branches of psychology. It was given currency by Piaget to describe the distinctive quality of children's vision and children's art, which is also described in the case of play by Wittgenstein:

> Here is a game played by children: they say that a chest, for example, is a house; and thereupon it is interpreted as a house in every detail. A piece of fancy is worked into it. And does the child now *see* the chest as a house? He quite forgets that it is a chest; for him it actually is a house. (There are some definite tokens of this.) Then would it not also be correct to say he *sees* it as a house?[13]

This attitude of play is obviously displayed by children in whichever continent. One of its essential aspects is a certain tolerance for conceptual chaos. As the educational psychoanalyst Anton Ehrenzweig has put it, 'A scribble can represent a great number of objects that would look very different to the analytic spectator. [But] however "abstract" the infant's drawing may appear to the adult, to [the child itself] it is a correct rendering of a concrete individual object.'[14] The European typically finds this not only a feature of the mentality of children but also of the tribal cultures which it conquered around the world.

The same thing is acutely true of the syncretistic style of Latin American cinema – to Old World eyes. Relatively and in fact, the films which seem the most exuberantly Latin American often display in their seeming formlessness – whether fiction or documentary – a much higher tolerance than European cinema for visual disorder, apparently haphazard bricolage and narrative or argumentational looseness. This is obvious in the complaints of the more tight-arsed critics, who cannot help seeing the film-makers concerned as still somehow savage and unformed, the way that generations of European colonisers saw the indigenous cultures they conquered and enslaved. At best, their attitude to them is paternalist.

At the same time, of course, these films exert a powerful and hypnotic fascination. What seems to have happened here is a fusion of elements of the symbolic languages of clashing cultures – in which the *conquistador* culture witnesses a counter-definition of its own tenets because the Other challenges the myth that it projects upon history. This is a question both of artistic style and of something more than style – in the same way as the modernist revolutions in European art, which created the succession of 'isms' that progressively fractured and fragmented traditional forms in every medium until no return seemed

Joseito Fernández

possible. It is a similar process which becomes a liability of the artistic imagination throughout Latin America, in whatever medium. Syncretistic features are equally much an essential element of the novel of the so-called literary 'boom' of post-war years, of which *A Hundred Years of Solitude* by Gabriel García Marquez, is only – if deservedly – the best known paradigm, the style which is known as magical realism. In the same way, once before, at the end of the nineteenth century, the style of the *modernista* poets was formed. At different moments, poets and film-makers have all proclaimed the creation of a new symbolic language, fit to express the true voice of the continent.

In Cuba, the poet Roberto Fernández Retamar focused on a powerful symbol for this phenomenon. He wrote, in 1971, a second key essay of Cuban revolutionary aesthetics, entitled *Caliban*. The old Caliban, he said, the base, deformed half-man half-fish of Shakespeare's last play, was dead, a new one was being born. He is not the only Caribbean intellectual to see Caliban this way. He refers himself in his essay to a number of others, including George Lamming, Edward Braithwaite and Aimé Cesaire.

Why Caliban? Who is he? His name, as numerous scholars tell, is an anagram of 'canibal', which derives from *caríbal*, carib, Caribbean. All sorts of historical evidence reveals that *The Tempest* alludes to the 'discovery' of the Americas: Shakespeare's island is the poetic symbol of the islands where Columbus first landed and where an English ship was wrecked in 1609, providing the Elizabethan playwright with a first-hand account upon which to draw. It was, moreover, a topical play, for the conquest of the New World, and in England especially the renewed project for the colonisation of Virginia, was a burning question of the day.

The central theme of the play, to modern Caribbean eyes, is the utter opposition between master and slave, coloniser and colonised. Implacable realist that he was, says Fernández Retamar, Shakespeare created in the figure of Caliban the other face of the nascent bourgeois world. He takes the noble savage from his contemporary Montaigne and turns him into the pathetic figure that the European coloniser produced in those they conquered and brutally exploited. The attitude of the coloniser is roundly represented in Prospero:

> I pitied thee,
> Took pains to make thee speak, taught thee each hour
> One thing or other: when thou didst not, savage,
> Know thine own meaning, but wouldst gabble like
> A thing most brutish, I endow'd thy purposes
> With words that made them known.

And the attitude of the rebellious slave in Caliban's reply:

> You taught me language; and my profit on't
> Is, I know how to curse. The red plague rid you
> For learning me your language!

269

*The Tempest* has exerted particular fascination in Latin America ever since the Argentinian Juan Rodó wrote an essay at the turn of the century on the nature of Latin American culture, entitled *Ariel*. His interpretation of the play followed traditional lines: Caliban was base, Ariel was the imprisoned spirit of creativity. The twist in the tail was that Rodó identified Caliban with the United States of America, the imperialist power in the north which, as his contemporary Martí explained, had come to represent the major threat to the integrity of Latin America. In the second half of the century, Rodó's version has been overturned. The imperialists have become Prospero, the tyrannical and sadistic foreign duke who exercises power through magic. Caliban is his militant anti-colonialist opponent.

Ariel also changes – Prospero's other slave, his houseboy, who just as Caliban performs Prospero's physical labour, carries out his spiritual desires. Previously, Ariel, who openly demands from Prospero his liberty, was seen as the symbol of the enslaved creative spirit, the symbol of everything aspiring, in contrast to Caliban's baseness. But now the Caribbean novelist George Lamming calls him Prospero's intelligence agent: 'the archetypal spy, the embodiment – when and if made flesh – of the perfect and unspeakable secret police'.[15] In the version of the play which the Martinique poet Aimé Cesaire wrote for a black theatre company in 1969, Ariel becomes a mulatto; and having carried out Prospero's wishes against his own better judgment and defiantly made his scruples known, Prospero replies, 'Here we go! Your crisis! It's always the same with you intellectuals!' But at least Ariel now has a choice: either to continue serving Prospero, or to turn his back on him and join with Caliban in the real liberation struggle.

Aspects of the Caliban theme found expression in Cuban cinema during the course of the 70s in a series of films about slavery in which the image of the slave is powerfully deconstructed: Sergio Giral's trilogy, *El otro Francisco*, *Rancheador* and *Maluala*, Alea's *La ultima cena*, plus an assortment of documentaries. They are films in which the figure and historical personage of the slave is seen in an entirely new light.

*El otro Francisco*, on which Alea and García Espinosa collaborated with the director and Héctor Veitía in writing the script, is (as we saw earlier) a piece of deconstruction that has been worked upon its source, a romantic abolitionist novel of 1839; not a free adaptation, but the product of a careful critical operation. The North American film theorist Julianne Burton puts this film forward, along with *Girón* and *De cierta manera*, as a paradigm of the subversion of the dominant phenomenon of cinema as spectacle. *Girón* 'simultaneously imitates and subverts the blood-and-guts war movie'; *De cierta manera* 'subverts the Hollywood romance'; and *El otro Francisco* 'critiques the historical melodrama.'[16] *Rancheador* is similarly based on a literary source, *Diario de un Rancheador* ('Diary of a Rancher') by Cirilo Villaverde (who also wrote the much better known *Cecilia Valdés* on which Humberto Solás based his epic, but less than successful, *Cecilia* of 1983). Villaverde, in turn, based his novel on the diary of a certain Francisco Estévez, a hunter of runaway slaves in the pay of the landowners. The film adopts a different aesthetic strategy. Cast in the form of an orthodox but ingeniously crafted narrative, *Rancheador* pictures Estévez as one of the bloodiest and most ambitious of mercenaries. He not only hunts down slaves in their *palenques*, hidden communities in the hills, but he employs his henchmen in repressing outbursts of rebellion black or white, slave or free. His behaviour threatens to expose the manoeuvres of the sugar landowners who employ him, in their factional conflicts with the smallholding coffee growers. He tries to vindicate himself by setting out to hunt for the legendary woman leader of the runaway slaves, Melchora. But Melchora is a mythological personage, a symbol to the slaves of their freedom, a psychological weapon of combat. In his blind and obsessional fury, Estévez commits a series of crimes that begin to contradict the class interests which he serves, and his employers, ever ready to sacrifice their bloodiest servants when necessary, abandon him to his destruction. Though it undoubtedly has elements in it of an epic western, this is actually much less of a genre movie than this description makes it sound, first because of the dialectical analysis of the historical forces involved, and secondly because of the potent Afrocuban symbolism of the myth of Melchora and its effect, among other things, in dissolving the individualism of the story's heroes into the collective.

This is also a strategy adopted in *Maluala*, which deals with the least-documented area of the history of slavery. The film's title is the name of a *palenque*, or settlement of escaped slaves, one of a group of such settlements somewhere in the eastern, mountainous part of the island, though exact time and place remain unspecified. The story describes how the Spanish set out to divide the leaders of the *palenques* against each other, with considerable but not total success. The three films of the trilogy taken together show a development of consciousness from singular to collective, from individual resistance to collective struggle, from suicide to battle. Combining professional and non-professional actors, and with music by Sergio Vitier, *Maluala* shared the top prize for fiction at the first Havana international film festival in 1979 with the Brazilian Geraldo Sarno's *Coronel Delmiro Gouveia*.

Alea's film *La ultima cena* ('The Last Supper') is a subtle, ironic fable, an allegory of the religious hypocrisy of a plantation owner towards his slaves, set in a time just after the Haitian revolution of 1795. The Cuban landowners are suddenly instilled with the fear of slave rebellion at the same time that the disruption of agriculture in Haiti offers them the chance to improve their position in the international market, but only on condition that they buy more slaves and intensify their exploitation, which only increases, of course, the dangers of rebellion. The Count of Casa Bayona, brilliantly played by Nelson Villagra, is a sensitive man, whose stomach turns at the sight of the treatment his overseer metes out to a runaway slave, Sebastian, when he is punished by having his ear cut off. The Count, who sees himself as a source of protective Christian love towards his slaves, would rather they accepted their lot with humility. Accordingly he selects twelve of them, including the runaway, for an Easter ritual: first he symbolically washes their feet – very symbolically, since touching

*La ultima cena*

the black men's feet offends his delicate constitution – and then he wines and dines them the evening before Good Friday.

What follows is a *tour de force* of black comedy. As Philip French reports, 'At the centre of the movie is a modern re-creation of the Last Supper that inevitably brings to mind the beggars' blasphemous celebration of the Eucharist in *Viri-diana*. But Alea's mentor, Buñuel, contrived that scene to produce a brief shocking frisson. Here it is the occasion for an extended, sinuous debate on the human condition in which the pious Christian, not his insulted and injured guests, brings the precepts of his religion into question... He has a little trouble in explaining to some of his guests the difference between transubstantiation and cannibalism, and not all of his temporary disciples understand his Franciscan sermon about the need to embrace their misery joyfully. But they think he's a grand, generous fellow, and when he frees an aged bondslave (who immediately asks if he can stay on anyway), they're convinced of his good faith. However, after the Count slumps on the table asleep, the supper's Judas-figure comes into his own. He is, of course, the slave Sebastian who regales the company with a forceful parable of his own about Truth and Dishonesty, and how decapitated Truth put on the head of Lies and went around the world deceiving people.'[17]

This parable of Sebastian's is his African reply to the Christian myth of Genesis and the Fall. 'When Olofi made the world he made it complete with day and night, good and bad, Truth and Lie. Olofi was sorry for Lie, who was ugly, and gave him a machete to defend himself. One day Truth and Lie met and had a fight. Lie cut off Truth's head. Headless, Truth took Lie's head. Now Truth goes around with the body of Truth and the head of Lie.' The Count's explana-tion of transubstantiation is similarly translated by his listeners, one of whom acts out the tale of an African family fallen on bad times. In order to get money to buy food, a father sets out to sell his son into slavery, but his son turns on him and sells him in place of himself. Whereupon the family turn on the son and deliver him up to the authorities, who sell him in turn into slavery, and they end up that way eating twice as much. What we get in this long scene is a dialogue between master and slave – an extraordinary achievement by the scriptwriters, Tomás González and María Eugenia Haya as well as Alea himself – a meta-dialogue of symbolic meanings, which, the North American critic Dennis West observes, enacts 'the profound and intricate Hegelian dialectic of lordship and servitude traced in *The Phenomenology of Mind*'.[18]

This dialogue is prepared by the early scenes of the film, and especially the relationships between the three men who administer the Count's estate, the overseer, the priest and the sugarmaster. The clergyman preaches moral platitudes to the slaves while grumbling about the godlessness of the overseer. The overseer, however, is much more the Count's *alter ego*, which some of the slaves realise perfectly well. (The ones who don't are those who, round his table, continue to believe in the Count's good faith.) The most equivocal of the three is the sugarmaster, an educated Frenchman with a scientific mind, analysing and improving the methods of refining sugar. He develops a system of burning cane-waste for fuel to replace the depleted forests. He explains to the Count that a nice new piece of English machinery would only be worth purchasing if he also got more slaves to increase production. Sympathetic to the suffering of the slaves – he later conceals the fugitive Sebastián from the slave-hunter – the sugarmaster teases the priest about the secrets of his art, which, he says, come from the mysteries of nature herself. To the priest's cautious enquiry if such beliefs are not a little like witchcraft, he responds with the question whether the church is not also witchcraft, and dangles a little bag containing the substances needed for the transmutation of raw cane juice into refined sugar, taunting him with its mystery: 'It seems that what is to become white must first be black.' But there's no magic in the substance: it's *caca de poule*, chicken shit. It's all up here, he says, tapping his head. He shows off the products: decreasing shades of brown and finally pristine white. But not all of it, he says, is capable of being purified, just like souls in purgatory.

And then it is that we come to the grotesque comedy of the supper, and at its centre, a key symbolic gesture: 'Hegel's notion of recognition,' writes West, 'means that the master depends on his bondsman for acknowledgement of his power, indeed for assurance of his very selfhood. As the Count reiterates his order that Sebastian recognise him [the Judas parallel] the camera emphatically dollies in on their juxtaposed faces, and a tense silence reigns. The slave's eventual answer is to spit in the master's face – a brutal refusal to recognise the other's lordship and the graphic expression of the bondsman's true self-consciousness: in spite of his actual bondage, the slave's mind is his own.'

# References

1. First published in *Cine Cubano* No.42/3/4, 1967; translated in M. Chanan ed., *Twenty-five Years of the New Latin American Cinema*, BFI/Channel 4, 1983.
2. 'Meditations on Imperfect Cinema... Fifteen Years Later', tr. M. Chanan, *Screen* Vol.26 No.3-4, 1985, p.93.
3. Rigoberto López, 'Hablar de Sara, de cierta manera', *Cine Cubano* No.93, pp.110-1.
4. Bullitta in *Hablemos de Cine* No.54.
5. *Granma* 14 April 1972.
6. 'Murder on the Way', *New Statesman* 18 April 1980.
7. Arthur MacEwan, *Revolution and Economic Development in Cuba*, Macmillan, 1981, p.117.
8. Jorge Edwards, *Persona Non Grata*, tr. Harding, Bodley Head, 1976, p.229.
9. Quoted in María Teresa Linares, *La música popular*, Instituto del Libro, 1970, p.18.
10. Colina and Díaz Torres, op.cit., p.23.
11. During a viewing of the film with T.G. Alea in Havana, July 1984.
12. Carpentier, op.cit., p.24.
13. Wittgenstein, *Philosophical Investigations*, Basil Blackwell, 1963, p.206.
14. Anton Ehrenzweig, *Psychoanalysis of Artistic Vision and Hearing*, Routledge and Kegan Paul, 1953, p.6.
15. George Lamming, *The Pleasures of Exile*, Michael Joseph, 1960, p.99.
16. Julianne Burton, 'Marginal Cinemas and Mainstream Critical Theory', *Screen*, Vol.26 Nos.3-4, 1985, p.14.
17. 'Crucified in Cuba', *Observer* 11 March 1979.
18. Dennis West, 'Slavery and Cinema in Cuba: The Case of Gutiérrez Alea's 'The Last Supper', *The Western Journal of Black Studies* Vol.3 No.2, Summer 1979.

# 14
# ONE WAY OR ANOTHER

*Movies for entertainment – De cierta manera – by way of an epilogue*

In 1974, Julio García Espinosa got involved with the Italian film critic Guido Aristarco in an altercation about what was going on in Cuban cinema. The occasion was the *Rencontres Internationales pour un Nouveau Cinéma* in Montreal, a gathering of some seventy-five radical film-makers from all over the world, together with critics, distributors and political activists given to using film. There were, reported John Hess in the North American film journal *Jump Cut*, several areas of awkward political disagreement which came to light during the course of the event, especially a series of misunderstandings between European and Latin American participants which reflected, he said, their very different relationships to the institutional structures of both film industry and state in the two continents. It was clearly a variation on this theme when the Italian criticised Cuban cinema for the peril of allowing the portrayal of triumphalist heroes rather too much like those of socialist realism. It is not to deny that the nature of the heroic icon may well be a barometer of certain critical aspects of a society, to say that Aristarco's criticism seemed not only to the Cubans but to other Latin Americans present to be schematic and unjust. To be sure, it was true of some of the early Cuban films like *El joven rebelde*, but it could hardly be said to apply to the astonishing output of the late 60s – *Memorias del subdesarrollo*, *Lucía*, and others; though it is also the case that in one or two of the very latest films at the time, like *El hombre de Maisinicú* ('The Man From Maisinicú, dir. Manuel Pérez, 1973), the problem was beginning to crop up again. There was some general discussion about the question, but García Espinosa provided a more considered reply in his own paper to the meeting, where he stepped back to look at the whole problem of militant cinema in the particular situation of a third world revolution in power.

'We controlled the means of production and the cinemas,' he began, 'but after ten years we had to recognise that we weren't yet the masters of these cinemas because, quite simply, one cannot show only revolutionary films in them.'[1] It was necessary, he explained, to undertake first a preliminary stage in the decolonisation of the screens in terms of the concrete choice of films available on the international market, and the first step was that Cuban audiences were able to see films from everywhere, not just North American films like before the Revolution. But there was a problem: the majority of films they found themselves showing left a great deal to be desired ideologically speaking. The situation, he admitted, led to absurdities, like showing Japanese films just because at least the faces of the heroes weren't white. He was saying implicitly that whatever it was in Cuban cinema Aristarco found to be suspicious about, it didn't come, as the Italian was arguing, from some kind of mythical leftist aesthetic orthodoxy, it was a material consequence of the colonisation of the screens by the capitalist metropolis. Jorge Fraga has recently pointed out that the problem has got worse: there were many films in the 60s that were ideologically acceptable. In the 80s, mainstream cinema has come to be more and more dominated by violence and pornography.[2]

The Cubans had been able, said García Espinosa, to resolve the problem of informing people more adequately about the society they lived in. But a cinema, he suggested, which provides its audience with more authentic and relevant information is relatively easy to accomplish. What remains the greater challenge is entertainment. The explosion of the technologies of mass communications in the 60s, he said, had produced a highly paradoxical situation in Cuba. All over the world people were seeing – mostly on the small screen – a growing range of highly informative documentary images. Although there was much in their form of presentation and contextualisation that needed to be questioned, the problem in Cuba, because of the isolation forced upon it, was that the images which reached them from abroad were virtually all fictional. Cuban film-makers were consequently confronted with a battle between two kinds of image, two types of cinema, documentary and fiction, which appeared fundamentally like a struggle between authenticity and falsehood. The audience continued however – and why not? – to reach for the fictional image, to satisfy what are after all perfectly real needs for the dramatisation of experience, which there have always been aesthetic forms to satisfy. This, said García Espinosa, was a most difficult and delicate problem for them.

.The truth is that a number of Cuban features during the 70s could be said to have succumbed before this problem by adopting the weak solution. In a way, this is because the very thing García Espinosa had warned about in introducing the idea of *cine imperfecto* had come to pass. Cuban film-makers had grown so much more confident in their control over the medium that they now took the very codes of Hollywood narrative and started playing around with them. The result was a series of films which included, in 1973, *El extraño caso de Rachel K.* ('The Strange Case of Rachel K.', dir. Oscar Valdés) and *El hombre de Maisinicú*; *Patty Candela* (dir. Rogelio París) in 1976; and a year later, Cortázar's *El brigadista* and another film by Manuel Pérez, *Rio Negro*. To put it crudely, these are all films which swap around the baddies and the goodies and play a few narrative tricks, and end up as Cuban versions of genre movies. Since – except for *Rio Negro* – they are all based on real people and events, this has an effect of mythologising recent Cuban history.

The first is a *film noir*, following the lines of a newspaper investigation, which tries rather too self-consciously to use the iconography of the genre as a kind of pathetic fallacy for the doom-laden mood of the time. It is set in 1931, a year before the fall of the dictator Machado. Ignoring a police raid on a meeting of tobacco workers, the press becomes obsessed with the sordid murder of a French nightclub dancer. While the workers' leader is assassinated in prison, the murder investigation threatens to reveal corruption in high places, and Machado is forced to silence the newspapers. *El hombre de Maisinicú* is an adventure story about an undercover counter-agent in the Escambray mountains in the early 60s who infiltrates and destroys a band of counter-revolutionaries trying to re-establish contact with the CIA. It is offered as a film of homage to a secret hero of the Revolution. The entire tale is told in flashback, starting with his death. The intention was that of distancing the spectator but the effect is the opposite. It only reinforces the dead man's heroic character.

In a similar vein, *Patty Candela* is an espionage movie about operations against the CIA in 1961, which shifts its point of view from that of the conspirators to that of the Cuban security forces, but then finds it necessary to tack on an epilogue. *Rio Negro*, Manuel Pérez's second feature, is a Cuban western set on a ranch in the Escambray at the time of the Bay of Pigs, in which Tirso, a revolutionary militiaman, son of a peasant whose land was seized in the bad years before the Revolution, slugs it out with Chano, a counter-revolutionary who had been involved in the land seizure. The greatest delights in this last film are the superb performances of Sergio Corrieri as the self-searching Tirso, and the Chilean actor Nelson Villagra as the thwarted Chano, but the genre format – and especially the spectacular shoot-out with which the film ends – overwhelms the attempt that had been made to mould the character of Tirso differently from the conventional genre hero, above all by introducing contradictions in his personality and a level of political discourse which Hollywood would never permit. Sergio Corrieri, like Nelson Villagra an actor of exceptional qualities, internationally renowned for the lead in *Memorias del subdesarrollo*, also played the Man from Maisinicú. After these films he withdrew from screen acting, to avoid getting typecast as Cuba's principal male lead.

If the descriptions of these films are unfair – too brief and schematic – there is nonetheless a visual feature in several of them which is both annoying and symptomatic: a constant, frequently ragged and often unnecessary use of the zoom lens, rather more intrusive than the smoother and more facile zooming which became virtually a trademark of Hollywood movies in the 70s. This weakness for the zoom is present in quite a lot of Cuban cinema. It is found, for example, in the style developed by Santiago Alvarez's principal cameraman, Iván Napoles; and indeed it clearly derives from the rough sponteneity of many of the best Cuban documentaries. It is quite a different matter, however, where fiction is concerned, not at all the same as the feverish hand-held style previously developed by Jorge Herrera – though he photographed some of these films too. Combined with quite conventional colour, it becomes in these films a style that is only too close to Hollywood, which in this respect, however, it still cannot hope to equal.

However, the fundamental difficulty in these films (except perhaps *Rachel K.*) is that of trying to portray the very real anonymous heroism which many people showed during the course of the Revolution, in a form inseparable from the traditional imagery of *machismo*. *El brigadista* shows perhaps most clearly what the dangers are of this approach, because it is a film of adolescent adventure and initiation, on a model whose original, perhaps, is Tom Sawyer. The crux of the difficulty is contained in a pair of incidents which reveal the obverse of *machismo*: the implications it has for the imagery of women. In the first, our young hero Mario meets with a girl by chance at night; they are carried off by adolescent dreams of first love, and Mario pledges himself to her with the gift of his watch – it doesn't work but he tells her 'it's like a ring'. In the second, he is almost seduced by the wife of a *gusano* whom he visits in her house quite legitimately as the village teacher, while her husband is in the swamps with an armed band of counter-revolutionaries. There is a clear and unfortunate equation at work here, in which revolutionary *brigadista* equals romantic idealism equals the danger of corruption, which can only come as an act of treachery on the part of a woman tainted by sharing her bed with a traitor to the Revolution. Both these women, the virgin and the adulteress, have virtually no other presence in the film than this, and both are the crudest of misogynist stereotypes.

These were all successful films with the audience – some more than others – and how they came to be made is that, on principle, ICAIC frowns upon aesthetic conformism and doesn't consider there's any a priori reason why such approaches should not be tried. At the same time there are other films, which though not as immediately arresting as those which immediately preceded, still attempt to come to terms more critically with the problems of narrative and representation. Manuel Octavio Gómez, for example, did so twice in the mid-70s, in *Ustedes tienen la palabra* ('Now It's Up to You', 1974) and *Una mujer, un hombre, una ciudad* ('A Man, A Woman, A City', 1977). These two films, both of them highly accomplished, are concerned with issues which, although of universal concern, are also subjects of particular political debate within the Cuban revolutionary process: the administration of justice and the problems of urban renewal. This makes for certain difficulties in assessing them. A lot of our recent film theory, as John Hess points out in discussing these films in *Jump Cut*, condemns conventional narrative means as hopelessly tainted by bourgeois ideology, which the imperfect cinema thesis largely seems to confirm. It is consequently pretty easy to pick out various films which offend from both points of view. But with these two films we find ourselves in an uncertain position to judge how effectively they may conduct a political dialogue with the audience; which in Hess's opinion suggests that they raise questions about the universal applicability of anti-narrative theories. At any rate, if bourgeois films, he says, 'include politics and social issues at all, it is usually as a background theme which the film-maker soon abandons in order to concentrate on the moral and romantic concerns of a few central characters. Manuel Octavio Gómez's two films, however, move in the opposite direction. They open with moral questions and move out to the underlying historical and political questions.'[3]

*Ustedes tienen la palabra*

*Ustedes tienen la palabra* deals with fictional events seven years earlier than the year of its release. Eight years have passed since the overthrow of Batista. The heroic struggle against imperialist military intervention is past, the October crisis is history, the remaining counter-revolutionary bandits have been routed. The Revolution has entered resolutely on the tasks of reconstruction. The institutionalisation of the new Communist Party has begun. But the new society is still only in process of formation and old attitudes persist.

It opens with one of those pre-title sequences which has become a hallmark of Cuban cinema: a fire rages at night in a wood, a large thatched building burns. People rush around trying to put it out. Following the titles we find ourselves among the ruins of the building: it has been turned into a court of law and a trial is in progress of a group of people accused of arson – counter-revolutionary sabotage. The camera roams across the shell of the building, a warehouse in the Rio Palmas Forestry Collective, and as it emerges how the arsonists had tried to do their dirty work elsewhere and failed, the trial broadens out to become a general investigation by the community of itself. The first of the accused was before the revolution a manager for the previous owner of the land, who now lives in the United States. The second was the same man's chauffeur. They deny their guilt, and, as the trial proceeds to uncover an intricate story, it becomes clear that in a way their particular guilt is not the main issue. For the film becomes a Brechtian demonstration of the real concerns of popular justice – it brings to mind the atmosphere of the prologue to *The Caucasian Chalk Circle* – which is not so much a matter of facts and sworn evidence as the investigation of the state of consciousness in the community, as well as the circumstances of the crime and the political nature of another kind of guilt – the guilt of those whose lack of consciousness allowed the crime to happen in the first place. As the story is pieced together through flashbacks corresponding to the successive stories told by defendants and witnesses, the investigation takes in the lack of proper planning and economic controls in the collective, the disorganisation of the labour process, the improper use of resources, and poor communication between the union and the administration. A central fact, immediately obvious to the Cuban viewer, is the absence in the collective of a Party caucus. According to Leopoldo Perdomo reviewing the film in *Juventud Rebelde*, the film reveals five kinds of deficiency, which also include the persistence of certain negative religious attitudes.[4]

But this makes the film sound schematic and even doctrinaire, which it certainly is not. In fact every effort was taken to avoid it being so. It was shot on location with the active participation of local people who contributed to the script, especially, according to the assistant director Fernando Pérez, in the scenes of the assembly and in the staging of the fire.[5] To achieve greater authenticity, the film was shot in 16mm and then blown up to 35 for cinema release, like *De cierta manera* by Sara Gomez, which allowed the cameraman, Pablo Martínez, a more than usually flexible and fluid and hence intimate style of filming. It is true that the narrative is linear, but as Manuel Octavio Gómez himself explained, in *La primera carga...*, the interviews and the reportage themselves produced the analysis; in *Los días de agua*, the successive subjective visions of each character provided more and more information for an under-standing of certain facts; in this film, the narrative simply follows the lines of the judicial inquiry.[6] Yet the flashbacks are not as simple in their internal structure as this implies. They are a means of fusing the incompleteness of the various individual points of view of the protagonists; on occasion they even begin with one character and end with another. The result is that while the film foregrounds individual behaviour, it does not psychologise it. At the same time, instead of the mechanical notion that people's behaviour will change as a result of improve-ments in economic planning and efficiency and material improvement in their conditions of life, the film poses the question exactly the other way round: how are these improvements to come about if the imperfect state of people's con-sciousness impedes the achievement of the more rational organisation of production?

The plot of *Una mujer, un hombre, una ciudad* is somewhat more complex and diffuse. Gómez takes up material he filmed nine years earlier in 1968 for a documentary on the rapidly growing port and industrial town of Nuevitas in the province of Camagüey – the city of the title – and uses it as the context for two parallel biographies. Marisa, the town's director of housing, has been killed in a car accident. Miguel, a young Havana-trained sociologist, reluctantly returns to his native city to replace her, he believes, temporarily. He becomes increasingly obsessed, however, with finding out who Marisa was, and as he talks to the people who knew her, family, friends and colleagues, the film develops, as John Hess points out, a format of flashbacks over her life resembling that of *Citizen*

*Kane*. He starts out, Hess observes, with very personal reasons for conducting this investigation. The ghost of Marisa's exemplary political life suffocates him. Every one he talks to describes Marisa in glowing terms and he feels unfavourably compared with her. But he cannot comprehend the records she has left behind, cannot figure out the basis on which she allocated housing and thinks she did it subjectively, with none of the scientific methods and rigour he has learnt at the university in Havana: and 'he wants to prove her wrong to validate himself'.

As he discovers more and more about Marisa, however, and at the same time becomes increasingly involved with the city and its people, he begins to change. He becomes uncomfortable with his Havana friends, including his architect wife, whose lack of relationship, personal or political, with the people for whom her apartments are intended, utterly contrasts with Marisa. In the end he decides to abandon Havana and his wife and stay in Nuevitas. The critique of the post-revolutionary Havana intelligentsia which the film thus elaborates makes it a successor to the concerns of *Memorias del subdesarrollo*. It is also directed towards the difference between the theory that is taught in the academy, including the misconceptions of various new administrative practices, and the reality to which they have to be applied.

Moreover, in contrast to the stereotypical portrayal of women in the genre films, Gómez clearly takes the question of women in the Revolution very seriously – and has found in Idalia Anreus an ideal actress for the character of Marisa, full of nervous energy and determination, just as she so marvellously accomplished the role of Tulipa ten years earlier. We find her, immediately after the Revolution, arguing for the right of women to work in the docks. Her husband supports her in finding another job when the male dockworkers force the women to quit but, as Hess remarks, when she becomes increasingly involved with her work and starts attending long meetings after hours, her husband rebels and asks her to quit. She refuses and the marriage ends. Although she then finds herself unable to handle an involvement with another man, John Hess is substantially right (he exaggerates a bit) that Gómez has somewhat idealised her character: 'Since she basically serves... as a symbol of the revolutionary woman, of the New Woman, he portrays her as morally superior to everyone else. She exhibits the greatest sensivity to the problems of ordinary people and the greatest possible commitment to the Revolution. She can stand up to men with a great deal of strength... and can articulate the needs of... other women, children, the sick, the uneducated peasants and workers. Nonetheless, her basic role... is passive; she becomes an example, a symbol. She does not propel the plot foward but serves as the locus of moral values... the model revolutionary woman as imagined by men.'

Hess concludes his account of these two films by observing that, in contrast, *De cierta manera* ('One Way or Another') by Sara Gómez is a unique example of a Cuban film where the female lead is an ordinary person with no symbolic baggage to carry around with her. By tragic mischance, Sara Gómez is the only Cuban director whose work we can see as a whole – but an imperfect whole, like the imperfect cinema she practised: she died, from asthma, as *De cierta manera*, her first feature, was being edited; it was completed under the supervision of Alea and García Espinosa.

The editing, at the moment of her death, was well advanced. Most sequences were already cut, and the commentary had been planned, though not all of it written. However, her death obviously delayed completion, which was further held up by technical problems in the laboratory, including damage suffered by the negative. In the end, the negative had to be sent to Sweden to be treated and then blown up to 35mm, and the result was that the film was not released for a couple of years.[7] Some observers find it difficult to believe that there wasn't something deliberate in this delay, and that ICAIC was uncomfortable about the film's critique of macho values. This could well be true, but it doesn't have to enter into any explanation of the delay. Cuba is a Latin American country, in the experience of the present writer more efficient to film in than any other; but people in Cuba still have a quite different, less anxious, sense of time to that of the over-programmed metropolis. It does not require sinister motives to explain how the technical problems alone which the film encountered could have taken two years to solve.

Sara Gómez trained as a musician, but after six years at the Havana Conservatory she decided, she said, that she didn't want to be 'a middle-class black woman who played the piano'.[8] She got a job as a journalist and then joined ICAIC as an assistant director, working with Alea, Fraga, and on a visit to Cuba, Agnès Varda. Then, between 1964 and *De cierta manera* in 1974, she made ten documentaries, most of them no longer than ten minutes' duration, on a range of subjects which include popular culture and traditions, the mechanisation of tobacco production, music, civic education, traffic accidents, child care, pre-natal attention, popular democracy and labour relations. What emerges is a body of work largely concerned with the same kinds of theme as her final film. It also demonstrates the acquisition of an exceptional economy of means in communication.

*Ire a Santiago* (1964), which takes its title from a poem by Lorca, is a fond and gentle portrait of Santiago de Cuba and its people. Its style of shooting (the photography is by Mario García Joya), editing, and informal voice-over commentary, make it perhaps the most striking 'free cinema' documentary ever produced in Cuba. It has a very personal quality which is reflected in the credits: as in one or two other films, Mario García Joya is listed under his nickname Mayito, and the director lists herself as 'Sarita', the name by which everyone in ICAIC speaks of her, till today. A year later came *Excursion a Vuelta Abajo* ('Trip to Vuelta Abajo'), which describes tobacco culture in a village in the province of Pinar del Río and the changes brought about by the Revolution. Curiously, it is more of an apprentice work than the first film, but it is notable for including in the focus of its social observation aspects which are unusual for the emerging pattern of the Cuban documentary; for example, the way it foregrounds the image of women workers in the fields, at a time when the subject had not yet drawn the attention of historians. It is true of all of Sara Gómez's films that she gives a stronger presence to women and black people than you get with a number of less conscientious directors within ICAIC.

Her third film was *Y . . . tenemos sabor*, which has already been discussed, and is one of the most delightful Cuban music documentaries in a quarter century. Then came a trio of films on the Isle of Pines, which the Revolution renamed the Isle of Youth when it decided to turn it over to youth and education. The last of the three, *Isla de Tesoro* ('Treasure Island', 1969) is a short, poetic, celebratory film essay, which simply crosscuts between shots of the Model Penitentiary of the pseudo-Republic years, where Fidel was imprisoned by Batista, and the production of citrus fruit, which ends up being packed and labelled as 'Treasure Island Grapefruit Produce of Cuba'. The two films which precede it, *En la otra isla* ('On the Other Island', 1967) and *Una isla para Miguel* ('An Island for Miguel', 1968), are her two most extraordinary documentaries, among the most extraordinary by any Cuban director.

The first and longer of them (at forty minutes) is a loose collection of individual portraits of people in the island: a seventeen-year-old girl who wants to be a hairdresser; a man of the theatre who works as a cowboy during the day, runs a theatre group in the evenings; another agricultural worker who used to be a tenor in Havana; an ex-seminarist; a girl at the reformatory; the woman at the reformatory responsible for her. The interviews – and as a result the structure of the film – have unusual qualities. Cubans are people who, from the evidence of Cuban cinema, are always eager to talk to cameras and microphones, but rarely in the manner we see here. Sara Gómez clearly had a remarkable way of gaining the trust of her subjects, and drawing out of them stories and reflections which go far beyond most other documentaries. The tenor, for example, speaks of the experience of racism he had in Havana as a black singer wanting to sing leading operatic roles. The interview, which is a two-shot of the both of them, sitting very informally in the open air, ends with him asking his interviewer, 'Sara, do you think one day I'll sing Traviata?' Other interviews touch further awkward subjects, above all questions of delinquency and re-education, and the difficulties of life for children in a reformatory or re-education camp. The girl, Manuela, whose father has been imprisoned as a CIA agent, while her mother has gone to the States, describes her own experience, and Cacha, her supervisor, answers questions very frankly about the need to treat inmates as adults, especially in the matter of sexual relations. This is also one of the handful of Cuban films which make self-reference to the camera and the business of filming, along the lines of García Espinosa's call in 'Imperfect Cinema'. Clapper boards are seen, the film has captions which say what comes next. The most striking moment of this kind tells us that Cacha, the supervisor, is going to comment on the interview with Manuela afterwards. The effect is to have us see the subjects in the film as integral human beings and representatives of particular social roles at the same time, and in a mutually illuminating way: it helps the viewer to make a judgment about the dialectic between the individual and the social. The same is true of *Una isla para Miguel*, which, beginning with a hearing before the disciplinary assembly at one of the re-education camps, is a case study of the boy being disciplined. It includes memorable interviews with Miguel's mother, in their poorest of homes, she and her countless children abandoned by her husband; and with his best buddy. A supervisor comments dramatically, 'They are rebels without a cause, our task is to give them the cause'. Although in our own countries we are nowadays used to television reports which probe similar topics about reformatories and their inmates, this is somewhat rare footage for Cuba – which is a great pity. These reformatories are not the same as the UMAP camps (Military Units to Augment Production) in the two years 1965 to 67, which were set up in a wave of sectarian fervour to rehabilitate those who were deemed social misfits: drug users, Jehovahs Witnesses, hippies and gays – people thought to be easy marks for CIA activity. What these films show is very far from the exploitation of fears inflamed by the constant threat of external attack, but a serious humane approach to the real problems of socially marginal individuals. If there had been more films of this kind, the Revolution would be less susceptible to attacks abroad on the grounds of irrational inhumanity towards social dissidents.

The next two films deal with public subjects. *Poder local, poder popular* ('Local Power, Popular Power', 1970) and *Un documental a proposito del transito* ('A Documentary About Traffic', 1971). The first is political and expository, and the only film of hers that is both too long, and in its structure, unwieldy; the second is a sociological and technical investigation of the problems of city traffic, inevitably somewhat prosaic. The next two, *Atención pre-natal* and *Año Uno* ('Pre-natal Attention' and 'First Year', both 1972, each ten minutes) are most remarkable, from the point of view of a masculine viewer, for the way they address themselves directly to women, about preparing to give birth and about lactation during the baby's first year of life, ignoring the presence of any chance male viewer, although they were made for general screening. *Sobre horas extras y trabajo voluntario* ('On Overtime and Voluntary Work', 1973) addresses everyone. Also a very short film, it is politically more effective than the longer essay on popular power. The theme, of course, needs far less exposition – it goes back to Che Guevara in the 60s. Together with *Isla de tesoro* the film of Sara Gómez that is closest in style to Santiago Alvarez, its stance is boldly agitational: there must be a struggle against the unnecessary use of overtime, but also, at the same time, against wasteful voluntary work which isn't properly organised.

Nearly all her films, then, were – as imperfect cinema requires – socially and politically functional: we find that the style and idiom of the film is subordinate to its purpose, never the other way round. Whenever possible a radical aesthetic is explored, but emerges from within, so that the film can be readily grasped and still communicate on a popular level. Her last work, *De cierta manera* is nothing if not an aesthetically radical film in this manner. Above all, it mixes different modes of filmic discourse, fiction and documentary, in the most original way, not merely by alternating them but by using real people to play themselves alongside

professional actors. Moreover, these real people appear both as themselves –
documentary material about them tells us who they are – and as characters within
the story. None of this is at all forced; it arises from the familiarity both of Sara
Gómez herself, and of Cuban audiences, with a whole range of forms in both
documentary and fiction.

Two things can be said about this. First, it is an answer to the problem of the
battle between the two forms of fiction and documentary of which García
Espinosa spoke in Montreal. In fact, to find a way of integrating them was an
endeavour of Cuban film-makers which first clearly surfaced in the late 60s with
films like *Memorias del subdesarrollo* and *La primera carga al machete*. Manuel
Octavio Gómez pursued the attempt in *Una mujer, un hombre, una ciudad*
through incorporating his own documentary material of a few years earlier.
There are yet other examples, like Manuel Herrera's *Girón* of 1972, which adopts
the format of a wide-screen war movie to present the results of an exhaustive
documentary investigation of the events. The second comment is that what *De
cierta manera* achieves is a veritable interpenetration of the two forms of address, a
teasing synthesis, which makes it a prime example of the process of syncretism.
The only problem of the film as finished is a miscalculation over the commentary, which imitates the didactic documentary in its use of a certain kind of
formal sociological language. It is intended, according to Rigoberto Lopez, 'as an
element of distanciation, and at the same time, to amplify the analysis'.[9] But as
Julia Lesage remarks in her perceptive piece on the film in *Jump Cut* (the same
issue as John Hess's article on the films of Manuel Octavio Gómez), it has a
tendency to sound pompous and grating.[10] (I don't think this is reducible,
however, to insensitivity on the part of Alea and García Espinosa in the course of
finishing the film: the commentary, Alea told me, was what Sara Gómez herself
intended – though one would like to think that, had she lived, she might have
had second thoughts, at least as far as the tone of its delivery is concerned.)

Another feminist commentator on the film, Annette Kuhn, finds that the way
the film takes up and in various ways combines the two different conventions of
film realism undercuts the normal relationship a viewer has with either on its
own. It is a form of deconstruction, she says, which works by setting up
expectations and then cutting them off, leaving the film with 'no single internally
consistent discourse'.[11] I think this is only partly true. I think it is demonstrable
that while the film is deconstructional in the way she describes, its internal
discourse is quite consistent – it speaks to us from within the quite particular
experience of the Cuban Revolution. For a third commentator, Ann Kaplan, the
'juxtaposition of two cinematic strategies forces the spectator to become aware of
his/her need for narrative. For as one watches, one becomes impatient with the
documentary sections; one always wants to get back to the story.'[12] I think
probably this effect is in certain respects less acute with the Cuban audience,
because of its considerable familiarity with the range of documentary styles
which have been discussed in this book. But it is true, as she says, that the
question of the power of narrative film preoccupies Cuban film-makers and
critics; that this is because Cuban audiences continue to respond strongly to

classical Hollywood cinema; and that what Sara Gómez is attempting in this film is to give a moral lesson in a pleasurable way. The film in fact is hugely pleasurable, and zips along (it runs only seventy-two minutes), brimming with lightness and good humour, however jarring the jumps. On the contrary, the jar of the jumps becomes part of the pleasure.

For *De cierta manera* is a revolutionary love story, which means a film about the growing relationship between a man and a woman which refuses to isolate their elective affinity from the social determinants which have not only made them what they are, but continue to affect them as they get to know each other. Nor does their relationship follow a smooth course but pride and conflict interrupt it, the result not of the mysterious qualities of the irreducible personality but the expression in the individual of class background, cultural inheritance and personal history, refracted through the impact of the Revolution. The central protagonists are Mario (played by Mario Balmaceda, who also played Miguel in *Una mujer, un hombre, una ciudad*), a worker at a bus factory, and Yolanda (Yolanda Cueller), a primary school teacher from a lower middle-class background.

The setting of the film is Mario's beat. In 1961, in one of the Revolution's first major projects to tackle the country's enormous housing problem, five new neighbourhoods were built for people living in Las Yaguas, a Havana slum that was one of the worst. The new neighbourhoods were constructed by the same people who were to live in them, who belonged to the dominantly black lumpen classes. One of these districts is Miraflores, where our two protagonists live and work. For Yolanda, it's a confusing place: 'How do I feel?' she asks in a Godardian testimony to camera, 'Well, not very good. I graduated from different schools. Then I came here, and all this was a different world, one I thought no longer existed.'

All of this we learn early in the film, amid a sequence of commentary over documentary images, which begin with a dramatic shot of demolition that serves as a thematic image for the whole picture. Here and in subsequent commentaries the film develops the thesis that rehousing is only a start. By itself it can do little to improve the life of people previously consigned to subsistence in the belts of squalor and poverty that still surround all other major cities throughout Latin America. With rehousing must come the provision of employment, education and health care. Even these things only make up the groundwork. Revolutionary change involves cultural regeneration, but this is not an automatic process. It requires a struggle to overcome the habits, customs, beliefs and values of the old society. And in the case of the marginal classes, without even a tradition of participation in trade union and political activity, their hermetic culture contains a high degree of resistance and inertia towards such changes; hence the persistence of certain anti-social attitudes within the Revolution.

To focus the problems, the film investigates the Abacuá religious society (a phenomenon which has also been examined in a number of Cuban documentaries on various subjects where the Abacuá influence can be felt, like music, such as the Oscar Valdés film, *La rumba*). Mario and Yolanda are conversing on a hillside, talking about Mario's background and adolescence. He was lucky, he

*De cierta manera*

says, to have been conscripted into the army, because military service saved him
at the moment he was thinking of 'going'. 'Leaving the country?' asks Yolanda.
'No, no, what for? "Going" means taking the oath.' 'What oath?' 'When I was a
kid I wanted to be a *ñañigo*.' 'A *ñañigo*!' Yolanda repeats in horror, to which
Mario responds, 'You think they eat babies on St. Barbara's Day, right?' and the
film shifts to a documentary sequence on the Abacuá to which the *ñañigo*
belongs. The Abacuá is a secret society, a heritage of the religious practices and
beliefs conserved in the legends, rites, symbols and language of the slaves. The
society took form during the nineteenth century in the marginal population of
the ports of Havana and Matanzas, where it not only fulfilled religious functions
but also became a mutual help association which defended the rights of its
members (white as well as black). However, as an exclusively male domain, it
'epitomises the social aspirations, norms and values of male chauvinism in Cuban
society'. The sequence which informs us of all this is not merely a convenient way
of instructing us about it. It also serves to teach us that Yolanda's horror has
elements of social prejudice in it, and that Mario is a man aware of the need to
fight free of its influence.

Male chauvinism takes its toll in the problems that Yolanda encounters in her
workplace. She is criticised by fellow teachers for her lack of sympathy in her
dealings with 'La Mejicana', the mother of one of her pupils, Lazaro, a somewhat delinquent child. La Mejicana and Lazaro are real people; Lazaro is the
eldest of five children in a fatherless family. As La Mejicana explains to Yolanda,
she had a fight with her husband in 1962 and has not heard from him since. A
narration in the film tells us that 'Around 53% of the family units in a group of

287

341 people were headed by women, a characteristic of marginal families whose marital instability indexes are high.'

Machismo takes another form where Mario works. In fact the film opens – and apart from an epilogue, closes – with a workers' assembly at Mario's factory which is called upon to examine the case of a buddy of Mario's, Humberto. Humberto has been missing from work – he skived off in order to go and get laid, though only Mario knows this. Humberto tells the assembly that he went to visit his dying mother at the other end of the island. Humberto is in many ways Mario's *alter ego*. Different aspects of the old marginal culture survive in each of them, but more rigidly and individualistically in Humberto, for whom the pursuit of personal whim justifies the evasion of social responsibility towards his fellow workers and dissimulation in the interests of private gratification. In Mario's case, the predominant survival of marginalism is found in his adherence to the code of loyalty – not giving Humberto away. But in the assembly, Mario feels provoked by Humberto's behaviour and spills the beans, which we witness in the opening sequence and then finally come to understand at the end when we see it again in context. When this happens, we recognise one of the members of the workers' council that presides over the assembly as Mario's father, Candito, whom we know to be a good revolutionary and critical of Humberto because he's been before the council three times already. And what we've learnt from Candito makes it clear that Mario has exploded because he is confused by a conflict of loyalties, the old code of loyalty to his buddy and the new social code of the Revolution and loyalty among compañeros.

The film opens and leads back to this explosive moment of rupture, and the love story is contained within this trajectory. The two strands stand in opposition to each other: an old friendship and an old code of behaviour is shattered, while a new relationship is formed on the basis of new codes of behaviour, antagonistic to the first. For his part, Humberto is clear about this. At one point he tells Mario, 'The teacher's brainwashed you, made you a Komsomol!' Mario, however, remains confused. In the epilogue, after he has turned against his former buddy, he says 'I acted like a woman, turning him in.' Here the film not only refuses to idealise its 'hero' but quite the opposite: it wants to be sure we know he's done the right thing for totally the wrong reason – not because he *has* acted 'like a woman' but because that's what he tells himself. This judgment upon him to which the whole course of the film has brought us is reinforced by remarks in the epilogue, in the scene in which workers from the assembly discuss what has happened. These are real workers from the bus factory where the film was made, and this unscripted discussion is another index of imperfect cinema in practice, for these are no longer simply actors in a story, but representatives of the audience watching the film, who show the audience what it is to be, as in Cortázar's *Por primera vez*, at the same time participant observers and observant participators in the dramas of daily life.

*De cierta manera* is seen, with great justification, by critics in the metropolis as a feminist film, but in Cuba the term 'feminism' isn't part of the vocabulary of revolutionary endeavour because of overtones of antagonistic confrontation between men and women which are regarded as unwelcome – an indication, perhaps, of the degree to which Cuban society is still patriarchal. Mario, in the film, has not yet escaped the thought structures of machismo because although he knows he has been in their grip, and is fighting against them, he can still only imagine that to break them is to be womanish, rather than revolutionary. The struggle for women's equality in Cuba, the film is telling us (not women's rights: the Revolution has given them these already), is a struggle against machismo which has to be joined by men and women together, within the Revolution, because machismo is one of the symptoms of underdevelopment. We can see this more clearly if we map out the way a whole series of elements in the film comprise a surprisingly symmetrical set of structural oppositions. First, Humberto and Lazaro are the film's two delinquents; an absent mother is associated with one, an absent father with the other. Second, there are conflicts between Mario and Humberto on the one hand, and Yolanda and Lazaro on the other. Linked to these two conflicts is a further pair of antagonisms, between Humberto and Candito, and between Lazaro and his mother La Mejicana. But since Humberto is Mario's *alter ego*, what you get symbolically are two conflicts between child and parent, one in Mario's sphere, one in Yolanda's, making a square. Within the square are various other parallels, especially between the factory and school, as the two central protagonists' places of work, and between the workers' assembly in the one, and in the other, Yolanda's meeting with her fellow teachers:

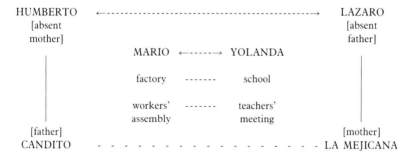

Certain other features fall within this pattern too, such as relations of authority: Candito's authority over Humberto, and Yolanda's over Lazaro, arise from their positions within the institutions they belong to, factory and school, in Candito's case as an elected representative, in Yolanda's because teachers are expected to concern themselves with their pupils' well-being.

These institutional settings are important elements in the socio-spatial discourse of the film – the way the film maps the social relationships it portrays on to the spaces, physical and institutional, in which they occur: the factory, the school, the street, the home and other places where the film unfolds. Each location corresponds to a different kind of social encounter, each kind of social encounter involves a different aspect of a character's social existence, and

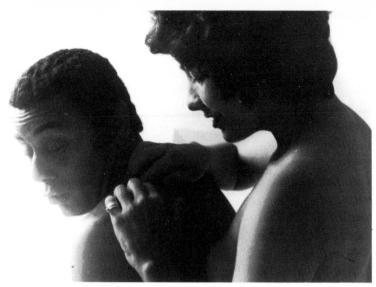

Mario Balmaceda and Yolanda Cueller in *De cierta manera*

therefore calls forth different behaviour. The way the film handles these differences and contrasts is manifold and paradigmatic, exposing the poverty of traditional narrative plotting which ignores everything about its characters that falls outside the particular set of motivations concentrated in the conventional plot and its linear trajectory. The socio-spatial discourse of a conventional narrative movie, though it always exists – actions always *take place*, every scene has a setting – is subordinate to the designs of the plot, and location is a colouring rather than part of the film's very fabric. But not here. Just as Miraflores, the district, is almost a character in the film in its own right, so too the individual locations contribute their own character to the dialectic of action and interaction. The narrative system of the film is thus a constant movement of many points, not a single unfolding line, and the character of each protagonist is not a predefined entity which can only change according to the exigencies of the plot, but a living field of possibilities arising from the constraints and sanctions of the different social spaces which these people inhabit. This is why Sara Gómez is able so successfully to introduce real persons alongside fictional ones, not as non-professional actors but as themselves, people 'with their own name and sur-name', to borrow a phrase from the neorealist Zavattini.

Only two locations in *De cierta manera* require special comment because they carry specific local connotations. The first is the bedroom where Mario and Yolanda have been making love, which probably only a Cuban audience would instantly recognise as a room in one of the *posadas* or *albergues* which the government erected after the Revolution to alleviate one of the problems of the housing shortage: these are hostels where couples can hire rooms by the hour.

The conversation in this scene is a function of the fact that the room is neutral territory in which couples meet as equals, at least to an extent that might not be possible in their own rooms in an overcrowded house where privacy is elusive.

In the second, the scene acquires a crucial dimension of irony if you know the location's symbolic connotations. At the end of the film, when Mario makes his remark about behaving like a woman, he is talking with a workmate in a public garden, underneath a statue of General Maceo. The General sits astride a horse with enormous balls. The irony arises because to say in Cuba that someone has the balls of Maceo's horse is to say that he's more macho than everyone else. 'After all, it's men who made the Revolution,' says Mario, and the location silently asks, 'What kind of boast is that?'[13]

The particular significance within this scheme of the institutional settings is twofold. On the one hand, this is where the ethics of the Revolution establish the standards against which other forms of behaviour must be measured. It is as if the film is an inquiry into the extent to which revolutionary ethics have become generalised, entering even the more informal, more enclosed, less public spaces in which people live out their private lives, spaces where it is much more difficult to root out the old values. At the same time, the different worlds of factory and school are contrasted in the film as the different realms of the central pair, Mario and Yolanda. They seem therefore to represent the two realms of male and female. The division is a symbolic arrangement which reveals a pattern of interdependence, fractured moieties which seek completion in each other, symbolised by the elective affinity between Mario and Yolanda. The difficulty, revealed by the parallel conflicts in the story, is that the forms of bonding in

*De cierta manera*: Mario and Yolanda

which people either find themselves or engage – family, friendship, sexual love – can become either wholesome or, when social codes conflict, antagonistic. In the case of the love-bond, antagonism usually comes less from determinate differences of class background, cultural inheritance and personal history, but when one partner refuses to accept the challenge of the other to change. But in the film and in Cuban society, the major force for change comes from beyond either partner: it comes from the dynamics of the Revolution. Marginalism, underdevelopment, machismo, are forms of disruption inherited from the past. And if the Revolution can hardly tolerate them, neither can it accept any solution to the problems they create that only intensifies antagonism. No society can be totally free from coercion, but coercion must be tempered by collective responsibility, for otherwise the Revolution would be denying its own character. It must therefore be part of the character of revolutionary ethics – and *De cierta manera* is above all a film about revolutionary ethics – that it recognises conflict and negation as productive, according to the laws of dialectical logic. This is a very consistent and coherent position.

The film remains a solitary example of a Cuban feature directed by a woman. Things are finally beginning to change, however: half of a new batch of documentary directors appointed in 1984 are women. *De cierta manera* has also left its mark in other ways. In 1979, Pastor Vega completed his first feature, co-scripted by Ambrosio Fornet, *Retrato de Teresa* ('Portrait of Teresa'), with Daysi Granados in the title role. This turned out to be ICAIC's most controversial film in twenty years. Teresa leads not just a double life but a triple life: housewife, factory worker and factory cultural secretary. Cuban audiences were shocked to see her physically fighting off her uncomprehending husband, whom eventually she leaves. It is a film which repays attention; but not here, for it already belongs to a new period in Cuban cinema which is yet too recent for retrospective historical study. Perhaps, too, a new period in Cuba's social development, for a few years later the controversies continued when the Brazilian feminist series *Malu Mulher* (seen in Britain on Channel Four) was shown on Cuban television. On that occasion, people began to be critical of the commentary of Party representatives, who argued that the series was an excellent dramatisation of the problems of women in the capitalist countries of Latin America but without direct parallels in Cuba, and different opinions were aired. This represents one of the strongest challenges that Cuban film-makers are now facing.

There remain a handful of feature films of the 70s which have not been discussed, including a Buñuelesque comedy by Alea, *Los Sobrevivientes* ('The Survivors', 1979), and *La tierra y el cielo* ('Heaven and Earth', 1976), a gentle tale about Haiti made with the Haitian community in Cuba by Manuel Octavio Gómez in 1976. The other two are by Humberto Solás, *Un día de noviembre* ('A Day in November', 1972) and *Cantata de Chile* (1975). The former is an oddity: the contemporary story of a young Cuban revolutionary who discovers he has a fatal illness and is forced to reassess his life. The film is deeply personal but not too successful. In the atmosphere of the early 70s, just after the detention of Padilla, an unusual season of distrust of artistic indulgence, ICAIC felt it was best to delay the release of the film. When it was premiered a year and a half later, the decision was also ICAIC's: the director now felt the film was too weak, and would not have minded, he told the present author, if nobody saw it. *Cantata de Chile* is a different matter altogether, and the absence of discussion here is a real lacuna. A film of the most profound solidarity with the defeat of the popular forces in Chile, with music by Leo Brouwer (though not his best), Solas here composes an aural and visual hymn against foreign exploitation from the *conquistadores* and their oppression of the Auracanians, to the cold and hateful British owners of the nitrate mines where Chilean workers went on strike in 1907. *Cine solidaridad, cine rescate, cine militante,* imperfect cinema, even *Variety* had to admit it is 'visually and narratively stunning'. There are finally one or two films that begin to appear in the catalogue of a new variety, like *El rey de Joropo* by the Venezuelan Carlos Rebolledo, and *El recurso del metodo* by the Chilean Miguel Littin. These are the first co-productions with film-makers in Latin America. This is also the beginning of an entirely new phase in Cuban cinema, which belongs with the creation at the end of the decade of an annual film festival in Havana, the International Festival of the New Latin American Cinema. For after a decade of restriction, Cuba is re-entering and rebuilding its international projection. Throughout the continent, the revolutionary stimulus of the Sandinista victory in Nicaragua is, among its many other effects, redoubling the resolution of Latin American film-makers not in any way to slacken their resolution, and by means of pooled resources and mutual commitment, to mount the best and strongest reply to the beast in the north on the screen that they can.


When the Cuban Revolution decided to create a film industry out of nothing, naturally it took a number of years for the new film-makers to find their feet. They were the years in which the cultural politics of the Revolution were forged. As Ambrosio Fornet, a cultural historian who is now the Film Institute's literary adviser has recalled:

> At the triumph of the Revolution, the first thing we found was that for the first time we had the means of disseminating our culture, that is to say, we had publishers, a Film Institute, centres of investigation – but the question was, now that we've got these resources, what culture shall we disseminate? What concept of culture – what concept of the relationship between the writer, the intellectual, and the people? Because we had been formed – the majority of intellectuals – in a tradition that was based in European and North American culture, which means in social terms, in a bourgeois cultural tradition. Few of us were Marxists. So the first question we had to pose was, what concept of culture are we going to defend? We didn't have the answer, it wasn't written anywhere, no angel descended with it from heaven. We had to find the answer

Humberto Solás                    Alfredo Guevara

in practice, in the revolutionary process itself. Obviously this produced clashes and conflicts between those who in some way continued defending the old concept of culture and the position of the intellectual in society, and those who wanted to defend a new sense and concept of culture. For the first time, the people, through the Revolution, had come into close-up, so to speak, in the scenario of history and were transforming the bases of society. It seemed impossible to many of us in a situation like this that the traditional concept of culture should remain untouchable. A large group of us thought, we cannot simply defend what in occidental culture are called the eternal values, because we had discovered that eternal values didn't exist. Eternal values are historical values, and they were changing. And obviously, in contact with this changing reality, we also changed our conceptions.[14]

Throughout this period ICAIC played a leading role in the ideological confrontations through which the cultural politics of the Revolution were defined. It developed and defended positions against both the sometimes near-hysterical attacks of liberals who feared the encroachment of the state, and the mechanical application of schemes for socialist realism on the part of more orthodox and traditional Marxists associated with the old guard of the pre-revolutionary Communist Party. Fidel Castro's critique of cultural liberalism in the address given to a meeting in Havana in 1961, known as 'Words to the Intellectuals', was the occasion on which he pronounced the famous formula, 'Within the Revolution everything, against it, nothing.' Less well known is the success of ICAIC's rebuttal of the same sectarian and bureaucratic forces that Fidel was to attack almost a year later in another crucial speech. In their journal *Cine Cubano* and in various national cultural assemblies, Alfredo Guevara and others spelt out the reasons forcefully and articulately. They argued that economic criteria of productivity could not be applied to artistic work, which could not be reduced either to the purely didactic functions of propaganda; nor, they said, should the audience be refused the right to see the work of progressive European film-makers because they supposedly dealt in the portrayal of bourgeois decadence. Moreover, ICAIC defended the right of its members to experiment in the most varied styles and techniques.

Not all the films that were made during this period were released. Creating the space for the film-makers to learn on the job, some of the films that went into production failed to run the course and were aborted. Countries with established film industries rely on a combination of apprenticeship and film schools to develop new film-makers, yet film industries all over the world still end up with disasters on their hands. This is no more than a consequence of the inherent risks of the medium, of the costliness of film production and the need to cut your losses when necessary. There can be no surprise if the same thing happened in ICAIC, where the urgency of the cultural needs of the Revolution made taking risks the only sane policy. Accusations have been made of censorship and autocracy, but it would have been counterproductive to have spent money on completing films which too clearly displayed their apprentice nature. Not all the film-makers, by any means, whose work was interrupted in this way, lost their enthusiasm and commitment to the Revolution and decided to leave.

Bit by bit, mostly through intelligent improvisation and critical reflection on the results, Cuba's revolutionary cinema defined its aims and the means by which to achieve them. Primarily moulded by practice and the exigencies of the revolutionary process, there has constantly been something of a tension between practice and theory. But there always is, and for the Cubans it has mostly been a creative tension. Through it, rather than against or in spite of it, Cuban film-makers have attempted to undermine the adverse power of the dream screen constructed by cultural imperialism, especially the mendacious projection of the mythical American Dream, by building on what started as the audience's spontaneous change of perspective in order to create both a more critical disposition in the audience and a radical film language.

Here the film-makers were aided by the experience both of guerrilla warfare and of the popular militia created by the Revolution after it took power, which provided the underpinning for a number of films which used experimental cinematic techniques explicitly to demystify the iconography of warfare as portrayed in conventional Hollywood cinema. This impulse, combined with the experience of their own revolution, also resulted in films of other people's revolutions, especially the Vietnamese, unparalleled in their strength and expressivity. Some of these were films which, in the process, explored the very edges of film language. In particular, this is the case with the work of Santiago Alvarez, in films like *Hanoi Martes 13* and *79 primaveras*, as well as in other examples, on different themes, like *LBJ* and *Despegue a las 18:00*.

But the sense of formal experiment was contagious. It was in any case a product of revolutionary upheaval, and was also manifest in other creative work like music and writing. The result was a series of exhilarating films at the end of the 60s which did exuberant things with both the visual and the narrative dimensions of the screen, including Julio García Espinosa's *Las aventuras de Juan Quin Quin*, T.G. Alea's *Memorias del subdesarrollo*, *Lucía* by Humberto Solás, and *La primera carga al machete* of Manuel Octavio Gómez. More than a style, these films implied a radically new attitude to film, which, partly influenced by the Cubans, was also developing throughout Latin America: in fiction, in the work of Glauber Rocha in Brazil, Jorge Sanjinés in Bolivia, Miguel Littin in Chile, and many others; and in documentary, in the films of Fernando Solanas and Octavio Getino in Argentina, Jorge Silva and Marta Rodríguez in Colombia and too many more to mention, for documentary was an essential component in the process. In 1970 Julio García Espinosa gave to this movement the name imperfect cinema, in an essay that is both key and highly polemical. More than a decade later, just before he became Alfredo Guevara's successor as head of ICAIC, he explained the philosophy behind the concept:

Just as we have to learn things even from the metropolis which is so much ahead of the underdeveloped countries, so we have to learn from their cinema too. But just as in our social aspirations we're looking for better means of human self-fulfilment, so we have to search for the appropriate cinema. For me, the societies of the great metropolis are marked by an economy of waste, and to this economy of waste there corresponds a culture of waste. Such a diabolical system has been created that people think that to make the most of their lives they have to be wasteful of things. And the question is how really to live a full life. So in the face of a culture of waste you have to search for a culture of true liberation. It's not possible to propose the idea of a New Economic Order without a new culture as well. Because in the underdeveloped world, suffering so much scarcity, people still often think that they have to achieve the same levels of consumption as the developed countries, and that's a lie. We cannot – the world cannot – aspire to such levels of consumption. Therefore the culture has to provide new ways of feeling and enjoying life, different from irrational consumption. This is the basis of imperfect cinema. Since we're creating a society which although it's full of imperfections will finally achieve a new kind of human productiveness, I suggested a cinema which although it has imperfections is essentially much more consistent with real human needs.[15]

There was, however, a peculiarity in Cuban cinema. Unlike the case of wars of liberation that have been fought since theirs, the Cubans had hardly any authentic images of their own guerrillas in action, their own masses on the streets. The war in Vietnam was filmed from both sides. The Chilean film-makers of Popular Unity created a living film image of their reality as they struggled against North American destabilisation of Allende's government. In both Nicaragua and El Salvador, revolutionary cinema comes out of the trenches of warfare itself, a political weapon aimed against the disinformation of the media system of late capitalism. In the Cuban case this kind of material is somewhat sparse. It has had to be reconstructed.

Sergio Giral                    Pastor Vega

This reconstruction was undertaken in several ways, including experiments in both fictional and documentary re-enactment. They have also ranged through the history of the hundred years struggle to build up an imaginary archive, with portraits of both the anonymous and the historical protagonists of this history. As they did so, an idiosyncratic form of self-reference appeared in Cuban cinema, with film-makers borrowing from each other's films, taking clips of reconstructed scenes to insert into their own films instead of reconstructing them afresh. It is a device which Santiago Alvarez is very fond of, because his entire style of documentary is based on the idea of collage, of using whatever images there are to hand of something you wish to refer to, be they newsreel, photographs, newspaper clippings, old engravings, or feature films. And from its fondness for Santiago Alvarez, the Cuban audience is well versed with the idea of images being used as quotes, with connotation as well as denotation, not to be read as literal portrayals but more obliquely, and often more ironically, as allusions – or symptomatically, as the sociologist Erving Goffman calls it.

But Alvarez is not by any means the only one to use these symptomatic images, nor is the manner of their use always simple and straightforward. It becomes a much more subtle question when the film from which the image is quoted is not documentary but fiction, and this has been done regularly. It is sometimes difficult to work out quite what effect these quoted images tend to have in the different contexts in which they occur, and it is not as if there are rules about it. Different directors do the same things for different reasons. Undoubtedly there can be something hermetic about the practice and it is not always easy to know how the Cuban audience sees such images. But the fact that this process has occurred is one of the most intriguing things about Cuban cinema, and speaks strongly for it. The Cuban film-makers who created ICAIC set out to provide the Revolution with a new way of seeing, of looking and of watching. They were not interested in using cinema simply to reflect a given world but wanted to be able to intervene with their projected images and help to reshape it. To do this it was necessary to create all kinds of images of things which had previously been hidden, rendered invisible by the selectivity of the camera's gaze. They undertook to accomplish this task with wide historical sweep, and in the process re-enacted episodes from Cuban history going back to the seventeenth century. They have helped to bring this history alive in the ordinary citizen. The play with which they quote each other's films is not a closed or academic game, but the expression of a country creating a new sense of identity for itself.

All this became possible because the film-makers resolved to create new identities for themselves as a working group, as Julio García Espinosa explained in Montreal in 1974. A revolution, he reminded his listeners, does not do away with industry. It occurs to no worker to do away with factories and industrial production. What disappears, comes to an end, is the private ownership of the means of production and the relations of production they entail. And once the revolution is in power, only the productive capacity offered by a film industry gives the chance of responding to the enormous demand there is for all sorts of films, didactic and educational and for entertainment. A delicate aspect to the problem comes from the contrast with pre-revolutionary conditions, in which the politicised film-maker is forced to work with artisanal means, and elaborates theories to justify this way of working. Very often, this produces the idea that the best way of producing a militant cinema consistent with the need for it, is not to become integrated with the system, but to remain in direct contact with trades unions and the workers at the base, and of learning not to be authoritarian, in order to illuminate the distance between the film-maker and the spectator; the rest follows.

Clearly, García Espinosa continued – and this, he said, was elementary – we still want to be producing militant films, a revolutionary cinema, we want to be in contact with the base, the worker, the peasant. But we no longer believe we can do this without working through an industrial structure. We don't, as intellectuals and artists, achieve proletarian consciousness simply by going along to factories and union meetings, filming the life and conditions of the workers, necessary as all these things are, unless our consiousness is subjected to the same determinants as those workers, and that means, through the experience of our own labour process.

Not that García Espinosa and others thought this was automatic. The nature of the labour process and the relations of production were a subject of active discussion and experiment within ICAIC, and ways of working underwent successive modifications in response to the evolution of socialist principles of productive relations. Working methods were developed in which apprenticeship and a constant sharing of experience through debate and discussion supported the endeavours of one and all. The abolition of capitalist relations of production through the amalgamation in one enterprise of what were previously a number of small companies buying and selling each other's services among themselves, favoured the streamlining of relations between members of different

298

Julio Garcia Espinosa                Santiago Alvarez in London

departments of the film crew. A particularly productive example was the creation of a special effects department which brought the processes of rostrum camera animation together with those of the optical camera which is conventionally attached to the laboratory. The department was created out of economic necessity: without streamlining the production process, it would simply not have been possible to accomplish the necessary amount of work. But the whole stylistic evolution of the newsreel and the documentary which Santiago Alvarez pioneered, with its integration of combined effects, would not have been possible otherwise.

Another instance of the changes ICAIC has brought about is the case of the composer. The composer has become more integrated into the editing process. In the standard practices which rule in Hollywood, the music for a film is composed afterwards, when the editing is almost finished, and a special music editor, working in the cutting room, prepares a music cue sheet for the composer with the timings and visual cues which the composer needs. At ICAIC, to keep the costs of production as economical as possible, they don't have special music editors. The composers must prepare the cue sheets for themselves. But this is a great advantage from an aesthetic point of view. The great problem with the standard practices of Hollywood and its imitators is the effect they have on the segmentation of creative input. At ICAIC, composers may not work any slower than in Hollywood, but by themselves working through the film with the director and editor their relationship to the evolving film is much more fluid. At the same time, with the creation of the Grupo Sonora Experimental in the late 60s, and the reintegration of the composer with the performing group, ICAIC fostered a much more fluid relationship with the musicians who record the music. In this entire process, ICAIC has in strong measure succeeded in creating an identity for itself, which it has successfully projected upon the screen across the great diversity of its output.

Compare ICAIC as the author of its films with the Hollywood studios as the authors of theirs. The difference is inscribed in the title sequences of the films themselves. This needs a quick excursus into film history. In the beginning, there were no film titles. Films appeared on a screen like moving snapshots. They had names, which to start with were descriptive, like 'Train Arriving at a Station' or 'Teasing the Gardener' but they didn't appear on the screen as titles. (You may see them now with titles, but these were added later.) The first lettering to be printed onto the moving image on the screen was in the form of trade marks, intended to establish rights of ownership to prevent piracy. In this way, and there's something very symbolic about it, the first signs of authorship were company names. Then, very rapidly, it is true, came the first title cards, which stood at the head of the film like the title page of a book. One or two of them were true silent film titles, like 'The ? Motorist'. Soon these title cards came to be decorated with borders round the words, and they began to appear between successive scenes, with the kind of information about time and place you get in theatre programmes. Next, they were used to carry snippets of dialogue, and therefore interrupted the flow of the image. For a long time during all this, there were often still no individual names on the screen to signify authorship, neither of the actors in front of the camera nor the people behind it. These credits were introduced only gradually over the years.

Long before they were all there, the titles of films had ceased to be simply descriptive. They became literary, borrowing the title of books and plays and inventing their own. Yet they remained, together with the credits, outside the body of the film, coming before and after the first and last images, again like title pages in a book and the various bits of information they carry – including the copyright claim.

Eventually, and increasingly so after the coming of sound, titles were formed into sequences at the beginning of the film with decorative motifs intended to create the appropriate mood for the film to follow. The information included in these title sequences varied; many of the credits were relegated to the end. But there are certain things they always contained – the names of the stars, the director, the producer, the photographer, the composer, the editor, in an order that became so crucial that it became a contractual matter, particularly with the stars. And always, there was the production company. In modern day feature production, title sequences have become so elaborate that you get title sequence specialists, freelance individuals or separate companies. Naturally they become entitled to their own credit – at the end, not during the title sequence itself of course.

In the course of these developments, the titles and credits of the film have changed their status. To begin with, the logical properties of the medium allow them to be displayed to the audience in the same way as in a book, but unlike, say, a play or a piece of music, where the title and the credits do not belong to the presentation itself but stand to it as an appendage. The first semiological fact about film titles, then, is that they are signs that a film is not performed, but manufactured. But then these signs of manufacture are ingested by the medium to become part of the spell it seeks to weave the moment the screen lights up. And eventually what happens is that they get pushed into the weave of the film, as pre-title sequences appear. The Cubans are especially fond of pre-title sequences; they have virtually become *de rigueur*.

There is subtle difference, however, between the opening of a Cuban film on a Cuban screen, and Hollywood cinema. The Cuban pre-title sequence is a way of reasserting the primacy of the immediacy of the image over the signs of its authorship. In the cinemas of the metropolis, as well as in many other countries, even the most magical opening to a pre-title sequence is generally preceded by two things: the announcement of the distribution company (lions and gongs and globes and things) – and the Censorship certificate. In Cuba, there are neither. ICAIC is its own distributor, and it signs on with 'ICAIC presents' wherever the film-maker decides to put it. It presents itself, in other words, not as the entity which merchandises the film or which classifies it, but as an author among the authors. Moreover, the logo which identifies ICAIC is not a fixed trademark, but varies according to the preferences of the graphic designer.

Twenty-five years on from the Victory, the Cuban cinema audience today has some very distinctive characteristics. ICAIC undertakes extensive audience investigations and there are interesting statistics, but what most impresses the commentator on Cuban cinema is not so much a matter of formal investigation but what you gather from watching films with Cuban audiences and considering how they react. And this is an audience that is highly reactive. The relationship with the screen is a strong one, stronger than we have grown used to in the cinemas of London or Paris or New York. When it comes to genre cinema it doesn't miss a trick: at particular twists and devices, it gasps aloud in one voice; it's equally quick to share a joke. Much of the time it is also an audience, again in comparison with general levels of informedness in the metropolis, which is well capable of deciding for itself what to think, whatever its continued attachment to models from the past; for ICAIC has made continuing efforts, through television programmes, criticism and the whole aficionado film movement, including a resurgence of aficionado cine on 8mm, to provide audiences with critical tools to sharpen their enjoyment. Cuban film-makers are in an enviable position: they are making films with the knowledge that it matters and that what they produce will be actively taken up. Indeed, although audience attendance in Cuba has fallen rapidly in the last couple of years – a trend which follows the increasing provision of other opportunities for cultural participation as well as because of television – Cuban films themselves gather the biggest audiences. They thereby continue to stimulate discussion and debate throughout the land.

# References

1.  *Rencontres Internationales pour un Nouveau Cinéma*, Cahiers No. 3, Montreal 1975, p.25.
2.  'Discussion with Jorge Fraga', *Undercut* No.12, 1984.
3.  John Hess, 'The personal is political in Cuba', *Jump Cut* No.20, p.15.
4.  *Juventud Rebelde* 1 April 1974.
5.  *Granma* 15 March 1974.
6.  Interview in *Romances* April 1974.
7.  Conversation with T.G. Alea, Havana, June 1984.
8.  Quoted in Rigoberto López, op.cit.
9.  *Ibid*.
10. Julia Lesage, 'One Way or Another: The Revolution in Action', *Jump Cut* No.19 (December 1978), p.33.
11. Annette Kuhn, *Women's Pictures, Feminism and Cinema*, Routledge and Kegan Paul, 1982, p.163.
12. E. Ann Kaplan, *Women & Film, Both Sides of the Camera*, Methuen, 1983, p.193.
13. Conversation with Jorge Sotolongo, Oberhausen, 1981.
14. In *New Cinema of Latin America I – Cinema of the Humble*, dir. Michael Chanan, 1983.
15. In *New Cinema of Latin America II – The Long Road*, dir. Michael Chanan, 1983.

# INDEXES

A NOTE ON THE INDEXING

What do you index in a book like this? The most scholarly thing would be everything, but this would have become unwieldy. The General Index therefore contains: 1) all proper names; 2) names of film and related companies of all nationalities; 3) names of the main Cuban and various international organisations (though not all: ICAIC itself isn't indexed; the CIA is but not UNESCO); 4) all titles of publications and pieces of music referred to in the text – with publications these are generally cross-indexed with English titles and authors – other than film titles which are recorded in the Film Title Index following. There is also 5) a selection of Spanish terms, connected with Cuba, film, and music. Historical events are not indexed; this is an historical essay, but not a work of general history.

About Spanish names, readers are reminded that these are frequently double-barrelled, the patronymic first, the matronymic second. Following Spanish practice, they are indexed under the patronymic. People are not consistent about this, however, and there are cross-references where someone is known by their matronymic.

M. C., Windsor, 7 August 1985

303

GENERAL INDEX